CAMBRIDGE TEXTS IN THE
HISTORY OF POLITICAL THOUGHT

AQUINAS: POLITICAL WRITINGS

D1073403

CAMBRIDGE TEXTS IN THE
HISTORY OF POLITICAL THOUGHT

Series editors

RAYMOND GEUSS, *Reader in Philosophy, University of Cambridge*
QUENTIN SKINNER, *Regius Professor of Modern History in the
University of Cambridge*

Cambridge Texts in the History of Political Thought is now firmly established as the major student textbook series in political theory. It aims to make available to students all the most important texts in the history of western political thought, from ancient Greece to the early twentieth century. All the familiar classic texts will be included, but the series seeks at the same time to enlarge the conventional canon by incorporating an extensive range of less well-known works, many of them never before available in a modern English edition. Wherever possible, texts are published in complete and unabridged form, and translations are specially commissioned for the series. Each volume contains a critical introduction together with chronologies, biographical sketches, a guide to further reading and any necessary glossaries and textual apparatus. When completed the series will aim to offer an outline of the entire evolution of western political thought.

For a list of titles published in the series, please see end of book.

ST THOMAS AQUINAS
POLITICAL WRITINGS

EDITED AND TRANSLATED BY

R.W. DYSON

CAMBRIDGE
UNIVERSITY PRESS

PUBLISHED BY THE PRESS SYNDICATE OF THE UNIVERSITY OF CAMBRIDGE
The Pitt Building, Trumpington Street, Cambridge, United Kingdom

CAMBRIDGE UNIVERSITY PRESS
The Edinburgh Building, Cambridge CB2 2RU, UK
40 West 20th Street, New York, NY 10011-4211, USA
477 Williamstown Road, Port Melbourne, VIC 3207, Australia
Ruiz de Alarcón 13, 28014 Madrid, Spain
Dock House, The Waterfront, Cape Town 8001, South Africa

http://www.cambridge.org

First published 2002

Printed in the United Kingdom at the University Press, Cambridge

Typeface Ehrhardt MT 9.5/12 pt   *System* LaTeX 2ε [TB]

A catalogue record for this book is available from the British Library

Library of Congress Cataloguing in Publication data

Thomas, Aquinas, Saint, 1225?–1274.
[Selections. English. 2002]
Political writings/Thomas Aquinas; edited and translated by R.W. Dyson.
p.   cm. – (Cambridge texts in the history of political thought)
Includes bibliographical references and index.
ISBN 0 521 37569 X – ISBN 0 521 37595 9 (pb.)
1. Political science – Early works to 1800.   2. Law – Philosophy – Early works
to 1800.   3. Justice – Early works to 1800.   I. Dyson, R. W.   II. Title.
III. Series.
JC121.T42   2002
320 – dc21   2002025748

ISBN 0 521 37569 X hardback
ISBN 0 521 37595 9 paperback

FOR JESS

*Ne glorieris de die crastino, quia nescis
quid pariturus sit dies*

Contents

Contents

Contents

Contents

Contents

Contents

Preface

This book has taken a long while to complete, and has accrued many debts. In particular, I mention Professor Antony Black and Dr P. J. Fitzpatrick who, as always, shared their scholarship with me without stint. I mention also the editorial staff of the Cambridge University Press, and above all Virginia Catmur, to whose amazing skills as a copy-editor this volume, like my edition of Augustine's *De civitate Dei* in the same series, owes so much. Finally, I thank my colleagues and students at the University of Durham for their unfailing support, encouragement and stimulation.

R. W. Dyson
Durham
Michaelmas Term, 2002

Abbreviations

<table>
<tr><td>BE</td><td>Blackfriars Edition: i.e. Summa theologiae, trans. Thomas Gilby et al. (61 vols., London and New York, 1964–80)</td></tr>
<tr><td>CIC</td><td>Corpus iuris canonici, ed. E. Friedberg (2 vols., Leipzig, 1879)</td></tr>
<tr><td>CICiv.</td><td>Corpus iuris civilis, ed. P. Krueger, Th. Mommsen, R. Schoell and G. Kroll (Berlin, 1872–7)</td></tr>
<tr><td>DE</td><td>Dominican Edition: i.e. Summa theologica, trans. Fathers of the English Dominican Province (2nd, rev. edn., 22 vols., London, 1912–36)</td></tr>
<tr><td>NCE</td><td>New Catholic Encyclopaedia (New York and London, 1967)</td></tr>
<tr><td>PG</td><td>Patrologiae cursus completus, series Graeca, ed. J.-P. Migne (Paris, 1857ff)</td></tr>
<tr><td>PL</td><td>Patrologiae cursus completus, series Latina, ed. J.-P. Migne (Paris, 1844ff)</td></tr>
<tr><td>SCG</td><td>St Thomas Aquinas, Summa contra gentiles, ed. C. Pera, P. Marc and P. Caramello (Turin and Rome, 1961–7)</td></tr>
</table>

Introduction

St Thomas Aquinas

St Thomas was born in 1225[1] into a wealthy and influential south-Italian family. Landulph, his father, was Count of Aquino; Theodora, his mother, Countess of Teano; the family was related to the Emperors Henry VI and Frederick II, and to the Kings of Aragon, France and Castile. He began his education in 1230 as an oblate at the Benedictine monastery of Monte Cassino, where his uncle, Landulph Sinibaldi, was Abbot. In 1238 he entered the *Studium generale* at Naples. In 1245, despite great opposition from his family, he became a member of the Dominican order and went to the University of Paris, where the German theologian Albertus Magnus introduced him to the study of Aristotle. In 1248 he followed Albertus to Cologne. Between 1252 and 1256, as part of his preparation for his *licentia docendi*, he compiled his *Scripta super libros sententiarum*, the treatise on the *Sentences* of Peter Lombard, which had become a standard part of medieval university education. He received his licence to teach in 1256. The next eighteen years were spent teaching and studying at Paris, Naples, Orvieto, Viterbo and Rome. His *Summa contra gentiles* – a manual for missionaries to the Moslems and Jews of Spain and north Africa – was completed at Orvieto in 1264. He began the *Summa theologiae* at Rome in 1266 and worked on it until forced by ill health to desist in 1273. During a final stint at the University of Paris between 1269 and 1272 he wrote twelve commentaries on the works of Aristotle, including the *Ethics* and *Politics*.

---

[1] St Thomas's earliest biographer, Peter Calo (1300) gives 1227 as his date of birth. See D. Prümmer, *Fontes Vitae S. Thomae Aquinatis, notis historicis et criticis illustrati* (Toulouse, 1911), pp. 28; 45. Fr Prümmer accepts 1227, but 1225 seems more likely on the whole.

It is a remarkable fact that St Thomas's literary output was compressed into a life of only forty-nine years. Not surprisingly, in view of his ferocious workload, he suffered a sudden and debilitating illness – perhaps a stroke – at Naples in December 1273. The story that he ceased work on the *Summa* because of some mystical experience is apparently due to the fact that the onset of this illness came while he was saying Mass. Evidently in a weakened condition he left Naples in February 1274 to attend the second Council of Lyons. He died at the Cistercian abbey of Fessa Nuova on 7 March 1274. He was canonised by Pope John XXII in 1323.

In 1277, a number of propositions representing his views were officially condemned by the Church. Even after his canonisation, St Thomas did not enjoy the status he was later to be accorded. The virtually exclusive place occupied by Thomist doctrines in Catholic philosophical education during most of the twentieth century is due to the encyclical *Aeterni patris* (4 August 1879) of Pope Leo XIII, which recommended scholastic philosophy, and especially the work of St Thomas, as an antidote to the threat of liberal thought in the Church. 'Let carefully chosen teachers strive to implant the doctrine of Thomas Aquinas in the minds of students, and set forth clearly his soundness and excellence over others. Let the universities ... illustrate and defend this doctrine, and use it for the refutation of prevailing errors.'[2]

Notes on the edition

Anyone who sets out to compile a work of this kind is confronted by a problem of selection. It is inevitable that not everyone will approve of how the problem has been solved. My brief was to present the essence of what St Thomas has to say about government, politics and related matters, and to do so in a book of fairly restricted size. This brief has governed my selection in two ways. First, I have thought it necessary to choose, as far as possible, material of a kind accessible to readers who have no specialised background in scholastic philosophy. There seemed no point in including passages so recondite as to be unintelligible without an apparatus of commentary more extensive than space would permit. Second, where St Thomas says the same thing more than once, I have avoided repetition by selecting the passages which, in my estimation, make the point most clearly and economically. The result is a volume

[2] *Acta Leonis XIII*, 283–5 (Rome, 1879).

which defines St Thomas's 'political thought' in terms of the following: the longish fragment usually called *De regimine principum*; the letter to the Duchess of Brabant usually called *De regimine Iudaeorum* (here included as part of Chapter 5); extensive extracts from the *Summa theologiae*, including the whole of the non-biblical parts of the so-called 'Treatise on Law';[3] and two excerpts from the *Scripta super libros sententiarum*. It will be as well to say something about each of these in turn.

De regimine principum, 'On the Government of Princes' – known in a number of manuscript sources as *De regno*, 'On Kingship' – is part (Book I and the first six and a half chapters of Book II) of a much larger treatise, the rest of which is attributed to Tolommeo of Lucca (Bartolomeo Fiadoni). It is dedicated *ad regem Cypri*, 'to the King of Cyprus', the king in question probably being Hugh II of Lusignan, who appears to have had a particular affection for the Dominican order. There has been a good deal of dispute over the authorship and authenticity of *De regimine principum*, but the view still prevailing is that St Thomas abandoned the treatise after the death of its dedicatee in December 1267, and that Tolommeo subsequently continued and finished it.[4] It is St Thomas's longest strictly political piece, dealing mainly with kingship and tyranny, and containing in its final chapters some discussion of the material conditions necessary to found a successful kingdom. Book I is closely based on Aristotle's *Politics*. What there is of Book II reflects an acquaintance with two texts influential in the middle ages: Vitruvius's *De architectura* and Vegetius's *Epitoma rei militaris*.

De regimine Iudaeorum ('On the government of Jews'), known alternatively as *De regimine subditorum* ('On the government of subjects'), is not

[3] The misleading expression *Tractatus de legibus* is sometimes used to refer to *Summa theologiae* IaIIae 90–108.
[4] The whole treatise is available in an edition and English translation by J. M. Blythe, *On the Government of Rulers:* De Regimine Principum. *Ptolemy of Lucca with Portions Attributed to Thomas Aquinas* (Pennsylvania, 1997). A conspectus of the manuscript tradition and some account of the difficulties which it presents is given by I. T. Eschmann, OP, 'A Catalogue of St Thomas's Works', in E. Gilson, *The Christian Philosophy of St Thomas Aquinas* (New York and London, 1961), pp. 412ff. On questions of authorship, date and authenticity, see especially M. Browne, 'An sit authenticum opusculum S. Thomae "De regimine principum"', *Angelicum* 3 (1926), pp. 300ff; A. O'Rahilly, 'Notes on St Thomas IV: *De regimine principum*', *Irish Ecclesiastical Record* 31 (1929), pp. 396ff; 'Notes on St Thomas V: Tholomeo of Lucca, Continuator of the *De regimine principum*', *Irish Ecclesiastical Record* 31 (1929), pp. 606ff; W. Mohr, 'Bemerkungen zur Verfasserschaft von *De regimine principum*', in J. Möller and H. Kohlenberger (eds.), *Virtus politica* (Stuttgart and Bad Cannstatt, 1974); J. Echard, 'S. Thomas de Aquino', in Quétif-Echard, *Scriptores Ordinis Praedicatorum* I (Paris, 1719), pp. 511ff. See also A. Black, *Political Thought in Europe, 1250–1450* (Cambridge, 1992), p. 22.

strictly speaking a contribution to 'political theory'. From the historian's point of view, it is an interesting example of political advice given by a medieval intellectual to a concerned and evidently pious personage. In particular, it is an illustration of the social and political status of Jews in mid-thirteenth-century Europe, and of the Church's attitude to the important economic question of usury: an issue with which St Thomas deals in a more technical way in the *Summa* (at IIaIIae 78: see pp. 220ff, below). It also has something to say about the sale of offices. It is addressed *ad ducissam Brabantiae*, 'to the Duchess of Brabant', although there is doubt over who this Duchess was, and therefore over the exact dating of the letter. She may have been Aleyde or Alix of Brabant, who was regent of the duchy after the death of her husband Henry III in 1261 until her son, John I, came of age in 1267. Or she may have been Marguerite, daughter of Louis IX, who married John I in February 1270 and died in 1271. The former seems more likely, but we cannot be certain; nor, of course, is the question a particularly important one.[5]

The great preponderance of what is here offered consists of material excerpted from St Thomas's great *Summa theologiae*. The passages from it, and the two passages from his treatise on the *Sentences*, have been chosen to illustrate his views on obedience (Chapter 2); law (Chapter 3); right, justice and judgment (Chapter 4); property relations (Chapter 5); war, violence and sedition (Chapter 6), and the interactions between religion and politics so central to medieval political thought (Chapter 7). Although I have been selective – more selective, on the whole, than I would have wished to be – I have let the author of the *Summa* speak with an uninterrupted voice as far as possible. To reproduce whole *Quaestiones* may seem to present the reader with much that is irrelevant to 'political thought' as the term is usually understood; but this, I contend, is not a valid objection. That St Thomas thought it right to consider such questions as (for instance) 'whether natural contingents are subject to the eternal law' (IaIIae 93:5: p. 109, below) *is* relevant to our understanding of how he thought about law. To pick and choose only those bits and pieces which fit our preconceived ideas of what a theory of law should look like would be to betray our author. Moreover, the excessive condensation practised by some of St Thomas's previous editors – particularly, though not only,

---

[5] For the manuscript evidence and a list of editions, see Eschmann, 'Catalogue', p. 422; see also P. Glorieux, 'Le *De Regimine Judaeorum*: hypothèses et précisions', *Divus Thomas* 39 (1936), pp. 153ff.

Professor d'Entrèves[6] – gives a distorted picture of St Thomas's literary and philosophical method. It fails to show the movement and expression of his thought within the highly formal structure of the *Summa*; and such failure is a short-changing both of St Thomas and of his modern students. I have, therefore, selected; but, with a few exceptions, I have not abridged the selected passages.

De regimine principum and *De regimine Iudaeorum* are straightforward and comparatively undemanding pieces. By contrast, and despite the care taken in choosing them, at least some of the passages from the *Summa* are likely to present the reader with problems. Putting the matter generally, these problems are of two kinds. First, as a distinguished medievalist has observed, modern education does not equip us to understand scholastic thought;[7] nor does it dispose us to be sympathetic towards its agendas. The twenty-first-century reader wonders why it ever occurred to anyone to be interested in some of the things to which St Thomas devotes pages of careful analysis. He is steeped in Aristotle, Roman law, the Bible and the Fathers: we are not. His intellectual objectives, and the presuppositions, beliefs and attitudes which he takes for granted in his audience, are of a kind almost wholly foreign to us. We are unaccustomed to the language of scholasticism and the subtle distinctions and analyses which it enables its exponents to make. This kind of difficulty will be felt especially in some parts of Chapter 3 and in the long and technical discussion of right, justice and judgment in Chapter 4. Second, St Thomas's writing tends to be obscure apart from the intractability of his subject matter. He is often repetitious, clumsy and opaque, and inclined to spend a great deal of time on points which seem to us trivial. It should be remembered that much of the *Summa* was written in haste, often by the expedient of dictating to several copyists at once, working in different rooms;[8] and in an age when material could be committed to paper only by manual and laborious means, opportunities for polishing and revision were limited. I make no apology for including material of this difficult and sometimes unflattering kind. There is no virtue in suppressing St Thomas's

---

[6] *Aquinas: Selected Political Writings*, ed. with an Introduction by A. P. d'Entrèves; trans. J. G. Dawson (Oxford, 1959).

[7] Janet Coleman, *A History of Political Thought from the Middle Ages to the Renaissance* (Oxford, 2000), p. 86.

[8] The author of a fourteenth-century catalogue, quoted by Fr Eschmann, 'Catalogue', p. 430, remarks that *semper secum habebat quatuor scriptores, et in dubiis semper orabat*: 'he always had four secretaries with him, and in doubtful matters always prayed'.

literary weaknesses merely for the sake of allowing his strengths to seem greater.

The *Summa* does, however, have a completely predictable literary and intellectual structure: a form which grew out of the practice of oral disputation in the medieval universities. The whole work is divided into three parts: Prima, Secunda and Tertia. The Second Part is divided into two sub-parts of its own: Prima Secundae ('the first part of the second part', customarily abbreviated as IaIIae) and Secunda Secundae ('the second part of the second part', or IIaIIae). Each part is divided into *quaestiones* ('questions'), each of which contains a number of *articuli* ('articles'). With rare exceptions, each *articulus* has four elements: (a) several *obiectiones*; (b) a short statement of an opposite view beginning with, and known by, the words *Sed contra*; (c) St Thomas's general *Responsio* or reply; (d) his specific replies to the original *obiectiones*, each beginning with the words *ad primum/secundum/tertium* [*argumentum*] (usually abbreviated in references to *ad 1*, *ad 2*, *ad 3*, etc.). The *obiectiones* are 'objections' in the sense of being arguments 'raised up against' the conclusion that St Thomas wishes to reach. References to the *Summa* usually take the following form or some variant of it: IaIIae 60:4 ad 1. This example (taken at random) expands into: Prima Secundae, *Quaestio* 60, *articulus* 4, reply to *obiectio* 1. A little practice will equip the reader to decode these references easily.

The translations have been made according to a principle which is surprisingly often disregarded: that the translator's duty is to transmit what the original author said, rather than what the translator thinks he ought to have said. It is not the translator's business to improve on the original; one has no right to paraphrase one's way out of difficulties; one certainly has no right to import clandestine elements of political correctness, or to modify religious or moral sentiments of which one does not approve. If the original is difficult, the translation should reflect that difficulty. My translations are, as far as possible, accurate representations of St Thomas's own words and arguments. I have departed from literalness only where the consequence of not doing so would have been unintelligibility. The result is not always an easy read. At places where I have anticipated that the text will mystify the non-specialist, I have provided as much in the way of gloss and annotation as there was room for. The best advice that can be given to the student is to keep at it. St Thomas's intellectual habits and literary peculiarities do become clearer with repeated readings and acclimatisation. Also, a close acquaintance with Aristotle's *Ethics* and *Politics* is an indispensable prerequisite, and the secondary sources mentioned in the Bibliography will aid understanding further. A special problem is presented by St Thomas's habit of cross-referencing his remarks to other passages in the *Summa*: passages which, in many cases, are not included in this volume. These cross references can be looked up in either of the complete English translations of the *Summa* mentioned in the Bibliography.

St Thomas's political thought

The most obvious feature of St Thomas's philosophy taken as a whole is the extent to which it is informed by the ideas and thought-patterns of Aristotle: of 'the Philosopher', as St Thomas almost always calls him. In this respect, St Thomas is the most distinguished member of a relatively new intellectual movement. Until the late twelfth and early thirteenth centuries, the political and ethical thought of Aristotle was unknown in the West. This fact is due largely, though not entirely, to the triumph of neoplatonism as mediated through the writings of St Augustine. Some of Aristotle's logical writings were known through the sixth-century Latin translations of Boethius (480–525), but the study of his ethical and political works was for many years the province of Arab commentators, chief among whom were Avicenna (980–1037) and Averroes (1126–96). That these works became increasingly known in the West during the thirteenth century is due to the translational and exegetical activity of a handful of adventurous scholars, notably Gerard of Cremona (d. 1187), Michael Scotus (d. 1235), Albertus Magnus (d. 1280) and William of Moerbeke (d. 1286). This renewed study of Aristotle – the 'recovery' of Aristotle, as it is called – came to be associated especially with the University of Paris. As we have noted, it was here, under the tutelage of Albertus Magnus, that St Thomas began to be acquainted with him.

Not surprisingly, the Church regarded the 'recovery' of Aristotle with hostility. Apart from his own paganism, the fact that Aristotle had been so much handled by Arab scholars was enough to infect him with the taint of Islam. The interpretations of Averroes were perceived as being particularly at odds with the fundamentals of Christianity; but they found a Latin champion nonetheless, in the person of Siger of Brabant (1240–81), Professor of Philosophy at the University of Paris. Repeated ecclesiastical censures culminated in 1270, when thirteen Aristotelian propositions were condemned as heretical by Bishop Etienne Tempier of Paris, a condemnation repeated and extended in 1277. Almost the whole of St Thomas's professional life was therefore passed in an atmosphere of hostility towards Aristotle. Despite this atmosphere – perhaps because of it – St Thomas became convinced that it is possible to reconcile the teachings of Aristotle with those of the Church. Aristotle, though he lacked the advantage of divine revelation, and though his understanding of truth was to that extent defective, had carried intellectual investigation as far as unaided reason can go. When his conclusions are properly understood and corrected by the addition of revealed truth, the resulting synthesis of reason and revelation will be an intellectually complete system. So St Thomas believed. To produce such a synthesis, and to do so by the kind of minute philosophical analysis that we find exemplified in the *Summa*, became his life's work.

As we might expect, therefore, his political thought differs much from the predominantly Platonist and Augustinian orientation of earlier generations. For St Augustine and those who wrote under his inspiration, earthly politics is on the whole a regrettable and squalid business. At best, it is a necessary evil. Political arrangements are inseparable from the sinful condition of fallen man. Government would not have come into existence at all had the Fall not occurred. It originates in human greed and in the desire which men have to dominate one another. Its redeeming feature is that it functions to limit and control man's destructive impulses, to punish the sinful and to test the faith of the righteous. Earthly peace and justice are uneasy, transient and unstable. They are pale copies of the true peace and justice laid up in heaven, which will be realised only after the end of earthly history, when the City of God enters into its inheritance of eternal bliss. Meanwhile the world grinds on through the war, greed, strife and pain generated by the ceaseless attempts of fallen men to triumph over one another.[9] Especially during the so-called Investiture Controversy of 1075–1122, the idea gathered momentum that the only thing which can redeem human government from being wholly sinful is the complete submission of earthly princes to the spiritual power: that is, to the guidance and censure of the Church, ruled over by the Supreme Pontiff in Rome.[10] This kind of political theory sets the predominant tone of political debate in the Latin West down to the thirteenth century and, in many respects,

---

[9] See R. W. Dyson, *The Pilgrim City: Social and Political Ideas in the Writings of St Augustine of Hippo* (Woodbridge, Suffolk, 2001); H. A. Deane, *The Social and Political Ideas of St Augustine of Hippo* (New York and London, 1963).

[10] See, e.g., Brian Tierney, *The Crisis of Church and State, 1050–1300* (Englewood Cliffs, N.J., 1980) pt 11; G. Tellenbach, *Church, State and Christian Society at the Time of the Investiture Contest* (Oxford, 1948).

beyond. An oft-quoted watchword of the hierocratic theorists of the thirteenth century comes verbatim from Augustine's *De civitate Dei* (2:21): 'True justice, however, does not exist other than in that commonwealth whose founder and ruler is Christ.'

The 'recovery' of Aristotle equips St Thomas to forge a new kind of political theory: a political theory which we may characterise as milder and more optimistic precisely because it lacks Augustine's stringent insistence on the unworthiness of this world and its ends. In this sense, St Thomas's remarks may be taken as a turning-point in the history of political thought. Augustine, with his eyes fastened upon on the world to come – the transcendent other world of the Christian platonist – had found the present world unnatural, sin-laden, destructive and disordered, and its politics harsh and coercive merely. To Augustine, the individual is aligned either with earth or with heaven. To be the ally of the one is to be estranged from the other. St Thomas, by contrast, finds nothing to quarrel with in the rational, humane and ordered world depicted by the Philosopher. He never explicitly disagrees with Augustine; but he sees no irreconcilable tension between the acquisition of present goods on earth and the achievement of eternal ones in heaven, provided that the former are directed towards the latter and the latter are not neglected in favour of the former. The interests of this world and the next can coexist. St Thomas quotes with approval the famous maxim of Aristotle, that 'man is by nature a political animal' (Ia 96:4 (p. 4, below); *De regimine principum* 1:1 (p. 6, below)). This is a maxim which runs counter to the Augustinian insistence that God 'did not intend that His rational creature, made in His own image, should have lordship over any but irrational creatures: not man over man, but man over the beasts' (*De civitate Dei* 19:15). To be sure, man has a true and final end of which Aristotle knew nothing. His true destiny is eternal beatitude with God in heaven. But earthly wellbeing, as far as it goes and as long as it is valued at its proper worth, is both possible and desirable, and the political means by which it is secured are valid. Even the rule of unbelievers over the faithful is legitimate provided that it is not scandalous or dangerous to the faith. Dominion and rule were introduced by human law; but the Divine law, which is of grace, does not abolish the human law, which arises from natural reason. Of itself the distinction between believers and unbelievers does not remove the authority of unbelievers over the believer (IIaIIae 10:10 (p. 270, below)).

Life on earth, then, is not the welter of misery that St Augustine depicted, and the achievement of earthly wellbeing is an end which, though limited and secondary, is positive and worthwhile, and of which human beings have no reason to be ashamed. The achievement of such earthly wellbeing requires government; but this is not 'Augustinian' government. It is not ordained to do little more than hold the lid on human destructiveness by force and fear. It is a benevolent administration suited to the kind of sociable and co-operating creature that man is by nature. No one is able to provide himself with all the necessaries of life: we need to co-operate in order to secure the benefits of a division of labour. Though rational, we are in some ways more vulnerable than the beasts, who are equipped by nature with the means of defence or flight and who know by instinct what is harmful to them. There may be more than one way to achieve our ends, and we need to be guided wisely towards them just as a ship needs to be steered into harbour. These are facts which have nothing to do with sin. They are facts of human nature simply. They are the facts which make it necessary for a community to be knit together in a collective purpose by wise leadership directed to the common good (see *De regimine principum* 1:1 (pp. 5ff, below)). The purpose of secular government is not suppression and punishment, but the achievement of earthly wellbeing.

Nor is earthly wellbeing only a matter of bodily protection and economic satisfaction. An ordered and co-operative life with others of our own kind can be a positive source of happiness and virtue. '[T]he end for which a community is brought together is to live according to virtue; for men come together so that they may live well in a way that would not be possible for each of them living singly. For the good is life according to virtue, and so the end of human association is a virtuous life' (*De regimine principum* 1:15). What St Thomas has to say about obedience at IIaIIae 104 (p. 57, below) is in some ways ill expressed; but in essence it is straightforward. Subjection is not foreign to our nature. Just as it is natural for material objects to be moved by stronger forces of nature, so is it natural for human beings to be moved by the commands of their natural superiors. Obedience is the virtue which reinforces all the other virtues in us. The subjection of inferiors to superiors is part of the divinely willed order, and it is God's will that we should obey our natural superiors in all that they can lawfully command: in all, that is, that does not contravene His will. Christians must not suppose that the fact of their having become Christians exempts them from obedience to the secular powers.

At *De regimine principum* 1:3 (p. 10, below), St Thomas holds that the kind of leadership which our condition requires is best provided by a king. Kingship, because it is government by one, is the most natural and therefore the best kind of government. Its archetype is God's government of the universe, and we see it mirrored everywhere in nature. St Thomas follows Aristotle in referring to the 'king' bee. It is the most efficient kind of government because a king's power is undivided and his freedom of action unlimited. The king has no one to compromise with, dissent from or consult. Also, although monarchy perverted into tyranny is the worst kind of bad government, monarchy is the form of government least likely to become perverted because it is not subject to the kind of internal stresses which subvert government by several (*De regimine principum* 1:6 (p. 16, below)). The discussion of governmental forms in *De regimine principum* is left incomplete, and St Thomas abandoned the treatise before taking the subject up again. In the *Summa*, he recommends a kingship tempered or limited by elements of democracy and oligarchy (IaIIae 105:1 (p. 52, below)), an arrangement also hinted at in *De regimine principum* 1:7 (p. 17, below). This, of course, reflects Aristotle's preference for mixed government. St Thomas follows Aristotle in supposing that this kind of government will derive stability from the fact that it will please all sections of the community.

But the Christian king must understand that his function is not merely to rule externals. In the final analysis his task is to create conditions within which men will be able to achieve the supernatural end which lies beyond earthly prosperity and wellbeing. Whatever he does must have material benefit only as an intermediate goal. His ultimate aim must be the virtue and salvation of his subjects. His true reward is not any material gain; nor is it the passing glory which comes from the renown of men. It is the eternal blessedness of heaven (*De regimine principum* 1:9–16 (pp. 24ff, below)). This kind of thing is, of course, a stock in trade of ecclesiastical writers. Such pious advice to rulers goes back to St Augustine's famous panegyric on Christian emperors at *De civitate Dei* 5:24, a passage which St Thomas approvingly paraphrases at *De regimine principum* 1:9 (p. 26, below):

> [W]e do not call Christian princes happy because they ruled for a longer time, or because they died in peace and left behind sons to rule as emperors, or because they subdued the enemies of the commonwealth, or because they were able to avoid and suppress uprisings against them by the citizens. Rather, we say that they are happy if they rule justly; if they prefer to govern wicked desires more than any people whatsoever; if they do these things not out of craving for empty glory, but from love of eternal felicity. We say that, for the time being, such Christian emperors are happy in hope and that, in time

to come, when that to which we now look forward has arrived, they will be so in possession.

It is at first sight odd that, despite his interest in how rulers should behave, St Thomas does not offer an extended treatment of the question of 'Church and State'. An obvious explanation is the fact that he was not himself involved in any particular political controversy. The major medieval treatises dealing with the question of *regnum* and *sacerdotium* were, after all, without exception produced as contributions to a specific dispute. St Thomas's several remarks may be regarded as evidence of a consistent if unelaborated position (see *De regimine principum* 1:15 (p. 39, below); IIaIIae 12:2 (p. 276, below); and *Scripta super libros sententiarum* 11, Dist. 44, quaest. 3, art. 4 (p. 277, below)). He states in a general way that the Supreme Pontiff is the representative of Christ on earth; that the king should submit to the spiritual guidance of the priesthood; that in certain cases he is subject to the temporal authority of the Church; that spiritual and temporal power come together in the Supreme Pontiff; and that the subjects of a king who apostasises from the faith can be released from their oath of fealty to him. His fullest statement is as follows (p. 278, below):

> Spiritual and secular power are both derived from the Divine power, and so secular power is subject to spiritual power insofar as this is ordered by God: that is, in those things which pertain to the salvation of the soul. In such matters, then, the spiritual power is to be obeyed before the secular. But in those things which pertain to the civil good, the secular power should be obeyed before the spiritual, according to Matthew 22:21: 'Render to Caesar the things that are Caesar's.' Unless perhaps the spiritual and secular powers are conjoined, as in the pope, who holds the summit of both powers: that is, the spiritual and the secular, through the disposition of Him Who is both priest and king, a priest for ever according to the order of Melchizedek.

The conclusion to which this and related passages point is that St Thomas subscribed to the *ratione peccati* doctrine usually associated with Innocent III's decretal *Novit*:[11] that the jurisdiction of kings is separate from that of popes; that popes should not ordinarily interfere in temporal affairs; but that they may judge and punish kings 'by reason of sin'. This, broadly speaking, was the standard position of the papacy between the pontificates

---

[11] See especially Tierney, *The Crisis of Church and State*, pt 111, ch. 4; see also S. R. Packard, *Europe and the Church under Innocent III* (New York, 1927); H. Tillmann, *Pope Innocent III* (Amsterdam, 1978); J. A. Watt, *The Theory of Papal Monarchy in the Thirteenth Century* (London, 1965).

of Innocent III (1196–1216) and Boniface VIII (1294–1303), and it would be surprising had St Thomas held any other view. The fact that he does not elaborate it or illustrate it with the standard historical examples is not, in itself, remarkable.

Because, for St Thomas, politics is a benign and positive activity, and civic happiness a worthwhile end, he takes a different view of tyranny from the 'traditional' Augustinian one. For Augustine, the power of even the cruellest tyrant has a divine origin and therefore a kind of divine validity. God has bestowed power upon the tyrant to punish sinners and try the faith of the righteous. If we find ourselves under a tyrant, we should reflect that this is no more than our sinful condition deserves, and submit with as good a grace as we can muster. The only exception arises if the tyrant requires us to do something plainly contrary to God's will. In such a case – if, say, he requires us to sacrifice to an idol – our proper course is to decline to obey and suffer the consequences. We may not resist. Augustine will countenance nothing more than civil disobedience. Where we cannot in conscience obey, we should follow the example of the martyrs.[12] St Thomas, by contrast, though his thought on the subject is not wholly divested of Augustinian elements, does not regard tyranny simply as a divinely intended punishment; nor does he hold that the right to disregard a tyrant's commands extends only to those commands which directly contradict the divine will. Kings exist to do more than merely suppress wickedness and test faith. They exist to secure a common good or a public interest. If, therefore, instead of this, the king devotes himself to his own private good – if he becomes a tyrant in the sense specified in Book III of Aristotle's *Politics* – he has betrayed the purpose for which God appointed him, and his people have no obligation to obey. They can, indeed, take action against him – on one occasion (IaIIae 96:4 ad 3 (p. 145, below)) St Thomas uses the word *resistere* – in appropriate circumstances.

What action St Thomas thinks them entitled to take is not entirely clear, at least partly because he himself does not think the question amenable to a straightforward answer. Some commentators have thought him inconsistent or pusillanimous on this issue. In his relatively youthful *Scripta super libros sententiarum*, speaking with apparent approval of the assassination of Julius Caesar, he seems to subscribe to a version of tyrannicide, at least when the tyranny is extreme and no other course of action is available (p. 72, below). At *De regimine principum* 1:7 (p. 17, below), he takes the view

---

[12] See Dyson, *The Pilgrim City*, ch. 2.

that action may be taken against tyrants, but only by those who are in some sense authorised to do so: either because they have a formal 'kingmaking' role, or because they are carrying out the will of an oppressed community. Tyrants may not be overthrown merely on the private judgment of someone who happens not to like the king. Those who think otherwise are a source of danger to everyone. Again, at *De regimine principum* 1:7 (p. 17, below) and in the *Summa* (IIaIIae 104:6 ad 3 (p. 71, below); IIaIIae 42:2 ad 3 (p. 250, below)) he holds that tyranny of a relatively mild kind ought to be tolerated and that action should be taken only where the harm involved in doing so is not greater than the advantages which taking action may be expected to secure. We may read these statements in conjunction with what he says about war and violence (Chapter 6): that wars waged to repel aggression or escape oppression, and reasonable force used in self-defence and without malice, are morally justified, but that one must always be careful not to do more damage than one averts. His position on the question of tyranny is not really inconsistent with itself or with his general view of how people who are threatened or aggrieved ought to behave; nor, strictly, does he fudge the issue. His remarks, taken together, add up to an intelligible position of cautious conservatism which recognises that extreme measures may be justified sometimes but should be avoided if at all possible.

St Thomas's willingness to engage in a positive spirit with the institutions and practices of the secular world is illustrated also by his attitude to private property and his interest in some of its minutiae (Chapter 5). He does not abandon the traditional belief which St Ambrose and St Augustine had taken over from the Roman Stoics that by nature all things are common. Departing once more from the Augustinian view of things, however – although, again, without overt disagreement – he does not associate private property merely with sin and greed and fallen human nature. It is by human law that we possess property; but our possession of it is justified by reference to practical considerations which are entirely benign. Human laws regulating property ownership are additions to, but not departures from, the law of nature. If there were no private property the earth's resources would not be as well managed as when they are owned and cared for by determinate individuals. Individuals will inevitably bestow more care on what belongs to them than they will on common property. This is not because human beings are sinful or depraved, but because our view of things is by nature limited or partial. If there were no laws to make clear who owns what, quarrels would occur more frequently than they do.

The institution of property therefore has a contribution to make to our earthly wellbeing, and offences against property are sins as well as crimes. St Thomas discusses the nature of such offences with a degree of detail which no earlier Christian writer had thought it worthwhile to bestow. His discussion of usury in particular shows the influence on his mind of non-Christian streams of thought. Whereas the patristic objection to usury had been on straightforward biblical and humanitarian grounds – the bible condemns usury; usurers are heartless creatures who exploit the misfortunes of others[13] – St Thomas's objection is grounded in Aristotle's account of the nature of money and its use and a technical analysis of the Roman law idea of *res fungibilia* (IIaIIae 78 (p. 220, below)).

It should be noted that St Thomas's account of private property differs from what we may call 'modern' doctrines of property in one significant respect. For St Thomas, what human laws confer is the right to expropriate property from nature and manage it responsibly. They do not confer an unlimited right of acquisition and use. This distinction between ownership and use is effectively absent from modern doctrines of property, but it is important to understand it. Again, it is derived from Aristotle. We are entitled to as much property as we need to enable us to meet our earthly needs comfortably. But what we have in excess of these needs we owe as a matter of moral duty to the poor. Private ownership exists as a convenience superimposed by human law upon the law of nature; but 'things pertaining to human right cannot take anything away from natural right or Divine right.' The conclusion therefore follows that in the event of a necessity

> so urgent and clear that [it] must be met at once by whatever means are to hand – for example, if a person is in immediate danger and no other help is available – anyone can then lawfully supply his own need from the property of another by taking it either openly or in secret; nor, properly speaking, does this have the character of theft or robbery . . . Properly speaking, to take and use another's property secretly in a case of extreme necessity does not have the character of theft, because that which someone takes in order to support his own life becomes his own by reason of that necessity. (IIaIIae 66:7 *responsio* & ad 2 (pp. 216f, below))

St Thomas is content to leave the actual distribution of surplus property to the conscience of the individual proprietor. In a modern guise, however,

---

[13] See Dyson, *The Pilgrim City*, ch. 3(d).

his argument would no doubt find expression as an argument in favour of progressive or redistributive taxation.

The best known and most discussed aspect of St Thomas's political writing is his analysis and typology of law (Chapter 3). He distinguishes four kinds of law: eternal law, natural law, human law and Divine law. The idea of natural law in particular – although, of course, not new – is given a detailed philosophical treatment unprecedented in Christian and pagan literature; although it will be noticed that St Thomas's philosophical orientation when dealing with law is much more Platonist than Aristotelian. The reader will encounter difficulties here, partly because of the nature of the subject matter and partly because of St Thomas's own modes of expression; but it is not difficult to express the pith of what he has to say.

Law, he holds, is a 'rule and measure' of reason. This is a definition which he proposes several times with slight variations. He conceives of law as being a kind of rational pattern somewhat after the fashion of Plato's forms or ideas. Any relationship between a superior and an inferior involves a kind of picture in the mind of the superior of what the inferior should do or be. For instance, before he actually makes anything, the craftsman has in his mind an idea – a rational pattern – of what his product will be like. In the case of a relationship between ruler and subjects, the idea which the ruler has in his mind of what his subjects should do is what we call law. It is the 'rule and measure' which governs their acts, and when they act as they should, they 'participate' in it in the way that a table 'participates' in the idea of a table which the carpenter has in his mind. Because God is the supreme Governor of everything, the rational pattern of the government of the universe which exists in His mind is 'law' in the most general and comprehensive sense. This rational pattern in God's mind is what St Thomas calls the eternal law, and to it everything in the created universe is subject. The eternal law, he says, 'is nothing but the rational pattern of the Divine wisdom considered as directing all actions and motions' (IaIIae 93:1 *responsio* (p. 102, below)).

Inasmuch as mankind is part of the order of the universe, it follows that there must be a portion or section of the eternal law which relates to his own conduct specifically. This is the *lex naturalis*, the 'natural' law, the 'law of nature'. There is a broad sense in which all animals have a 'natural' law: the sense, that is, in which all sentient creatures have an instinctive urge to protect and reproduce themselves. But the natural law to which men are subject is not the mere instinct to survive and breed. It is prescriptive; it tells us what we ought to do. The natural law tells us to do good and avoid evil. It tells us to live at peace with our neighbours. It is 'natural' to us, at least partly, in the sense that we are by nature creatures to whom its prescriptions are rationally obvious. We do not have to learn about them or have them legislated for us: to all human beings, pagans included, they simply 'stand to reason'.

We are, then, creatures able by nature to tell right from wrong: able, as it were, to read off the pattern of right conduct from the rational nature of the universe. Why, in that case, is it also necessary for us to have human laws? To this question, Augustine had given a predictable answer: sin has so effaced the natural law from our hearts that we now need human law to repress our destructiveness by force and fear. St Thomas – again without explicitly disagreeing with Augustine – gives a quite different account. The law of nature is clear to us, he says, but its provisions are too general to furnish us with an immediate guide to conduct. We know that we ought to do good and avoid evil; but we do not necessarily know what is good or evil in specific circumstances; nor do we know what to do with people who do evil: what punishments should be and who should incur them. This difference between our awareness of the general principles of the natural law and our need for detailed rules of behaviour creates the gap which needs to be filled by human laws. Human laws are specific inferences made by practical reasoning from the natural law. They are derived from it in much the same way as, in scientific or speculative reasoning, we infer particular conclusions from general principles. Some human laws are so close to the general principles of nature that we find them shared by all known peoples. These laws are what Roman law traditionally designates as the *ius gentium*. Other, more particular, 'civil' laws may be peculiar to a given political community and, to that extent, separated from the natural law by a longer chain of reasoning. But all human law properly so called takes its character as law from the fact that it reflects, however remotely, the general principles of the natural law. Thus, human laws can be changed or dispensed from in order to suit changing times or exceptional circumstances; but the general principles of the natural law cannot be changed and must always be honoured. Moreover, St Thomas shares with Aristotle the belief that, if we are required by human law to conform outwardly to standards of virtuous conduct, this can form genuinely virtuous habits in us. Human law can in this way also be a force in moral education.

By the same token, 'laws' which are not derived from the natural law – laws which are unjust in the sense of oppressing those subject to them or failing to secure their good – are not really laws at all, and so we are not bound to obey them. They have, St Thomas says (IaIIae 96:4, *responsio* (p. 144, below), more the character of violence than of law. And so a condition here arises similar to the one that we noted in connection with tyranny. We should obey even unjust laws if the consequences of disobedience would be worse than any good which disobedience might secure. But we are not *obliged* to obey, simply because the 'laws' in question are not really laws, and so cannot oblige. (The point is more obvious in Latin than in English, inasmuch as *lex*, 'law', is related etymologically to *ligare*, to bind.) Once again, the Augustinian doctrine that we normally have no rights against the existing order is challenged, albeit tentatively, by a new affirmation: that we are entitled to expect the existing order to exhibit a certain moral quality, namely, justice, in the absence of which it has no claim to our allegiance.

The fourth and final kind of law is the Divine law. The Divine law differs from human law in that it is not derived by a process of rational inference from the more general principles of nature; nor do all its precepts 'stand to reason'. It is part of the eternal law, but it is the law of revelation, made accessible to us through the teaching of scripture and the Church. Divine law is a separate and autonomous field of law. Human law must not contravene it; but human law is not derived from it. Why do rational creatures need a revealed law over and above the natural and human laws? The answer is that human law is concerned only with justice in things relating to our public or social life. Eternal salvation requires that we be virtuous in our private acts and intentions also. The Divine law regulates those aspects of our conduct that no one can see; it punishes us insofar as we are sinners rather than merely criminals; it guides us in those duties which are religious rather than civic.

Broadly speaking, then, St Thomas develops the kind of legal theory which is called 'intellectualist' rather than 'voluntarist'. He thinks that law derives the morally important aspects of its character not from the will or command of a legislator, but from the rational content which it embodies; and legislative pronouncements which depart from, or which fail to institutionalise, the natural law simply do not have the character of law. Promulgation and command are important parts of what make law a reality, and there is a formal or technical sense in which even bad laws are laws; but no one who commands or promulgates something against nature makes law in the proper sense. Ultimately, the value of law depends upon the validity with which it is inferred from eternal and invariable moral principles; nor is it necessarily the province of the Church to define the meaning and application of these principles. Under the tutelage of Aristotle, the human legislator is given a dignity which, according to the Augustinian mode of understanding, he could not have.

What general evaluation may be given of St Thomas's political thought? On the one hand, it must be said that St Thomas has been in some ways overrated as a philosopher. The encyclical *Aeterni patris* did not, strictly speaking, appoint him as the 'official' philosopher of the Catholic Church; but it might as well have done so. Down to the 1960s, Catholic philosophical and theological education was dominated almost wholly by the 'Angelic Doctor' and those who wrote and thought under his aegis. The conferment upon him of such a status by a Church so authoritarian in its approach to intellectual enquiry effectively placed St Thomas beyond criticism for the best part of a century. Only since the late 1960s has solid and disinterested Aquinas scholarship become possible, and now that the odour of sanctity has dissipated, frank acknowledgment of his faults is possible. As we have remarked, his literary style is often difficult. He is prone to the pursuit of elaborate and distracting side issues. His arguments tend to be clouded by needlessly subtle and sometimes trivial distinctions: this is a criticism which has perhaps been levelled too much against scholasticism in general, but it is not wholly undeserved. Ultimately, of course, he is intellectually dishonest; perhaps it would be more charitable to say that he is innocently tendentious. He is committed in advance to a closed system of religious and moral beliefs, and his 'philosophical' arguments are without exception devised with a view to supporting and confirming those beliefs.

On the other hand, it is not the historian's business to reproach St Thomas for sharing the attitudes, beliefs and prejudices of every other thirteenth-century Christian intellectual; and we have to grant that the work of reconciling Aristotle and the Christian faith is an enterprise of heroic proportions. The fact that so much of it now seems quaint and misguided is hardly the point. Specifically in regard to political theory, we may make three remarks. First, St Thomas was by far the ablest and most active of those responsible for reintroducing the political and ethical thought of Aristotle into the educational curriculum of the Latin West. This in itself is a fact of considerable significance. Second, and as a direct consequence of the rehabilitation of Aristotle, he was largely responsible for a wholesale re-evaluation of political activity and participation as worthwhile activities apart from any connection with the Church. At the cost of some oversimplification, we may say that, in this regard, he helped to make 'modern' normative political theory possible. Third, although he himself abstains from an extended treatment of 'Church and State', he made available the intellectual equipment by which his successors – notably Marsilius of Padua – were at last to begin to unravel the long-established interweaving of secular and spiritual themes in European political discourse. These facts establish him in a place of the first importance in the history of political thought.

A brief chronology of St Thomas's life

ca. 1225	Born in the castle of Rocca Secca, near Aquino.
1230	Began his education at the Abbey of Monte Cassino.
1238	Entered the *Studium generale* at Naples.
1245	Joined the Dominican Order; went to Paris to study with Albertus Magnus.
1248	Went to Cologne with Albertus Magnus.
1252–6	Studying at the University of Paris. Working on *Scripta super libros sententiarum*.
1256	Received his *licentia docendi*, i.e. his licence to teach: his 'Master's Degree'. *Scripta super libros sententiarum* completed.
1259–68	Teaching at Paris, Naples, Orvieto, Viterbo and Rome.
1264	*Summa contra gentiles* completed.
1266	*Summa theologiae* begun.
1267	*De regimine principum* possibly abandoned on the death of its dedicatee; finished some years later by Tolommeo of Lucca.
1269–72	Teaching at Paris; *Commentaries* on Aristotle.
1272–3	Teaching at the Dominican *Studium* at Naples. Sudden illness, December 1273; *Summa theologiae* discontinued.
1274	Died 7 March, Fessa Nuova.

Bibliography

Primary sources

The standard text of the *Summa theologiae* is the *editio Leonina* – i.e. the edition prepared by members of the Dominican Order at the command of Pope Leo XIII. This is in vols. IV–VIII of *S. Thomae Aquinatis opera omnia iussu Leonis XIII edita cura et studio Fratrum Praedicatorum* (Rome, 1888–1948). The same text, with or without critical apparatus, can be consulted in numerous subsequent editions.

De regimine principum and *De regimine Iudaeorum* are in R. M. Spiazzi, *S. Thomae Aquinatis opuscula philosophica* (Turin and Rome, 1951). R. M. Spiazzi has also edited St Thomas's commentary on Aristotle's *Politics*, as *In octo libros politicorum Aristotelis expositio* (Turin and Rome, 1966).

Scripta super libros sententiarum is in vols. VI–VIII of *S. Thomae opera omnia* (25 vols., Parma, 1852–73; repr. New York, 1948–9).

The whole of the *Summa theologiae* is available in the following English translations:

Summa theologica, trans. Fathers of the English Dominican Province (2nd, rev. edn, 22 vols., London, 1912–36) (the 'Dominican Edition': see table of abbreviations).

Summa theologiae, trans. Thomas Gilby *et al.* (61 vols., London and New York, 1964–80) (the 'Blackfriars Edition'). This is a bilingual edition printed with the Leonine edition of the Latin text *verso* (without *apparatus criticus*) and the English translation *recto*.

The earlier translation is literal and, for the most part, accurate. The translation by Fr Gilby and others is so free and colloquial as to be almost a paraphrase.

A comprehensive catalogue of St Thomas's works, compiled by I. T. Eschmann, OP is printed in E. Gilson, *The Christian Philosophy of St Thomas Aquinas* (see below), pp. 381ff.

Secondary sources

Biographies

For a scholarly biography of St Thomas see J. A. Weisheipl, *Friar Thomas d'Aquino: His Life, Thought and Works* (Oxford, 1975). G. K. Chesterton's *St Thomas Aquinas: the Dumb Ox* (New York and London, 1956) is hagiography, but not without value.

St Thomas and Aristotle

There is a useful account of the 'recovery' of Aristotle by Fernand van Steenberghen: *Aristotle in the West: The Origins of Latin Aristotelianism* (New York, 1970); see also van Steenberghen, *Thomas Aquinas and Radical Aristotelianism* (Washington, D.C., 1980); C. J. Nederman, *Medieval Aristotelianism and its Limits: Classical Traditions in Moral and Political Philosophy* (Aldershot, 1997); C. Flüeler, *Rezeption und Interpretation der Aristotelischen 'Politica' im späten Mittelalter* (Amsterdam and Philadelphia, 1992).

General studies of St Thomas

For a general, though highly tendentious, account of St Thomas's philosophy, see E. Gilson, *The Christian Philosophy of St Thomas Aquinas* (New York and London, 1961); see also F. C. Coplestone, *Aquinas* (Harmondsworth, 1970); A. Kenny, *Aquinas* (Oxford, 1980); J. Pieper, *A Guide to Thomas Aquinas* (Notre Dame, Ind., 1987); M. de Wulf, *The System of St Thomas Aquinas* (Cambridge, Mass., 1922); B. Davies, *The Thought of Thomas Aquinas* (Oxford, 1992).

Moral philosophy

On St Thomas's moral philosophy generally see R. M. McInerny, *Ethica Thomistica: The Moral Philosophy of St Thomas Aquinas*

(Washington, D.C., 1982); G. Stevens, 'Moral Obligation in St Thomas', *The Modern Schoolman* 40 (1962–3), pp. 1ff. For St Thomas's understanding of Aristotle's treatment of the virtues, see Harry Jaffa, *Thomism and Aristotelianism* (Chicago, 1952); see also R. Sokolowski, *The God of Faith and Reason* (Notre Dame, Ind., 1982); J. Pieper, *The Four Cardinal Virtues: Prudence, Justice, Fortitude, Temperance* (New York, 1965).

Natural law

On natural law in St Thomas see R. A. Armstrong, *Primary and Secondary Precepts in Thomistic Natural Law Teaching* (The Hague, 1966); D. J. O'Connor, *Aquinas and the Natural Law* (London, 1967); J. Finnis, *Natural Law and Natural Rights* (Oxford, 1982); A. P. d'Entrèves, *Natural Law* (London, 1950). More generally, see Y. Simon, *The Tradition of Natural Law: A Philosopher's Reflections* (New York, 1965); P. E. Sigmund, *Natural Law in Political Thought* (Cambridge, Mass., 1971).

St Thomas's political thought

J. Finnis, *Aquinas: Moral, Political and Legal Theory* (Oxford, 1998); T. Gilby, *Principality and Polity: Aquinas and the Rise of State Theory in the West* (London, 1958); E. L. Fortin, 'St Thomas Aquinas', in Leo Strauss and Joseph Cropsey (eds.), *A History of Political Philosophy* (Chicago, 1981), pp. 223ff; J. Tooke, *The Just War in Aquinas and Grotius* (London, 1965); J. Dunbabin, 'The Reception and Interpretation of Aristotle's *Politics*', in N. Kretzmann, A. Kenny and J. Pinborg (eds.), *The Cambridge History of Later Medieval Philosophy* (Cambridge, 1982); J. I. Catto, 'Ideas and Experience in the Political Thought of Aquinas', *Past and Present* 71 (1976), pp. 3ff.

Medieval political thought

A. Black, *Political Thought in Europe, 1250–1450* (Cambridge, 1992); J. M. Blythe, *Ideal Government and the Mixed Constitution in the Middle Ages* (Princeton, N.J., 1992); R. W. and A. J. Carlyle, *A History of Medieval Political Theory in the West* (Edinburgh and London, 1903–36); Janet Coleman, *A History of Political Thought from the Middle Ages to the Renaissance* (Oxford, 2000); M. S. Kempshall, *The Common Good in Late Medieval Political Thought* (Oxford, 1999); C. H. McIlwain, *The Growth of Political Thought in the West* (New York, 1932); J. B. Morrall, *Political Thought in Medieval Times* (London, 1958); W. Ullmann, *Principles of Government and Politics in the Middle Ages* (London, 1961); *A History of Political Thought: The Middle Ages* (Harmondsworth, 1965).

Government and politics

(a) *Summa theologiae* Ia 96: Concerning the dominion which belonged to man in the state of innocence

articulus 3:[1] *Whether men were equal in the state of innocence*[2]

It seems that all men were equal in the state of innocence.

obiectio 1: For Gregory says: 'Where we do not sin, we are all equal.'[3] But in the state of innocence there was no sin. Therefore all were equal.

obiectio 2: Moreover, similarity and equality are the basis of mutual love, according to Ecclesiasticus 13:19: 'Every beast loveth its like; so also every man him that is nearest to himself.' Now in that state there was among men abundant love, which is the bond of peace. Therefore all were equal in the state of innocence.

obiectio 3: Moreover, when the cause ceases, the effect ceases also. But the inequality which now exists among men seems to arise, on the side of God, from the fact that He rewards some and punishes others; and, on the side of nature, from the fact that some are born weak and disadvantaged by some defect of nature, whereas others are strong and perfect. But this would not have been so in the primitive state.

sed contra: It is said at Romans 13:1 that the things which come from God are ordered. But order seems to consist especially in disparity; for Augustine says: 'Order is the disposition of equal and unequal things in such a way as to give to each its proper place.'[4] Therefore in the primitive

---

[1] This *quaestio* has four articles, the first two of which are: 'Whether man in the state of innocence was lord of the animals'; and 'Whether man was lord of all other creatures'.

[2] I.e. would all men have been equal had the Fall not occurred?

[3] *Moralia* 21:15 (*PL* 76:203).

[4] *De civitate Dei* 19:13.

state, in which everything was entirely proper, there would have been found disparity.

responsio: It is necessary to say that in the primitive state there would have been some disparity, at least as regards sex, because without diversity of sex there would be no generation; and similarly as regards age, for some would have been born of others; nor were those who mated sterile. Moreover, as regards the soul, there would have been diversity in the matter of righteousness and knowledge. For man worked not of necessity, but by the free will which equips the man who has it to apply his mind either more or less to the doing or willing or understanding of something. Hence some would have become more proficient in righteousness and knowledge than others.

There might have been bodily disparity also. For the human body was not so totally exempt from the laws of nature as not to receive from external sources varying degrees of advantage and help; for its life also was sustained by food. And so nothing prevents us from saying that, according to the different dispositions of the air and the different positions of the stars, some would have been born more robust in body than others, and greater and more beautiful and more fair; although even in those who were surpassed in these respects, there would have been no defect or sin either in soul or body.

ad 1: By these words Gregory intends to exclude the disparity which exists as between righteousness and sin from which it comes about that some persons are made subject to the coercion of others as a punishment.[5]

ad 2: Equality is the cause of equality in mutual love. Yet there can be greater love between unequals than between equals, even if not an equal reciprocation. For a father naturally loves his son more than a brother loves his brother, although the son does not love his father as much as he is loved by him.

ad 3: The cause of disparity could lie on the side of God [even in the state of innocence]: not, indeed, because He would punish some and reward others, but because He might exalt some above others, so that the beauty of order might shine forth all the more brightly among men. Disparity might arise also on the side of nature in the manner

[5] I.e. he does not mean to say that where there is no sin there is no inequality, but that such inequality as there is is not penal.

described in the body of the article, without there being any defect of nature.

articulus 4: Whether in the state of innocence man would have had dominion over man

It seems that in the state of innocence man would not have had dominion over man.

obiectio 1: For Augustine says at *De civitate Dei* 19: 'God did not intend that His rational creature, made in His own image, should have lordship over any but irrational creatures: not man over man, but man over the beasts.'[6]

obiectio 2: Moreover, that which was introduced as a punishment for sin would not have existed in the state of innocence. But the fact that man is subject to man was introduced as a punishment for sin. For after sin it was said to the woman (Genesis 3:16): 'Thou shalt be under thy husband's power.' Therefore in the state of innocence man would not have been subject to man.

obiectio 3: Moreover, subjection is opposed to liberty. But liberty is one of the foremost blessings, and would not have been lacking in the state of innocence, where, as Augustine says at *De civitate Dei* 14, 'nothing was absent that a good will might seek'.[7] Therefore man would not have had dominion over man in the state of innocence.

sed contra: The condition of man in the state of innocence was not more exalted than the condition of the angels. But among the angels some have dominion over others, and so one order is called 'Dominations'.[8] Therefore it was not contrary to the dignity of the state of innocence that one man should be ruled by another.

responsio: 'Dominion' is understood in two ways. In one way, it is contrasted with servitude; and so a master [*dominus*] in this sense is one to whom someone is subject as a slave. In another way, dominion is understood as referring in a general way to [the rule of] any kind of subject

---

[6] *De civitate Dei* 19:15.
[7] *De civitate Dei* 14:10.
[8] Cf. Colossians 1:16; Ephesians 1:21. The earliest and most influential Christian treatise on the 'orders' of the angels is Ps.-Dionysius, *De caelesti hierarchia* (*PG* 3; and see *Pseudo Dionysius: the Complete Works*, ed. and trans. C. Luibheid *et al.* (New York, 1987)). For St Thomas's discussion of the angelic orders see Ia 108:6.

3

whatsoever; and in this sense even he who has the office of governing and directing free men can be called a master. In the first sense, therefore, one man could not have had dominion over other men in the state of innocence; but, in the second sense, one man could have had dominion over others even in the state of innocence. The reason for this is that a slave differs from a free man in that the latter 'exists for his own sake', as is said at the beginning of the *Metaphysics*, whereas a slave is subordinated to another.[9] One man is therefore the master of another as his slave when he treats the one whose master he is as a means to his own – that is, to the master's – advantage. And since every man's proper good is desirable to himself, and, consequently, it is a sorrowful thing to anyone to cede to another a good which ought to be his own, therefore such dominion cannot exist without pain on the part of the subject; and so such dominion could not have existed in the state of innocence as between one man and another.

On the other hand, one man is the master of another as a free subject when he directs him either towards his own good, or towards the common good. And such dominion would have existed in the state of innocence between man and man, for two reasons. First, because man is by nature a social animal,[10] and so in the state of innocence would have lived a social life. But there cannot be social life among a multitude of people save under the direction of someone who is to look to the common good; for many, as such, seek many things, whereas one attends only to one. And so the Philosopher says at the beginning of the *Politics* that wherever many things are directed to one end, there is always found one at the head, directing them.[11] Second, if one man were pre-eminent over all the others in knowledge and righteousness, it would be inconsistent [with the idea of moral pre-eminence] for such pre-eminence not to be directed to the benefit of others, according to 1 Peter 4:10: 'As every man hath received grace, ministering the same one to another.' Hence Augustine says at *De civitate Dei* 19: 'For it is not out of any desire for mastery that just men command; rather they do so from a dutiful concern for others';[12] and: 'This is prescribed by the order of nature: it is thus that God created man.'[13]

By this are shown the replies to all the *obiectiones* which proceeded from the first mode of dominion.

[9] *Metaphysics* 1:2 (982b26).
[10] See n. 17, below.
[11] *Politics* 1:5 (1254a28).
[12] *De civitate Dei* 19:14.
[13] *De civitate Dei* 19:15.

(b) *The treatise 'De regimine principum' or 'De regno'*[14]

Preface

The author sets forth his intention in writing to the king of Cyprus[15] As I considered with myself what I should undertake that would be worthy of royal majesty and in keeping with my calling and office, it occurred to me that what I might offer a king above all would be a book written on the subject of kingship, in which I should, to the best of my powers, diligently draw out both the origin of a kingdom and what pertains to the king's office, according to the authority of Divine scripture, the teachings of the philosophers, and the examples given by those who praise princes, relying for the beginning, progression and completion of the work upon the aid of Him Who is King of kings and Lord of lords, by Whom kings reign: the Lord, 'a great God, and a great King above all gods' (Psalm 95:3).

Book I

Chapter I: That it is necessary for men who live together to be subject to diligent rule by someone To fulfil this intention, we must begin by explaining how the title 'king' is to be understood. Now in all cases where things are directed towards some end but it is possible to proceed in more than one way, it is necessary for there to be some guiding principle, so that the due end may be properly achieved. For example, a ship is driven in different directions according to the force of different winds, and it will not reach its final destination except by the industry of the steersman who guides it into port. Now man has a certain end towards which the whole of his life and activity is directed; for as a   creature who acts by intelligence, it is clearly his nature to work towards some end.[16] But men can proceed towards that end in different ways, as the very diversity of human efforts and activities shows. Man therefore needs something to guide him towards his end.

Now each man is imbued by nature with the light of reason, and he is directed towards his end by its action within him. If it were proper for man to live in solitude, as many animals do, he would need no other guide towards his end; for each man would then be a king unto himself, under God, the supreme King, and would direct his own actions by the light of reason divinely given to him. But man is by nature a social and

[14] See Introduction, p. xix.
[15] The chapter headings which appear in this treatise are the additions of a later editor.
[16] Aristotle, *Ethics* 1:7 (1098a5).

political animal, who lives in a community [*in multitudine vivens*]:[17] more so, indeed, than all other animals; and natural necessity shows why this is so. For other animals are furnished by nature with food, with a covering of hair, and with the means of defence, such as teeth, horns or at any rate speed in flight. But man is supplied with none of these things by nature. Rather, in place of all of them reason was given to him, by which he might be able to provide all things for himself, by the work of his own hands.[18] One man, however, is not able to equip himself with all these things, for one man cannot live a self-sufficient life. It is therefore natural for man to live in fellowship with many others.

Moreover, other animals are endowed with a natural awareness of everything which is useful or harmful to them. For example, the sheep naturally judges the wolf to be an enemy. Some animals even have a natural awareness which enables them to recognise certain medicinal plants and other things as being necessary to their lives. Man, however, has a natural understanding of the things necessary to his life only in a general way, and it is by the use of reason that he passes from universal principles to an understanding of the particular things which are necessary to human life. But it is not possible for one man to apprehend all such things by reason. It is therefore necessary for man to live in a community, so that each man may devote his reason to some particular branch of learning: one to medicine, another to something else, another to something else again. And this is shown especially by the fact that only man has the capacity to use speech, by means of which one man can reveal the whole content of his mind to another.[19] Other animals express their feelings to each other in a general way, as when a dog shows his anger by barking and the other animals show their feelings in various ways; but one man is more able to communicate with another than any other animal is, even those which are seen to be gregarious, such as cranes, ants and bees.[20] Solomon, therefore, is thinking of this at Ecclesiastes 4:9 where he says: 'Two are better than one, because they have the reward of mutual companionship.'

[17] Aristotle, *Politics* 1:2 (1253a2). St Thomas's 'man is by nature a social and political animal' – *Naturale autem est homini ut sit animal sociale et politicum* – is taken from William of Moerbeke's Latin translation of the *Politics*. On the whole it conveys the meaning of Aristotle's ὁ ἄνθρωπος φύσει πολιτικὸν ζῷον better than the literal translation 'political animal' would. See also p. 9, below. 'Community' is probably as close as one can get to what St Thomas usually means by *multitudo*.

[18] Aristotle, *De partibus animalium* 4:10 (687a19).

[19] Aristotle, *Politics* 1:2 (1253a1).

[20] Aristotle, *Historia animalium* 1:1 (488a10).

If, therefore, it is natural for man to live in fellowship with many others, it is necessary for there to be some means whereby such a community of men may be ruled. For if many men were to live together with each providing only what is convenient for himself, the community would break up into its various parts unless one of them had responsibility for the good of the community as a whole, just as the body of a man and of any other animal would fall apart if there were not some general ruling force to sustain the body and secure the common good of all its parts. Solomon is thinking of this at Proverbs 11:14 where he says: 'Where there is no governor, the people shall be scattered.' This accords with reason; for individual interests and the common good are not the same. Individuals differ as to their private interests, but are united with respect to the common good, and such differences have various causes. It is fitting, therefore, that, beyond that which moves the individual to pursue a good peculiar to himself, there should be something which promotes the common good of the many. It is for this reason that wherever things are organised into a unity, something is found that rules all the rest.[21] For by a certain order of Divine providence all bodies in the material universe are ruled by the primary, that is, the celestial, body, and all bodies by rational creatures.[22] Also, in one man the soul rules the body, and, within the soul, the irascible and concupiscible appetites are ruled by the reason.[23] Again, among the

[21] Aristotle, *Politics* 1:5 (1254a28).
[22] For St Thomas's cosmology see *SCG* 3:23; for the main classical origin of this cosmology see Aristotle, *De caelo* 1–2 *passim*. See also *SCG* 3:78.
[23] For St Thomas's explanation of this terminology, which the reader will encounter several times, see e.g. Ia 80:1–2; 81:1–3; IaIIae 9:2; 17:2. Scholastic psychology posits three parts of the soul: appetite, reason, and will. The soul is correctly ordered when reason controls the appetite and commands the will. The idea is, of course, in essence the same as the account of individual justice given by Plato at *Republic* 434D–449A. 'Appetite' is the name given by St Thomas to all strivings or drives, or (to give *appetitus* its literal meaning) all 'seekings' after something. Appetites can be conscious or unconscious, intellectual or sensitive. 'Sensitive' appetites – i.e. appetites arising from sensation – tend towards particular objects desired by the senses. They are 'concupiscible' insofar as they are directed towards a sensible good or strive to avoid a sensible evil; they are 'irascible' if the striving encounters an obstacle to be overcome. Concupiscible appetites include such things as love, hate, desire, aversion, joy and grief; irascible appetites such things as hope, despair, fear and anger. The movements of the appetites are the cause of emotions. 'Intellectual' or 'rational' appetite is the same thing as will. It differs from the sensitive appetite because it tends of itself towards the good as such, and therefore necessarily towards God as the Supreme Good. Sin occurs when an 'object moves the sensitive appetite, and the sensitive appetite inclines the reason and will' (IaIIae 85:1). At Ia 81:2 the terms 'concupiscible' and 'irascible' are attributed to Nemesius (*De natura hominis* 16; 17 (*PL* 40:672; 676)) and Damascene (*De fide orthodoxa* 2:12 (*PG* 94:928)). There is a useful synopsis at *NCE* 1, *s.v.* 'Appetite'. See also E. Gilson, *The Christian Philosophy of St Thomas Aquinas*, pt II, ch. 8.

members of the body there is one ruling part, either the heart or the head, which moves all the others.[24] It is fitting, therefore, that in every multitude there should be some ruling principle.[25]

Chapter II: The various forms of lordship or government But where matters are directed towards some end, there may be one way of proceeding which is right and another which not right; and so we find that the government of a community can be directed both rightly and not rightly.[26] Now something is directed rightly when it is led to its proper end, and not rightly when it is led to an end which is not proper to it. But the end proper to a community of free men is different from that of slaves. For a free man is one who is the master of his own actions, whereas a slave, insofar as he is a slave, is the property of another.[27] If, therefore, a community of free men is ordered by a ruler in such a way as to secure the common good, such rule will be right and just inasmuch as it is suitable to free men. If, however, the government is directed not towards the common good but towards the private good of the ruler, rule of this kind will be unjust and perverted;[28] and such rulers are warned by the Lord at Ezekiel 34:2, where He says: 'Woe be to the shepherds that do feed themselves' – because they seek only gain for themselves. 'Should not the shepherds feed the flocks?' Shepherds must seek the good of their flock, and all rulers the good of the community subject to them.

If, therefore, government is exercised unjustly by one man alone, who, in ruling, seeks gain for himself and not the good of the community subject to him, such a ruler is called a tyrant, a name derived from [the Greek word τυραννίς, which means] 'force', because he oppresses with power, and does not rule with justice.[29] Hence, among the ancients all men of power were called 'tyrants'.[30] If, however, unjust government is exercised not by one but by several, when this is done by a few it is called 'oligarchy', that is, 'rule by the few'; and this comes about when, by reason of their wealth, the few oppress the people, and it differs from tyranny only with respect

[24] Aristotle, *Metaphysics* 5:1 (1013a5).
[25] Cf. John of Salisbury, *Policraticus* 5:2.
[26] Aristotle, *Politics* 3:6 (1279a17).
[27] Aristotle, *Metaphysics* 1:2 (982b25).
[28] Aristotle, *Politics* 3:7 (1279a22); *Ethics* 8:10 (1159b31).
[29] Isidore of Seville, *Etymologiae* 9:3 (*PL* 82:344); although, like so many medieval etymologies, this one is not correct.
[30] Augustine, *De civitate Dei* 5:19.

to number. Again, if wrongful government is exercised by the many, this is named 'democracy', that is, 'rule by the people'; and this comes about when the common people oppress the rich by force of numbers. In this way the whole people will be like a single tyrant.

Similarly, it is proper to distinguish the various kinds of just government. For if the administration is in the hands of a certain section of the community [*aliquam multitudinem*], as when the military class [*multitudo bellatorum*] governs a city or province, this is commonly called polity.[31] If, again, administration is in the hands of a few but virtuous men, rule of this kind is called aristocracy: that is, 'the best rule', or 'rule of the best men' [*optimorum*], who for this reason are called aristocrats [*optimates*]. And if just government belongs to one man alone, he is properly called a king. Hence the Lord, at Ezekiel 37:24, says: 'And David my servant shall be king over them, and they all shall have one shepherd.' It is clearly shown by this verse that it is the nature of kingship that there should be one who rules, and that he should be a shepherd who seeks the common good and not his own gain.[32]

Now since it is fitting for man to live in a community because he would not be able to provide all the necessaries of life for himself were he to remain alone, it must be that a society of many men will be perfect to the extent that it is self-sufficient in the necessaries of life. The self-sufficient life is certainly present to some extent in the family of one household, with respect, that is, to the natural activities of nourishment and the procreation of children and other things of this kind; and one locality may be sufficient in all those things belonging to a particular trade; and a city, which is a perfect [i.e. a complete] community, is sufficient in all the necessaries of life.[33]

---

[31] This sentence does not lend itself to exact translation. In the context, I cannot see what *aliquam multitudinem*, 'a certain multitude', can mean other than 'a section of the community'. 'The military class' is a pretty free translation of *multitudo bellatorum*, but I could not think of a better way of conveying what St Thomas seems to mean. Aristotle's use of the word 'polity' is ambiguous, and Aquinas has inherited this ambiguity with the term. Aristotle's chief meaning seems to be rule by a fairly numerous middle class, because he thinks that a constitution midway between rule by the few and rule by the many will be most stable (cf. *Politics* 3:7 (1279a37); 4:8 (1293b33); 4:11 (1295a31)). St Thomas here seems to be remembering the passage at *Politics* 3:7 (1279b1), where Aristotle says that the shared excellence of good government by the many is likely to be military and that the franchise will be related to the bearing of arms. One cannot help feeling that St Thomas has rather missed the point. But he refers to polity again at the beginning of ch. IV, as the good form of rule by the many.

[32] The threefold classification of good and bad constitutional forms given here and in the preceding paragraph is derived from Aristotle's *Politics* 3:7 (1279a25).

[33] Aristotle, *Politics* 1:2 (1252b9).

But this is all the more true of a single province, because of the need for common defence and mutual assistance against enemies.[34] Hence, he who rules a perfect community, that is, a city or province, is properly called a king; but he who rules a household is not a king, but the father of a family. He does, however, bear a certain resemblance to a king, and for this reason kings are sometimes called the 'fathers' of their people.

From what we have said, therefore, it is clear that a king is one who rules over the community of a city or province, and for the common good. Hence Solomon, at Ecclesiastes 5:8, says: 'The king commands all the lands subject to him.'

Chapter III: That it is more beneficial for a community of men living together to be ruled by one than by many Having said these things, we must next ask whether it is more suitable for a province or city to be ruled by many or by one. This can be answered by considering the end of government itself. For it must be the task of anyone who exercises rule to secure the wellbeing of whatever it is that he rules. For example, it is the task of the steersman to preserve the ship from the perils of the sea and to guide it into a safe harbour. But the good and wellbeing of a community united in fellowship lies in the preservation of its unity. This is called peace,[35] and when it is removed and the community is divided against itself, social life loses its advantage and instead becomes a burden. It is for this end, therefore, that the ruler of a community ought especially to strive: to procure the unity of peace. Nor may he rightly wonder whether he ought to bring about peace in the community subject to him, any more than the physician should wonder whether he ought to heal the sick entrusted to him: for no one ought to deliberate about an end for which he must strive, but only about the means to that end.[36] Thus the Apostle, commending the unity of the faithful people, says at Ephesians 4:3: 'Be ye solicitous for the unity of the Spirit in the bond of peace.' The more effectively government preserves the unity of peace, therefore, the more beneficial it is; for we call something 'more beneficial' when it leads more effectively to its end. Clearly, however, something which is itself one can bring about unity more effectively than something which is many can, just as the most

---

[34] This sentence is, of course, St Thomas's gloss on Aristotle, made as a concession to the fact that he is talking about medieval kingdoms rather than Greek city-states.

[35] Augustine, *De civitate Dei* 19:13.

[36] Aristotle, *Ethics* 3:3 (1112b13).

effective cause of heat is that which is itself hot.[37] Government by one is therefore more advantageous than government by several.

Moreover, it is clear that a plurality of rulers will in no way preserve a community if they are wholly at odds with one another. Some kind of unity is required as between a plurality of individuals if they are to govern anything whatsoever, just as a group of men in a boat cannot pull together as one unit unless they are in some measure united.[38] But a plurality is said to be united to the degree that it approaches to one. It is therefore better for one to rule than many, who only approach to one.

Again, those things are best which are most natural, for in every case nature operates for the best; and in nature government is always by one. Among the multitude of the body's members there is one part which moves all the others, namely, the heart; and among the parts of the soul there is one force, namely the reason, which chiefly rules; also, there is one king of the bees,[39] and in the whole universe one God is the Maker and Ruler of all. And this accords with reason, for every multitude is derived from unity. Thus, if those things which come about through art do so by imitation of those which exist in nature, and if a work of art is better to the degree that it achieves a likeness to what is in nature,[40] it is necessarily true in the case of human affairs that that community is best which is ruled by one.

This appears also to be borne out by experience. For provinces or cities which are not ruled by one man toil under dissensions and are tossed about without peace, so that the complaint which the Lord made through the prophet (Jeremiah 12:10) may be seen to be fulfilled: 'Many pastors have destroyed my vineyard.' By contrast, provinces and cities governed by a single king rejoice in peace, flourish in justice and are gladdened by an abundance of things. Hence the Lord promises His people through the prophets that, as a great gift, He will put them under one head and that there will be one prince in the midst of them.[41]

Chapter IV: That just as the rule of one is the best when it is just, so its opposite is the worst; and this is proved by many reasons and arguments But just as the rule of a king is the best, so the rule of a tyrant is the worst. Now

---

[37] Cf. *SCG* 4:76:4; *Summa theologiae* Ia 103:3.
[38] Cf. Aristotle, *Politics* 3:4 (1276b20).
[39] Aristotle, *Historia animalium* 5:21 (553b6).
[40] Aristotle, *Physics* 2:2 (194a21).
[41] Cf. Jeremiah 30:21; Ezekiel 34:23; 37:25.

democracy is the opposite of polity, since, as is apparent from what has been said, rule is in each case exercised by the many;[42] and oligarchy is the opposite of aristocracy, since in each case it is exercised by the few; and tyranny of kingship, since in each case it is exercised by one. But it has been shown already that kingship is the best form of government.[43] If, therefore, that which is the opposite of the best is the worst, tyranny is necessarily the worst.[44]

Again, a power which is united is more efficient at bringing about its purposes than one which is dispersed or divided. For many men united at the same time can pull what no one of them would be able to pull if the group were divided into its individual parts. Therefore, just as it is more beneficial for a power which produces good to be more united, because in this way it is able to produce more good, so is it more harmful for a power which produces evil to be united than divided. But the power of an unjust ruler produces evil for the community inasmuch as it replaces the good of the community with a good peculiar to himself. Therefore, just as, in the case of good government, rule is more beneficial to the extent that the ruling power is more nearly one, so that kingship is better than aristocracy and aristocracy than polity; so the converse will be true in the case of unjust rule: that is, it will be more harmful to the extent that the ruling power is more nearly one. Tyranny is therefore more harmful than oligarchy and oligarchy than democracy.

Again, what renders government unjust is the fact that the private good of the ruler is sought at the expense of the good of the community. The further it departs from the common good, therefore, the more unjust will the government be. But there is a greater departure from the common good in an oligarchy, where the good of the few is sought, than in a democracy, where the good of the many is sought; and there is a still greater departure from the common good in a tyranny, where the good of only one is sought. A large number comes closer to the whole than a small one, and a small one closer than only one. Tyranny, therefore, is the most unjust form of government.

The same thing becomes clear from a consideration of the order of Divine providence, which disposes all things for the best. For goodness arises in things from one perfect cause, as from the working together of everything that can assist in the production of good; whereas evil arises

---

[42] Ch. II; and see n. 31.
[43] Ch. III.
[44] Aristotle, *Ethics* 8:10 (1160b9).

singly, from individual defects.[45] For there is no beauty in a body unless all its members are properly disposed, and ugliness arises when even one member is improperly so. And so ugliness arises for many reasons and from a variety of causes, whereas beauty does so in one way and from one perfect cause; and this is true in all cases of good and evil, as if it were by the providence of God that good should be the stronger because coming from a single cause, while evil should be the weaker because coming from many. It is fitting, therefore, that just government should be exercised by one man alone, so that it may for this reason be stronger. But if the government should fall away into injustice, it is more fitting that it should belong to many so that it may be weaker, and so that they may hinder one another. Among the forms of unjust rule, therefore, democracy is the most tolerable and tyranny is the worst.

The same conclusion is especially apparent if one considers the evils which arise from tyranny. For when the tyrant, despising the common good, seeks his own private good, the consequence is that he oppresses his subjects in a variety of ways, according to the different passions to which he is subject as he tries to secure whatever goods he desires. For one who is in the grip of the passion of greed will seize the property of his subjects; hence Solomon says at Proverbs 29:4: 'The just king makes rich the earth, but the greedy man destroys it.' If he is subject to the passion of wrath, he will shed blood for no reason; hence it is said at Ezekiel 22:27: 'Her princes in the midst thereof are like wolves ravening their prey, to shed blood.' The wise man admonishes us that such rule is to be shunned, saying (Ecclesiasticus 9:13), 'Keep thee far from the man that hath power to kill': that is, because he kills not for the sake of justice, but through power and from the lust of his own will. There will, therefore, be no security, but all things uncertain, when the law is forsaken; nor will it be possible for any trust to be placed in that which depends upon the will, not to say the lust, of another. Nor does such rule oppress its subjects in bodily matters only, but it impedes them with respect to their spiritual goods also; for those who desire to rule their subjects rather than benefit them put every obstacle in the way of their progress, being suspicious of any excellence in their subjects that might threaten their own wicked rule. Tyrants 'suspect good men rather than bad, and are always afraid of another's virtue'. [46] Tyrants therefore endeavour to

[45] Romans 8:28; Ps.-Dionysius, *De divinis nominibus* 4:30 (*PG* 3:729).
[46] Sallust, *Bellum Catilinae* 7:2.

prevent their subjects from becoming virtuous and increasing in nobility of spirit, lest they refuse to bear their unjust dominion. They prevent the bond of friendship from becoming established among their subjects, and hinder them from enjoying the rewards of mutual peace, so that, for as long as they do not trust one another, they will not be able to unite against a tyrant's rule. For this reason, tyrants sow discord among their subjects, nourish strife, and prohibit those things which create fellowship among men, such as wedding-feasts and banquets and other such things by which familiarity and trust are usually produced among men.[47] They also endeavour to prevent anyone from becoming powerful or rich, because, suspecting their subjects according to their own evil conscience, they fear that, just as they themselves use power and riches to do harm, so the power and wealth of their subjects will be used to do harm to them in return. Hence Job (15:21) says this of the tyrant: 'The sound of dread is ever in his ears, and even when there is peace' – that is, even when no ill is intended towards him – 'he is ever suspicious of treacheries'. For this reason, then, when rulers who ought to cultivate the virtues in their subjects look upon their subjects' virtues with wretched envy and do everything in their power to impede them, few virtuous men will be found under a tyrant. For according to what the Philosopher says, brave men are found among those who honour the bravest;[48] and, as Cicero says, 'Things which are despised by everyone always fail and have little strength.'[49]

It is, indeed, natural that men who are nourished in a climate of fear should degenerate into a servile condition of soul and become fearful of every manly and strenuous act. This is shown by the experience of those provinces which have remained long under a tyrant. Hence the Apostle says at Colossians 3:21: 'Fathers, provoke not your children to anger, lest they be discouraged.' And Solomon is thinking of these harmful effects of tyranny when he says (Proverbs 28:12): 'When the wicked reign, men are ruined': because, that is, subjects fall away from the perfection of virtue through the wickedness of tyrants. And he goes on to say (29:2): 'When the wicked beareth rule, the people mourn'; and again (28:28): 'When the wicked rise, men hide themselves' in order to escape the cruelty of tyrants. And no wonder; for a man who rules without reason according to the lusts of his own soul is no different from a beast. Hence Solomon says (Proverbs 28:15): 'As a roaring lion and a hungry bear, so is a wicked ruler over the

---

[47] Cf. Aristotle, *Politics* 5:11 (1313a39).
[48] *Ethics* 1:3 (1095b28); 3:8 (1116a20).
[49] *Tusculanae disputationes* 1:2:4.

De regimine principum

poor people.' And so it is that men remove themselves from a tyrant as from cruel beasts, and to be subject to a tyrant seems the same as to be mauled by a ferocious animal.

Chapter V: How varied the forms of government were among the Romans; and that their commonwealth sometimes prospered under the government of many Because both the best and the worst can occur in a monarchy – that is, under government by one – the evil of tyranny has rendered the dignity of kingship odious to many. For sometimes those who desire to be ruled by a king fall victim instead to the savagery of tyrants, and a great many rulers have exerted tyrannical sway under the pretext of royal dignity. Clear examples of this appear in the case of the Roman commonwealth. For the kings were expelled by the Roman people when they could no longer bear the burden of their rule, or, rather, of their tyranny. They then instituted for themselves consuls and other magistrates by whom they commenced to be ruled and guided, wishing to exchange kingship for aristocracy; and, as Sallust remarks, 'It is incredible to recall how swiftly the city of Rome grew once she had achieved her liberty.'[50] For it often happens that men living under a king are reluctant to exert themselves for the common good, no doubt supposing that whatever they do for the common good will not benefit them but someone else who is seen to have the goods of the community under his own power. But if no one person is seen to have such power, they no longer regard the common good as if it belonged to someone else, but each now regards it as his own. Experience therefore seems to show that a single city governed by rulers who hold office for one year only can sometimes accomplish more than a king can even if he has three or four cities, and that small services exacted by kings bear more heavily than great burdens imposed [on itself] by a community of citizens. This principle was exemplified during the emergence of the Roman commonwealth; for the common people were enlisted into the army and paid wages for military service, and when the common treasury was not sufficient to pay the wages, private wealth was put to public use to such an extent that not even the senators retained anything made of gold for themselves apart from one gold ring and one seal each, which were the insignia of their rank.[51] Presently, however, the Romans became exhausted by the continual quarrels which eventually grew into civil wars, and the liberty which they had so striven to attain was then snatched from

---

[50] Sallust, *Bellum Catilinae* 7:3; cf. Augustine, *De civitate Dei* 5:12.
[51] Livy 36; cf. Augustine, *De civitate Dei* 3:19.

their hands by those civil wars, and they began to be under the power of the emperors: who at first would not allow themselves to be called kings, because the name of king was odious to the Romans. Some of these emperors faithfully pursued the common good, as kings should, and the Roman commonwealth was increased and preserved by their efforts. Most of them, however, were tyrants to their subjects and weak and ineffective in the face of their enemies, and these brought the Roman commonwealth to naught.

A similar process occurred in the case of the people of the Hebrews. At first, while they were ruled by judges they were plundered on all sides by their enemies, for each man did only what was good in his own eyes. Then, at their own request, kings were divinely given to them;[52] but because of the wickedness of the kings they fell away from the worship of the one God and finally were led away into captivity. Peril lurks on either side, therefore: either the best form of government, kingship, may be shunned because tyranny is feared, or, if the risk is considered worthwhile, royal power may change into a wicked tyranny.

Chapter VI: *That tyrannical government more often arises from the rule of many than from that of one; and so government by one is better* Now when it is necessary to choose between two alternatives both of which involve danger, one should certainly choose that which is accompanied by the lesser danger. But if monarchy is changed into tyranny, less evil flows from this [process of change] than when the government of a number of the best men becomes corrupt. For the dissension which often follows government by several persons is contrary to the good of peace, which is the foremost goal of any social community; but this is a good which is not taken away by tyranny, for the tyrant only takes away some of the goods of individual men – unless the tyranny is so excessive that it ravages the whole community. The rule of one is therefore to be preferred to that of many, though perils flow from each.

Again, it seems clear that we ought to avoid that alternative from which great danger is more likely to follow. But the greatest dangers to a community more often follow from the rule of many than from the rule of one. For where there are many it is likelier that one of them will fail to be concerned with the common good than where there is only one. And whenever one out of a number of governors ceases to labour for the common good, there arises a danger of dissension in the community of their subjects; for where

---

[52] Judges 2 *passim*; 1 Samuel 12:13f.

there is dissension among princes, a consequence of this is that dissension in the community may ensue. If, however, one man rules, he will more often attend to the common good, or, if he turns aside from the task of securing the common good, it does not immediately follow that he will set about oppressing his subjects and become an extreme tyrant, which, as we have shown above,[53] is the worst kind of bad government. The perils which arise out of government by many are therefore more to be avoided than those which arise out of government by one.

Again, the rule of many turns into tyranny more rather than less frequently than that of one. For when dissension arises under the rule of several persons, it often happens that one man rises superior to the others and usurps to himself sole dominion over the community. This can plainly be seen to have happened from time to time, for in almost every case government by many has ended in tyranny; and this appears very clearly in the example of the Roman commonwealth. For when it had long been administered by several magistrates, there arose plots, dissensions and civil wars, and it fell victim to the most cruel tyrants. Indeed, if one gives diligent attention both to what has been done in the past and to what is being done now, it will be found universally that tyranny has been exercised more often in lands governed by many than in those governed by one.[54] If, therefore, kingship, which is the best form of government, seems to be worthy of avoidance mainly because of the danger of tyranny, and if tyranny tends to arise not less but more often under the government of several, the straightforward conclusion remains that it is more advantageous to live under one king than under the rule of several persons.

Chapter VII: The conclusion is that the rule of one man is the best simply. It is shown how a community should conduct itself in relation to him so as to remove the opportunity of his becoming a tyrant, but that even tyranny is to be tolerated for the sake of avoiding a greater evil It is clear from what we have said, therefore, that the rule of one, which is the best, is to be preferred, but that it can turn into a tyranny, which is the worst. It is therefore necessary to labour with diligent care to provide the community with a king who is of such a kind that it will not fall victim to a tyrant. First, then, it is necessary that the character of the man elevated to kingship by those to whom the duty of doing this belongs should be such that it is not

---

[53] Ch. IV.   [54] Aristotle, *Politics* 5:10 (1310b14).

probable that he will decline into tyranny. Hence Samuel, commending God's providence in appointing a king, says, at 1 Samuel 13:14: 'The Lord hath sought Him a man after His own heart.' Next, once the king has been appointed, the government of the kingdom should be so arranged as to remove from the king the opportunity of becoming a tyrant; and, at the same time, his power should be restricted so that he will not easily be able to fall into tyranny. How these things can be done will have to be discussed in subsequent chapters.[55] Finally, we must consider what should be done if the king does become a tyrant.

If, however, the tyranny is not excessive, it is more advantageous to tolerate a degree of tyranny for the time being than to take action against the tyrant and so incur many perils more grievous than the tyranny itself. For it may happen that those who take such action prove unable to prevail against the tyrant, and succeed only in provoking the tyrant to even greater savagery. Even when those who take action against a tyrant are able to overthrow him, this fact may in itself give rise to many very grave dissensions in the populace, either during the rebellion against the tyrant or because, after the tyrant has been removed, the community is divided into factions over the question of what the new ruling order should be. Again, it sometimes happens that a community expels a tyrant with the help of some other ruler who, having achieved power, snatches at tyranny himself and, fearing to suffer at the hands of another what he has himself done to another, forces his subjects into a slavery even more grievous than before. It is often true in cases of tyranny that a subsequent tyrant proves to be worse than his predecessor; for, while not undoing any of the troubles inflicted by his predecessor, he devises new ones of his own, out of the malice of his own heart. Thus, at a time when all the people of Syracuse desired the death of Dionysius, a certain old woman continually prayed that he would remain safe and sound and might outlive her. When the tyrant came to know of this, he asked her why she did it. She said to him: 'When I was a girl, we suffered the oppression of a tyrant, and I longed for his death. Then he was slain, but his successor was even harsher, and I thought it a great thing when his rule came to an end. But then we began to have a third ruler who was even more savage: you. And if you were to be taken from us, someone still worse would come instead.'[56]

---

[55] St Thomas discontinued the treatise before coming to any such discussion. His thoughts on this subject are given at IaIIae 105:1 (pp. 52ff below).

[56] Valerius Maximus 6:2:2; John of Salisbury, *Policraticus* 7:25.

If, however, a tyranny were so extreme as to be intolerable, it has seemed to some that it would be an act consistent with virtue if the mightier men were to slay the tyrant, exposing themselves even to the peril of death in order to liberate the community. Indeed, we have an example of such a thing in the Old Testament. For a certain Ehud slew Eglon, king of Moab, with a dagger 'fastened to his thigh',[57] because he oppressed the people of God with a harsh bondage; and for this deed Ehud was made a judge of the people. But this is not consistent with apostolic doctrine. For Peter teaches us to be subject with all fear not only to good and gentle masters, but also to those who are ill disposed, 'For this is thankworthy, if a man for conscience toward God endure grief, suffering wrongfully' (1 Peter 2:18f). Thus, when many Roman emperors tyrannically persecuted the faith of Christ, a great part of the community, both nobles and ordinary people, were converted to the faith and are now praised because, offering no resistance, they suffered death for Christ with patience and courage, as appears clearly in the case of the holy legion of Thebes.[58] Moreover, Ehud should be adjudged to have slain an enemy of the people rather than a ruler, albeit a tyrannical one; and so also we read in the Old Testament that those who slew Joash the king of Judah were themselves slain (although their children were spared, according to the teaching of the law) even though he had turned aside from the worship of God.[59] For it would be a perilous thing, both for a community and its rulers, if anyone could attempt to slay even tyrannical rulers simply on his own private presumption. Indeed, the wicked expose themselves to such peril more often than good men do. For the lordship of a just king is usually no less a burden to the wicked than that of a tyrant; for, according to the saying of Solomon at Proverbs 20:26: 'A wise king scattereth the wicked.' What is more likely to come of such presumption, therefore, is peril to the community through the loss of a king than relief through the removal of a tyrant.

It seems, then, that steps are to be taken against the scourge of tyranny not by the private presumption of any persons, but through public

---

[57] I.e. with a concealed dagger: see Judges 3:14ff; cf. John of Salisbury, *Policraticus* 8:20.

[58] I.e. the Roman legion consisting of 6,666 Christian soldiers martyred 22 Sept. 286 by the emperor Maximian when they followed the example of their leader St Maurice in refusing to sacrifice to idols. The legend is found at *Acta sanctorum*, Sept. VI: 895. It is preserved in a number of versions, the best known of which is that of St Eucherius, Bishop of Lyons (434–50). See *NCE* 14, *s.v.* 'Theban Legion'.

[59] 2 Kings 14:5f.

authority.[60] First of all, in cases where it belongs by right to a community to provide a ruler for itself, that community can without injustice depose or restrain a king whom it has appointed, if he should abuse royal power tyrannically. Nor should such a community be thought disloyal if it acts to depose a tyrant even if the community has already pledged itself to him in perpetuity; for the tyrant who has failed to govern the community faithfully, as the office of king requires, has deserved to be treated in this way. Thus the Romans who had accepted Tarquin the Proud as their king, then ejected him from the kingship because of his and his sons' tyranny, and substituted a lesser power, that is, the consulate. So also Domitian, who succeeded the mildest of emperors, Vespasian, his father, and Titus, his brother, was slain by the Roman Senate when he exercised tyrannical power, and all the wicked things that he had inflicted upon the Romans were justly and wholesomely revoked and made void by decree of the Senate.[61] Thus it came about that Blessed John the Evangelist, the beloved disciple of God, who had been sent away into exile on the island of Patmos by Domitian, was brought back to Ephesus by special senatorial decree.[62]

If, however, the right to provide a community with a king belongs to some superior, then a remedy against the wickedness of a tyrant must be sought from him. Thus when Archelaus, who began to reign in Judea in place of his father Herod, imitated the wickedness of his father, the Jews made complaint against him to Augustus Caesar, by whom his power was first reduced, the title of king being removed from him and half his kingdom divided between his two brothers; then, when this did not keep his tyrannical behaviour in check, he was banished into exile by Tiberius Caesar to Lyons, a city of Gaul.[63]

If, however, there can be no human aid at all against a tyrant, recourse must be had to God, the King of all, who is 'a refuge in time of trouble' (Psalm 9:9). For it is within His power to turn the heart of the cruel tyrant

---

[60] Cf. IIaIIae 42:2 ad 3 (p. 250, below); and *Scripta super libros sententiarum* II:44:2:2 (p. 72, below); and see Introduction, p. xxix.

[61] Verbal resonances suggest that St Thomas is here relying on Augustine, *De civitate Dei* 5:12 and 21; although Augustine does not mention the assassination of Domitian, which perhaps comes from Eutropius 7:23.

[62] See Revelation 1:9; Eusebius of Caesarea, *Historia ecclesiastica* 3:18 and 20.

[63] Josephus, *Bella Iudaica* 2:6f. But Josephus says that it was Augustus, not Tiberius, who exiled Archelaus, and that he was exiled to Vienne, not Lyons. St Thomas gets his – rather garbled – information here second-hand, from the *Glossa ordinaria* on Matthew 2:22 (*PL* 114:78). See Biographical Glossary, *s.v.* 'Archelaus'.

towards gentleness, according to what Solomon says at Proverbs 21:1: 'The king's heart is in the hand of the Lord: He turneth it whithersoever He will.' He it was Who turned the cruelty of the king of the Assyrians to gentleness when he was preparing death for the Jews.[64] He it was Who changed the cruel King Nebuchadnezzar so effectively that he became a proclaimer of the Divine might: 'Now', he said, 'I, Nebuchadnezzar, praise and extol and honour the King of heaven, all Whose works are truth, and His ways judgment; and those that walk in pride He is able to abase' (Daniel 4:37). As for those tyrants whom He deems unworthy to be converted, He can remove them from our midst or reduce them to a lowly condition, according to what the wise man says (Ecclesiasticus 10:14): 'The Lord hath cast down the thrones of proud princes, and set up the meek in their stead.' He it is Who, seeing the affliction of His people in Egypt and hearing their cries, cast down the tyrant Pharaoh and his army into the sea.[65] Not only did He eject the proud Nebuchaznezzar whom we have just mentioned from his kingdom, but He also drove him out from the company of men like a beast.[66] Nor, indeed, is His hand now so weakened that He cannot set His people free from a tyrant. For He promised His people through Isaiah (14:3) that He would give them rest from their labour and confusion and from the harsh bondage in which they served. And through Ezekiel (34:10) He said: 'I will deliver my flock from their mouth' – that is, from those shepherds who feed only themselves. But if men are to deserve such benefit from God they must cease from sin, because it is as a punishment for their sin that ungodly men are given power over them. For the Lord says through Hosea (13:11): 'I gave thee a king in mine anger'; and at Job 34:30 it is said that 'He maketh a man who is an hypocrite to rule because of the people's sins.' Guilt, therefore, must first be taken away, so that the scourge of tyranny may cease.

Chapter VIII: The holy Doctor here asks whether honour or glory above all ought to motivate a king in ruling; and he presents opinions as to what view should be held on this question Since, then, according to what we have now said, it is the king's task to seek the good of the community, and since the king's duty would seem unduly onerous if some good personal to himself were not provided in return, we must now consider what a suitable reward for a good king might be.

[64] Esther 15:11.
[65] Exodus 14:23ff; 15:1, 4.
[66] Daniel 4:28ff.

It has seemed to some that this reward is nothing else than honour and glory. Hence Cicero asserts that 'the ruler of a city should be flattered with glory'.[67] The reason for this seems to be indicated by Aristotle in the book *Ethics*: 'A ruler for whom honour and glory are not sufficient will in consequence become a tyrant.' [68] For the desire to seek their own good is present in the souls of all men. If, therefore, the prince were not content with honour and glory, he would seek pleasure and riches, and so would fall to plundering and injuring his subjects.

If we accept this view, however, a number of unwelcome consequences follow. First, it would be too weighty a burden if kings were to undergo such great labour and anxiety for so fragile a reward. For there seems to be nothing in human affairs more fragile than the honour and glory bestowed by the favour of men, because these things depend upon human opinion, and there is nothing more changeable in the life of mankind. Thus it is that the prophet Isaiah (40:6) calls such glory 'the flower of the field'. Next, the desire for human glory takes away greatness of soul; for he who seeks the favour of men must necessarily subserve their wishes in everything that he says or does, and so, for as long as he strives to please men, he becomes the servant of each of them. For this reason the same Cicero in the book *De officiis* says that we should beware of the desire for glory, for it destroys that liberty of spirit which ought above all to be the goal of the great-souled man;[69] and nothing is more fitting to a prince who is appointed to accomplish good purposes than greatness of soul. Human glory is therefore an unsuitable reward for the office of king.

Also, if such a reward is set before princes, this is at the same time harmful to the community. For it belongs to the duty of the good man to hold glory and other temporal goods in contempt. A man of virtue and strength of soul ought to despise glory, and indeed life itself, for the sake of justice; and hence arises the remarkable conclusion that, while glory follows virtuous acts, it is in itself a virtuous act to despise glory, and that a man is rendered more glorious by his contempt for glory, according to the opinion of Fabius, who says: 'He shall find true glory who despises it';[70] and Sallust said of Cato: 'The less he sought glory the more it followed him';[71] and, again, the disciples of Christ showed themselves

[67] *De republica* 5:7:9; Augustine, *De civitate Dei* 5:13.
[68] *Ethics* 5:6 (1134b7).
[69] *De officiis* 1:20:68.
[70] Livy 22:39.
[71] Sallust, *Bellum Catilinae* 54:6; Augustine, *De civitate Dei* 5:12.

to be ministers of God in both glory and shame, in disgrace and good reputation alike. That glory which good men despise is therefore not a suitable reward for the good man. If, then, it were the only reward appointed for good princes, it would follow that good men would not allow themselves to be made princes or, if they did, would do so unrewarded.

Moreover, dangerous evils arise from the desire for glory. For many have brought the liberty of their fatherland under the power of an enemy when they have sought immoderate glory in the commerce of war and have perished along with their army. Hence Torquatus, a prince of Rome, wishing to show how important it is to avoid such danger, slew his own son who, even though he had triumphed over an enemy, had in the ardour of youth been goaded into fighting against orders. He did this lest more evil should come from the example of disobedience than benefit from the glory of slaying an enemy.[72]

There is another vice closely related to the desire for glory, namely, dissimulation. For it is difficult to pursue those true virtues to which alone honour is due, and few manage to do so; but, desiring glory, many pretend to be virtuous. In this way, as Sallust says, 'Ambition has made many a mortal false. They have one thing shut up in their bosom, but another ready on their tongue, and they have more appearance than prowess.'[73] But our Saviour Himself calls such people hypocrites, that is, dissimulators, who do good that they may be seen by men.[74] Therefore, just as it is perilous for the community if the prince should seek pleasure and wealth as his rewards and so become predatory and overbearing, so also is it perilous when the love of glory has him in its grip and he therefore becomes presumptuous and deceitful.

As to the sayings of the wise,[75] therefore, it is clear that they wish to suggest not that honour and glory are the reward of the prince as if these things were to be sought as the chief goal of the good king, but that it is at all events more tolerable for him to seek glory than to desire riches or pursue pleasure. For this vice is closer to virtue because, as Augustine says, the glory which men desire is nothing more than the judgment of men when they think well of their fellows.[76] The desire for glory therefore has some vestige of virtue about it, inasmuch as it does at any rate seek to

[72] Augustine, *De civitate Dei* 5:18.
[73] *Bellum Catilinae* 10:5.
[74] Matthew 6:5.
[75] I.e. the statements of Cicero and Aristotle quoted in the second paragraph of this chapter.
[76] *De civitate Dei* 5:12.

win the approval of good men and to avoid displeasing them. Given that so few achieve true virtue, therefore, it would seem more tolerable to choose as a ruler one who is at least restrained from overt wrongdoing by his fear of the judgment of men. For one who desires glory either exerts himself to follow the true path of virtuous action so as to secure the approval of men, or at any rate tries to secure it even if only by fraud and artifice.[77] But one who wishes to dominate merely, if he lacks the desire for glory and is not afraid to displease men of right judgment, will more often seek to obtain what he loves through open crimes, surpassing even the beasts in the vices of cruelty and luxury. This is clear in the case of Nero Caesar, whose love of pleasure was so great, as Augustine says, that one would have thought him capable of no manly act, and whose cruelty was such that one would have supposed him incapable of any kindness.[78] Again, the matter is expressed clearly enough by what Aristotle says in the *Ethics* about the great-souled man: that he does not seek honour and glory as something great, as if they were a sufficient reward for virtue, yet he is content to receive nothing more from men.[79] For of all earthly rewards the highest seems to be the testimony rendered to a man for his virtue by other men.

Chapter IX: The Doctor here shows what is the true end of a king, which ought to motivate him to rule well Since, therefore, worldly honour and the glory of men are not a sufficient reward for the anxieties of royal office, it remains to inquire what a sufficient reward might be. Now it is fitting that the king should look to God for his reward; for a minister looks to his lord for the reward of his ministry, and a king governing his people is a minister of God, as the Apostle says at Romans 13:1 and 4: that there is no power but of the Lord God, and that 'he is the minister of God, a revenger to execute wrath upon him that doeth evil'; and in the Book of Wisdom (6:5) kings are described as the ministers of God. Kings, therefore, must look to God for the reward of their ministry. Now God does occasionally reward kings for their ministry with temporal goods; but such rewards are common to good and wicked kings alike,[80] and so the Lord says at Ezekiel 29:18: 'Nebuchadrezzar king of Babylon caused his army to serve a great service against Tyrus: yet he had no wages, nor his army, for Tyrus, for the service

---

[77] Sallust, *Bellum Catilinae* 11:1f; Augustine, *De civitate Dei* 5:12; 19.
[78] *De civitate Dei* 5:19.
[79] *Ethics* 4:3 (1124a16).
[80] Augustine, *De civitate Dei* 1:8.

that he had served against it' – that is, for that service in respect of which, according to the Apostle, the power is 'the minister of God, a revenger to execute wrath upon him that doeth evil'. As to the reward, He then adds: 'Therefore thus saith the Lord God: Behold, I will give the land of Egypt unto Nebuchadrezzar king of Babylon; and he shall take her spoil, and it shall be the wages of his army.' If, therefore, wicked kings, who fight against the enemies of God without intending to serve God but only out of hatred and greed, are repaid by the Lord with a reward so great that He gives them victory over their foes, places kingdoms beneath them and sets plunder before them to bear away, what will He do for good kings who rule the people of God with pious intent, and repulse His enemies? He promises them not an earthly reward merely, but an eternal one; nor is this found anywhere but in Himself, as Peter says to the shepherds of the people of God at 1 Peter 5:2ff: 'Feed the flock of God which is among you, and when the chief Shepherd' – that is, the King of kings, Christ – 'shall appear, ye shall receive a crown of glory that fadeth not away'. And of this Isaiah says (28:5): 'The Lord shall be a garland of exultation and a crown of glory for His people.'

Again, this is shown by reason. For there is implanted in the minds of all who have the use of reason the understanding that blessedness is the reward of virtue. For virtue in anything whatsoever is described as that which makes that which has it good, and renders what it does good; moreover, everyone, in acting well, is striving to achieve what he most desires, and that is to be happy: something that it is not possible not to wish for.[81] We may properly suppose, therefore, that the reward of virtue is that which makes a man blessed.[82] But if the task of virtue is to act well, and it is the king's duty to rule his subjects well, the reward of the king will also be that which causes him to be blessed. And we must now consider what this may be. Now we say that blessedness is the ultimate end of desire; for the motion of desire does not continue into infinity: if it did, desire would by its very nature be futile, for it would not be possible to traverse infinities.[83] Also, because an intellectual nature desires that which is universally [i.e. wholly] good, it will be able to be made truly happy only by a good such that, once it is achieved, no good remains which might be the object of any further desire. Hence blessedness is called the perfect

---

[81] Aristotle, *Ethics* 2:6 (1106a15).
[82] It should be noted that, in this discussion, St Thomas is using the words 'blessed' (*beatus*) and 'happy' (*felix*) as synonyms. The synonymy is more natural in Latin than in English.
[83] Cf. *SCG* 3:25:9.

good, as comprehending all desirable things in itself.[84] But no earthly good can do this. For those who have riches will desire to have more, and the same is clearly true of all other things. Even if more things are not sought, men will at any rate want what they have to be permanent (or to be succeeded in due course by other things; for nothing permanent is to be found among earthly things). No earthly thing, therefore, can be that which pacifies desire. Nor, then, can any earthly thing cause the king to be blessed and so be a suitable reward for him.

Moreover, the final perfection and complete good of anything depends upon something superior to itself. For instance, bodies are rendered better by the addition of something better, and worse by being mixed with something worse. If silver is mixed with gold, the silver becomes better, whereas it is made impure by the admixture of lead. Now it is clear that every earthly thing is inferior to the human mind and that blessedness is the final perfection and complete good of man, at which all men desire to arrive. There is therefore nothing earthly by which a man may be made blessed; nor, then, is there anything earthly which is a sufficient reward for a king. For, as Augustine says, we do not call Christian princes happy because they ruled for a longer time, or because they died in peace and left behind sons to rule as emperors, or because they subdued the enemies of the commonwealth, or because they were able to avoid and suppress uprisings against them by the citizens. Rather, we say that they are happy if they rule justly; if they prefer to govern wicked desires more than any people whatsoever; if they do these things not out of craving for empty glory, but from love of eternal felicity. We say that, for the time being, such Christian emperors are happy in hope and that, in time to come, when that to which we now look forward has arrived, they will be so in possession.[85] Nor is there any other created thing which could make a man blessed and which could be singled out as the king's reward. For the desire which is present in anything whatsoever leads it back always to its source: to the cause from which it derives its being.[86] But the cause of the human mind is nothing but God, Who made it in His own image.[87] God alone, therefore, can satisfy the desire which is in a man and make a man blessed, and so be a suitable reward for a king.

[84] Aristotle, *Ethics* 1:1 (1094a18).
[85] Paraphrased from Augustine, *De civitate Dei* 5:24.
[86] Cf. *SCG* 3:25:10f; Augustine, *Confessiones* 1:1.
[87] Cf. Genesis 1:26.

Again, the human mind is capable, through the intellect, of knowing, and, through the will, of desiring, a universal good. But a universal good is not found except in God. There is therefore nothing which can make a man blessed by fulfilling his desire except God, of Whom it is said at Psalm 103:5: 'He fills with good things the desires of thy heart.' It is in this, therefore, that the king must place his hope of reward. With this in mind, then, King David says at Psalm 73:25: 'Whom have I in heaven but Thee, and besides Thee what do I desire on earth?' Then, answering this question, he goes on (vs. 28): 'But it is good for me to draw near to God. I have put my trust in the Lord God.' He it is Who gives to kings not only that temporal wellbeing by which He preserves men and beasts alike, but also that salvation of which He says through Isaiah (51:6): 'My salvation shall be for ever', by which He saves men and leads them to a condition of equality with the angels.

It can, therefore, truly be said that honour and glory are the rewards of a king: for what worldly and passing honour can resemble that honour by which a man becomes a citizen [of the kingdom of God] and a member of God's household, and through which he is numbered among the children of God and attains with Christ to the inheritance of a heavenly kingdom?[88] This is the honour of which King David spoke with longing and wonder at Psalm 139:17: 'Thy friends, O God, are made exceedingly honourable.' Again, what glory of human praise can be compared to that which is produced not by the treachery of flattering tongues and deceitful human opinion but by the inward testimony of conscience, and confirmed by the testimony of God, Who promises to those who confess Him that He will acknowledge them in the glory of the Father before the angels of God?[89] Those who seek such glory shall find it, and the glory of men, which they do not seek, shall follow them, as we see from the example of Solomon, who not only received the wisdom which he sought from the Lord, but was made glorious above all other kings.[90]

Chapter x: The holy Doctor here declares that the reward of kings and princes is the highest degree of heavenly blessedness; and this is shown by many reasons and examples It remains to consider further the excellence of that degree of heavenly blessedness which is obtained by those who discharge the

---

[88] Ephesians 2:19.
[89] Matthew 10:32; Luke 12:8.
[90] 1 Kings 10:23.

duties of kingship worthily and laudably. For if blessedness is the reward of virtue, it follows that a greater degree of blessedness will be owed to greater virtue. Now that virtue is especially great by which a man is able to direct not only himself, but others also;[91] and such virtue will be greater in proportion to the number of those who are to be governed. For as, in the case of bodily strength, someone is deemed stronger by reason of the number of men he can defeat or the amount of weight he can lift, so too greater virtue is required to regulate a household establishment than to govern oneself, and much greater still to rule a city and a kingdom. To discharge the duty of kingship well therefore requires outstanding virtue, and so an outstanding degree of blessedness ought to be its reward.

Again, in all arts and powers, those who can direct others well are more deserving of praise than are those who conduct themselves well under the direction of another. In the speculative sciences it is a greater thing to pass the truth on to others by teaching than it is to be able to understand what is taught by others. In the practical arts too, the architect who designs a building is regarded more highly and retained at a higher fee than is the builder who works with his hands according to the architect's direction. And in the commerce of war the glory of victory more readily attends the prudence of the general than the courage of the soldier. And what is true of the teacher in relation to the sciences and the architect in relation to building and the general in relation to war is true also of the ruler of a community in relation to the virtuous acts of its individual members. The king is therefore worthy of a greater reward if he governs his subjects well than any one of his subjects is if he conducts himself well under the king.

Moreover, if virtue is that quality by which a man's work is rendered good, it seems that a greater degree of virtue will be needed to secure a greater amount of good. But the good of a community is greater and more Divine than the good of one man.[92] This is why harm to one person may sometimes be tolerated if it contributes to the good of the community, as when a thief is put to death in order to secure the community's peace. God Himself would not permit there to be evil in the world if He did not bring forth good from it, for the benefit and beauty of the universe.[93] And it belongs to the office of a king studiously to procure the good of the whole community. A greater reward, therefore, is due to the king for good rulership than to a subject for good behaviour.

[91] Aristotle, *Ethics* 5:1 (1129b31); *Rhetoric* 1:9 (1366b3).
[92] Aristotle, *Ethics* 1:3 (1094b7); cf. *SCG* 3:71:7.
[93] Cf. *SCG* 3:71:7; Augustine, *Enchiridion* 27; 96.

This will become even clearer if we consider some more particular aspects of the matter. For a private person is praised by men and considered worthy of reward by God if he sustains the needy; if he brings peace to those who are quarrelling; if he rescues the oppressed from the strong: if, in short, he contributes to the welfare of anyone by some help or counsel. How much more, therefore, is he to be praised by men and rewarded by God who gladdens a whole province with peace, restrains the violent, preserves justice, and disposes the actions of men by means of his laws and precepts?

Also, the magnitude of the king's virtue appears from the great likeness which it bears to that of God, since he does in his kingdom what God does in the world. Hence, at Exodus 22:28 the judges of the community are called gods. Among the Romans too the emperors were called gods. But something is more acceptable to God the closer it comes to imitating him; which is why the Apostle admonishes us at Ephesians 5:1: 'Be ye therefore imitators of God, as dear children.' But if, according to the opinion of the wise man (Ecclesiasticus 13:15), 'every beast loves his like', then, according to the principle that causes have a certain likeness to that which they cause, it follows that good kings are most acceptable to God and worthy of the greatest rewards from Him. At the same time again, to use the words of Gregory: What is a tempest upon the sea if not also a tempest in the mind? For when the sea is calm, even one who is unskilled can steer a ship rightly; but when the sea is disturbed by the waves of a tempest, even the skilled sailor may come to grief. Hence also it is often true in the occupation of government, that the practice of a good work is lost, which was preserved in times of peace.[94] For, as Augustine says, it is very difficult for rulers not to be lifted up by the tongues of those who accord them sublime honours or pay court to them with an excessive humility, and to remember that they are but men.[95] We read at Ecclesiasticus 31:8ff: 'Blessed is the man that hath not gone after gold nor put his trust in money nor in treasures; who might offend, and hath not offended, or done evil, and hath not done it.' It is in this way that the faithful man is found: tried, as it were, by the virtue of his own works. Hence, according to the proverb of Bias, 'Power shows the man.'[96] For many who seemed virtuous while they were in a lowly station have fallen away from virtue as soon as they have reached the summit of power.

[94] Paraphrased from Gregory, *Regulae pastoralis* 1:9 (*PL* 77:22).
[95] *De civitate Dei* 5:24.
[96] Quoted in Aristotle, *Ethics* 5:1 (1130a1).

It is, then, the very difficulty which confronts princes in acting well that makes them worthy of greater reward and renders them more excusable in the sight of men and more easily deserving of forgiveness from God if they sometimes sin through weakness: provided only, as Augustine says, that they do not neglect to offer to the true God the sacrifice of humility and contrition and prayer for their sins.[97] In this matter we have the example of Ahab, king of Israel, whose sins were many, yet of whom the Lord said to Elijah (1 Kings, 21:29): 'Because he humbleth himself before me, I will not bring the evil in his days.'

But it is not only by reason that it is shown that kings should receive an outstanding reward. This is also confirmed by Divine authority. For it is said at Zechariah 12 that in the day of blessedness, when 'the Lord shall defend the inhabitants of Jerusalem' – that is, the vision of eternal peace[98] – all houses shall be like unto the house of David, for all will be kings and will reign with Christ, as members with the Head. But 'the house of David shall be as of God', because by his faithful rule he performed the office of God among the people; so that as his reward he shall draw nigh unto God and cleave to Him.[99] This was also foreseen by the gentiles, as in a dream, inasmuch as they believed that the rulers and preservers of their cities were transformed into gods.

Chapter XI: That the king and prince should strive after good government because this is good and useful for himself; and that the opposite attends the rule of the tyrant The reward of heavenly blessedness set before kings if they acquit themselves well in governing is so splendid that they must keep diligent watch over themselves to ensure that they do not turn into tyrants. For nothing should be more desirable to them than to be carried over from the state of royal honour in which they are lifted up on earth into the glory of the heavenly kingdom. Tyrants err indeed who forsake justice for the sake of some earthly advantage: who deprive themselves of the great reward which they might have obtained by ruling justly. No one, no matter how stupid or unbelieving, can fail to see how foolish it is to lose such great and eternal goods for the sake of such small and temporal ones.

---

[97] *De civitate Dei* 5:24.

[98] An etymology universally accepted in the Middle Ages, on the strength of Hebrews 7:2, but probably false: see *NCE* 7, *s.v.* 'Jerusalem'.

[99] Zechariah 12 *passim*, and especially vs. 8; but one wonders what the point of so awkward and inaccurate a paraphrase is supposed to be.

We must add also that the temporal advantages for the sake of which tyrants forsake justice come much more readily to kings who preserve justice. First, indeed, it would seem that, among worldly things, there is nothing worthier to be preferred than friendship; for it is friendship which, by bringing virtuous men together as one, preserves and promotes virtue. All men, no matter what their walk of life, have need of a friendship which neither forces itself insolently upon them in time of plenty nor deserts them in adversity. It is friendship which brings the greatest pleasures: so much so that, without friends, even the most delightful things are made tedious. Love makes troublous things easy and almost turns them into nothing; nor is any tyrant so cruel that he is not delighted by friendship. For when Dionysius, the former tyrant of Syracuse, was about to slay one of the two friends called Damon and Pythias, the one who was to be slain asked for a delay so that he might go home and put his affairs in order, and the other one of the friends gave himself up to the tyrant as a pledge of his return. As the appointed day approached and the other did not return, everyone reproached the hostage for his folly; yet he declared that he had no fears at all as to the constancy of his friend, and at the very hour when he was to be slain, his friend returned. Full of admiration at the spirit of the two men, the tyrant revoked the punishment because of the steadfastness of their friendship, asking moreover that he might be received as a third member of that friendship.[100] But no matter how much they may desire it, tyrants cannot secure this good of friendship. For when they do not seek the common good but their own, there is little or no communion between them and their subjects. Such communion is cemented more firmly by friendship than by anything else. For whether men are brought together by natural origin, or by similarity of custom, or by any other kind of common fellowship, we see that all are united by the bond of friendship.[101] The friendship between a tyrant and his subjects, however, is small; or, rather, it does not exist at all. For the subjects, oppressed by the injustice of tyranny and aware that they are not loved, but despised, certainly do not themselves love; nor have tyrants any reason to complain if they are not loved by their subjects, for they do not exhibit towards them the kind of behaviour for which anyone deserves to be loved.

But good kings, who work studiously to achieve the common benefit and who understand that it is their task to secure greater advantages for their subjects, are loved by most of their subjects because they themselves have

---

[100] Valerius Maximus 4:7:1.   [101] Aristotle, *Ethics* 8:9 (1159b25).

shown love for them. There is no malice in a community greater than that which arises when hatred is shown to friends, and benefactors are repaid with evil for good. But from this love comes the fact that the kingdoms of good kings are stable; for their subjects do not refuse to expose themselves to any peril whatsoever for their sake. An instance of this appears in the case of Julius Caesar, of whom Suetonius tells us that his regard for his soldiers was so great that, hearing of the death of some of them, he cut neither his hair nor his beard until he had avenged them.[102] Such gestures made the soldiers so exceptionally devoted to him and so strenuous in his service that when some of them were made prisoners and it was put to them that they might save their lives by taking up arms against Caesar, they refused to do so. Octavian Augustus also, who was most modest in his use of authority, was so highly regarded by his subjects that, when he was dying, many of them gave instructions that the victims which they had set aside for their own sacrifices should be offered so that he might be allowed to remain alive.[103]

It is not easy, therefore, for the dominion of a prince whom the people are so greatly united in loving to be disturbed; which is why Solomon says at Proverbs 29:14: 'The king that faithfully judgeth the poor, his throne shall be established for ever.' The dominion of a tyranny, however, cannot endure for long, because it is hated by the community; for it is not possible to preserve for any length of time that which is repugnant to the wishes of so many. Men seldom come to the end of this present life without suffering some adversity; but, in time of adversity, there can be no lack of opportunity to rise up against a tyrant, and where the occasion is present, there will be no lack of someone out of the many to make use of the opportunity. Moreover, the people will willingly support the rebel; nor will one who has achieved the favour of the community easily fail to accomplish his task. It can seldom happen, therefore, that the dominion of a tyrant is prolonged for any great length of time.

This is shown even more clearly if one considers how the lordship of a tyrant is preserved. For it cannot be preserved through love, since, as is clear from what we have noted already, the community subject to him has little or no affection for a tyrant. Nor can a tyrant count on the loyalty of his subjects; for we find that most people are not so much restrained by the virtue of loyalty that they will not throw off the yoke of undeserved

---

[102] Suetonius, *Iulius* 67f.   [103] Suetonius, *Augustus* 59.

servitude if they can. According to the opinion of most, perhaps, it will not be reputed a breach of faith if the wickedness of a tyrant is averted by any means whatsoever. The conclusion remains, therefore, that the rule of the tyrant is sustained by fear alone; and so it is that tyrants strive by every means to make themselves feared by their subjects. But fear is a weak foundation. For those who are subdued by fear will, if an occasion arises when they may do so with hope of impunity, rise up against their rulers in a manner which will be all the more ardent the more they have been constrained against their will and through fear alone, just as water, when forcibly compressed, will burst forth all the more vigorously when it finds an outlet. Fear itself does not lack peril, for many have been driven to despair by fear, and a man who despairs of his own wellbeing will fling himself all the more boldly into any undertaking. The dominion of the tyrant therefore cannot endure for long.

This conclusion is no less clear from example than from reason. Whether we consider the records of antiquity or the events of modern times, we seldom find that the dominion of a tyrant has lasted long. Hence also Aristotle, in his *Politics*, having listed a number of tyrants, shows that the dominion of all of them came to an end in a short time and that, if some of them did reign for longer than others, this was because they did not carry their tyranny to extremes but in many respects imitated the moderation of kingship.[104]

Again, this is made even clearer by a consideration of the Divine judgment. For as is said at Job 34:30: 'He maketh a man who is an hypocrite to rule because of the people's sins.' For no one can be more truly called 'an hypocrite' than one who assumes the duty of a king and then shows himself to be a tyrant; for a hypocrite is said to be one who represents himself as being something that he is not, as is usually done in plays. God, therefore, permits tyrants to rule as a punishment for the sins of their subjects. And such punishment is usually called in the scriptures the wrath of God. Hence the Lord says through Hosea (13:11): 'I will give thee a king in my wrath.' But unhappy is the king who is given to his people in the wrath of God, because his lordship cannot stand firm; for 'God will not forget to show mercy, nor will He in anger shut up his mercies' (Psalm 77:10). On the contrary, it is said through Joel (2:13) that: 'He is gracious and merciful, and repenteth Him of the evil.' God, therefore,

---

[104] *Politics* 5:12 (1315b11).

does not permit tyrants to reign for long; rather, after the tempest brought down upon the people by them, He restores calm by their overthrow. Hence it is said at Ecclesiasticus 10:14: 'The Lord hath cast down the thrones of proud princes, and set up the meek in their stead.'

Still more clearly does it appear from experience that kings acquire greater riches through justice than tyrants do by robbery. For the dominion of tyrants displeases the whole multitude subject to them, and so the tyrant has need of many attendants to give him protection against his subjects; and it is necessary for him to spend more on these than he can wring from his subjects.[105] The dominion of a king, however, because it is pleasing to his subjects, has all the subjects as its guardians, who protect it, and there is no need to spend anything on them. On the contrary, in times of necessity they will give freely to kings more than tyrants would be able to exact; and thus is fulfilled what Solomon says at Proverbs 11:24: 'Some' – kings, that is – 'divide their own goods for the benefit of their subjects, and grow rich; others' – that is, tyrants – 'seize what is not their own, and are always in want'. Similarly again, it comes about through the just judgment of God that those who heap up riches spend them to no good purpose; or, indeed, they are justly taken from them. For as Solomon says at Ecclesiastes 5:9: 'A covetous man shall not be satisfied with money, and he that loveth riches shall receive no fruit from them.' Again, he says at Proverbs 15:27: 'He that is greedy of gain troubleth his own house.' To kings who seek justice, on the other hand, riches are added by God, as to Solomon who, when he sought wisdom to discern judgment, received the promise of abundant riches.[106]

It would seem superfluous to speak of fame. For who would doubt that good kings, not only during life, but more so after death, in a certain sense live in the praises of men, and are grieved for by them; whereas the name of evil men is forgotten at once or, if they have been outstanding in their wickedness, they are remembered with hatred? Hence Solomon says at Proverbs 10:7: 'The memory of the just is blessed, but the name of the wicked shall rot': for it is either forgotten or remains only as a stench.

Chapter XII: That even such worldly goods as riches, power, honour and fame come more readily to kings than to tyrants; and of the ills which tyrants incur even in this life From what we have said, therefore, it is clear that

---

[105] Aristotle, *Politics* 3:14 (1284a25).   [106] 1 Kings 3:5ff.

stability of power, riches, honour and fame come more readily to the wish of kings than to tyrants, and that the prince who would attain these things unworthily falls away into tyranny; for no one falls away from justice unless he is drawn by some desire for gain. Moreover, a tyrant is deprived of the most excellent blessedness which is due to good kings as their reward; and, what is more grievous, he acquires for himself by way of punishment the greatest degree of torment. For if someone who robs one man, or delivers him into slavery, or slays him, deserves the greatest punishment, whether, indeed, it be death by the judgment of men or eternal damnation by the judgment of God, how much more is the tyrant to be deemed worthy to suffer worse penalties, who has robbed all men everywhere, worked against the liberty of all, and slain all and sundry to please his own will?

Such men, moreover, seldom repent. Puffed up with pride, forsaken by God as the due reward of their sins, and spoiled by the adulation of men, it is rare that they are able to make proper satisfaction. For when could they restore all those things which they have taken beyond their just due? There is no doubt that they ought to make restitution; but when could they recompense those whom they have oppressed and unjustly injured in every way? Added to their impenitence, moreover, is the fact that they consider all those things lawful which they have been able to do with impunity and without opposition. Not only do they make no attempt to repair the evil that they have done, but by the authority of their actions they make shameless sinning into a custom which they then transmit to their posterity, and so they are held guilty in the sight of God not only of their own misdeeds, but also of those of the others to whom they have left behind the example of sinning before God. And their sin is aggravated by the dignity of the office which they have received. For just as an earthly king punishes his ministers more grievously if he finds them opposed to him, so will God punish more heavily those whom He makes the executors and ministers of His rule if they act unworthily and change the judgment of God into bitterness. Hence also it is said to wicked kings at Wisdom 6:4ff: 'Because, being ministers of His kingdom, ye have not judged aright, nor kept the law, nor walked after the counsel of God: horribly and speedily shall He come upon you; for a sharp judgment shall be to them that be in high places. For to him that is little, mercy is granted, but the mighty shall be mightily tormented.' And it is said to Nebuchadnezzar through Isaiah (14:15): 'Yet thou shalt be brought down to hell, to the sides of the pit. They that see thee shall narrowly look upon thee, and consider thee' as one plunged into the depths of punishment. If, therefore, temporal goods come to kings in abundance, and a state of surpassing blessedness is prepared for them by God, whereas tyrants who long for many temporal goods are frustrated and are subject moreover to many perils and, what is worse, are deprived of eternal goods and marked out for the most grievous punishments: those who assume the duty of ruling must strive vehemently to show themselves as kings to their subjects, not tyrants.

We have, then, now said enough to show what a king is, that it is advantageous for a community to have a king, and, moreover, that it is advantageous to him to show the community subject to him that he is a king, not a tyrant.

Chapter XIII: He proceeds to show what the duties of a king are; he shows also that, according to the way of nature, the king in his kingdom is like the soul in the body and God in the world Following on from what we have said, it is necessary now to consider what the duty of the king is and what sort of person the king should be. And because it is true that art imitates nature[107] and that it is from natural things that we learn how to act according to reason, it would seem best to infer the duties of a king from the forms of government which occur in nature.

Now among natural things there is found both a universal and a particular form of government. The universal form is that according to which all things are contained under the government of God, Who governs all things by His providence. The particular form of government is very similar to the Divine government, and it is found within man, who for this reason may be called a lesser world, because within him is found an example of universal government.[108] For just as all corporeal creatures and all spiritual powers are contained under the Divine rule, so also the members of the body and the other powers of the soul are ruled by reason; and so the place of reason in man is, in a certain sense, like the relation of God to the world. But because, as we have shown above,[109] man is by nature a social animal who lives in community, this similarity with Divine rule is found in man not only inasmuch as the individual man is ruled by reason, but also inasmuch as a community is ruled by the reason of an individual man; for it is this which belongs especially to the duty of the king. Something similar is found in the case of certain animals who live

---

[107] Aristotle, *Physics* 2:2 (194a21).
[108] Aristotle, *Physics* 8:2 (252b24); Gregory, *Homilia in evangelia* 29:2 (*PL* 76:1214).
[109] Ch. 1.

socially, such as bees, among whom there is said to be a king;[110] but rule of this kind does not come about through reason, but through an instinct of nature implanted in them by the Supreme Ruler.

Let the king understand, therefore, that he has received the duty of being to his kingdom what the soul is to the body and what God is to the world. If he reflects diligently upon this, he will on the one hand be fired with zeal for justice when he considers that he has been appointed to exercise judgment in his kingdom in the place of God; and, on the other, he will acquire kindness and clemency, for he will look upon all those subject to his government as though they were his own members.

Chapter XIV: From the similarity between Divine and human government, it follows that the king should act towards his subjects in his kingdom in the way that God does in distinguishing each thing according to its proper order and activity, and in the way that the soul does [in relation to the body] It is, therefore, necessary to consider what God does in the world; for in this way it will become clear what the king should do. Now God's work in relation to the world must be considered under two general aspects. First, He made the world; second, He governs the world that He has made. Again, the soul has two functions in relation to the body; for, first, the power of the soul gives form to the body, and, second, the body is ruled and moved by the soul. Now it is the second of these activities which more properly belongs to the duty of the king; for the task of governing pertains to all kings, and the title 'king' [*rex*] is derived from the fact that he directs the government [*a gubernationis regimine*].[111] But the first activity does not belong to all kings, for not every king founds the city in which he reigns; many carry on the activity of ruling in a kingdom or city which has been founded already. It must be borne in mind, however, that if there had not been someone in the beginning to found a city or a kingdom, there would be no place in the world for royal government. The founding of a city or kingdom must therefore also be considered as falling within the duty of the king. For some have founded the cities in which they ruled, as Ninus did Nineveh and Romulus Rome.[112] Similarly again, it pertains to the duty of government to protect what is governed and to make use of it for the purpose for which it was established. But the ruler will not be able to

---

[110] Aristotle, *Historia animalium* 5:21 (553b6).
[111] Isidore of Seville, *Etymologiae* 1:29 (*PL* 82:105); 9:3 (*PL* 82:341f).
[112] Cf. Augustine, *De civitate Dei* 16:17.

understand the duties of government fully if he does not know the reason why it was instituted.

Now the reason for the foundation of a kingdom can be inferred from the example of the creation of the world. In this connection, we must first consider the creation of things themselves; then the orderly distribution of the parts of the world; then we see how the different species of things are distributed in the various parts of the world: the stars in the heaven, birds in the air, fish in the waters, animals on the earth; and finally we see how abundantly Divine providence gives to each of them whatever it needs. Moses has expressed this rational order of creation subtly and with care. For he first considers the creation of things, saying: 'In the beginning, God created the heaven and the earth' (Genesis 1:1). He then describes how all things were distinguished by the Divine command according to their proper order: that is to say, day from night, the heights from the depths, the sea from dry land. Next he describes how the heavens were adorned with stars, the sea with fish, and the earth with animals, and, finally, how dominion over the earth and its creatures was assigned to man; and the use of plants, he says, was given by the Divine providence to mankind and animals alike.

Now the founder of a city cannot create men and dwelling-places and all the other things necessary to support life out of nothing; rather, it is necessary for him to make use of things which already exist in nature, just as the other arts receive the materials with which they work from nature, smiths making use of iron and the builder of wood and stone. One who wishes to found a city or a kingdom must therefore first of all choose a place suitable to the preservation of the health of the inhabitants; fertile enough to provide them with sufficient food; pleasant enough to give them enjoyment; and well defended enough to afford them protection against enemies.[113] Even if some of these advantages are absent, the place will be suitable in proportion as the foregoing conditions, or at any rate the most necessary of them, are fulfilled. Then, having chosen the site, it is necessary for the founder of a city or a kingdom to divide it up in such a way as to supply all the needs which must be met if the kingdom is to be complete. For example, if a kingdom is to be founded, it will be necessary to provide locations suitable for the establishment of towns, farms and castles, and centres will need to be set up for the pursuit of learning, the training of soldiers and the conduct of commerce; and so on with the other

---

[113] See Book II, below.

38

things which the perfecting of a kingdom requires. Again, if a city is to be established, it will be necessary to provide places suitable for worship, for the administration of justice and for the pursuit of the various trades. Then, it will be necessary to group men together in suitable locations in the city according to their various occupations. Finally, it will be necessary for the needs of each man to be supplied in a fashion appropriate to his condition and standing: otherwise neither city nor kingdom could endure for long.

Stated briefly, then, these are the things which pertain to the duty of a king in founding a city or kingdom, arrived at by analogy with the creation of the world.

Chapter XV: That the government of a king is like the Divine government, and that such government may be compared to the steering of a ship. Also, a comparison is here made between priestly and royal dominion Just as the foundation of a city or kingdom can fittingly be inferred from the example of the creation of the world, so also can the proper government of the former be inferred from the government of the latter. First of all, however, it must be noted that to govern is to guide what is governed in a suitable fashion to its proper end. Thus a ship is said to be governed when it is steered on its right course to port by the industry of the sailors. If, therefore, something is directed towards an end external to itself, as a ship is to harbour, the duty of its governor will be not only to preserve the thing itself, but also to guide it towards its final end; whereas if there were something with no end outside itself, then the sole task belonging to the ruler would be the preservation of the thing itself in perfect condition.

But nothing of the latter kind [i.e. nothing with no end outside itself] is found in the world [*in rebus*] apart from God, Who is the end of all things; and the care of that which is directed towards an end outside itself is beset with a number of difficulties. For perhaps there is one person whose responsibility it is to preserve the thing itself and another whose task is to lead it towards a higher perfection, as in the case of the ship, from which we have drawn an example of government. For the carpenter has the task of repairing any damage which the ship has sustained, whereas the mariner bears the responsibility for guiding the ship to port. And so it happens also in the case of a man. For the physician has the task of preserving a man's life in a healthy condition; the steward has to supply him with the necessaries of life; the task of the teacher is to see to it that he understands the truth; and that of the moral counsellor is to ensure that he lives according to reason. And if man were not directed towards some good external to himself, the foregoing forms of care would suffice.

But there is a certain extraneous good which awaits man after he has lived this mortal life: namely, the final blessedness to which he looks forward in the enjoyment of God after death. For as the Apostle says (2 Corinthians 5:6): 'While we are in the body, we are absent from the Lord.' The Christian man, then, for whom that blessedness has been won by the blood of Christ, and for the attainment of which he has received the earnest of the Holy Spirit, has need of another, spiritual, care by which he is guided towards the harbour of eternal salvation. And this is the kind of care shown to the faithful by the ministers of the Church of Christ.

We must make the same judgment in regard to the end of the whole community as we do of one person.[114] If the end of man were some good existing only in himself, therefore, the final end of government would similarly be to acquire and preserve that good for the whole community. Thus if that ultimate end, whether of one man or of a community, were the life and health of the body, the physicians would have the duty of governing. And if the final end were abundant wealth, the steward would be king of the community. And if the good were that the community might achieve knowledge of the truth, the king would have the duty of a teacher. But it seems that the end for which a community is brought together is to live according to virtue; for men come together so that they may live well in a way that would not be possible for each of them living singly. For the good is life according to virtue, and so the end of human association is a virtuous life.[115]

An indication of this lies in the fact that only those who share with one another in the task of living well are deemed to be parts of a community. For if men came together for the sake of life merely, both animals and slaves would have a part in civil society; if for the sake of acquiring wealth, all those engaged in commerce together would belong to one city.[116] But we see that only those are counted as members of a community who are guided in living well under the same laws and by the same government. But because the man who lives according to virtue is also directed towards a further end, which, as we have already said above, consists in the enjoyment of the Divine, the end of the whole community of mankind must therefore be the same as it is for one man. The final end of a multitude

[114] Aristotle, *Politics* 7:2 (1324a5; 1325b31).
[115] Aristotle, *Ethics* 2:1 (1103b3); *Politics* 1:2 (1252b27); 3:9 (1280b5).
[116] Aristotle, *Politics* 3:9 (1280a25).

united in society, therefore, will not be to live according to virtue, but through virtuous living to attain to the enjoyment of the Divine. Now if it were possible to achieve this end through natural human virtue alone, it would necessarily belong to the king's duty to guide men to this end; for, as we suppose, it is to the king that the supreme ruling power in human affairs is entrusted, and government is of a higher order according to the finality of the end to which it is directed. For we find that it is always the one who has responsibility for the final end who directs those who carry out the tasks leading to the final end.[117] For example, the captain whose responsibility it is to direct the navigation of the ship commands him who constructs the ship to make the kind of ship most suitable for his purposes; and the citizen who makes use of arms gives orders to the blacksmith as to what kind of arms he is to forge. But because the enjoyment of Divinity is an end which a man cannot attain through human virtue alone, but only through Divine virtue, according to the Apostle at Romans 6:23: 'The grace of God is eternal life', it is not human but Divine rule that will lead us to this end. And government of this kind belongs only to that King Who is not only man, but also God: that is, to our Lord Jesus Christ, Who by making men sons of God, has led them to the glory of heaven.

This, then, is the government given to Him, which shall not pass away and by reason of which He is called in Holy Scripture not only priest but king. As Jeremiah says (23:5): 'A king shall reign and be wise.' Hence a royal priesthood is derived from Him; and, what is more, all who believe in Christ, insofar as they are His members, are called kings and priests.[118] The administration of this kingdom, therefore, is entrusted not to earthly kings, but to priests, so that spiritual and earthly things may be kept distinct; and in particular to the Supreme Priest, the successor of Peter, the Vicar of Christ, the Roman Pontiff, to whom all the kings of the Christian people should be subject, as if to the Lord Jesus Christ Himself. For those who are responsible for intermediate ends should be subject to one who is responsible for the ultimate end, and be directed by his command. Since the priesthood of the gentiles and the worship of their gods existed only for the sake of acquiring those temporal goods which are entirely directed to the good of the community and which it is therefore the duty of kings to secure, it was suitable that the priests of the gentiles[119] should be subject

---

[117] Aristotle, *Ethics* 1:1 (1094a10).
[118] Cf. 1 Peter 2:9; Hebrews 7 *passim*.
[119] Like medieval authors in general, St Thomas tends to use 'gentile' to mean 'heathen' rather than 'non-Jewish'.

to their kings. Again, under the old law, those who embraced the true religion were promised temporal goods not by demons, but by God; and so we read that, under the old law, priests were subject to kings. But under the new law there is a higher priesthood, by which men are conducted towards heavenly goods; and so, under the law of Christ, kings must be subject to priests.

For this reason it came about by the wondrous dispensation of Divine providence that in the city of Rome, which God foresaw would be the principal seat of the Christian people in time to come, the custom gradually grew up that the rulers of the city should be subject to the priests. For as Valerius Maximus declares:

> Even in matters relating to the dignity of the highest majesty, our city has always affirmed that all things should be placed after religion. For this reason, holders of secular authority have never doubted that they ought to serve sacred authority, thereby showing their belief that the government of human affairs will be properly conducted only by those who are good and constant servants of the Divine power.[120]

Again, because it was to come to pass also that the religion of the Christian priesthood would flourish with particular vigour in Gaul, Divine providence permitted that the gentile priests of the Gauls, who were called Druids, should be the interpreters of the law throughout Gaul, as Caesar relates in the book which he wrote on the Gallic war.[121]

Chapter XVI: That the king should govern his subjects in such a way that they live according to virtue in their pursuit of both their final and intermediate ends. Also, an account is here given of those things which promote living well and of those which impede it, and of what remedy the king is to apply to such impediments Just as the life that men live here, when they live well, is directed, as to its end, towards the blessed life in heaven for which we hope, so all the particular goods which men obtain, whether wealth or profit or health or skill or learning, are directed, as to their end, to the good of the community. If, therefore, as we have said,[122] he who is responsible for a final end must govern those who are responsible for the things directed towards that end and must direct them by his command, it is clear that the king, just as he must be subject to the lordship and

---

[120] Valerius Maximus 1:1:9.
[121] *De bello Gallico* 6:13.
[122] Ch. XV.

governance administered by the priestly office, must rule over all human occupations and direct them by his own command and rule.

Now whoever has the task of bringing to completion something which is directed towards an end must make sure that his work is suited to that end. For example, the smith forges the kind of sword that is fit to fight with, and the builder lays out the kind of house that is suitable for living in. And because the end of our living well at this present time is the blessedness of heaven, the king's duty is therefore to secure the good life for the community in such a way as to ensure that it is led to the blessedness of heaven: that is, by commanding those things which conduce to the blessedness of heaven and forbidding, as far as it is possible to do so, those which are contrary to it. But we learn the way to true blessedness, and the obstacles to it, from the Divine law, the duty of teaching which belongs to the priests, according to Malachi 2:7: 'For the priest's lips should keep knowledge, and they should seek the law at his mouth.' And so the Lord commands at Deuteronomy 17:18–19:

> And it shall be, when he sitteth upon the throne of his kingdom, that he shall write him a copy of this law in a book out of that which is before the priests of the tribe of Levi, and it shall be with him, and he shall read therein, all the days of his life, that he may learn to fear the Lord his God, to keep all the words of this law and these statutes, to do them.

The king, therefore, being instructed in the Divine law, must strive with special care to ensure that the community subject to him lives well; and this task may be divided into three parts. First, he must establish the good life in the community subject to him; second, he must preserve it once it is established; third, having preserved it, he must strive to improve it. But the good life for each man requires two things. The first and chief requirement is activity according to virtue, for virtue is that quality by which we live well.[123] The other requirement is secondary and, as it were, instrumental: namely, a sufficiency of bodily goods, the use of which is necessary to virtuous conduct.[124]Man himself is made a unity by natural causation; but the unity of a community, which is called peace, must be brought about by the industry of the ruler. So, then: to establish the good life for a community requires three things: first, that the community be established in the unity of peace; second, that the community united by

---

[123] Augustine, *De libero arbitrio* 2:19.   [124] Aristotle, *Ethics* 1:8 (1099b1).

the bond of peace be guided to act well – for just as a man cannot act well unless we presuppose the unity of his parts, so a multitude of men who are at odds with one another because they lack peace will be prevented from living well; and, third, it requires that, through the industry of the ruler, there be a plentiful supply of those things necessary to living well.

When, therefore, the good life has been established in the community by the duty of the king, he must next consider how to preserve it. Now there are three things detrimental to the permanence of the public good; and one of these arises from the nature of things. For the good of the community should not be established for a particular length of time only, but should be as it were perpetual. But men, because they are mortal, do not endure perpetually; nor, while they are alive, do they always have the same degree of vigour, for human life is subject to many changes, and men are not equally capable of fulfilling the same duties throughout the whole of life. Another obstacle to the preservation of the public good arises from within, and consists in perversity of will; for some people are negligent in carrying out the duties which the commonwealth requires, or even damage the peace of the community when they transgress against justice and disturb the peace of others. And the third obstacle to the preservation of the commonwealth comes from an external cause, when the peace is undone by the invasion of enemies, and sometimes the kingdom or city which has been founded is destroyed. In relation to the three foregoing causes, therefore, the task of the king has a threefold character. The first has to do with the succession of men: that is, with the replacement of those who preside over the various duties. For just as the Divine government ensures that corruptible things, which cannot remain the same for ever, are renewed by the production of others to replace them, and in this way preserves the integrity of the universe, so by the efforts of the king the good of the community subject to him will be preserved when he takes care to ensure that successors take the place of those who are faltering. Second, he should restrain the men subject to him from iniquity by means of laws and commands, penalties and rewards, and lead them to do virtuous works, taking his example from God, Who gave men a law, and Who rewards those who observe it and requites with punishment those who transgress it. Third, it is the king's task to furnish the community subject to him with protection against enemies; for taking measures against internal perils will bring no benefit if it is not possible for it to be defended against external ones.

So, then, a third thing remains as belonging to the duty of the king if he is to ensure the good of the community: he must be careful to secure its improvement. This will be done in each of the ways mentioned above if he corrects what is disordered, if he supplies what is lacking, and if he strives to perfect whatever can be done better. Hence the Apostle, at 1 Corinthians 12:31, admonishes the faithful always to 'covet earnestly the best gifts'.

These, then, are the things which belong to the duty of a king; but it is necessary to treat of each of them more carefully.

Book II

Chapter 1: How it pertains to the king to found cities or castles in order to achieve glory; that he must choose temperate places for this purpose; and what advantages there are for kingdoms when this is done, and disadvantages when it is not First, then, it is especially necessary to expound the king's duty in relation to the founding of a kingdom or city. For as Vegetius says: 'The mightiest nations and the most renowned princes could seek no greater glory than to found new cities or to broaden their sway by transferring those established by others into their own names';[125] which, indeed, accords with the teaching of sacred scripture, for it is said at Ecclesiasticus 40:19 that 'the building of a city will confirm a name'. The name of Romulus would be unknown today had he not founded Rome.

In founding a city or kingdom, a region must be selected which, if there is a choice, should be temperate; for those who dwell there will derive many benefits from the temperateness of the region. First, men derive soundness of body and length of life from the temperateness of a region. Because health consists in a certain temperateness of the humours, health will be preserved in a temperate place, since like is preserved by like.[126] If, however, there is excessive heat or cold, the body will necessarily be changed by the quality of the air. Hence by a kind of natural impulse certain animals remove themselves to a warm place during a cold period and vice versa, in order to achieve a temperate condition from the disposition of each place at each time.[127]

---

[125] *Rei militaris instituta* 4, prologue.
[126] Aristotle, *Physics* 7:3 (246b4).
[127] Aristotle, *Historia animalium* 7:12 (596b23).

45

Again, since animal life is a matter of heat and moisture, if heat is intense natural moisture is soon dried up and life fails, just as a lamp is soon extinguished if the fuel poured into it is quickly consumed when the flame is too high. Hence in certain very hot regions of Ethiopia, men are not able to live for more than thirty years. But in regions which are excessively cold, natural moisture is easily frozen and natural heat soon extinguished.[128]

Next, the temperateness of a region gives many opportunities for success in war, by which human society is rendered secure. For as Vegetius remarks:

> All nations which are close to the sun and dried up by the excessive heat are said to have more wisdom but less blood, and so they do not have the constancy and courage necessary for close combat, for those who know that they have little blood fear wounds. On the other hand, peoples of the north, who are removed from the heat of the sun, lack prudence but are overflowing with a great deal of blood, and so are very ready to go to war. But those who dwell in temperate regions are supplied with plenty of blood, and so are contemptuous of wounds and death; but they do not lack prudence, and this both preserves orderliness in the camp and promotes strategic thought in battle.[129]

Finally, a temperate region is of no little benefit to political life. For as Aristotle says in his *Politics*, those races who dwell in cold places are full of spirit, but are greatly deficient in intellect and art. For this reason they remain free, but they do not live politically, and cannot rule their neighbours because of their lack of prudence. Those who dwell in hot places are intellectual and accomplished in matters of learning, but they lack spirit, and so they become subjects and remain in a servile condition. But those who dwell in temperate places have both spirit and intellect, by reason of which they both remain free and are specially able to live politically, and they know how to rule others.[130]

A temperate region should therefore be chosen for the founding of a city or kingdom.

Chapter II: That kings and princes ought to choose places for the founding of cities or castles where the air is wholesome; and he shows how and by what signs

---

[128] Cf. Aristotle, *Parva naturalia*, 'De longitudine et brevitate vitae' 5 (466a20).
[129] *Rei militaris instituta* 1:2.
[130] Paraphrased from Aristotle, *Politics* 7:7 (1327b23).

such a place is to be known After the choice of region, it is necessary to choose a suitable place for building the city; and it seems that wholesome air is the first requirement here. For before any kind of social life comes natural life itself, and this is preserved by wholesome air.

As Vitruvius teaches, the healthiest place will be 'elevated, not foggy, not frosty, and facing regions of the heaven which are neither hot nor cold; finally, it should not be close to marshy ground'.[131] The elevation of a place usually confers wholesomeness upon the air, because a high place is exposed to the blowing of the winds, by which the air is rendered pure. Also, the vapours which are released from the earth and the waters by the power of the sun's rays are multiplied more in valleys and low-lying places than in high ones, so that in high places the air is found to be more refined. Moreover, such refinement of the air, which avails greatly for free and pure breathing, is hindered by the fogs and frosts which usually abound in very damp places, so that places of this kind are found to be contrary to health. Also, because marshy places abound with excessive dampness, the place chosen for the building of a city ought to be far away from marshy ground.

> For when the morning breezes arrive at that place when the sun rises, the fogs which arise from the swamps will be added to them and they will spread abroad the exhalations of the venomous marshland creatures mixed with the fogs, and so make the place pestilential. It is, however, reasonable to construct walls in places close to the sea provided that they face north or thereabouts [and so are not exposed to extremes of temperature] and the marshes are more elevated than the sea shore; for if ditches are made the water will then be able to drain out to the shore, and when, in storms, the sea flows back into the marshes, it will not allow marsh animals to be born. And if certain animals come down from higher places, they will be killed by the unaccustomed saltness.[132]

It is also necessary for the place intended for a city to be temperately disposed as regards heat and cold according to the various aspects which it presents to the regions of the heavens. 'For it will not be healthy if the walls, especially those built near the sea, face south.' For such places will be cold in the morning, because the sun does not shine on them, but at noon they will be very hot because of the sunshine. Places which face west are cool or even cold when the sun rises, but warm at noon and hot in

---

[131] *De architectura* 1:4.   [132] *Ibid.*

47

the evening because of the continuous heat and shining of the sun. Those which face east will be moderately warm in the morning, because the sun is directly opposite them; nor will the heat be much increased at noon, because the sun does not shine directly on them; but in the evening they will be cold because the rays of the sun will then be completely behind them. From the converse of what was said of those facing south, there will be the same or similar temperatures when the location of the city faces north. But we can learn from experience that it is unhealthy to move to a warmer place, for 'bodies which are brought from cold regions into warm ones cannot endure, but are dissolved, because the heat dissolves their natural virtues by sucking up their moisture.' Hence even in wholesome places, 'summer renders bodies infirm'.[133]

Since suitable food is required for bodily health, it is necessary to investigate this aspect of the matter when considering the wholesomeness of the place chosen for the building of a city; for the condition of those born in a place can be discovered from the quality of their food. The ancients customarily explored this question by means of the animals nourished there. For since both men and other animals make common use of those things which the land produces as food, it follows that if the entrails of slaughtered animals are found to be in good condition, men too may be wholesomely nourished in the same place. But if the parts of slaughtered animals appear to be diseased, this can reasonably be taken to show that the place in question is not a healthy dwelling-place for men either.[134]

As well as temperate air, wholesome water is required; for the health of the body depends especially upon those things which are used by men most often. Clearly, it is essential to life that we draw in air every day by breathing, which is why its wholesomeness will especially contribute to the body's health and wellbeing; and, by the same token, because, among the things that we take by way of nourishment, we use water most often, both as drink and food, nothing apart from the purity of the air is more pertinent to the healthfulness of a place than the wholesomeness of its water.

There are other signs that a place can be considered healthful: namely, if the faces of the men who live there appear to have a good colour; if their bodies are robust and their limbs well made; if their children are many and lively; and if there are many old people. Conversely, if men's faces

---

[133] *Ibid.*   [134] *Ibid.*

appear deformed, if their bodies are weak, if their limbs are exhausted or diseased, if their children are few and ill, and if old people are few, it cannot be doubted that the place is deathly.

Chapter III: That the king must construct the city to have a plentiful supply of food, for without this a city cannot be perfect; and he distinguishes two ways in which this may be done, of which the first is more to be commended Again, the place chosen for the building of a city should be one which not only preserves the health of those who dwell there, but suffices also for an abundant supply of food.[135] For it is not possible for a community of men to dwell where there is not plenty of food. Hence, as Vitruvius records, when the most distinguished architect Xenocrates demonstrated to Alexander of Macedon that he could construct a city of elegant appearance on a certain mountain, Alexander asked him whether there were fields there able to provide that city with a plentiful supply of grain. When he found that these were lacking, he retorted that anyone who built a city in such a place would be worthy to be cursed; for: 'Just as a newborn infant can be neither fed nor induced to grow without a nurse's milk, so a city cannot support a large populace without an abundance of food.'[136]

Now there are two ways in which a city can be provided with a plentiful supply of things. One is through the fertility of the region, which produces an abundance of all the things necessary for human life. The other is through trade, by which the things necessary for life are brought in from various other parts. But it may be clearly established that the first way is more suitable. For the more excellent something is, the more it is found to be self-sufficient, since that which lacks something is shown to be deficient. But a city is more fully self-sufficient if its surrounding region is adequate to furnish it with the necessaries of life, whereas a city which lacks something acquires these things through trade. For a city is more excellent if it has an abundance of things from its own territory than if it has such abundance through trade, since the first way seems to be more secure. For the transportation of food can easily be hindered by the events of war and the various hazards of the road, and so the city may be overcome through lack of food.

---

[135] Vitruvius, *De architectura* 1:5.

[136] Vitruvius, *De architectura* 2, prologue. According to Vitruvius the architect is Dinocrates of Rhodes. The spelling Xenocrates is no doubt a copyist's error. See Bibliographical Glossary *s.v.* 'Dinocrates'.

This [self-sufficiency] is also more beneficial to civic life. For a city which needs much trade to sustain it must also of necessity suffer continual contact with foreigners. But according to the teaching of Aristotle, association with foreigners commonly corrupts the morals of the citizens because men from foreign parts, nurtured on other laws and usages, inevitably behave differently in many ways from the customs of the citizens, and when their example influences the citizens to act in similar ways, civic life is disturbed.[137]

If the citizens themselves are devoted to trade, the way is thrown open to many vices. Because the practice of commerce especially involves the pursuit of gain, greed is introduced into the citizens' hearts by commerce; and so it comes to pass that all things in the city are made venal.[138] When good faith has departed the place is laid open to frauds; when the public good is despised, everyone pursues his own advantage, zeal for virtue ceases, and everyone puts profit before the honour of virtue. Hence in such a city civic life will necessarily be corrupted.

Also, commerce is more at odds with military prowess than are most other occupations. Merchants rest in the shade without toil, and while they enjoy delights their spirits grow soft and their bodies are rendered weak and unfitted for military exertions.[139] This is why, according to the civil law, knights are forbidden to engage in commerce.[140]

Finally, a city is usually more peaceful if its people come together only rarely and if few dwell within the city walls. When men frequently gather together, this gives occasion for disputes and provides the matter for seditions. According to what Aristotle teaches, it is more beneficial for people to be occupied outside the cities than to dwell always together within the city walls.[141] But if the city is devoted to trade, it is then greatly necessary for the citizens to reside within the city and engage in trade there.

It is therefore better for a city to be plentifully supplied with food from its own fields than for it to be totally given over to commerce. It is not, however, fitting to exclude merchants from the city altogether, because a place cannot easily be found which so abounds in all the things necessary for life that it does not need to have some things brought in from elsewhere. Also, when things are especially abundant in the same place, many people suffer

---

[137] Aristotle, *Politics* 5:3 (1303a25); 7:6 (1327a13).
[138] Aristotle, *Politics* 1:9 (1257b21).
[139] Cf. Vegetius, *Rei militaris instituta* 1:3.
[140] *CICiv.: Codex* 1:12:34.
[141] *Politics* 6:4 (1318b10).

loss if they cannot be transported to another place through the activity of merchants. Hence it is fitting for the perfect city to practise trade in moderation.

Chapter IV: The region which the king chooses for a city or castle must be arranged in such a way as to have pleasant features: which the citizens should be encouraged to enjoy in moderation, however, since they are often a cause of dissoluteness, by which the kingdom is undermined The place chosen for the building of cities should delight the inhabitants with its pleasantness. For a multitude of inhabitants will not readily forsake a pleasant place, nor will they readily flock to a place which lacks pleasantness, for no man can for long endure a life from which pleasure is absent. Broad fields in the plains, fruitful trees, mountains visible nearby, graceful groves and flowing water: all these things will contribute to such pleasantness. But too much in the way of pleasantness leads men to enjoy delights to excess, and this is harmful to cities in many ways. Thus, delights should be enjoyed in moderation, primarily because men devoted to delights become dull in their senses. Pleasure immerses their souls in sensations, so that they cannot exercise free judgment with respect to delightful things; and so, according to the opinion of Aristotle, prudent judgments are corrupted by pleasure.[142]

Again, excessive pleasures cause one to fall away from honest virtue; for nothing leads more readily than pleasure to an immoderate increase by which the mean of virtue is corrupted.[143] This is partly because it is the nature of pleasure to induce greed, so that one who has taken moderate pleasure is precipitated into the blandishments of disgraceful delights in the way that dry wood is kindled by a small flame. Partly also it is because pleasure does not satisfy the appetite; on the contrary, a pleasure once tasted produces a thirst for more. Hence it pertains to the office of virtue to see to it that men abstain from excessive pleasures, for by shunning excess one arrives more easily at the mean of virtue.

Consequently again, men excessively devoted to pleasure grow weak in spirit and become irresolute in confronting any hardship, in tolerating labour and in facing danger. Hence also delights greatly harm the conduct of war; for, as Vegetius says in the book *De re militari*: 'They fear death less who know that they had fewer delights in life.'[144]

[142] *Ethics* 6:5 (1140b13).
[143] *Ethics* 2:6 (1106b35).
[144] *Rei militaris instituta* 1:3.

Those who are unrestrained in their enjoyment of delights eventually become slothful and, neglecting necessary studies and their proper business, care only for the pursuit of pleasure, in the course of which they lavishly dissipate what others have previously gathered. Then, reduced to the condition of paupers, and because they cannot bear to be without their accustomed delights, they become thieves and robbers in order to have the means of satisfying their longing. It is, therefore, harmful for a city to abound in excessive delights, whether these arise from the disposition of the place or from some other causes.

Moderate pleasure, therefore, is appropriate to human association, as a kind of spice whereby the human spirit may be restored.[145]

(c) *Summa theologiae* IaIIae 105:1: Concerning the reason for the judicial precepts [of the Old Testament][146]

articulus 1: Whether the old law enjoined suitable precepts concerning rulers

It seems that the old law did not enjoin suitable precepts concerning rulers.

obiectio 1: For, as the Philosopher says, 'the ordering of a people depends for the most part upon the chief ruler'.[147] But the law contains no precept concerning the appointment of a 'chief ruler', although we find prescriptions there concerning lesser rulers: for example (Exodus 18:21): 'Provide out of all the people wise men', etc.; and (Numbers 11:16): 'Gather unto me seventy men of the ancients of Israel'; and (Deuteronomy 1:13): 'Let me have from among you wise and understanding men', etc. The law therefore did not provide sufficiently for the rulers of the people.

obiectio 2: Moreover, as Plato says: 'The best gives of the best.'[148] But the best kind of order for a commonwealth or any nation is rule by a king, because this is the kind of government which most closely resembles the Divine government by which God has ruled the world from the

---

[145] See Introduction, p. xix.

[146] This *Quaestio* has four articles. The other three are: 'Whether the judicial precepts made suitable provision for living together'; 'Whether the judicial precepts made suitable provision concerning foreigners'; and 'Whether the old law established suitable precepts concerning household relations'.

[147] *Politics* 3:6 (1278b10).

[148] Cf. *Timaeus* 29A; E.

beginning.[149] Therefore the law should have set a king over the people, and they should have not been allowed any choice in the matter; although in fact they were given a choice (Deuteronomy 17:14f): 'When thou shalt say, I will set a king over me, thou shalt set him', etc.

obiectio 3: Moreover, according to Matthew 12:25, 'Every kingdom divided against itself is brought to desolation.' This saying proved true in the case of the Jewish people, whose destruction was encompassed when the kingdom was divided. But the law should seek above all to secure the general welfare of the people. It should therefore have forbidden the division of the kingdom between two kings, nor should this arrangement have been introduced even by Divine authority; yet it is said to have been introduced by the authority of the prophet Ahijah the Shilonite (1 Kings 11:29ff).

obiectio 4: Moreover, just as priests are appointed for the benefit of the people in things pertaining to God, as stated at Hebrews 5:1, so rulers are established for the benefit of the people in human affairs. But certain things were set aside as a means of support for the priests and Levites of the law, such as tithes and first-fruits and many similar things. In the same way, therefore, certain things should have been provided for the support of the rulers of the people, especially since they were forbidden to accept gifts, as is stated clearly at Exodus 23:8: 'And thou shalt take no gift, for the gift blindeth the wise and perverteth the words of the righteous.'

obiectio 5: Moreover, just as kingship is the best form of government, so is tyranny the most corrupt.[150] But when the Lord appointed a king, he established a tyrannical law; for it is said at 1 Samuel 8:11: 'This will be the right of the king that shall reign over you: he will take your sons', etc. The law therefore did not make suitable provision with regard to the appointment of rulers.

sed contra: The nation of Israel is congratulated on the beauty of its order (Numbers 24:5): 'How goodly are thy tents, O Jacob, and thy tabernacles, O Israel.' But the goodly ordering of a nation depends upon the right establishment of its rulers. The law therefore made proper provision for the people with regard to its rulers.

responsio: Two things are to be considered with regard to the good ordering of government in a city or nation. The first is that all should

---

[149] Cf. p. 11, above.   [150] See pp. 11ff, above.

have some share in the government; for an arrangement of this kind secures the peace of the people, and all men love and defend it, as is stated at *Politics* II.[151] The other thing to be considered is the kind of rule, or the ordering of government. Of the different kinds of rule which the Philosopher discusses at *Politics* III,[152] the foremost are kingship, in which one man governs according to virtue, and aristocracy, that is, the power of the best men, in which a few govern according to virtue. Hence the best ordering of government in any city or kingdom is achieved when one man is chosen to preside over all according to virtue; when he has under him others who govern according to virtue; and when such government nonetheless belongs to all, both because all are eligible for election to it and because it is elected by all. Such a 'polity' is the best form of government inasmuch as it is a benign mixture of kingship, because there is one man who presides; of aristocracy, because it is the rule of several according to virtue; and of democracy, that is, popular power, because the rulers can be elected from the people and it belongs to the people to elect the rulers.[153]

Now it was this form of government which was instituted according to the Divine law. For Moses and his successors governed the people in such a way that each of them was ruler over all. But they chose seventy-two elders according to their virtue. For it is said at Deuteronomy 1:15: 'I took out of your tribes men wise and honourable, and appointed them rulers'; and this was aristocracy. But this arrangement was also democratic in that they were chosen from all the people. For it is said at Exodus 18:21: 'Provide out of all the people wise men', etc. Also, they were chosen by the people; for it is said at Deuteronomy 1:13: 'Let me have from among you wise men.' Hence it is clear that the [old] law provided for the best form of government.

ad 1: This people [i.e. the people of Israel] was ruled under the special protection of God; hence it is said at Deuteronomy 7:6: 'The Lord thy God hath chosen thee to be a special people unto Himself.' This is why the Lord reserved to Himself the appointment of the chief ruler. For this, too, did Moses pray (Numbers 27:16): 'May the Lord the God of the spirits of all the flesh provide a man that may be over this multitude.' Thus, by the command of God Joshua was set over them to succeed Moses; and it is said of each of the judges who came after Joshua that God 'raised up a saviour'

---

[151] *Politics* 2:6 (1270b17).
[152] *Politics* 3:5 (1279a32).
[153] Cf. *Politics* 3:7 (1279a37); 4:8 (1293b33); 4:11 (1295a31).

for the people, and that 'the Spirit of the Lord' was in them (Judges 3:9, 10, 15). Hence the Lord did not leave the choice of a king to the people, but reserved it to Himself, as appears from Deuteronomy 17:15: 'Thou shalt set him king over thee whom the Lord thy God shall choose.'

ad 2: Kingship is the best form of government for a people for as long as it does not become corrupt. But because the power granted to a king is so great, it is easy for kingship to degenerate into tyranny unless he to whom such power is granted is a man of perfect virtue; for, as the Philosopher says at *Ethics* IV, 'No one but the virtuous man can bear himself well in good fortune.'[154] But perfect virtue is found only in a few, and the Jews in particular were prone to cruelty and avarice, which vices above all cause men to become tyrants. And so the Lord did not at first institute for them kings having supreme power, but a judge and governor to protect them. Later, however, at the request of the people, he gave them a king, as though in anger, as is clear from what He said to Samuel at 1 Samuel 8:7: 'They have not rejected thee, but me, that I should not reign over them.'

Nonetheless, as regards the institution of kingship, He did lay down the manner of election from the beginning (Deuteronomy 17:14ff); and in doing so He made two provisions: that is, that in making their choice they should look to the Lord's judgment and not make a man of another nation their king (vs. 15), because such kings usually have little love for the people over whom they rule, and consequently do not care for them. And, second, He ordained how kings should conduct themselves when appointed: that is (vs. 16f), that they should not multiply chariots and horses or wives or great riches, because it is through greed for such things that princes fall away into tyranny and forsake justice. He also laid down how they should conduct themselves towards God: that is (vs. 19), that they should always read and think upon the law of God, and live always in the fear and obedience of God. He also laid down how they should conduct themselves in relation to their subjects: that is (vs. 20), that they should not proudly despise them or oppress them or turn aside from justice.

ad 3: The division of the kingdom and the number of the kings was a punishment inflicted upon the people for their many rebellions, especially against the just rule of David, rather than a benefit conferred upon them for their advantage. Hence it is said at Hosea 13:11: 'I will give you a king

---

[154] *Ethics* 4:3 (1124a30).

in my wrath'; and at Hosea 8:4: 'They have reigned, but not by me; they have been princes, and I knew it not.'

ad 4: The priestly office was handed down in succession from father to son so that it might be held in greater esteem than it would have enjoyed if the priesthood could be held simply by any member of the populace; for honour was to be given to the priests out of reverence for the Divine worship. Hence it was necessary to put certain things aside for them, in the form of both tithes and first fruits, and also oblations and sacrifices, so that they might be provided with a means of support. Rulers, on the other hand, were chosen from among the people, as stated above; and so they had their own possessions as a means of support: all the more so since the Lord forbade even a king to have excessive wealth or to make too great a show of magnificence, partly because [otherwise] he could hardly avoid the excesses of pride and tyranny arising from such things, and partly because, if the rulers were not unduly wealthy, and if their office involved much toil and care, the ambition of the common people would not be tempted by it and a cause of sedition would not arise.

ad 5: This was not a right given to the king by Divine institution; rather, it was foretold that kings would usurp that right by degenerating into tyrants and oppressing their subjects. This is shown by the words which follow (vs. 17): 'and ye shall be his servants.' This signifies tyranny, for a tyrant rules his subjects as though they were his servants. Samuel spoke these words to discourage the people from asking for a king; but, as the passage goes on (vs. 19): 'the people refused to obey the voice of Samuel'. It may happen, however, that even a good king may take away the sons of his subjects and make them tribunes and centurions, and may take many other things for the sake of the common welfare, without thereby becoming a tyrant.

2

Obedience

(a) *Summa theologiae* IIaIIae 104: On obedience

We come next to obedience; and here there are six things to consider:

1. Whether one man is bound to obey another
2. Whether obedience is a specific virtue
3. How it relates to other virtues
4. Whether God is to be obeyed in all things
5. Whether subjects are bound to obey their rulers in all things
6. Whether the faithful are bound to obey the secular powers

articulus 1: *Whether one man is bound to obey another*

It seems that one man is not bound to obey another.

obiectio 1: For nothing should be done contrary to Divine ordinance. But it is a Divine ordinance that man should be ruled by his own counsel, according to Ecclesiasticus 15:14: 'God made man from the beginning, and left him in the hand of his own counsel.' Therefore one man is not bound to obey another.

obiectio 2: Moreover, if someone were bound to obey another, the will of the one commanding him would be the rule of his conduct. But the only rule of human conduct is the Divine will, which is always right. Therefore man is bound to obey no one except God.

obiectio 3: Moreover, the more freely service is given, the more acceptable it is. But what a man does out of duty is not freely given. Therefore if a man were bound by duty to obey others in performing good works, his good works would be rendered less acceptable by the fact that they were done under obedience. Therefore one man is not bound to obey another.

sed contra: It is commanded at Hebrews 13:17: 'Obey them that have the rule over you, and submit yourselves.'

responsio: As the actions of natural things proceed from natural powers, so do human actions proceed from the human will. In the natural order, it happens of necessity that higher things move lower things by the excellence of the natural power divinely given to them. Hence in human affairs also superiors must move inferiors by their will, by virtue of a divinely established authority. But to move by reason and will is to command. And so just as in the divinely instituted natural order lower natural things are necessarily subject to higher things and are moved by them, so too in human affairs inferiors are bound to obey their superiors by virtue of the order of natural and Divine law.

ad 1: God has left man 'in the hand of his own counsel', not as though it were lawful for him to do everything that he might wish, but because, unlike non-rational creatures, he is not compelled by natural necessity to do what he ought to do, but has the free choice of proceeding according to 'his own counsel'. And just as he must proceed according to his own counsel in doing other things, so also must he do so in the matter of obeying his superiors. For as Gregory says: 'When we humbly yield ourselves up to the voice of another, we overcome ourselves in our own hearts.'[1]

ad 2: The Divine will is the first rule by which all rational wills are regulated; but it is according to the divinely instituted order that one will should stand closer to this will than another. And so the will of the one man who commands can be as it were a second rule to the will of the other who obeys.

ad 3: Something can be judged to be done freely in two ways. In one way, with reference to the deed itself: that is, because a man is not bound to do it. In another way, with reference to the doer: that is, because he does it of his own free will. Now a deed is rendered virtuous and praiseworthy and meritorious [not by the mere fact that it is done, but] chiefly by the way in which it proceeds from the will. And so even where there is a duty of obedience, if someone obeys with a ready will, his merit is not on that account diminished, especially in the sight of God, Who sees not only the outward deed, but also the inward will.

---

[1] *Moralia* 35:14 (*PL* 76:765).

articulus 2: *Whether obedience is a specific virtue*[2]

It seems that obedience is not a specific virtue.

obiectio 1: For the opposite of obedience is disobedience. But disobedience is a general sin; for Ambrose says that 'sin is disobedience of the Divine law'.[3] Therefore obedience is not a specific virtue, but a general one.[4]

obiectio 2: Moreover, every specific virtue is either theological or moral.[5] But obedience is not a theological virtue, since it is not contained under faith, hope or charity. Similarly, it is not a moral virtue, since it does not occupy a mean between excess and deficiency: for the more obedient one is, the more one is praised.[6] Therefore obedience is not a specific virtue.

---

[2] St Thomas wishes to say that obedience in its primary aspect is a 'specific' virtue (*specialis virtus*, but 'special virtue' does not quite capture what is meant) inasmuch as it is the 'species' of justice, or of deference to superiors, which is deployed when we obey a specific command: see the *sed contra* and *responsio*. See also n. 4 below.

[3] *De paradiso* 8 (*PL* 14:292).

[4] I.e. St Ambrose's comment seems to imply that obedience consists not in compliance with a particular command but in a general readiness to keep the Divine law. The reply (ad 1, below) is that obedience has both a 'specific' and a 'general' aspect: primarily specific insofar as it involves compliance with a particular command, but general insofar as it consists in a general willingness to comply.

[5] For St Thomas's treatment of 'theological' and 'moral' virtues, see especially IaIIae 55–62. As with Aristotle, his use of the word 'virtue' is broader than the modern English acceptation of the term. For St Thomas, as for Aristotle, a virtue may be defined as 'a characteristic disposition of something to act in the manner proper to itself'. He distinguishes three kinds of virtue: intellectual, moral and theological. The intellectual virtues are more or less the same as they are in Aristotle (see *Ethics* 6:1ff (1139a1)), having intellectual activities, both theoretical and practical, as their objects. 'Acquired' moral virtues are habitual dispositions to pursue a mean lying between excess and deficiency (cf. *Ethics* 2:6 (1107a1)), the four 'cardinal' virtues – i.e. the virtues from which all other virtues come – being prudence, fortitude, temperance and justice. The theological virtues are faith, hope, charity and the 'infused' moral virtues. For St Thomas's full treatment of all this, see IaIIae 49–67. For 'acquired' and 'infused' virtue, see p. 97 n. 93 below; also *NCE* 14 *s.v.* 'Virtue'. More generally, see Gilson, *The Christian Philosophy of St Thomas Aquinas*, pt III, ch. 1. The reader who wishes fully to understand what St Thomas says should also read Books II–VI of Aristotle's *Nicomachean Ethics*.

[6] I.e. since it is evidently not possible for anyone to err by being too obedient, it seems that obedience cannot be a 'mean' between excess and deficiency, and so is not a moral virtue according to Aristotle's definition. St Thomas answers this (ad 2, below) in two ways, both of which are presumably intended to be valid in suitable circumstances. (i) Obedience is a mean between disobedience on the one hand and, on the other, obeying someone whom, or a command which, one should not obey. (ii) The mean of obedience lies between excess on the part of the one who withholds obedience from a superior and deficiency on the part of the superior who is not obeyed.

obiectio 3: Moreover, Gregory says that 'the less it has of its own will, the more meritorious and praiseworthy obedience is'.[7] But every specific virtue is the more to be praised the more it has of its own will, because, as is said at *Ethics* 11, virtue requires willing and choosing.[8] Therefore obedience is not a specific virtue.[9]

obiectio 4: Moreover, virtues differ in species according to their objects. But the object of obedience seems to be the command of a superior, of which, it seems, there are as many kinds as there are degrees of superiority [i.e. as there are kinds of superior]. Therefore obedience is a general virtue, comprising many specific virtues.[10]

sed contra: Obedience is deemed by certain persons to be a part of justice, as stated above.[11]

responsio: A specific virtue is assigned to all good works which are praiseworthy in a specific way, for it is the property of a virtue to render a work good.[12] Now obedience to a superior is due according to the divinely instituted order of things, as has been shown,[13] and is consequently a good, since good consists in 'mode, species and order', as Augustine says in the book *De natura boni*.[14] But this act is praiseworthy in a specific way by reason of its object. For while inferiors must defer to their superiors in many ways, this one, that they are bound to obey their commands, is

---

[7] *Moralia* 35:14 (*PL* 76:765).

[8] *Ethics* 2:4 (1105a31).

[9] I.e. in the sense that obedience is a 'specific' virtue as distinct from a general willingness to comply, its exercise must involve a positive act of will and choice. But Gregory seems to suggest (and see also ad 3, below) that obedience is a negative act involving submission to the will of someone else, and that the virtue of obedience is proportionate to the degree of submission required. The reply (ad 3) is the obvious one: that submission to a superior will is itself an act of will, even if the submission is very easy because agreeable.

[10] I.e. because we obey different kinds of superior in different ways, it seems that obedience is better understood as 'general' – that is, as a 'genus' of several virtues – than as one 'specific' virtue. (Notice, however, that this is a different sense of 'general' from the one used in *obiectio* 1. Here 'general' means 'generic' whereas in *obiectio* 1 and at ad 1 it means 'indeterminate'. For this distinction, see IIaIIae 58:6, *responsio* (p. 179, below).) The answer (ad 4, below) is that obedience itself is one, but that, because we obey different people for different reasons, according to the kind of 'reverence' that we have for them, it has several causes. See also n. 27, below.

[11] IIaIIae 80.

[12] *Ethics* 2:6 (1106a1).

[13] Art. 1.

[14] *De natura boni* 3.

specific in relation to the rest.[15] Hence obedience is a specific virtue, and its specific object is a command: tacit or express; for the will of a superior, however it becomes known, is a tacit command, and obedience is seen to be all the readier when it is forthcoming as soon as the superior's will is understood, in anticipation of a direct command.

ad 1: There is nothing to prevent two specific aspects [of praiseworthiness] to which two specific virtues correspond from occurring together in the same material object. For example, a soldier who defends the king's castle completes both a work of courage by not shirking the peril of death for a good end, and a work of justice by rendering a service owed to his lord. So, then: the aspect of [praiseworthiness which is] obedience to a command can be present in any act of virtue, but it is not present in all acts of virtue, since not every act of virtue arises from obedience to a command, as noted above.[16] Similarly, certain virtuous acts sometimes consist in obedience to a command simply, and pertain to no other virtue, as is clear in the case of those things which are not evil except because they are forbidden.[17] So, then: if obedience is taken in its primary sense, as being concerned formally and intentionally with the aspect of command, it will be a specific virtue, and disobedience will be a specific sin. If the virtue of obedience is to be present in this sense, a work of justice or some other virtue must be performed with the specific intention of fulfilling a command; and disobedience requires that one act in such a way as to treat a command with contempt. If, however, obedience is taken to mean a general readiness to carry out any action which one can be commanded to do, and if disobedience is taken to mean the lack of such readiness for any reason whatsoever, then obedience will be a general virtue, and disobedience a general sin.

ad 2: Obedience is not a theological virtue, since its object is not God; rather, its object is the command, whether express or implied, of any superior whatsoever: that is, the simple word of a superior indicating his will, which the obedient subject obeys promptly, according to Titus 3:1: 'Admonish them to be subject to princes, and to obey at a word', etc. It is, however, a moral virtue, since it is a part of justice, and it observes a mean

---

[15] I.e. obedience is that 'species' of deference to superiors which consists in obeying their commands. See n. 2, above.

[16] IaIIae 96:3 (p. 141, below).

[17] E.g. driving on one side of the road rather than the other is intrinsically neither 'evil' nor 'virtuous'. The 'virtue' of driving on the 'right' side of the road therefore lies in nothing other than obedience to the law which tells us which side to drive on.

between excess and deficiency. An excess of it is measured not according to quantity, but according to other things: insofar, that is, as someone obeys either one whom he ought not, or in some matter where he ought not, to obey, as stated above concerning religion.[18] Alternatively, we can say that, as in the case of justice, where the excess is in the person who retains another's property, and the deficiency is in the person who does not receive his due, as the Philosopher says at *Ethics* v,[19] so too obedience occupies the mean between excess on the part of him who withholds the obedience due to his superior, since he exceeds in fulfilling his own will, and deficiency on the part of the superior, who does not receive obedience. Accordingly, then, obedience will be a mean, but not between two kinds of vice, as was stated above in the case of justice.[20]

ad 3: Obedience, like every other virtue, requires that the will be prompt towards its proper object and not towards that which is repugnant to it. Now the proper object of obedience is a command proceeding from the will of another. Hence obedience renders a man's will prompt in fulfilling the will of another: namely, the giver of the command. If that which he is commanded to do is willed by him for its own sake even apart from its being commanded, as happens in the case of agreeable things, he tends towards it at once by his own will and seems to comply not by reason of the command, but by reason of his own will. But when that which is commanded is in no way willed for its own sake, but, considered in itself, is repugnant to his own will, as happens in the case of disagreeable things, then it is quite clearly not fulfilled except by reason of the command. Hence Gregory says that 'obedience requires little or no effort when it has its own will in agreeable things': because, that is, one's own will seems to tend principally not to the fulfilment of the command, but to the accomplishment of one's own wish; but that 'the effort is great in disagreeable or difficult things', because in this case one's own will tends to nothing apart from the command. But this must be understood only in relation to outward appearance. For, according to the judgment of God, Who searches the heart, it may happen that even in agreeable matters obedience, while having something of its own will, is no less praiseworthy on that account: if, that is, the will of him who obeys tends no less devoutly to the fulfilment of the command.

---

[18] IIaIIae 92:2.
[19] *Ethics* 5:4 (1132a10).
[20] IIaIIae 58:10 ad 2 (below, p. 188).

ad 4: Reverence is a regard directly for a person of eminence, and so there can be various species of it according to the various aspects of eminence. Obedience, however, is a specific regard for the command of a person of eminence, and therefore it admits of only one aspect [namely, the specific aspect of command]. But since obedience is due to a person's command by reason of reverence for him, it follows that although all obedience to him is of one species, the causes from which it proceeds differ in species.[21]

articulus 3: *Whether obedience is the greatest of the virtues*

It seems that obedience is the greatest of the virtues.

obiectio 1: For it is said at 1 Samuel 15:22: 'Obedience is better than sacrifices.' But the offering of sacrifices belongs to religion, which is the greatest moral virtue of all, as shown above.[22] Therefore obedience is the greatest of all virtues.

obiectio 2: Moreover, Gregory says that 'obedience is the only virtue which implants the other virtues in the soul and protects them once implanted'.[23] But a cause is greater than its effect. Therefore obedience is greater than all the other virtues.[24]

obiectio 3: Moreover, Gregory says that 'evil should never be done out of obedience; yet sometimes for the sake of obedience we should put aside something good that we are doing'.[25] But one does not put anything good aside except for the sake of something better. Therefore obedience, for whose sake the good of the other virtues is to be put aside, is better than the other virtues.

---

[21] Cf. art. 3 ad 1, below; see also n. 10, above.

[22] IIaIIae 81:6.

[23] *Moralia* 35:14 (*PL* 76:765).

[24] The idea here (and see ad 2, below) is that obedience 'implants' the other virtues because it is through obeying virtuous commands that we form and maintain the habit of virtue. Essentially the same point is made by Aristotle at *Ethics* 2:1 (1103a30): 'We acquire the virtues in the same way as we do the arts: by exercising them first. For the things we have to learn before we can do them, we learn by doing them: for instance, men become builders by building and lyre-players by playing the lyre ... So too in States, legislators make the citizens good by forming habits in them: this is what every [good] legislator wishes to do.' St Thomas deals more explicitly with the relation between virtue and habit at IaIIae 92:1 (p. 96, below). See also n. 29, below. He does not mean by *habitus* quite what we mean by 'habit'. For our present purposes, however, the differences are probably too subtle to be worth dwelling on.

[25] *Moralia* 35:14 (*PL* 76:765).

sed contra: Obedience is worthy of praise because it proceeds from charity; for Gregory says that 'obedience should be practised not out of servile fear, but from the affection of charity; not from fear of punishment, but from love of justice'. Therefore charity is a greater virtue than obedience.

responsio: Just as sin consists in a man despising God and clinging to mutable things, so, on the other hand, the merit of a virtuous act consists in a man despising created goods and clinging to God as his end. Now an end is greater than the things which are directed to that end. Therefore if a man despises created goods so that he may cling to God, his virtue derives greater praise from his clinging to God than from his despising earthly goods. And so those virtues by which he clings to God in Himself – that is, the theological virtues – are greater than the moral virtues by which he despises some earthly good in order to cling to God. But among the moral virtues, the greater the thing which a man despises so that he may cling to God, the greater the virtue. Now there are three kinds of human goods which a man can despise for God's sake. The lowest of these are external goods; the goods of the body are intermediate; the highest are the goods of the soul; and among these last the foremost, in a sense, is the will, insofar as it is by his will that a man makes use of all other goods. And so, strictly speaking, the virtue of obedience, by which we despise our own will for God's sake, is more praiseworthy than the other moral virtues by which we despise other goods for God's sake. Hence Gregory says that 'obedience is rightly preferred to sacrifices, because by sacrifices is slain the flesh of another, whereas by obedience we slay our own will'.[26] Hence also all other acts of virtue whatsoever have merit in the sight of God only through being performed out of obedience to God's will. For if someone were to suffer even martyrdom, or to give all his goods to the poor, unless he directed those things to the fulfilment of the Divine will, which pertains directly to obedience, they could not be meritorious; just as they could not be if they were done without charity, which cannot exist without obedience. For it is said at 1 John 2:4f: 'He who saith that he knoweth God, and keepeth not His commandments, is a liar; but he that keepeth His word, in him in very deed the charity of God is perfected'; and this is because those who are God's friends wish to do and avoid what He wishes.

ad 1: Obedience proceeds from reverence, which shows worship and honour to a superior, and in this respect it is contained under different

---

[26] *Ibid.*

virtues, even though, considered in itself, as being concerned with the aspect of command, it is one specific virtue. Insofar, therefore, as it proceeds from reverence for a ruler, it is contained under respectfulness; whereas insofar as it proceeds from reverence for one's parents, it is contained under piety; and insofar as it proceeds from reverence for God, it is contained under religion, and pertains to devotion, which is the principal act of religion. For this reason, then, it is more praiseworthy to obey God than to offer sacrifice.[27] This is also because 'by sacrifices is slain the flesh of another, whereas by obedience we slay our own will', as Gregory says. In particular, in the case where Samuel spoke, it would have been better for Saul to obey God than to offer in sacrifice the fat animals of the Amalekites against the command of God.[28]

ad 2: All acts of virtue belong to obedience insofar as they arise from the carrying out of a command. Inasmuch, therefore, as acts of virtue cause or dispose the virtues by generating and preserving them, obedience is said to implant and protect all the virtues. It does not follow, however, that obedience is prior to all the virtues in an absolute sense, for two reasons. First, whereas an act of virtue can arise from obeying a command, someone may nonetheless perform the same act of virtue for some other reason than that he is commanded to. Moreover, if there is any virtue whose object is naturally prior to command, that virtue is said to be naturally prior to obedience also. This is clear in the case of faith, through which we come to know the sublime nature of the Divine authority by which the power to command rightly belongs to God. Second, because the infusion of grace and virtues must precede, even in time, all virtuous acts; and in this way obedience is not prior to all virtues either in time or by nature.[29]

---

[27] The point here refers back to the one made under art. 2:4 and ad 4, above (see also n. 10). Obedience is one 'specific' virtue, but it has several causes, and the merit of obedience is in proportion to the elevated nature of its cause. Obedience 'caused by' reverence for God is clearly more praiseworthy than obedience caused by anything else: without, however, being a different *kind of* obedience.

[28] 1 Samuel 15:2ff.

[29] This reply qualifies rather than 'answers' *obiectio* 2. The point is as follows. Obedience does indeed inculcate and strengthen virtuous behaviour; but the relationship of 'priority' between obedience and the other virtues is not an absolute or necessary one, for two reasons. (a) Not all virtuous acts are done in obedience to a command. In the specific case of faith, we do not have faith because we are obeying a command of God, since it is precisely through faith that we know that we ought to obey the commands of God. (b) Every virtuous act, including an act of obedience, presupposes that we already have at least some capacity to act virtuously. That capacity must therefore come to us by a kind of Divine gift rather than through a process of habituation. For the technical meaning of 'infusion' here, see n. 93 on p. 97.

ad 3: There are two kinds of good. On the one hand there is that good which man is bound to do as a matter of necessity: for example, to love God, or something of the sort; and such a good must in no way be set aside for the sake of obedience to anyone. But there is another kind of good, which man is not bound to do as a matter of necessity; and a man ought sometimes to set this kind of good aside for the sake of an obedience to which he is bound as a matter of necessity, since no man ought to do good by incurring fault. Nonetheless, as Gregory says, 'he who forbids his subjects any single good must necessarily grant them many others, lest the minds of those who obey perish utterly through being deprived of every good'.[30] And so the loss of one good by obedience can be recompensed by other goods.

articulus 4: *Whether God is to be obeyed in all things*

It seems that God is not to be obeyed in all things.

obiectio 1: For it is said at Matthew 9:30f that when the Lord healed the two blind men He commanded them, saying: 'See that no man know this. But they going out spread His fame abroad in all that country.' But they are not reproached for doing this. Therefore it seems that God is not to be obeyed in all things.

obiectio 2: Moreover, no one is bound to do anything contrary to virtue. But we find that God has commanded certain things which are contrary to virtue. For example, He commanded Abraham to slay his innocent son, as recorded at Genesis 22:2, and the Jews to steal the property of the Egyptians, as recorded at Exodus 11:2, which things are contrary to justice; and Hosea to take to himself a woman who was an adulteress (Hosea 1:2), which is contrary to chastity. Therefore God is not to be obeyed in all things.

obiectio 3: Moreover, whoever obeys God causes his own will to will whatever the Divine will wills. But we are not bound in all things to cause our own wills to will what the Divine will wills, as noted above.[31] Therefore man is not bound to obey God in all things.

---

[30] *Moralia* 35:14 (*PL* 76:766).

[31] IaIIae 19:10. For example, it is the sin of parricide to will the death of one's father. But it is God's will that one's father will die. In this case, therefore, a son is not bound to will what God wills. Similarly, God wills the damnation of some men; but no one is bound to will harm to himself; therefore no one is bound to will his own damnation. These examples are St Thomas's own.

sed contra: It is said at Exodus 24:7: 'All that the Lord hath said will we do, and be obedient.'

responsio: as stated above,[32] he who obeys is moved by the command of him whom he obeys as natural things are moved by their motive causes. Now just as God is the first mover of all things that are moved naturally, so also is He the first mover of all wills, as shown above.[33] And so just as all natural things are subject to the Divine motion by necessity of nature, so too all wills are bound to obey the Divine commands by a kind of necessity of justice.

ad 1: When the Lord told the blind men to conceal the miracle, He did not do so as intending to bind them with the force of a Divine command. Rather, as Gregory says, 'He gave to His servants who follow Him an example that even if they wish to conceal their virtue, it should be proclaimed nonetheless, that others may profit by their example.'[34]

ad 2: Just as God does nothing contrary to nature (since 'the nature of anything whatsoever is what God does in it', as noted in a gloss on Romans 11:24),[35] even though He does certain things contrary to the usual course of nature, so too God can command nothing contrary to virtue, since virtue and the righteousness of the human will consist principally in conforming to God's will and following His command even if it is contrary to the usual mode of virtue. Accordingly, therefore, the command given to Abraham to slay his innocent son was not contrary to justice, since God is the author of life and death. Similarly, it was not contrary to justice that He commanded the Jews to take the things belonging to the Egyptians, for all things are His and He gives them to whom He will. Nor was it contrary to chastity that Hosea was commanded to take an adulteress, because God Himself is the ordainer of human generation, and the proper way of using women is that which God appoints. Hence it is clear that the foregoing persons did not sin, either by obeying God or by willing to obey Him.

ad 3: Though a man is not always bound to will what God Himself wills, he is nonetheless always bound to will what God wills him to will. And man comes to know what this is chiefly through God's command; and so man is bound to obey God's commands in all things.

[32] Art. 1.
[33] IaIIae 9:6.
[34] *Moralia* 19:23 (*PL* 76:120).
[35] Peter Lombard, *Collectanea in omnes de Pauli apostoli epistolas, PL* 191:1488.

articulus 5: *Whether subjects are bound to obey their superiors in all things*

It seems that subjects are bound to obey their superiors in all things.

obiectio 1: For the Apostle says at Colossians 3:20: 'Children, obey your parents in all things'; and he then adds (vs. 22): 'Servants, obey in all things your masters according to the flesh.' By the same token, therefore, other subjects are bound to obey their rulers in all things.

obiectio 2: Moreover, rulers stand between God and their subjects, according to Deuteronomy 5:5: 'I stood between the Lord and you at that time, to show you the word of the Lord.' But nothing can pass from one point to another except by going through that which stands between. A ruler's commands must therefore be accorded the same repute as God's commands. Hence the Apostle says at Galatians 4:14: 'Ye received me as an angel of God, even as Christ Jesus'; and at 1 Thessalonians 2:13: 'When ye received the word of God which ye heard of us, ye received it not as the word of men, but as it is in truth, the word of God.' Therefore as man must obey God in all things, so too must he obey his superiors.

obiectio 3: Moreover, when religious make their profession, they take vows not only of chastity and poverty, but of obedience also. But a religious is bound to observe chastity and poverty in all things. Similarly, therefore, he is bound to obey in all things.

sed contra: It is said at Acts 5:29: 'We ought to obey God rather than men.' But sometimes the things commanded by a ruler are against God. Therefore rulers are not to be obeyed in all things.

responsio: As stated above,[36] one who obeys is moved by the command of the one who commands him as by a kind of necessity of justice, just as a natural thing is moved by the power of its mover by necessity of nature. But it can come about in two ways that a natural thing is not moved by its mover. In one way, because of some impediment produced by the stronger force of some other mover: for example, wood is not consumed by fire if the stronger force of water impedes it. In another way, if there is a defect of order as between moved and mover such that the former is subject to the latter's action in one respect but not in all: for example, a humour is sometimes subject to the action of heat with respect to being heated, but not with respect to being dried up or consumed. Similarly, it may come

---

[36] Art. 1 and 4.

about in two ways that a subject is not bound to obey his superior in all things. In one way, because of the command of a higher power. For as a gloss on Romans 13:2, 'Whosoever therefore resisteth the power, resisteth the ordinance of God', says:

> Is an overseer ever to be obeyed if what he requires is contrary to the command of the proconsul? And if the proconsul commands one thing and the emperor another, is there any doubt that the former ought to be disregarded and the latter served? Therefore if the emperor commands one thing and God another, you must disregard the former and obey God.[37]

In another way, an inferior is not bound to obey a superior if the latter commands him to do something with respect to which he is not subject to him. For Seneca says at *De beneficiis* III: 'If anyone supposes that slavery falls upon the whole man, he errs; for the better part of him is excepted. His body is subject and bound to his master, but his mind is his own.'[38] And so in matters pertaining to the inward movement of the will man is not bound to obey man, but God alone. Man is, however, bound to obey man in things which are to be done outwardly by means of the body. In things pertaining to the nature of the body – for example, in matters having to do with the support of the body or the generation of children – man is not bound to obey man, but only God, since all men are by nature equal. Hence servants are not bound to obey their masters, nor children their parents, in contracting marriage or preserving virginity or other things of that kind. But in things pertaining to the disposing of actions and human affairs, a subject is bound to obey his superior according to the scope of his authority: for example, a soldier must obey his commander in things pertaining to war, a servant his master in things pertaining to the performance of his work as a servant, a son his father in things pertaining to the orderly conduct of his life and the care of the household; and so on.

ad 1: When the Apostle says 'in all things', this is to be understood as meaning in all those things which rightfully belong to the power of a father or master.

ad 2: Man is subject to God absolutely, in all things both inward and outward, and so is bound to obey Him in all things. But subjects are not

---

[37] Peter Lombard, *Collectanea in omnes de Pauli apostoli epistolas*, PL 191:1505; Augustine, *Sermo* 62:8.
[38] *De beneficiis* 3:20.

subject to their superiors in all things absolutely, but only in particular things and in a determinate way. With respect to such things, the superior stands between God and his subjects; but in other things the subject is under God immediately, by Whom he is instructed either by the natural or the written law.

ad 3: Religious profess obedience with respect to the rule of life according to which they are subject to their superiors; and so they are bound to obey only in those matters which can pertain to that rule of life, and this obedience is sufficient for salvation. If they are willing to obey in other things also, this will pertain to the increase of perfection; provided, of course, that such things are not against God or the rule which they profess, for in that case obedience would be unlawful.

So, therefore, three kinds of obedience can be distinguished: one, sufficient for salvation, which obeys in those things where there is an obligation to do so; a second, perfect obedience, which obeys in all things lawful; and a third, indiscriminate obedience, which obeys even in things which are unlawful.

articulus 6: *Whether Christians are bound to obey the secular powers*

It seems that Christians are not bound to obey the secular powers.

obiectio 1: For a gloss on Matthew 17:25, 'Then are the children free', says: 'If in every kingdom the children of the king who reigns over that kingdom are free, then the children of that King to Whom all kingdoms are subject should be free in every kingdom.'[39] But Christians are made children of God by the faith of Christ, according to John 1:12: 'He gave them power to be made the sons of God, to them that believe in His name.' Therefore they are not bound to obey the secular powers.

obiectio 2: Moreover, it is said at Romans 7:4: 'You are become dead to the law by the body of Christ', and the law here spoken of is the Divine law of the Old Testament. But the human law by which men are made subject to the secular power is less than the Divine law of the Old Testament. Still more therefore, are men who have been made members of the body of Christ delivered from the law of subjection by which they were in bondage to secular princes.

---

[39] *Glossa ordinaria, PL* 114:145.

obiectio 3: Moreover, men are not bound to obey robbers who oppress them with violence. But Augustine says at *De civitate Dei* IV: 'Justice removed, then, what are kingdoms but great bands of robbers?'[40] Since therefore the dominion of secular princes is often exercised with injustice, or is derived from some unjust usurpation, it seems that obedience ought not to be given to secular princes by Christians.

sed contra: It is said at Titus 3:1: 'Admonish them to be subject to princes and powers', and at 1 Peter 2:13f: 'Be ye subject to every human creature for God's sake: whether it be to the king as supreme, or to the governors as sent by Him.'

responsio: The faith of Christ is the foundation and cause of justice, according to Romans 3:22: 'The justice of God which is by faith of Jesus Christ.' And so the order of justice is not removed by the faith of Christ, but strengthened. Now the order of justice requires that inferiors obey their superiors; otherwise the condition of human affairs could not be preserved. And so the faithful are not excused by the faith of Christ from the obligation to obey secular princes.

ad 1: As stated above,[41] the subjection by which one man is bound to another pertains to the body, not to the soul, which remains free. Now, in the condition of this life, we are redeemed by the grace of Christ from defects of soul, but not from defects of body, as the Apostle shows at Romans 7:23, where he says of himself that in his mind he served the law of God, but in his flesh the law of sin. And so those who are made children of God by grace are redeemed from the spiritual servitude of sin, but not from the corporeal servitude by which they are bound to serve temporal masters, as a gloss on 1 Timothy 6:1, 'Whosoever are servants under the yoke', etc., says.[42]

ad 2: The old law was a prefiguring of the New Testament, and so it had to cease with the coming of the Truth. The comparison with the human law by which one man is made subject to another man is therefore not valid; although by the Divine law also man is bound to obey man.

ad 3: Man is bound to obey secular princes insofar as the order of justice requires it. And so if princes have a ruling power which is not just but

[40] *De civitate Dei* 4:4.
[41] Art. 5.
[42] *Glossa ordinaria*, *PL* 114:631.

usurped, or if they command that which is unjust, their subjects are not bound to obey them, except perhaps accidentally, in order to avoid scandal or peril.

(b) *Scripta super libros sententiarum* II, Dist. 44, quaest. 2[43]

articulus 2: Whether Christians are bound to obey the secular powers, and tyrants in particular

It seems that Christians are not bound to obey the secular powers, and tyrants in particular.

obiectio 1: For it is said at Matthew 17:26: 'Then are the children free.' For if in every kingdom the children of the king who reigns over that kingdom are free, then the children of that King to Whom all kingdoms are subject should be free in every kingdom.[44] But Christians have been made children of God: 'For the Spirit Himself giveth testimony to our spirit, that we are the sons of God' (Romans 8:16). They are, therefore, everywhere free, and so are not bound to obey the secular power.

obiectio 2: Moreover, as stated above,[45] servitude was introduced by sin. But by baptism men are cleansed from sin. Therefore they are delivered from servitude; and so we arrive at the same conclusion as before.

obiectio 3: Moreover, a greater bond absolves from a lesser, as the new law has absolved us from observance of the old. But by baptism man is bound to God, and this obligation is a greater bond than that by which one man is bound to another in servitude. Therefore we are absolved from servitude by baptism.

obiectio 4: Moreover, anyone can lawfully take back what has been unjustly taken away from him if the opportunity to do so arises. But many secular princes have acquired dominion over their lands by tyrannical invasion. Therefore, when the opportunity of rebellion arises, we are not bound to obey them.

obiectio 5: Moreover, no one is bound to obey someone whom it is lawful, or even praiseworthy, to slay. But Cicero, in the book *De officiis*, defends

[43] This article was written approximately fifteen years before the similar art. 6 of IIaIIae 104 which immediately precedes it in this edition.
[44] *Glossa ordinaria, PL* 114:145.
[45] II:44:1:1.

those who slew Julius Caesar even though he was their friend and relative, because he usurped the rights of empire as a tyrant.[46] We are therefore not bound to obey such persons.

sed contra: 'Servants, be subject to your masters' (1 Peter 2:18); and further: 'He that resisteth the power, resisteth the ordinance of God' (Romans 13:2).

solutio: It must be noted that obedience consists in the observance of a command which it is our duty to observe. Now the cause of such duty is an order of authority having the power to coerce not only temporally but also spiritually, in conscience, as the Apostle says at Romans 13:1ff, because the order of authority descends from God, as the Apostle intimates in the same place. And so the Christian is bound to obey it insofar as it is 'of God', and not insofar as it is not. But authority can be said to be not of God for two reasons: either because of the way in which the authority was acquired, or because of the use to which the authority is put. As to the first, there are two ways in which this can be so: either because of a defect of the person, because he is unworthy, or because of a defect in the means by which power was acquired; that is, by violence or simony or some other unlawful mode of acquisition. The first defect is not an impediment to the acquisition of rightful authority; and because authority is always of God according to its form, which is the cause of our duty to obey it, their subjects are always bound to obey such rulers, however unworthy.[47] But the second defect is an impediment to rightful authority, for he who seizes power by violence does not become a ruler or lord truly; and so anyone can reject such authority when the opportunity arises, unless perhaps the ruler is subsequently made a true lord either by the consent of his subjects or by the authority of a superior.[48]

Now the abuse of authority can be of two kinds. First, when what is commanded by the ruler is contrary to the purpose for which the ruler

---

[46] *De officiis* 1:26.

[47] I.e. in terms of its 'formal cause' – i.e. its essence or nature: 'what it is' – authority comes from God rather than from the personal qualities of whoever exercises it. The nature of authority is therefore such that it must be obeyed even when exercised by the unworthy. For Aristotle's four causes see *Physics* 2:3 (194b16–195b30).

[48] The familiar distinction between *potestas* and *auctoritas*, power and authority, goes back to republican Rome; but medieval authors do not always observe the distinction strictly. St Thomas says in this sentence that we may reject the authority of someone who seizes power by violence. We should nowadays find it more natural to say that someone who seizes power by violence does not *have* any authority, which is why he need not be obeyed.

was appointed: for example, if some sinful act is commanded contrary to the virtue which the ruler is ordained to foster and preserve. In this case, not only is one not bound to obey the ruler, but one is bound not to obey him, as in the case of the holy martyrs who suffered death rather than obey the ungodly commands of tyrants. Second, when what is demanded goes beyond what the order of authority can require: if, for example, a master were to exact a payment which a servant is not bound to give, or something of the kind. In this case the subject is not bound to obey; nor, however, is he bound not to obey.

ad 1: Authority which is directed to the advantage of those subject to it does not take away the liberty of its subjects; and so there is no reason why those who are made children of God should not be subject to such authority. Alternatively, it can be said that Christ is here speaking of Himself and His disciples, who were neither of servile condition, nor did they have any temporal things from which they were obliged to pay tribute to their lords. And so it does not follow that all Christians may share in such liberty, but only those who follow the apostolic life, possessing nothing in this world and being free from the condition of servitude.

ad 2: Baptism does not immediately erase all the penalties consequent upon the sin of our first parents: for example, the necessity of death, and blindness,[49] or anything of this kind. Rather, it regenerates in us the living hope of that life in which all these things are to be taken away. Thus it is not fitting that someone who is baptised should at once be released from his servile condition, even though this condition is a penalty of sin.

ad 3: A greater bond does not absolve from a lesser except where the two cannot exist together: in the way, for example, that the darkness of error cannot exist simultaneously with truth. Hence with the coming of the truth of the Gospel, the darkness of the old law ceased. But the bond by which someone is bound in baptism can exist at the same time as the bond of servitude, and so does not absolve from it.

ad 4: Those who achieve ruling power by violence are not truly rulers; hence, nor are their subjects bound to obey them, except in the circumstances already mentioned.

[49] Cf. John 9:2.

ad 5: Cicero was speaking of a case where someone had seized dominion for himself by violence, either against the wishes of his subjects or by coercing them into consenting, and where they had no recourse to a superior by whom judgment might be passed on the invader. In such a case he who delivers his country by slaying a tyrant is to be praised and rewarded.[50]

[50] See Introduction, p. xxix.

3

Law

(a) *Summa theologiae* IaIIae 90: The essence of law

Here there are four things to consider:

1. Whether law is something belonging to reason
2. The end of law
3. Its cause
4. Its promulgation

articulus 1: *Whether law is something belonging to reason*

It seems that law is not something belonging to reason.

obiectio 1: For the Apostle says (Romans 7:23): 'I see another law in my members', etc. But nothing which belongs to reason is 'in' the members, for reason does not make use of any corporeal organ. Therefore law is not something belonging to reason.

obiectio 2: Moreover, there is nothing in reason but power, habit, and act.[1] But law is not a power of reason; similarly, it is not some habit of reason, because the habits of reason are the intellectual virtues, which have been spoken of above;[2] nor again is it an act of reason: if it were, law would cease when the activity of reason ceases; for example, when we are asleep. Therefore law is not something belonging to reason.

obiectio 3: Moreover, law moves those subject to it to act rightly. But, properly speaking, it is the function of will to move someone to act, as is shown by what has been said above.[3] Therefore law belongs not to reason,

[1] Cf. *Ethics* 2:5 (1105b20).
[2] IaIIae 57; and see n. 5 on p. 59, above.
[3] IaIIae 9:1.

but to will; and this is in accordance with what the Jurist says: 'What pleases the prince has the force of law.'[4]

sed contra: It is a function of law to command and prohibit. But to command pertains to reason, as noted above.[5] Therefore law is something belonging to reason.

responsio: Law is a kind of rule and measure of acts, by which someone is induced to act or restrained from acting; for 'law' [*lex*] is derived from 'binding' [*ligando*], because it obliges us to act.[6] Now the rule and measure of human acts is reason, which is the guiding principle of human acts, as is shown by what has been said above;[7] for it pertains to reason to direct to an end, which, according to the Philosopher, is the guiding principle in all matters of action.[8] Now that which is the principle in [i.e. the primary member of] any genus is the measure and rule of that genus: for example, unity in the genus of numbers, and the first movement in the genus of movements.[9] The conclusion is left, then, that law is something belonging to reason.

ad 1: Since law is a kind of rule and measure, it is said to be 'in' something in two ways. In one way, as in that which measures and rules; and because ruling and measuring are proper to reason, it follows that, in this way, law is in reason alone. In another way, as in that which is measured and ruled; and in this way law is in all those things which are inclined to something by reason of some law: so that any inclination arising from a law can be called a law, not essentially but as it were by participation. And it is in this latter way that the inclination of the members to concupiscence is called 'the law of the members'.[10]

ad 2: Just as, in outward actions, we can consider the activity itself and what the activity does – for instance, the work of building and the house built – so in the operations of reason we can consider the activity of reasoning

---

[4] *CICiv.*: *Digesta* 1:4:1.

[5] IaIIae 17:1.

[6] Cf. art. 4 ad 3.

[7] IaIIae 1:1 ad 3; 66:1.

[8] *Physics* 2:9 (200a22); *Ethics* 7:8 (1151a16).

[9] Cf. *Metaphysics* 5:28 (1024b1).

[10] Peter Lombard, *Sententiae* 2:30:8 (*PL* 192:722); cf. IaIIae 91:6 (p. 93, below). The idea here – and see also IaIIae 91:6, *responsio* (p. 94, below) – is that law, insofar as it is a rule (*regula*), is 'present by participation in', i.e. is exemplified in, anything which exhibits a 'regular' or 'regulated' pattern of behaviour.

itself, which is to understand and ratiocinate, and that which is produced by such activity. In the case of speculative reasoning, what is produced is first of all the definition; second, the proposition; third, the syllogism or argument. And since, according to what the Philosopher teaches in the *Ethics*,[11] practical reasoning also makes use of a kind of syllogism in determining a course of action, as noted above,[12] we therefore find that in practical reasoning there is something which stands in the same relation to actions as the proposition does to the conclusions in speculative reasoning. And such universal propositions of practical reason directed to actions have the character of law. These propositions sometimes come under active consideration, while sometimes they are held in the reason by means of a habit.[13]

ad 3: Reason receives its power of moving from the will, as stated above.[14] For it is because someone first wills an end that his reason then proceeds to issue commands concerning the things which are directed to that end. But in order that what it commands may have the character of law, the will itself must be in accord with some rule of reason. And it is in this way that we are to understand that the will of the prince has the force of law: otherwise [i.e. if it were not in accord with some rule of reason], the will of the prince would have more the character of iniquity than of law.

articulus 2: *Whether law is always directed to the common good*

It seems that law is not always directed to the common good as to its end.

obiectio 1: For it pertains to law to command and prohibit. But some commands are directed to particular goods. Therefore the end of law is not always the common good.[15]

[11] *Ethics* 7:3 (1147a24). On the – not entirely unproblematical – idea of the 'practical syllogism' in Aristotle see W. K. C. Guthrie, *A History of Greek Philosophy*, vol. VI (Cambridge, 1981), pp. 349ff. See also A. Broadie, 'The Practical Syllogism', *Analysis* 29 (1968–9), pp. 26ff.
[12] IaIIae 13:3; 76:1; 77:2 ad 4.
[13] Cf. IaIIae 94:1 (p. 114, below).
[14] IaIIae 17:1.
[15] St Thomas is here concerned with the question of how laws which affect particular individuals only – and for what he means by this see p. 138 n. 274, below – can at one and the same time secure a common good. At IaIIae 96:1 (p. 137, below), he addresses the same difficulty from the other direction by asking how general laws can sufficiently secure individual interests. The two articles may usefully be read together.

obiectio 2: Moreover, law directs man in his actions. But human actions are concerned with particular things. Therefore law is directed to some particular good.

obiectio 3: Moreover, Isidore says: 'If law is grounded in reason, whatever is grounded in reason will be law.'[16] But reason is the foundation not only of what is directed to the common good, but also of that which is directed to an individual's private good. Therefore law is not directed to the common good only, but also to the private good of an individual.

sed contra: Isidore says that law is 'composed for no private advantage, but for the common benefit of the citizens'.[17]

responsio: Law belongs to [reason, which is] the guiding principle of human acts because it is their rule and measure, as stated above.[18] Now, just as reason is the first principle of human acts, so reason itself must be guided by something which is the first principle of everything it does;[19] and it is to this guiding principle that law must chiefly and mainly be directed. Now the first principle in practical matters, which are the object of practical reasoning, is the final end:[20] and the final end of human life is happiness or blessedness, as noted above.[21] Law must therefore attend especially to the ordering of things towards blessedness. Moreover, since every part of something is ordered in relation to the whole as imperfect to perfect, and since one man is a part of a perfect [i.e. a complete or self-sufficient] community, law must attend to the ordering of individual things in such a way as to secure the common happiness. Hence the Philosopher, having first defined lawful acts, makes mention of both happiness and the political community; for he says at *Ethics* v that we call those lawful acts 'just which tend to produce and preserve happiness and its components for the political community',[22] the perfect community being, as he says at *Politics* I, the State.[23]

---

[16] *Etymologiae* 2:10; 5:3 (*PL* 82:130 and 199).
[17] *Etymologiae* 5:21 (*PL* 82:203).
[18] Art. 1.
[19] I.e. reason itself must be directed towards something or guided by some purpose.
[20] *Physics* 2:9 (200a22); *Ethics* 7:8 (1151a16).
[21] IaIIae 2:7; 3:1; 69:1; and see also *De regimine principum* 1:9 (p. 24, above). Here again, St Thomas uses *felicitas* and *beatitudo*, 'happiness' and 'blessedness', as synonyms.
[22] *Ethics* 5:1 (1129b17).
[23] *Politics* 1:1 (1252a5).

Now in every genus, that which is called the chief member of it is the guiding principle of the others, and the others are said to be ordered in relation to it:[24] fire, for example, which is chief among hot things, is the cause of heat in mixed bodies, and these are said to be hot in so far as they participate in fire. Hence, since law may be called chief of those things directed to the common good, it must be that any other precept having to do with a particular act can have the character of law only in so far as it is itself directed towards the common good. And so every law is directed to the common good.

ad 1: 'Command' signifies the application of law to those things which are regulated by law. Now the ordering of things towards the common good which it is the concern of law to bring about includes particular ends also; and it is in this way that commands are given with respect to certain particular matters.[25]

ad 2: Human actions are indeed concerned with particular things which do not belong to the same species or genus as the common good; but those particular things can nonetheless be directed [by the law] to the common good because the common good is the end which all men have in common.

ad 3: Just as in the case of speculative reasoning nothing is validly established other than by being inferred from indemonstrable first principles, so too in the case of practical reasoning nothing is validly established other than by being ordered to the final end, which is the common good; and whatever is grounded in reason in this latter sense has the character of law.

articulus 3: *Whether the reason of anyone whatsoever can make laws*

It seems that the reason of anyone whatsoever can make laws.

obiectio 1: For the Apostle says (Romans 2:14): 'When the Gentiles, who have not the law, do by nature those things that are of the law, these are a law unto themselves.' But he is speaking of everyone in general. Therefore anyone can make a law for himself.

---

[24] Cf. *Metaphysics* 5:28 (1024b1).

[25] I.e. even when the law's commands are 'directed to particular goods' they are so directed with a view to achieving the common good rather than a private or individual good. See n. 15, above.

obiectio 2: Moreover, the Philosopher says that 'the intention of the legislator is to lead men to virtue'.[26] But any man can lead another to virtue. Therefore the reason of any man can make laws.

obiectio 3: Moreover, just as the prince of a State is the State's governor, so each head of a family is the governor of his household. But a prince can make law in the State. Therefore any head of a family can make law in his own household.

sed contra: Isidore says at *Etymologies* v and in the *Decretum* that 'Law is an ordinance of the people whereby something is sanctioned by those of high birth in conjunction with the commons.'[27] It is therefore not the task of anyone whatsoever to make law.

responsio: Law properly so called looks first and foremost to the ordering of things to the common good. But to order something to the common good is the business of the whole community, or of someone acting on behalf of the whole community. Therefore to make law is either the business of the whole community, or it belongs to the public person who has care of the whole community; for, as in all things, the ordering of something to an end is the concern of him to whom the end belongs.

ad 1: As stated above,[28] law is present in someone not only as in one who rules, but also, by participation, as in one who is ruled. And it is in this latter way that each man is a law unto himself: in so far as he participates in the order that he receives from one who rules him. Hence also [the Apostle] adds (Romans 2:15): 'Who show the work of the law written in their hearts.'

ad 2: A private person cannot be entirely effective in leading another to virtue; for he can only admonish, and if his admonition is not accepted, he does not have the power to compel which law must have if it is to be effective in leading people to virtue, as the Philosopher says.[29] This power to compel is vested in the community or in the public person whose duty it is to inflict punishments, as will be said below;[30] and so the making of laws belongs to him alone.

---

[26] *Ethics* 2:1 (1103b3).
[27] *Etymologiae* 5:10 (*PL* 82:200); Dist. 2, c. 1: *Lex est constitutio* (*CIC* 1:3).
[28] Art. 1 ad 1.
[29] *Ethics* 10:9 (1180a20).
[30] IaIIae 92:2 ad 3 (p. 100, below); IIaIIae 64:3 (p. 255, below).

ad 3: Just as one man is part of a household, so a household is part of a State; and a State is a perfect community, as is said at *Politics* I.[31] And so just as the good of one man is not the final end, but is subordinated to the common good, so too the good of one household is subordinated to the good of the whole State, which is a perfect community. Hence he who governs a family can indeed make precepts or statutes of a kind, but these do not have the character of law properly so called.

articulus 4: *Whether promulgation is essential to law*

It seems that promulgation is not essential to law.

obiectio 1: For the natural law most certainly has the character of law. But the natural law needs no promulgation. Therefore it is not essential to law that it be promulgated.

obiectio 2: Moreover, it belongs properly to law to oblige someone to do or not do something. But the obligation to fulfil a law is binding not only upon those in whose presence it is promulgated, but upon others also. Therefore promulgation is not essential to law.

obiectio 3: Moreover, the obligation of law extends also to what is yet to be, since, as the laws state, 'laws impose a necessity upon future transactions'.[32] But promulgation is to those who are present. Therefore promulgation is not a necessary part of law.

sed contra: It is said in the *Decretum* that 'laws are established when they are promulgated'.[33]

responsio: Law is imposed upon others as a rule and measure, as stated above.[34] Now a rule and measure is imposed by being applied to whatever is ruled and measured by it. Hence, if a law is to acquire the binding force which is proper to law, it must be applied to the men who are to be ruled by it. Such application is made by its being brought to their notice by promulgation. Promulgation is therefore necessary for the law to acquire its force.

Thus from the four foregoing articles the following definition of law can be inferred: that it is nothing but a certain ordinance of reason for

---

[31] *Politics* I:I (1252a5).
[32] *CICiv.: Codex* 1:14:7.
[33] Dist. 4, c. 3: *In istis temporalibus* (*CIC* I:5)
[34] Art. I.

the common good, made and promulgated by him who has care of the community.

ad 1: The natural law is promulgated precisely by the fact that God has inserted it into the minds of men in such a way that they are able to know it naturally.

ad 2: Those who are not present when a law is promulgated are obliged to observe the law in so far as it is brought to their notice by others, or can be so brought, after it has been promulgated.

ad 3: Promulgation in the present time extends also into the future because of the enduring character of the written records through which the law is in a certain sense being promulgated continuously. Hence Isidore says that '"law" [*lex*] is derived from "reading" [*legendo*] because it is written down'.[35]

(b) *Summa theologiae* IaIIae 91: The various kinds of law

We come next to the various kinds of law; and here there are six things to consider:

1. Whether there is an eternal law
2. Whether there is a natural law
3. Whether there is a human law
4. Whether there is a Divine law
5. Whether the Divine law is one or several
6. Whether there is a law of sin

articulus 1: *Whether there is an eternal law*

It seems that there is not an eternal law.

obiectio 1: For every law is imposed on someone. But there was not someone from eternity on whom law could be imposed, for only God has existed from eternity. Therefore no law is eternal.

---

[35] *Etymologiae* 2:10 (*PL* 82:130); although the etymology given in the *responsio* of art. 1 is more likely to be the correct one.

obiectio 2: Moreover, promulgation is essential to law. But promulgation could not be from eternity, because there was no one to whom it could be promulgated from eternity. Therefore no law can be eternal.

obiectio 3: Moreover, law implies direction to an end. But nothing which is directed to an end is eternal, for only the final end itself is eternal. Therefore no law is eternal.

sed contra: Augustine says: 'That law which is called the Supreme Reason cannot be understood by anyone as other than immutable and eternal.'[36]

responsio: Law is nothing but a certain dictate of practical reason in the ruler who governs a perfect community, as stated above.[37] Now, on the supposition that the world is ruled by Divine providence, as was stated in the First Part,[38] it is clear that the whole community of the universe is governed by Divine reason. And so the rational pattern of the government of things [*ratio gubernationis rerum*] which is in God as Ruler of the universe, itself has the character of law. And since the Divine reason's conception of things is not subject to time but is eternal, as is said at Proverbs 8:23 ['I was set up from everlasting, from the beginning, before ever the earth was'], this kind of law must therefore be called eternal.

ad 1: Those things which have not yet come into being in themselves already exist in God inasmuch as they are foreknown and foreordained by Him, according to Romans 4:17: 'Who calleth those things which be not, as though they were.' So, therefore, the eternal concept of the Divine law has the character of an eternal law in so far as it is ordained by God to the government of things foreknown by Him.

ad 2: Promulgation is effected by word and writing; and, on the side of God, the eternal law is promulgated in both these ways, because the Divine word is eternal and the writing of the Book of Life is eternal. But the promulgation cannot be from eternity on the side of the creature who hears or reads.

ad 3: Law implies direction to an end when it is considered in relation to what it does: that is, the ordering of certain things to an end. Considered

---

[36] *De libero arbitrio* 1:6.
[37] IaIIae 90:1 ad 2 p. 77, above; 90:3 p. 80, above and 90:4 (p. 82, above).
[38] Ia 22:1 ad 2.

without reference to what it does, however – that is, considered simply in itself – law is not directed to an end: it is only contingently so, in a governor who has an end outside himself to which his law must of necessity be directed. But the end of the Divine government is God Himself, nor is His law something other than Himself. Hence the eternal law is not directed to any other end.[39]

articulus 2: *Whether there is a natural law in us*

It seems that there is not a natural law in us.

obiectio 1: For man is sufficiently governed by the eternal law. For Augustine says that 'the eternal law is that by which it is right that all things should be perfectly in order'.[40] But nature does not provide an abundance of what is superfluous, just as she does not fail to provide what is necessary. Therefore no law is natural to man.

obiectio 2: Moreover, it is by law that man is directed in his acts to an end, as noted above.[41] But the directing of human acts to their end is not a function of nature, as it is in the case of non-rational creatures, which act for an end solely by natural appetite; for man acts for an end by his reason and will. Therefore no law is natural to man.

obiectio 3: Moreover, the more free someone is, the less subject to law he is. But man is more free than all other animals, by reason of free will, which he has more fully than all other animals. Since, therefore, other animals are not subject to a natural law, nor is man subject to a natural law.

sed contra: A gloss on the verse, 'When the Gentiles, who have not the law, do by nature those things that are of the law',[42] says: 'Although they have no written law, they nonetheless have the natural law, by which each man understands what is good and what is evil, and is aware of it for himself.'[43]

---

[39] I.e. purpose is not intrinsic to law: it is the will of the legislator which gives law its purpose or direction. The eternal law expresses God's will; but it is not directed to any purpose as yet unrealised because, from the standpoint of God's eternal reason, there are no purposes as yet unrealised.

[40] *De libero arbitrio* 1:6.

[41] IaIIae 90:2 (p. 78, above).

[42] Romans 2:14.

[43] Peter Lombard, *Collectanea in omnes de Pauli apostoli epistolas, PL* 191:1345.

responsio: Law, because it is a rule and measure, can be in something in two ways, as stated above.[44] In one way, as in that which rules and measures; in another way, as in that which is ruled and measured, for something is ruled or measured in so far as it participates in rule or measure. Hence, since all things subject to Divine providence are ruled and measured by the eternal law, as is shown by what has been said,[45] it is clear that all things participate to some degree in the eternal law: that is, in so far as they derive from its being imprinted upon them their inclination to the activities and ends proper to them.

Now the rational creature is subject to Divine providence in a more excellent way than any other creature is, inasmuch as it participates in Providence by providing for itself and others. Hence it participates in the eternal reason, by virtue of which it has a natural inclination to the activity and end proper to it; and such participation of the rational creature in the eternal law is called the natural law.

Hence, when the Psalmist has said (Psalm 4:5f): 'Offer up the sacrifice of justice', he adds, as though to those asking what the works of justice are: 'Many say, Who showeth us good things?' And then, answering this question, he says: 'The light of Thy countenance, O Lord, is signed upon us': as if to say that the light of natural reason, by which we discern what is good and what evil, which is the function of the natural law, is nothing else than the impression of the Divine light in us.

It is therefore clear that the natural law is nothing but the rational creature's participation in the eternal law.

ad 1: This argument would be valid if the natural law were something different from the eternal law: whereas it is in fact only a participation in it, as stated in the body of the article.

ad 2: Every operation of both reason and will in us is derived from that which is according to nature, as noted above.[46] For every act of reason is derived from principles which are known naturally, and our every appetite in relation to means is derived from our natural appetite with respect to a final end.[47] And thus also the first direction of our acts towards their end must be in virtue of the natural law.

---

[44] IaIIae 90:1 ad 1 (p. 77, above).

[45] Art. 1.

[46] IaIIae 10:1.

[47] I.e. our every impulse to do something is governed by the natural desire that we have to achieve a purpose. For this use of 'appetite', see p. 7 n. 23, above.

ad 3: Even non-rational animals participate in the eternal reason in their own way, just as the rational creature does. But because the rational creature participates in the eternal law intellectually and rationally, only the rational creature's participation in it is called law in the proper sense, since law is something belonging to reason, as we have said above.[48] But non-rational creatures do not participate in it rationally, and so it cannot be called law in them, except in an analogous sense.

articulus 3: Whether there is a human law

It seems that there is not a human law.

obiectio 1: For the natural law is a participation in the eternal law, as stated above.[49] But through the eternal law all things are 'perfectly in order', as Augustine says.[50] Therefore the natural law is sufficient for the ordering of all human affairs. It is therefore not necessary for there to be a human law.

obiectio 2: Moreover, law has the character of a measure, as stated above.[51] But human reason is not a measure of things, but rather the converse, as is said in the *Metaphysics*.[52] Therefore no law can proceed from human reason.

obiectio 3: Moreover, a measure should be completely exact, as is said in the *Metaphysics*.[53] But the dictate of human reason in relation to matters of conduct is not exact, according to Wisdom 9:14: 'The thoughts of mortal men are fearful, and our counsels uncertain.' Therefore no law can proceed from human reason.

sed contra: Augustine posits two kinds of law, the one eternal and the other, which he calls 'human', temporal.[54]

responsio: Law is a kind of dictate of practical reason, as stated above.[55] Now a similar method of proceeding is found in both practical and

---

[48] IaIIae 90:1 (p. 76, above).

[49] Art. 2.

[50] *De libero arbitrio* 1:6.

[51] IaIIae 90:1 (p. 77, above).

[52] *Metaphysics* 9:9 (1053a31); i.e. what human reason can do depends on the nature of things; the nature of things does not depend on human reason.

[53] *Ibid.*

[54] *De libero arbitrio* 1:6 and 15.

[55] IaIIae 90:1 ad 2 (p. 77, above).

speculative reasoning; for each proceeds from principles to conclusions, as noted above.[56] Accordingly, it must be said that, just as, in speculative reasoning, we produce from naturally known indemonstrable principles the conclusions of the various sciences the knowledge of which is not imparted to us by nature, but discovered by effort of reason, so too human reason must necessarily proceed to derive from the precepts of the natural law, as from general and indemonstrable principles, certain arrangements of a more particular kind. And these particular arrangements, devised by human reason, are called human laws, provided that the other conditions belonging to the character of law are present, as stated above.[57] Hence Cicero says in his *Rhetoric* that 'justice had its origin in nature; then certain things became customary by reason of their utility; later still both the principles which proceeded from nature and those which had been approved by custom were sanctioned by fear and reverence for the law'.[58]

ad 1: Human reason cannot participate in the dictate of the Divine reason fully, but only in its own way and imperfectly. And so just as, in speculative reasoning, there is present in us a knowledge of certain general principles by virtue of our natural participation in the Divine wisdom, but not a specific knowledge of each single truth which the Divine wisdom contains; so too, in practical reasoning, man participates naturally in the eternal law in so far as he can derive from it certain general principles, but he does not know all the specific provisions which would apply in particular cases, even though these are in fact contained in the eternal law. And so there is a need for human reason to go further and establish laws which apply in particular cases.

ad 2: Human reason in itself is not the rule of things; but the principles which nature has implanted in it are general rules and measures of all things relating to human activity. It is of these things, and not of the nature of things in themselves, that natural reason is the rule and measure.

ad 3: The practical reason is concerned with practical matters, which are singular and contingent, but not with necessary things, as the speculative reason is. And so human laws cannot have that infallibility which the demonstrated conclusions of the sciences have; nor is it

---

[56] *Ibid.*
[57] IaIIae 90:1–4 (pp. 76ff, above).
[58] *De inventione* 2:53.

necessary for every measure to be entirely infallible and exact, but only to such a degree as is possible within its own particular genus.[59]

articulus 4: *Whether it was necessary for there to be a Divine law*

It seems that it was not necessary for there to be a Divine law.

obiectio 1: For, as stated above,[60] the natural law is a kind of participation of the eternal law in us. But the eternal law is a Divine law, as stated above.[61] Therefore there was no need for a Divine law in addition to the natural law and the human laws derived from it.

obiectio 2: Moreover, it is said at Ecclesiasticus 15:14 that God 'left man in the hand of his own counsel'. Now 'counsel' is an activity of reason, as noted above.[62] Therefore man was left to the government of his own reason. But a dictate of human reason is a human law, as stated above.[63] Therefore there is no need for man to be governed by another, Divine, law.

obiectio 3: Moreover, human nature is more self-sufficient than non-rational creatures are. But non-rational creatures do not have a Divine law in addition to the inclination implanted in them by nature. Still less, therefore, should the rational creature have a Divine law in addition to the natural law.

sed contra: David prayed to God to set His law before him, saying (Psalm 119:33): 'Teach me, O Lord, the way of Thy statutes.'

responsio: It was necessary for the direction of human life to have a Divine law in addition to the natural law and the human law. This is so for four reasons.

First: it is by law that man is directed in the performance of the acts proper to his final end; and, indeed, if the only end appointed for mankind were one which did not exceed the capacity of man's natural faculty, there would be no need for man to receive any direction from his reason over and above the natural law and the human law derived from

---

[59] Cf. *Ethics* 5:10 (1129b29).
[60] Art. 2.
[61] Art. 1.
[62] IaIIae 14:1.
[63] Art. 3.

it. But because mankind is ordained to the end of eternal blessedness, which exceeds the capacity of man's natural faculty, as noted above,[64] it was therefore necessary that, over and above the natural and the human law, he should be directed to his end by a law divinely given.

Second: thanks to the uncertainty of human judgment, especially in contingent and particular matters, it happens that different people judge human acts in different ways; and from this fact different and contrary laws arise. In order, therefore, that man might know without any doubt what to do and what to avoid, it was necessary for him to be directed in his proper acts by a law divinely given; for it is clear that such a law cannot err.

Third: man can make laws only in respect of those matters which he is able to judge. But man cannot judge inward acts, which are concealed, but only outward ones, which are apparent; and yet the perfection of virtue requires that man conduct himself rightly in acts of both kinds. And so human law could not sufficiently control and direct inward acts; rather, it was necessary for this purpose that a Divine law should supervene.

Fourth: as Augustine says,[65] human law cannot punish or prohibit all evil deeds, for in seeking to remove all evils, it would as a consequence remove many good things also; and so the securing of the common good which is a necessary part of human association would be impeded. In order, therefore, that no evil might remain unprohibited and unpunished, it was necessary that a Divine law, by which all sins are forbidden, should supervene.

And these four reasons are touched upon in Psalm 19:7, where it is said: 'The law of the Lord is perfect', that is, in that it permits none of the defilement of sin; 'converting the soul', because it directs not only outward, but inward acts also; 'the testimony of the Lord is sure', thanks to the certainty of its truth and righteousness; 'making wise the simple', inasmuch as it directs man to an end which is supernatural and Divine.

ad 1: Man's participation in the eternal law by way of the natural law is in proportion to the capacity of human nature. But man needs to be directed to his final, supernatural end in a higher way; and so a divinely given law is provided in addition, through which man participates in the eternal law in a higher way.

---

[64] IaIIae 5:5.   [65] *De libero arbitrio* 1:5.

ad 2: Counsel is a kind of inquiry; hence it must proceed from certain principles. Nor, for the reasons given in the body of the article, is it enough for it to proceed from principles implanted by nature, which are the precepts of the natural law; rather, there is a need for certain principles to be provided in addition: namely, the precepts of the Divine law.

ad 3: Non-rational creatures are not ordained to an end higher than that which is proportionate to their natural powers; and so the two cases are not similar.

articulus 5: *Whether there is only one Divine law*

It seems that there is only one Divine law.

obiectio 1: For where there is one king in one kingdom there is one law. But the whole human race is subject to God as to one king, according to Psalm 47:7: 'God is the King of all the earth.' Therefore there is only one Divine law.

obiectio 2: Moreover, every law is directed to the end which the legislator intends for those for whom he makes the law. But God intends one and the same thing for all men, according to 1 Timothy 2:4: 'He will have all men to be saved, and to come to the knowledge of the truth.' Therefore there is only one Divine law.

obiectio 3: Moreover, the Divine law seems to be closer to the eternal law, which is one, than to the natural law, inasmuch as the revelation of grace is of a higher order than natural knowledge. But there is one natural law for all men. So much more, therefore, is there only one Divine law.

sed contra: The Apostle says (Hebrews 7:11f): 'The priesthood being changed, there is made of necessity a change also of the law.' But the priesthood is twofold, as is said in the same place: that is, the Levitical priesthood and the priesthood of Christ. Therefore the Divine law is also twofold: that is, the old law and the new law.

responsio: Distinction is the cause of number, as stated in the First Part.[66] But we find that things can be distinguished in two ways. In one way, as those things which are altogether different in species: horse and ox, for example. In another way, as perfect and imperfect in the same species: for

---

[66] Ia 30:3; cf. *Metaphysics* 10:1 (1053a20).

instance, boy and man. And it is in this latter way that the Divine law is divided into the old law and the new law. Hence the Apostle (Galatians 3:24f) compares the state of man under the old law to that of a boy under a schoolmaster, but his state under the new law to that of a grown man who is no longer under a schoolmaster.

Now the perfection and imperfection of these two laws must be considered in relation to the three features of law already discussed.[67] First, the purpose of law is to be directed to the common good as to its end, as stated above.[68] But this good may be twofold. On the one hand, it may be sensible and earthly; and man was directly ordained to a good of this kind by the old law. Hence, at the very beginning of the law, the people were invited into the earthly kingdom of the Canaanites (Exodus 3:8, 17). On the other hand, it may be an intelligible and heavenly good: and, to this, man is ordained by the new law. Hence, at the very beginning of His preaching, Christ invited men into the kingdom of heaven, saying (Matthew 4:17): 'Repent, for the kingdom of heaven is at hand.' And so Augustine says that 'promises of temporal goods are contained in the Old Testament, and this is why it is called Old; but the promise of eternal life belongs to the New Testament'.[69]

Second, it pertains to law to direct human acts according to the order of justice; and in this respect also the new law surpasses the old law, since it directs the inward acts of the soul, according to Matthew 5:20: 'Unless your justice abound more than that of the Scribes and Pharisees, you shall not enter into the kingdom of heaven.' And so it is said that 'the old law restrains the hand, but the new law controls the mind'.[70]

Third, it pertains to law to induce men to observe its commandments. The old law did this by the fear of punishment, but the new law does it by the love which is poured into our hearts by the grace of Christ, bestowed in the new law, but prefigured in the old. Hence Augustine says that 'the little difference between fear [*timor*] and love [*amor*] is the difference between the law and the Gospel'.[71]

ad 1: As the father of a family gives different commands in his house to children and adults, so also the one King, God, in His one kingdom, gave one law to men while they were yet imperfect, and another more perfect

---

[67] IaIIae 90:1, 2, 3 (pp. 76ff, above); 91:1 ad 3 (p. 84, above); 3 (p. 87, above).

[68] IaIIae 90:2 (p. 78, above).

[69] *Contra Faustum* 4:2.

[70] Peter Lombard, *Sententiae* 3:40:1 (*PL* 192:838).

[71] *Contra Adimantum Manichaei discipulum* 17.

law when they had been led by the first law to a greater capacity for things divine.

ad 2: The salvation of mankind could not be achieved by any other means than through Christ, according to Acts 4:12: 'There is no other name given to men, whereby we must be saved.' And so the perfect law that brings all men to salvation could not be given until after the advent of Christ. But before His coming it was necessary to give to the people of whom Christ was to be born a law in which some of the rudiments of the righteousness necessary to salvation were contained, in order to prepare them to receive Him.

ad 3: The natural law directs man according to certain general precepts which apply to perfect and imperfect men alike, and so there is one natural law for all men. But the Divine law directs man in certain particular matters with respect to which perfect and imperfect men do not resemble each other. And so it was necessary for the Divine law to be twofold, as stated in the body of the article.

articulus 6: *Whether there is a 'law of lust' [lex fomitis]* [72]

It seems that there is not a law of lust.

obiectio 1: For Isidore says that law is 'grounded in reason'.[73] But lust is not grounded in reason; on the contrary, it deviates from reason. Therefore lust does not have the character of law.

obiectio 2: Moreover, every law is obligatory, so that those who do not observe it are called transgressors. But no one becomes a transgressor because he does not follow the promptings of lust: on the contrary, he is rendered a transgressor if he does follow them. Therefore lust does not have the character of law.

obiectio 3: Moreover, law is directed to the common good, as noted above.[74] But lust inclines us not to the common good, but to a private good of our own. Therefore lust does not have the character of law.

---

[72] See Peter Lombard, *Sententiae* 2:30:8 (*PL* 192:722); Damascene, *De fide orthodoxa* 4:22 (*PG* 94:1200). *Lex fomitis* is not capable of being translated literally. *Fomes* is 'tinder': the idea is that we 'flare up' and act irrationally under the influence of lust.

[73] *Etymologiae* 5:3 (*PL* 82:199).

[74] IaIIae 90: 2 (p. 78, above).

sed contra: The Apostle says (Romans 7:23): 'I see another law in my members, warring against the law of my mind.'

responsio: Law, as to its essence, is found in that which rules and measures, as stated above,[75] but is present by participation in that which is ruled and measured, so that every inclination or ordination found in things subject to law is itself called a law by participation; and this also is shown by what has been said above.[76] Now we find that those subject to law can receive an inclination from a legislator in two ways. In one way, in so far as he inclines his subjects to something directly, and from time to time assigns different men to different activities; and it is in this way that we can say that there is one kind of law for soldiers and another for merchants. In another way, in so far as he does this indirectly, as when a legislator dismisses a subject from his station and, as a consequence of this, the subject then passes [by default] into another order and comes under another kind of law: for instance, if a soldier is discharged from the army, he may become subject to rural or mercantile legislation.

So, then: under God as Legislator different creatures have different natural inclinations, so that what is a kind of law for one is against the law for another. For example, I might say that fierceness is a kind of law for a dog but against the law of a sheep or other gentle animal. The law of man, therefore, which is assigned to him by the Divine ordinance according to his proper condition, is that he should act according to reason. This law was so effective in the original state that nothing either beyond or against reason could take man unawares. But when man turned away from God, he fell under the influence of his sensual impulses. Indeed, this happens to each man individually the more he turns aside from the path of reason, so that he becomes in a certain sense like the beasts who are led by the impulse of sensuality, according to Psalm 49:20: 'Man, when he was in honour, did not understand: he hath been compared to senseless beasts, and made like to them.'

So, then, this very inclination of sensuality which is called lust, in other animals simply has the character of law (although only in so far as we may call 'law' what is an inclination subject to law). But in man it does not have the character of law in this way: rather, it is a deviation from the law of reason. But since, by Divine justice, man is destitute of original justice and the vigour of reason, this impulse of sensuality by which he is led has

---

[75] IaIIae 90:1 ad 1 (p. 77, above); 91:2 (p. 86, above).
[76] Art. 2. And see n. 10, above.

the character of law in so far as it is a penalty following from the fact that the Divine law has dismissed man from his proper station.[77]

ad 1: This argument is valid with respect to lust considered in itself, in so far as it inclines us to evil. But, as stated in the body of the article, it is not in this sense that it has the character of law, but rather in so far as it follows from the justice of the Divine law. It is as though we were to say that the law allows a nobleman to be condemned to hard labour for some misdeed.[78]

ad 2: This argument is valid with respect to law considered as a rule or measure: for it is in this sense that those who deviate from the law become transgressors. But lust is a law not in this sense, but by a kind of participation, as stated in the body of the article.

ad 3: This argument is valid with respect to lust considered in relation to what it inclines us to now, but not with reference to its origin. For if the inclination towards sensuality is considered simply in itself, as it exists in other animals, it is directed to a common good: namely, to the preservation of nature in the species or in the individual. And this is so even in man, to the extent that sensuality is subject to reason. But it is called lust in so far as it departs from the order of reason.[79]

(c) *Summa theologiae* IaIIae 92: The effects of law

We come next to the effects of law; and here there are two things to consider:

---

[77] I.e. lust has the character of law in that it 'governs' so much of what we do, but it is not assigned to man as law 'simply', or 'directly', as it is to other animals; rather, it is a punitive condition into which we have fallen because we have turned away from our 'proper' law of reason. In the *responsio*, St Thomas seems to suggest that we have fallen into it by default, in the way that a discharged soldier comes by default under some other kind of law; but at ad 1, lust is treated as though it were a punishment in a positive sense.

[78] This notion that lust is literally a punishment inflicted on mankind for sin originates with St Augustine. See e.g. *De civitate Dei* 14:19.

[79] The suggestion is that sexual desire is evil not in itself – it is, after all, necessary for 'the preservation of nature' – but only insofar as it 'departs from the order of reason' by which human beings are differentiated from the beasts: insofar, that is, as it is inordinate and uncontrolled. Again, this way of thinking originates with St Augustine, whose dislike of sex arises largely from the fact that sexual desire operates beyond the control of reason. The fact that our 'members' now 'disobey' us, he suggests, is part of the punishment for the disobedience of our first parents (see, e.g., *De civitate Dei* 14:20). He speculates at *De civitate Dei* 14:23ff that, had the fall not occurred, the reason would have had complete control of our sexual impulses: or, really, that they would not have been *impulses* at all.

1. Whether it is an effect of law to make men good
2. Whether the functions of law are to command, to forbid, to permit and to punish, as the Jurist says[80]

articulus 1: *Whether it is an effect of law to make men good*

It seems that it is not an effect of law to make men good.

obiectio 1: For men are good through virtue, since virtue is 'that which makes its possessor good', as is said at *Ethics* II.[81] But virtue comes to man from God alone, because it is He Who 'performs it in us without us',[82] as stated above in the definition of virtue.[83] Therefore law does not make men good.

obiectio 2: Moreover, law is of no profit to a man unless he obeys the law. But the very fact that a man obeys the law is due to his goodness. Goodness in man is therefore a prerequisite [rather than a consequence] of law. Therefore law does not make men good.

obiectio 3: Moreover, law is directed to the common good, as stated above.[84] But there are some who behave well in matters pertaining to the community who do not behave well in things relating to themselves.[85] Therefore it is not an effect of law to make men good.

obiectio 4: Moreover, some laws are tyrannical, as the Philosopher says in his *Politics*.[86] But a tyrant does not intend the good of his subjects, but only his own advantage. Therefore law does not make men good.

sed contra: The Philosopher says in the *Ethics* that the 'intention of every legislator is to make men good'.[87]

responsio: Law is nothing but a dictate of reason in the ruler by which his subjects are governed, as stated above.[88] Now the virtue of anything

---

[80] *CICiv.*: *Digesta* 1:3:7.
[81] *Ethics* 2:6 (1106a1).
[82] Peter Lombard, *Sententiae* 2:27:5 (*PL* 192:711).
[83] IaIIae 55:4.
[84] IaIIae 90:2 (p. 78, above).
[85] Cf. *Ethics* 5:1 (1129b33).
[86] *Politics* 3:11 (1282b12).
[87] *Ethics* 2:1 (1103b3).
[88] IaIIae 90:1 ad 2 (p. 77, above); 3 and 4 (pp. 8off, above).

which is a subject lies in its being properly subjected to that by which it is governed: for example, the virtue of the irascible and concupiscible appetites[89] consists in their being properly obedient to the reason. And so it is that the virtue of every subject consists in his being properly subject to his ruler, as the Philosopher says in the *Politics*.[90] But the purpose of every law is that it should be obeyed by those subject to it. Hence it is clear that the proper effect of law is to lead its subjects to their proper virtue; and since virtue is 'that which makes its possessor good', it follows that the proper effect of law is to make those to whom it is given good, either absolutely or relatively. For if the intention of the legislator is bent on true good, which is the common good regulated according to Divine justice, it follows that the effect of his law is to make men good absolutely. If, however, the intention of the legislator is bent on that which is not good absolutely, but useful or pleasurable to himself, or repugnant to Divine justice, then his law does not make men good absolutely, but only in a relative sense: that is, only in relation to that particular government.[91] In this latter sense good is found even in things which are bad of themselves: for instance, a man is called a 'good' robber because he operates in a fashion which is adapted to his end.[92]

ad 1: Virtue is twofold, as is shown by what has been said above: that is, acquired and infused.[93] Now acquiring the habit of virtuous action

---

[89] See p. 7 n. 23, above.

[90] *Politics* 1:13 (1260a20).

[91] *Politics* 3:4f (1277a20ff).

[92] Cf. Plato, *Republic* 351C.

[93] IaIIae 63:1–2; 65:2. The idea here is that we can achieve an approximate kind of virtue by ourselves, but that such 'acquired' virtue is not true virtue (a wicked man can be courageous, temperate, etc.) unless 'topped up', as it were, by Divine 'infusion'. The virtues, says St Thomas at IaIIae 63:1, 'both intellectual and moral, are in us by nature to the extent of a certain rudimentary aptitude, but not in their perfect completeness; the reason being that nature is limited to one fixed course of action, whereas the perfection of the virtues does not lead to one fixed course of action, but varies according to the diversity of matters and circumstances with respect to which the virtues come into play'. And at IaIIae 65:2: 'The moral virtues, considered as operating in man towards an end which does not exceed the natural faculty of mankind, may be acquired by human acts; and, so acquired, may be without charity, as they have been in many unbelievers. But considered as productive of good ordered to man's supernatural final end, they cannot have the perfect and true character of virtue, and cannot be acquired by human acts, but are infused by God; and such moral virtues cannot be without charity.' See also n. 24 on p. 63, above, for the relation between virtue and habit.

contributes to virtue of both kinds, but in different ways; for it causes acquired virtue, whereas it disposes us to receive infused virtue, and it preserves and promotes the latter when it is already possessed. And since law is given for the purpose of directing human acts, then, in so far as human acts conduce to virtue, law to that extent makes men good. Hence the Philosopher says in the *Ethics* that 'legislators make men good by habituating them to good works'.[94]

ad 2: It is not always through perfect goodness of virtue that someone obeys the law, but sometimes through fear of punishment, and sometimes merely because of the prompting of reason, which is a beginning of virtue, as noted above.[95]

ad 3: The goodness of any part is to be considered in terms of how it relates to the whole; hence Augustine says in the *Confessions* that 'any part is ugly that is not well adjusted to the whole'.[96] Since therefore every man is a part of the State, it is impossible for any man to be good unless he is well adjusted to the common good; nor can the whole of anything be properly composed unless its parts are well adjusted to it. Hence it is impossible for the common good of the State to be secured unless the citizens are virtuous: at least those whose business it is to rule, although it is enough for the good of the community if the other citizens are virtuous enough to obey the commands of their rulers. Hence the Philosopher says in the *Politics* that 'the virtue of a ruler is the same as that of a good man, but the virtue of the citizen is not the same as that of a good man'.[97]

ad 4: A tyrannical law, because not according to reason, is not strictly speaking a law, but rather a kind of perversion of law. Yet in so far as it has at least something of the character of law, its intention is still that the citizens should be good. Even if it has nothing of the character of law apart from being an ordinance made by a superior for his subjects, the superior's intention is still that the subjects will obey it, and hence be good: not absolutely, but at any rate with respect to that particular government.

---

[94] *Ethics* 2:1 (1103b3).
[95] IaIIae 63:1.
[96] *Confessiones* 3:8.
[97] *Politics* 3:4 (1277a20).

articulus 2: *Whether the functions of law are properly described
[as commanding, prohibiting, permitting and punishing]*[98]

It seems that the functions of law are not properly described when it is
said that the functions of law are to command, to prohibit, to permit and
to punish.

obiectio 1: For 'every law is a general precept', as the jurist Papinian says.[99]
Now 'command' and 'precept' are the same; but the other three headings
are therefore superfluous.

obiectio 2: Moreover, the effect of a law is to induce its subjects to be good,
as stated above.[100] But counsel aims at a higher good than command.[101]
Therefore it belongs to law to counsel more than to command.

obiectio 3: Moreover, just as a man is moved to do good deeds by punishment, so is he also by reward. Therefore if punishing is posited as one of
the effects of law, so too should rewarding be.

obiectio 4: Moreover, the intention of a legislator is to make men good, as
stated above.[102] But he who obeys the law merely through fear of punishment is not good, for 'although a kind of good deed may be done through
servile fear, which is fear of punishment, it is not done well', as Augustine
says.[103] It seems, therefore, that it is not proper for law to punish.

sed contra: Isidore says:[104] 'Every law either permits something, as: "A
brave man may demand his reward"; or prohibits something, as: "No
man may ask a consecrated virgin in marriage"; or punishes, as: "Let one
who commits a murder be put to death."'

[98] Here, as so often in the *Summa*, the point is apparently obscure and pedantic, but the underlying problem – that two major authorities appear to differ – is, for St Thomas, an important
one. If law is exhaustively defined as precept or command (as Papinian seems to say at
obiectio 1), in what way can we say also that it prohibits, permits and punishes, as Isidore
says in the *sed contra* and as is also said at *Digesta* 1:3:7? The answer (in the *responsio*) is that
commanding, prohibiting, permitting and punishing are the different aspects under which
the preceptive character of law manifests itself in relation to different kinds of human acts;
with the supplementary point (ad 1) that a prohibition is only a kind of negative precept.
[99] *CICiv.: Digesta* 1:3:1.
[100] Art. 1.
[101] Counsel 'aims at a higher good than command' because it encourages us to go beyond mere
duty. See n. 54 on p. 221, below, for what St Thomas means by this.
[102] Art. 1.
[103] *Contra duas epistolas Pelagianorum* 2:4.
[104] *Etymologiae* 5:19 (*PL* 82:202).

responsio: Just as a proposition is a dictate of reason asserting something, so a law is a dictate of reason preceptive of something. Now it is the proper task of reason to lead from one thing to another. Hence, just as, in the demonstrative sciences, reason leads us from certain principles to assent to a conclusion, so too it leads us by certain means to assent to a precept of law. Now the precepts of law are concerned with human acts, which the law directs, as stated above.[105] But there are three kinds of human acts; for, as stated above,[106] some acts are good generically: namely, acts of virtue; and the function of the law with respect to these is to prescribe or command, for the law prescribes all acts of virtue, as is said in the *Ethics*.[107] Some acts are evil generically: namely, acts of vice, and the function of the law with respect to these is to prohibit. Some acts are generically indifferent, and the function of the law with respect to these is to permit; and all acts which are neither good nor bad can be called indifferent. And fear of punishment is that of which law makes use in order to induce people to obey it; and to this extent punishment also is identified as an effect of law.

ad 1: Just as to cease from evil has something of the character of good, so prohibition has something of the character of a precept; and accordingly, taking 'precept' broadly, every law is called a 'precept'.

ad 2: To give counsel is not an act peculiar to law, for it can pertain even to a private person, who cannot make a law. Hence the Apostle, after giving a certain counsel, said (1 Corinthians 7:12): 'I speak, not the Lord.' And so it is not counted among the effects of law.

ad 3: To reward may also pertain to anyone: but to punish pertains to no one apart from the minister of the law, by whose authority the penalty is inflicted; and so to reward is not counted an act of law, but only to punish.

ad 4: Having first become accustomed to avoid evil and fulfil good through fear of punishment, one is sometimes led on to do so with delight and of one's own free will. Accordingly, law, even by punishing, leads men on to being good.[108]

---

[105] IaIIae 90:1 and 2 (pp. 76ff, above).

[106] IaIIae 18:8.

[107] *Ethics* 5:1 (1129b19).

[108] Once again, the reference is to the habituating influence of law in the creation of virtue. See n. 24 on p. 63.

(d) *Summa theologiae* IaIIae 93: The eternal law

Here there are six things to consider:

1. What the eternal law is
2. Whether it is known to all men
3. Whether all law is derived from it
4. Whether necessary things are subject to the eternal law
5. Whether natural contingents are subject to the eternal law
6. Whether all human affairs are subject to it

articulus 1: *Whether the eternal law is supreme reason existing in God*

It seems that the eternal law is not supreme reason existing in God.

obiectio 1: For there is only one eternal law. But there are many reasons in the Divine mind; for Augustine says that God 'made each thing according to its reasons'.[109] It seems, therefore, that the eternal law is not the same as reason existing in the Divine mind.

obiectio 2: Moreover, it is part of the character of law to be promulgated by word, as stated above.[110] But 'Word' is predicated of God personally [i.e. is the name of God the Son],[111] as noted in the First Part, whereas 'reason' is predicated of the [Divine] essence.[112] Therefore the eternal law is not the same as Divine reason.[113]

obiectio 3: Moreover, Augustine says: 'We see a law above our minds, which is called truth.'[114] But the law which is above our minds is the eternal law.

---

[109] *De diversis quaestionibus octoginta tribus* 46. The 'reasons' referred to (*rationes*) are Platonist 'exemplars' or 'ideas'. St Thomas's full discussion of such *rationes* is at Ia 15, where he quotes more fully from Augustine's *83 quaest.*, 46, as follows: 'Ideas are certain original forms or permanent and immutable models of things which are contained by the Divine intelligence. They are immutable because they themselves have not been formed, and that is why they are eternal and always the same. But though they themselves neither come to be nor perish, yet it is according to them that everything which can come to be or pass away, or which actually does come to be or pass away, is said to be formed.' See also Gilson, *The Christian Philosophy of St Thomas Aquinas*, pp. 125f.

[110] IaIIae 90:4 (p. 82, above); 91:1 ad 2 (p. 84, above).

[111] Cf. John 1:1–5.

[112] Ia 34:1.

[113] I.e. because it is the nature of law to be 'promulgated by word', it seems that the eternal law must be attributed specifically to God the Son, the 'word' through Whom God speaks to the world. But 'reason' is attributed to the Divine essence as such, not to any one Person of the Trinity. The eternal law therefore cannot be identical with Divine reason. See n. 122, below.

[114] *De vera religione* 30.

Therefore the eternal law is truth. But the idea of truth is not the same as the idea of reason. Therefore the eternal law is not the same as supreme reason.

sed contra: Augustine says that 'the eternal law is the supreme reason to which we must always conform'.[115]

responsio: Just as in every craftsman there pre-exists a rational pattern of the things which are to be made by his art, so too in every governor there must pre-exist a rational pattern of the order of the things which are to be done by those subject to his government. And just as the rational pattern of the things to be made by an art is called the art, or the exemplar of the products of that art, so too the rational pattern existing in him who governs the acts of his subjects bears the character of law, provided that the other conditions which we have mentioned above are also present.[116] Now God is the Creator of all things by His wisdom, and He stands in the same relation to them as a craftsman does to the products of his art, as noted in the First Part.[117] But He is also the governor of all the acts and motions that are to be found in each single creature, as was also noted in the First Part.[118] Hence just as the rational pattern of the Divine wisdom has the character of art or exemplar or idea in relation to all the things which are created by it, so also the rational pattern of the Divine wisdom bears the character of law in relation to all the things which are moved by it to their proper end. Accordingly, the eternal law is nothing but the rational pattern of the Divine wisdom considered as directing all actions and motions.

ad 1: Augustine is here speaking of the ideal reasons [*rationes*] which relate to the proper nature of each individual thing; and so there is found in them a certain distinction and plurality, according to the different ways in which they relate to things, as noted in the First Part.[119] But law is said to be directive of human acts by ordering them to the common good, as stated above.[120] And things which are different in themselves may be considered as one according as they are ordered to one common end. Hence the eternal law is one since it is the rational pattern of this order.

[115] *De libero arbitrio* 1:6.
[116] IaIIae 90:1–4 (pp. 76ff, above).
[117] Ia 14:8.
[118] Ia 103:5.
[119] Ia 15:2.
[120] IaIIae 90:2 (p. 78, above).

ad 2: In the case of any word, two aspects can be considered: namely, the word itself, and the meaning expressed by the word. For the spoken word is something produced by the mouth of man, but this word also expresses that which a human word is intended to signify. The same applies to the mental word of man, for this is nothing but a certain concept of the mind by which a man mentally expresses what he thinks. So then: the Divine word [i.e. God the Son], conceived by the intellect of the Father, is predicated of God personally; but all things that are in the Father's knowledge, whether they have to do with the essence or the persons or the works of God, are expressed by this word, as Augustine makes clear at *De Trinitate* xv.[121] Among the other things which are expressed by this Word, the eternal law itself is expressed by it, but it does not follow that the eternal law is predicated of God personally. It is, however, specially associated with the Son, on account of the close relation between 'reason' and 'word'.[122]

ad 3: The reason of the Divine intellect does not stand in the same relation to things as the reason of the human intellect does. For the human intellect is measured by things: that is, a human concept is not true simply in itself, but is said to be true by reason of its correspondence with things, for an opinion is true or false according to what a thing is or is not.[123] But the Divine intellect is the measure of things, since each thing has truth in it in so far as it represents the Divine intellect, as was stated in the First Part.[124] And so the Divine intellect is true in itself; and its reason is truth itself.

articulus 2: *Whether the eternal law is known to all men*

It seems that the eternal law is not known to all men.

obiectio 1: For, as the Apostle says (1 Corinthians 2:11): 'the things that are of God no man knoweth, but the Spirit of God'. But the eternal law is a kind of rational pattern existing in the Divine mind. Therefore it is unknown to all except God alone.

---

[121] *De Trinitate* 15:14.

[122] I.e. the Word expresses the *meaning* of the eternal law without *being* the eternal law, just as, in the ordinary sense of the terms, a word and its meaning are distinct. This enables us to say that God the Son expresses the eternal law (as is appropriate, since reason needs to be made accessible through verbal expression) without also saying that the eternal law is therefore an attribute of one person of the Trinity, rather than essential to the Divine nature as such. Technically: the eternal law is subsistently real in God, and by special attribution in the Son.

[123] *Metaphysics* 10:1 (1053a31); and see n. 52, above.

[124] Ia 16:1.

obiectio 2: Moreover, as Augustine says, 'the eternal law is that by which it is right that all things should be perfectly in order'.[125] But not all men know how all things are perfectly in order. Therefore not all men know the eternal law.

obiectio 3: Moreover, Augustine says that 'the eternal law is that upon which men cannot pass judgment'.[126] But, as is said at *Ethics* I, 'any man can judge well of what he knows'.[127] Therefore the eternal law is not known to us.

sed contra: Augustine says that 'knowledge of the eternal law is imprinted on us'.[128]

responsio: A thing may be known in two ways: in one way, in itself; in another way, by its effect, in which some likeness of the thing is found: for instance, someone not seeing the sun in its substance may know it by its radiance. So then, we must say that no one can know the eternal law as it is in itself, except God alone and the blessed who see God in His essence. But every rational creature knows it to a greater or lesser extent by its radiance. For every knowledge of truth is a kind of radiance and participation of the eternal law which is the immutable truth, as Augustine says.[129] And all men know the truth to some extent, at least as to the general principles of the natural law; and, as to its other commands, they participate in the knowledge of truth to a greater or lesser degree, and in this respect know the eternal law, some more and some less.

ad 1: 'The things that are of God' cannot be known to us as they are in themselves, but they are revealed to us through their effects, according to Romans 1:20: 'The invisible things of God are clearly seen, being understood by the things that are made.'

ad 2: Although each man knows the eternal law according to his own capacity, in the way explained in the body of the article, no one can comprehend it fully: for it cannot be totally revealed through its effects. Therefore it does not follow that anyone who knows the eternal law in the way just explained also knows the whole order of things by which they are 'perfectly in order'.

[125] *De libero arbitrio* 1:6.
[126] *De vera religione* 31.
[127] *Ethics* 1:3 (1094b27).
[128] *De libero arbitrio* 1:6.
[129] *De vera religione* 31.

ad 3: What it is to judge a thing can be understood in two ways. In one way, as when a cognitive power passes judgment with respect to its proper object, according to Job 12:11: 'Doth not the ear discern words, and the palate of him that eateth, the taste?' And it is of this kind of judgment that the Philosopher speaks when he says that 'anyone can judge well of what he knows': that is, by judging whether what is proposed is true. In another way, we speak of a superior using a kind of practical judgment to judge whether something subordinate to him should be thus or otherwise. And in this latter sense no one can pass judgment upon the eternal law.

articulus 3: *Whether every law is derived from the eternal law*

It seems that not every law is derived from the eternal law.

obiectio 1: For there is a law of lust, as stated above.[130] But this is not derived from that Divine law which is the eternal law, since to it belongs the 'carnal mind' of which the Apostle says (Romans 8:7), that 'it cannot be subject to the law of God'. Therefore not every law is derived from the eternal law.

obiectio 2: Moreover, nothing wicked can proceed from the eternal law, because, as stated above, 'the eternal law is that according to which it is right that all things should be perfectly in order.'[131] But some laws are wicked, according to Isaiah 10:1: 'Woe to them that make wicked laws.' Therefore not every law is derived from the eternal law.

obiectio 3: Moreover, Augustine says that 'the law which is framed for ruling the people, rightly permits many things which are punished by Divine providence'.[132] But the rational pattern of Divine providence is the eternal law, as stated above.[133] Therefore not even every right law proceeds from the eternal law.

sed contra: The Divine wisdom says (Proverbs 8:15): 'By me kings reign, and lawgivers decree just things.' But the rational pattern of the Divine wisdom is the eternal law, as stated above. Therefore all laws proceed from the eternal law.

[130] IaIIae 91:6 (p. 93, above).
[131] Art. 2, 2.
[132] *De libero arbitrio* I:5.
[133] Art. 1.

responsio: Law denotes a kind of reason directing acts towards an end, as stated above.[134] Now in all cases where there are movers ordered in relation to one another, the power of the second mover must be derived from the power of the first mover, since the second mover does not move except in so far as it is moved by the first. Hence we see the same thing in all who govern: that the plan of government is derived by secondary governors from the first governor, so that the plan of what is to be done in a State is derived from the king by way of his command to subordinate administrators; and, again, when things are to be made, the plan of what is to be made is derived from the designer to the lower craftsmen who work with their hands. Since, then, the eternal law is the plan of government in the Supreme Governor, all plans of government which are in lower governors must necessarily be derived from the eternal law. And these plans of lower governors are all other laws apart from the eternal law. Therefore all laws are derived from the eternal law in so far as they participate in right reason. Hence Augustine says that 'in temporal law there is nothing just and lawful but what man has drawn from the eternal law'.[135]

ad 1: Lust has the character of law in man in so far as it is a punishment resulting from Divine justice; and in this respect it is clear that it is derived from the eternal law. But in so far as it denotes an inclination to sin, it is contrary to the law of God, and does not have the character of law, as stated above.[136]

ad 2: Human law has the character of law in so far as it is according to right reason; and it is clear that, in this respect, it is derived from the eternal law. But in so far as it departs from reason, it is called a wicked law, and so has the character not of law, but of violence. Nevertheless even a wicked law, in so far as it retains some appearance of law through being enacted by one who has the power to make law, is derived from the eternal law; since, according to Romans 13:1, there is no power but of the Lord God.

ad 3: Human law is said to permit certain things, not as approving them, but as being unable to direct them. And many things are directed by the Divine law which human law is unable to direct, because more things are subject to a higher cause than to a lower one. Hence the very fact that

[134] IaIIae 90:1–2 (pp. 76ff, above).
[135] *De libero arbitrio* I:6.
[136] IaIIae 91:6 (p. 93, above).

human law does not concern itself with things which it cannot direct, comes under the ordination of the eternal law. It would be different were human law to approve of what the eternal law condemns. Hence it does not follow that human law is not derived from the eternal law, but that it cannot aspire to its perfection.

articulus 4: *Whether necessary and eternal things are subject to the eternal law*[137]

It seems that necessary and eternal things are subject to the eternal law.

obiectio 1: For whatever is rational is subject to reason. But the Divine will is rational, for it is just. Therefore it is subject to reason. But the eternal law is the Divine reason. Therefore God's will is subject to the eternal law. But God's will is eternal. Therefore eternal and necessary things are subject to the eternal law.

obiectio 2: Moreover, whatever is subject to a king is subject to the king's law. But, as is said at 1 Corinthians 15:25 and 28, the Son 'shall be subject to God and the Father when He shall have delivered up the Kingdom to Him'. Therefore the Son, Who is eternal, is subject to the eternal law.

obiectio 3: Moreover, the eternal law is the reason of Divine providence. But many necessary things are subject to Divine providence: for example, the stability of incorporeal substances and of the heavenly bodies. Therefore even necessary things are subject to the eternal law.

sed contra: Things that are necessary cannot be other than they are, and so have no need of restraint, whereas laws are imposed on men in order to restrain them from evil, as is shown by what has been said.[138] Therefore necessary things are not subject to the eternal law.

[137] The difficulty which St Thomas seems to have in mind here is as follows. We wish to say that everything is subject to the eternal law; and 'everything' must presumably include necessary and eternal things. But apparently this involves difficulties. It seems to require us to say that the Divine reason is subject to itself; that God the Son, who is of one nature with the Father, is at the same time subject to the Father (i.e. that God is subject to Himself); and that things which are necessary – i.e. which *cannot* be other than they are – are nonetheless subject to the direction of law. The answers given in the *responsio* and replies to the *obiectiones* are as follows: (a) in essence, the Divine reason *is* the eternal law; (b) the very fact that necessary things cannot be other than they are is part of the eternal law; (c) God the Son is subject to the Father only with respect to His human nature.

[138] IaIIae 92:2 (p. 99, above).

responsio: The eternal law is the rational pattern of the Divine government, as stated above.[139] Whatever is subject to the Divine government, therefore, is also subject to the eternal law; whereas anything not subject to the Divine government is not subject to the eternal law. This distinction can be understood from the things around us. For those things which can be done by man are subject to human government; but what pertains to the nature of man is not subject to human government: for example, that he should have a soul or hands or feet. So then, everything, whether contingent or necessary, that is in things created by God is subject to the eternal law, while things pertaining to the Divine nature or essence are not subject to the eternal law, but are really the eternal law itself.

ad 1: God's will can be spoken of in two ways. In one way, it can be spoken of as referring to the will itself; and in this way, since God's will is His very Essence, it is subject neither to the Divine government nor to the eternal law, but is the same thing as the eternal law. In another way, we can speak of the Divine will as being expressed in those things which God wills with respect to creatures. Now these things are subject to the eternal law in so far as the rational plan of them is in the Divine wisdom [which is the eternal law]. In reference to these things, God's will is said to be rational, though, considered in its own nature, it should rather be called reason itself.

ad 2: The Son of God was not made by God, but was naturally begotten of God; and so He is not subject to Divine providence or to the eternal law, but rather is Himself the eternal law by a kind of appropriation, as is shown by Augustine in the book *De vera religione*.[140] But He is said to be subject to the Father with respect to His human nature, with respect to which also the Father is said to be greater than He.[141]

The third objection we concede, because it is true in respect of those necessary things which are created.

ad 4 [i.e. the *sed contra*]: As the Philosopher says at *Metaphysics* v,[142] some necessary things have a cause of their necessity, and thus they derive from something else the fact that it is impossible for them to be other than they are. And this is in itself a most effective restraint; for whatever is

---

[139] Art. 1.
[140] *De vera religione* 31.
[141] Cf. John 14:28.
[142] *Metaphysics* 5:4 (1015b10).

restrained is generally said to be restrained in so far as it cannot do other than what it is disposed to do.

articulus 5: *Whether natural contingents are subject to the eternal law*[143]

It seems that natural contingents are not subject to the eternal law.

obiectio 1: For promulgation is essential to law, as stated above.[144] But a law cannot be promulgated except to rational creatures to whom it is possible for something to be announced. Therefore only rational creatures are subject to the eternal law, and therefore natural contingents are not.

obiectio 2: Moreover, 'Whatever obeys reason participates to some degree in reason', as is said at *Ethics* 1.[145] But the eternal law is supreme reason, as stated above.[146] Since, therefore, natural contingents do not participate in reason in any way, but are wholly non-rational, it seems that they are not subject to the eternal law.

obiectio 3: Moreover, the eternal law is entirely efficacious.[147] But in natural contingents defects occur. Therefore they are not subject to the eternal law.

sed contra: It is written (Proverbs 8:29): 'When He compassed the sea with its bounds, and set a law to the waters, that they should not pass their limits.'

responsio: We must speak otherwise of the law of man than of the eternal law which is the law of God. For the law of man does not extend itself to anything other than rational creatures subject to man. The reason for

---

[143] By 'natural contingents' here, St Thomas simply means 'non-rational creatures'. All things are subject to the eternal law. But we know that law in the ordinary sense is a rule of reason which needs to be promulgated to and received by rational creatures capable of understanding it (see IaIIae 90 *passim*). How, therefore, can non-rational creatures be subject to the eternal law? St Thomas's answer is that the eternal law is a higher-order law – a more encompassing law – which 'impresses an inward principle of action' on non-rational things: i.e. which imparts to non-rational things the capacity to act in the ways characteristic of them.

[144] IaIIae 90:4 (p. 82, above).

[145] *Ethics* 1:13 (1102b25).

[146] Art. 1.

[147] I.e. because the eternal law is identical with the Divine reason, it is infallible and indefectible. *Efficacissima* is perhaps not the most obvious choice of word; but St Thomas wants to express the idea that the eternal law can 'do' everything.

this is that [human] law directs the actions of those who are subject to the government of someone. (Hence, strictly speaking, no one imposes a law on his own actions.) But whatever is done regarding the use of non-rational things subject to man is done by the act of man himself moving those things; for such non-rational creatures do not move themselves, but are moved by others, as noted above.[148] And so man cannot impose laws on non-rational beings, however much they may be subject to him. But he can impose laws on rational beings subject to him, in so far as by his command or a pronouncement of any kind he imprints on their minds a certain rule which is a principle of action. And just as man, by such a pronouncement, impresses a kind of inward principle of action upon a man subject to him, so God imprints on the whole of nature the principles of its proper actions. And so, in this way, God is said to command the whole of nature, according to Psalm 148:6: 'He hath made a decree, and it shall not pass away.' And thus all movements and actions of the whole of nature are subject to the eternal law. Hence non-rational creatures are subject to the eternal law inasmuch as they are moved by Divine providence; but not, as rational creatures are, through an intellectual understanding of the Divine commandment.

ad 1: The impression of an inward active principle is to natural things what the promulgation of law is to men: because law, by being promulgated, imprints on man a directive principle of human action, as stated in the body of the article.

ad 2: Non-rational creatures neither participate in human reason, nor do they obey it, whereas they do participate in the Divine reason by obeying it, because the power of Divine reason extends over more things than the power of human reason does. And just as the members of the human body are moved by the command of reason and yet do not participate in reason, since they have no capacity of their own to apprehend reason, so too non-rational creatures are moved by God, without, however, being rational themselves.

ad 3: Although the defects which occur in natural things lie outside the order of particular causes, they nonetheless do not lie outside the order of universal causes, especially of the First Cause, which is God, Whose

---

[148] IaIIae 1:2.

providence nothing can elude, as stated in the First Part.[149] And since the eternal law is the rational pattern of the Divine providence, as stated above,[150] even the defects of natural things are therefore subject to the eternal law.[151]

articulus 6: *Whether all human affairs are subject to the eternal law*

It seems that not all human affairs are subject to the eternal law.

obiectio 1: For the Apostle says (Galatians 5:18): 'If ye be led by the Spirit, ye are not under the law.' But the righteous, who are the sons of God by adoption,[152] are led by the spirit of God, according to Romans 8:14: 'Whosoever are led by the spirit of God, they are the sons of God.' Therefore not all men are under the eternal law.

obiectio 2: Moreover, the Apostle says (Romans 8:7): 'The carnal mind is an enemy to God: for it is not subject to the law of God.' But there are many men in whom the carnal mind predominates. Therefore not all men are subject to the eternal law which is the law of God.

obiectio 3: Moreover, Augustine says that 'the eternal law is that by which the wicked deserve misery, the good, a life of blessedness'.[153] But those who are already blessed, and those who are already damned, are not in a state of deserving anything. Therefore they are not under the eternal law.

sed contra: Augustine says: 'Nothing is in any way removed from the sway of the laws made by the supreme Creator and Governor Who directs the peace of the universe.'[154]

---

[149] Ia 22:2.

[150] Art. 1.

[151] Cf. Ia 22:2 ad 2: 'Hence, corruption and defects in natural things are said to be contrary to some particular nature, yet they are in keeping with the plan of universal nature, inasmuch as a defect in one thing contributes to the good of another, or even to the universal good ... Since God, then, provides universally for all beings, it belongs to His providence to permit certain defects in particular effects, that the perfect good of the universe may not be hindered; for if all evil were prevented, much good would be absent from the universe. A lion would cease to live if there were no slaying of animals, and there would be no patience of martyrs if there were no tyrannical persecution.'

[152] Galatians 4:5; Ephesians 1:5; Romans 8:15; 23.

[153] *De libero arbitrio* 1:6.

[154] *De civitate Dei* 19:12.

responsio: There are two ways in which a thing is subject to the eternal law, as is shown by what has been said above.[155] In one way, in so far as it participates in the eternal law by way of knowledge. In another way, by acting and being acted upon [*per modum actionis et passionis*],[156] in so far as it participates in the eternal law by way of an inward motive principle; and in this second way, non-rational creatures are subject to the eternal law, as stated above.[157] But since, in addition to what it has in common with all creatures, the rational nature has some property peculiar to itself inasmuch as it is rational, it is therefore subject to the eternal law in both ways; for each rational creature has some knowledge of the eternal law, as stated above,[158] and each rational creature also has a natural inclination towards what is consonant with the eternal law; for 'we are adapted by nature to receive the virtues'.[159]

Both ways, however, are imperfect, and to a certain degree corrupted, in the wicked, because in them the natural inclination to virtue is depraved by vicious habits, and, moreover, the natural knowledge of good is darkened in them by the passions and habits of sin. But in the good both ways are found in more perfect form: because in them, over and above the natural knowledge of good, there is the added knowledge of faith and wisdom; and again, over and above the natural inclination to good, there is the added inward motive principle of grace and virtue.

So, then, the good are perfectly subject to the eternal law, as always acting according to it, whereas the wicked are subject to the eternal law, imperfectly as to their actions, indeed, since both their knowledge of good and their inclination to it are imperfect; but this deficiency in terms of how they act is made good by how they are acted upon [*suppletur ex parte passionis*]: that is, in so far as they suffer what the eternal law decrees concerning them, according as they fail to do what the eternal law requires. Hence Augustine says in the book *De libero arbitrio*: 'I esteem that the righteous act according to the eternal law';[160] and in the book

---

[155] Art. 5.
[156] *Passio* in this context means 'the capacity to be acted upon' – i.e. it refers to 'passivity' as distinct from 'activity'. Here and elsewhere in this *articulus* I have resorted to paraphrase simply because 'passion' would not be a helpful translation. With the single exception of the 'passion' of Christ, the idea of passion as meaning 'undergoing' or 'suffering' is extinct in modern English. But see n. 166, below.
[157] *Ibid*.
[158] Art. 2.
[159] *Ethics* 2:1 (1103a25).
[160] *De libero arbitrio* 1:15.

De catechizandis rudibus he says: 'Out of the just misery of the souls which forsook Him, God knew how to furnish the lower parts of His creation with most suitable laws.'[161]

ad 1: This saying of the Apostle can be understood in two ways. In one way, it can be taken to mean that someone may be under the law who, because he is not bound by it willingly, is subject to it as to a burden. Hence, a gloss on the same passage says that 'he is "under the law" who refrains from evil deeds through fear of the punishment threatened by the law, and not from love of virtue'.[162] But spiritual men are not 'under' the law in this way, because they fulfil the law willingly, through the charity which is poured into their hearts by the Holy Spirit. In another way, it can be taken to mean that the works of a man who is led by the Holy Spirit are the works of the Holy Spirit rather than his own. Hence, since the Holy Spirit is not under the law, just as the Son is not, as stated above,[163] it follows that such works, in so far as they are works of the Holy Spirit, are not under the law. And the Apostle bears witness to this when he says (2 Corinthians 3:17): 'Where the Spirit of the Lord is, there is liberty.'

ad 2: Considered in terms of how it acts, the 'carnal mind' cannot be subject to the law of God, since it inclines to actions contrary to the Divine law; but considered in terms of how it is acted upon [*ex parte passionis*], it is subject to the law of God since it deserves to suffer punishment according to the law of Divine justice. Nevertheless, in no man is the carnal mind so completely dominant that the whole good of his nature is corrupted by it: and so there remains in man the inclination to act in accordance with the eternal law. For it has been noted above that sin does not wholly destroy the good of nature.[164]

ad 3: The same cause both maintains something in its end and moves it towards that end. For example, gravity, which causes a heavy body to rest in a lower place, is also the cause by which it is moved to such a place. And so it must be said that just as it is according to the eternal law that some deserve blessedness and others misery, so is it by that same law that some are maintained in blessedness and others in misery. Accordingly both the blessed and the damned are under the eternal law.

---

[161] *De catechizandis rudibus* 18.
[162] Peter Lombard, *Collectanea*, on Galatians 5:18 (*PL* 192:158).
[163] Art. 4 ad 2.
[164] IaIIae 85:2.

(e) *Summa theologiae* IaIIae 94: The natural law

We come next to the natural law; and here there are six things to consider:

1. What the natural law is
2. What the precepts of the natural law are
3. Whether all virtuous acts belong to the natural law
4. Whether the natural law is the same for all men
5. Whether it is mutable
6. Whether it can be deleted from the mind of man

articulus 1: *Whether the natural law is a habit*

It seems that the natural law is a habit.

obiectio 1: For, as the Philosopher says,[165] 'there are three things in the soul: power, habit, and passion'.[166] But the natural law is not one of the soul's powers; nor is it a passion, as we may see by going through the passions one by one. Therefore the natural law is a habit.

obiectio 2: Moreover, Basil says that 'conscience' or *synderesis* 'is the law of our mind',[167] and this can only be understood as a reference to the natural law. But *synderesis* is a kind of habit, as was noted in the First Part.[168] Therefore the natural law is a habit.

obiectio 3: Moreover, the natural law abides in man always, as will be shown below.[169] But man's reason, to which law belongs, is not always engaged in thinking of the natural law. Therefore the natural law is not an act, but a habit.

sed contra: Augustine, in the book *De bono coniugali*, says that 'a habit is that by which something is done when needed'.[170] But the natural law is not of this kind, since it is in infants and in the damned who cannot act by it. Therefore the natural law is not a habit.

---

[165] *Ethics* 2:5 (1105b20).
[166] *Passio* here has the straightforward meaning of 'emotion' or 'feeling': cf. n. 156, above. For St Thomas's discussion of the meanings and ambiguities of *passio* see IaIIae 22–48.
[167] *In hexaemeron* 7 (*PG* 29:158); cf. Damascene, *De fide orthodoxa* 4:22 (PG 94:1200).
[168] Ia 79:12.
[169] Art. 6.
[170] *De bono coniugali* 21.

responsio: Something may be called a habit in two ways. In one way, properly and in its essence; and in this way the natural law is not a habit. For it has been stated above[171] that the natural law is something constituted by reason, just as a proposition is a kind of work of reason. But what someone does is not the same as that by which he does it; for someone makes a well-composed speech by the habit of grammar.[172] Since, then, a habit is that by which we act, a law cannot be a habit properly and in its essence. In another way, something which we hold by habit may be called a habit, just as that which we hold by faith may be called a Faith. And in this second way, since the precepts of the natural law sometimes come under active consideration by the reason, while sometimes they are in it only by habit, the natural law may be called a habit: just as, in speculative matters, the indemonstrable principles are not the habit itself by which we hold those principles, but are the principles which we hold by the habit.[173]

ad 1: The Philosopher is here intending to investigate the genus of virtue; and since it is clear that virtue is a guiding principle of action, he mentions only those things which are guiding principles of human actions: namely, powers, habits and passions. But there are other things in the soul besides these three: for example, certain acts, such as 'willing' in the person who wills; and 'things known' are in the person who knows; moreover its own natural properties are in the soul, such as immortality and other such things.

ad 2: *Synderesis* is called 'the law of our mind' because it is a habit containing the precepts of the natural law, which are the first principles of human acts.

ad 3: This argument proves that the natural law is held by habit; and this we concede.

As to the argument to the contrary, it must be said that a man is sometimes unable to make use of that which is in him by habit because of some impediment: for example, a man cannot make use of the habit of science by reason of his being asleep; and, similarly, a child cannot make use of

---

[171] IaIIae 90:1 ad 2 (p. 77, above).

[172] Cf. *Ethics* 2:5 (1105b5).

[173] I.e. St Thomas wishes to say that our disposition to observe the natural law is habitual, but that this disposition is not the natural law itself. It is only in a looser sense that we tend not to distinguish between something that we do habitually and the habit by which we do it.

the habit of reasoning from first principles by reason of his lack of years, or even of the natural law which is in him by habit.

articulus 2: Whether the natural law contains several precepts,
or only one

It seems that the natural law contains not several precepts, but only one.

obiectio 1: For law is a kind of precept, as noted above.[174] If therefore there were many precepts of the natural law, it would follow that there are also many natural laws.

obiectio 2: Moreover, the natural law is a concomitant of human nature. But human nature as a whole is one, and multiplex as to its parts. Therefore, either there is only one precept of the natural law, by reason of the unity of the whole, or there are many, according to the multiplicity of the parts, of human nature; in which case even things belonging to the concupiscible inclination[175] would belong to the natural law.

obiectio 3: Moreover, law is something belonging to reason, as stated above.[176] But reason in man is one only. Therefore there is only one precept of the natural law.

sed contra: The precepts of the natural law in man stand in relation to practical matters as the first principles do to matters of demonstration. But there are several indemonstrable first principles. Therefore there are also several precepts of the natural law.

responsio: As stated above, the precepts of the natural law are to the practical reason what the first principles of demonstrations are to the speculative reason, for both are self-evident principles. Now something is said to be self-evident in two ways: in one way, in itself, and, in another way, in relation to us. A proposition is said to be self-evident in itself if its predicate is contained in the idea of the subject;[177] although it may happen that someone who does not know the definition of the subject will not know that the proposition is self-evident in this sense. For example, the proposition, 'Man is a rational being', is self-evident in its very nature since anyone who says 'man', says 'a rational being'; yet to someone who does not know what

[174] IaIIae 92:2 (p. 99, above).
[175] See p. 7 n. 23, above.
[176] IaIIae 90:1 (p. 76, above).
[177] I.e. if it is what is nowadays called 'analytic'.

a man is, this proposition is not self-evident. Hence it is that, as Boethius says, certain axioms or propositions are generally self-evident to everyone;[178] and of this kind are those propositions whose terms are known to all men: for instance, that 'every whole is greater than its part', and, 'two things equal to the same thing are equal to each other'. But some propositions are self-evident only to the wise, who understand what the terms of the proposition signify. Thus to one who understands that an angel is not a body, it is self-evident that an angel is not confined to one particular place;[179] but this is not evident to the uninstructed, who cannot grasp it.

Now a certain order is to be found in those things which fall under the apprehension of mankind. For that which falls under apprehension first is 'being', the idea of which is implicit in all things apprehended. And so the first indemonstrable principle, based on the notion of 'being' and 'not-being', is that 'the same thing cannot be affirmed and denied at the same time'; and on this principle all other principles are based, as the Philosopher says at *Metaphysics* IV.[180] But as 'Being' is the first thing that falls under the apprehension absolutely, so 'good' is the first thing that falls specifically under the apprehension of the practical reason, which is directed to action, since every agent acts for the sake of an end which has the character of a good.[181] And so the first principle of practical reason, namely, 'good is that which all things seek', is based on the notion of good.[182] The first precept of law, therefore, is that 'good ought to be done and pursued, and evil avoided'. All other precepts of the natural law are based upon this, so that whatever the practical reason naturally apprehends as human goods [or evils] belong to the precepts of the natural law as things to be done or avoided.

Since, however, good has the character of an end and evil is its opposite, it follows that all those things to which man has a natural inclination are naturally apprehended by reason as being good, and consequently as things to be pursued, and their opposites as evil, and as objects to be avoided. The order of the precepts of the natural law is therefore according to the order of our natural inclinations. For in man there is, first, an

---

[178] *De hebdomadibus (PL* 64:1311).

[179] Cf. Ia 52.

[180] *Metaphysics* 4:3 (1005b29).

[181] I.e. just as we cannot apprehend anything at all without first having the idea that it 'is', so we cannot pursue any practical goal without first having the idea that the goal in question is good. The practical activity of making choices presupposes that we can know the difference between a good choice and a bad choice.

[182] *Ethics* 1:1 (1094a3).

inclination to a good according to the nature which he has in common with all substances: that is, inasmuch as every substance seeks the preservation of its own being according to its nature; and, according to this inclination, whatever is a means of preserving human life belongs to the natural law, and whatever impedes it is contrary to it. Second, there is in man an inclination to certain more specific ends which he has by nature in common with other animals; and, according to this inclination, 'those things which nature has taught to all animals'[183] are said to belong to the natural law, such as the union of male and female and the education of the young and similar things. Third, there is in man an inclination to a good specific to himself, belonging to his rational nature. Thus man has a natural inclination to know the truth concerning God and to live in society; and, accordingly, whatever pertains to this inclination belongs to the natural law: for instance, to shun ignorance, to avoid giving offence to those among whom one has to live, and other such things.

ad 1: All the precepts of the law of nature have the character of one natural law inasmuch as they can all be referred back to the one first precept [i.e. that good is to be done and evil avoided].

ad 2: All the inclinations of any parts whatsoever of human nature, for example, the concupiscible and irascible parts, in so far as they are ruled by reason, pertain to the natural law, and are reduced to the one first precept, as stated in the body of the article. Accordingly, the precepts of the natural law are many in themselves, but nonetheless share the same common root.

ad 3: Although reason is one in itself, it nonetheless directs all things relating to man. Accordingly, whatever can be ruled by reason is contained under the law of reason.

articulus 3: *Whether all acts of virtue are prescribed by the natural law*

It seems that not all acts of virtue are prescribed by the natural law.

obiectio 1: For, as stated above,[184]it is of the nature of law that it be directed to the common good. But some acts of virtue are directed to the private good of someone, as is clear especially in the case of acts of self-restraint

---

[183] *CICiv.*: *Digesta* I:I:I.   [184] IaIIae 90:2 (p. 78, above).

[which seem to benefit no one but oneself]. Therefore not all acts of virtue come under the natural law.

obiectio 2: Moreover, every sin is the opposite of some virtuous act. If therefore all acts of virtue belong to the natural law, it seems to follow that all sins are against nature; whereas this is in fact said only of certain specific sins.

obiectio 3: Moreover, those things which are according to nature are common to all men. But acts of virtue are not common to all men, for something that is virtuous in one man may be a vice in another. Therefore not all acts of virtue are prescribed by the natural law.

sed contra: Damascene says that 'the virtues are natural'.[185] Therefore virtuous acts also come under the natural law.

responsio: We can speak of virtuous acts in two ways: in one way, in so far as they are generically virtuous; in another way, in so far as they are acts of a certain specific kind.[186] If, then, we speak of acts of virtue considered simply as virtuous, all virtuous acts belong to the natural law. For it has been said[187] that everything to which a man is inclined according to his nature belongs to the natural law. Now each thing is naturally inclined to a mode of action that is suitable to it according to its form: for example, fire is inclined to give heat. Hence, since the rational soul is the proper form of man [i.e. since man is by nature a rational creature], there is in every man a natural inclination to act according to reason; and this is to act according to virtue.[188] So considered, therefore, all acts of virtue are prescribed by the natural law, since the reason of each man naturally tells him to act virtuously. But if we speak of virtuous acts considered specifically – considered, that is, in their proper species – not all virtuous acts are prescribed by the natural law, for many things are done virtuously which we are not in a primary sense inclined to do by nature but which, through the inquiry of reason, have been found by men to be advantageous to them in living well.[189]

---

[185] *De fide orthodoxa* 3:14 (*PG* 94:1045).
[186] Cf. *Ethics* 2:4 (1105b5).
[187] Art. 2.
[188] *Ethics* 1:7 (1098a16).
[189] An illustration used earlier can be pressed into service again. Reason has discovered that it is advantageous, and in that sense 'virtuous', for everyone to drive on the same side of the road. It is not specifically prescribed by the natural law that we should drive on the left-hand side or the right; but that we should do one or the other is required by the general principle that we should do good and avoid evil.

ad 1: Self-restraint comes into play in relation to the natural appetites for food, drink and sexual intercourse, which are indeed directed to the natural common good, just as other matters of law are directed to the moral common good.

ad 2: By the 'nature' of man we may mean either that which is peculiar to man; and, according to this sense, all sins, as being against reason, are also against nature, as Damascene makes clear:[190] or we may mean that nature which is common to man and other animals; and in this sense certain specific sins are said to be against nature: for example, sexual intercourse between men, which runs counter to the intercourse of male and female which is common to all animals, is especially said to be a vice against nature.

ad 3: This argument is valid with respect to acts considered in themselves. But it is because of the differing conditions of men [and not because of the nature of the acts themselves] that certain acts are virtuous for some, as being appropriate and suitable to them, while vicious for others, as being inappropriate to them.[191]

articulus 4: *Whether the natural law is the same in all men*

It seems that the natural law is not the same in all men.

obiectio 1: For it is stated in the *Decretum* that 'the natural law is that which is contained in the law and the Gospel'.[192] But this is not common to all men because, as is said at Romans 10:16, 'all do not obey the gospel'. Therefore the natural law is not the same in all men.

obiectio 2: Moreover, 'Those things which are according to the law are called just', as is said at *Ethics* V. But it is said in the same book that nothing is so just for all as not to vary for some.[193] Therefore also the natural law is not the same in all men.

obiectio 3: Moreover, as stated above,[194] everything to which a man is inclined according to his nature belongs to the law of nature. But different men are naturally inclined to different things: some to the appetite for

---

[190] *De fide orthodoxa* 2:4; 30 and 4:20 (*PG* 94:876; 976 and 1196).
[191] E.g. marriage is virtuous for laymen but not for religious: see p. 245, below.
[192] Dist. 1, Prologue (*CIC* 1:1).
[193] *Ethics* 5:1 (1129b12); 5:7 (1134b32).
[194] Art. 2 and 3.

pleasure, others to the desire for honours, and others to other things. Therefore there is not one natural law for all.

sed contra: Isidore says: 'Natural right [*ius naturale*] is common to all nations.'[195]

responsio: As stated above,[196] those things to which a man is inclined by nature belong to the natural law, and among these things it is a property of man to be inclined to act according to reason. Now reason proceeds from general principles to particular conclusions, as is made clear at *Physics* I.[197] But speculative reasoning differs from practical reasoning in the way that it does this. For speculative reasoning is concerned chiefly with necessary things which cannot be otherwise than they are, and so the truth is found just as surely in its particular conclusions as it is in its general principles; whereas practical reasoning is concerned with contingent things belonging to human actions, and so although there is a certain necessity in its general principles, the more we descend to particulars the more frequently do we find exceptions.

So, then: in speculative matters truth is the same in all men, both as to principles and as to conclusions; although the truth is not known to all as regards the conclusions, but only as regards the principles which are called common conceptions.[198] In matters of action, however, truth or practical rightness is not the same for all as to matters of detail, but only as to general principles; and where there is the same rightness in matters of detail, it is not equally known to all.

It is clear, then, that, as regards the general principles of reason, whether speculative or practical, truth or rightness is the same for all men, and is equally known to all. As to the particular conclusions of speculative reason, the truth is the same for all men, but is not equally known to all: for instance, it is true for all that the three angles of a triangle are equal to two right angles, although this is not known to all. But as to the particular conclusions of practical reason, truth or rightness is not the same for all, nor, where it is the same, is it equally known to all. For it is right and true for all to act according to reason, and from this general principle it follows as a particular conclusion that [for instance] goods left in the care of

---

[195] *Etymologiae* 5:4 (*PL* 82:199). *Ius* (right) and *lex* (law) are not, strictly speaking, synonyms; but for our present purposes they may be treated as if they were. See p. 158 n. 2, below.
[196] Art. 2 and 3.
[197] *Physics* 1:1 (184a16).
[198] Cf. Boethius, *De hebdomadibus* (*PL* 64:1311).

another should be restored to their owner. Now this is true in the majority of cases, but it can happen in a particular case that it would be harmful, and consequently unreasonable, to restore such goods: for instance, if someone claimed them in order to fight against his country.[199] And the more we descend to matters of detail, the more the general principle will be found to admit of exceptions: for instance, if one were to say that goods held on behalf of another should be restored on such and such a condition, or in such and such a way; because the greater the number of particular conditions added, the greater the number of ways in which the principle may fail to indicate whether it is right or not right to restore the goods in question.

So, then: we must say that the law of nature is the same for all with respect to its general principles, in terms of both rightness and knowledge; but that with respect to certain particulars which are as it were the conclusions of those general principles, it is the same for all in the majority of cases, in terms of both rightness and knowledge, but in some cases may fail: as to rightness, by reason of certain specific obstacles (just as natures subject to generation and corruption fail in some few cases because of some obstacle), and as to knowledge, because in some men the reason is perverted by passion, or evil custom, or a wicked disposition of nature: for example, robbery, although expressly against the natural law, was at one time not considered wrong among the Germans, as Julius Caesar relates in the book *De bello Gallico*.[200]

ad 1: The statement is not to be understood as meaning that everything contained in the law and the Gospel belongs to the natural law, since the law and the Gospel contain many things which go beyond nature; but that everything belonging to the natural law is fully contained in the law and the Gospel. Hence Gratian, when he had said that 'the natural law is that which is contained in the law and the Gospel', immediately added by way of explanation, 'by which everyone is commanded to do to others what he would have done to himself, and forbidden to do to others what he would not have done to himself'.

ad 2: The Philosopher's [second] statement is to be understood as applying to things which are naturally just not as general principles, but as conclusions drawn from them, having rightness in the majority of cases, but failing in some.

---

[199] Cf. Plato, *Republic* 331C.   [200] *De bello Gallico* 6:23.

ad 3: As, in man, reason rules and commands the other powers, so all the natural inclinations which belong to those other powers must be directed according to reason. Hence it is commonly held among all men that all the inclinations of men should be directed according to reason.

articulus 5: *Whether the natural law can be changed*

It seems that the natural law can be changed.

obiectio 1: For a gloss on Ecclesiasticus 17:9, 'He gave them instructions, and the law of life', says: 'He wished the law of the letter to be written, in order to correct the law of nature.'[201] But that which is corrected is changed. Therefore the natural law can be changed.

obiectio 2: Moreover, the slaying of the innocent, adultery, and theft are against the natural law. But we find these prohibitions changed by God: for example, when God commanded Abraham to slay his innocent son, as recorded at Genesis 22:2; and when he commanded the Jews to borrow and steal the vessels of the Egyptians (Exodus 12:35); and when He commanded Hosea to take to himself 'a wife of fornication', as recorded at Hosea 1:2. Therefore the natural law can be changed.

obiectio 3: Moreover, Isidore says that 'the possession of all things in common, and one liberty for all men, are matters of natural law.'[202] But we see that these things are changed by human laws. Therefore it seems that the natural law can be changed.

sed contra: It is said in the *Decretum*: 'The natural law begins with the origin of rational creatures; nor does it vary according to time, but remains immutable.'[203]

responsio: The natural law can be understood to be changed in two ways. In one way, by addition; and in this sense nothing prohibits the natural law from being changed, for many things advantageous to human life have been added over and above the natural law, both by the Divine law and by human laws. In another way, a change in the natural law can be understood to occur by subtraction, so that what was formerly according to the natural law ceases to be a part of the natural law. In this sense, the natural law is

[201] Rhabanus Maurus, *Commentariorum in Ecclesiasticum* 17:9 (*PL* 109:876).
[202] *Etymologiae* 5:4 (*PL* 82:199).
[203] Dist. 5, Prologue (*CIC* 1:7).

entirely immutable as to its first principles; but in its secondary principles –
which, as we have said,[204] are certain particular conclusions derived from
the first principles – although the natural law is not changed in most cases,
where what it prescribes is right, it may nonetheless be changed in some
particular instance and in a few cases because of some special reasons
hindering the observance of such precepts, as stated above.[205]

ad 1: The written law is said to be given for the 'correction' of the natural
law either because something that was lacking in the natural law is supplied
by the written law, or because the law of nature was corrupted in the hearts
of some men with respect to certain things, so that they esteemed those
things good which are naturally evil, and such corruption stood in need
of correction.

ad 2: All men, guilty and innocent alike, die the death of nature, and
this death of nature is inflicted by the Divine power by reason of original
sin, according to 1 Samuel 2:6: 'The Lord killeth and maketh alive.' And
so without any injustice the command of God can inflict death upon
any man whatsoever, guilty or innocent. Similarly, adultery is intercourse
with another man's wife, allotted to him by the divinely given law of God.
Hence to approach any woman by Divine command is neither adultery
nor fornication. The same argument applies to theft, which is the taking
of another's property. For whatever is taken by the command of God,
to Whom all things belong, is not taken against the will of its Owner,
which is what theft is.[206] Nor is it only in human affairs that whatever is
commanded by God is right; but in natural things also whatever is done
by God is in some way natural, as stated in the First Part.[207]

ad 3: Something is said to be naturally right in two ways. In one way,
because there is a natural inclination to do it: for example, not to injure
another; in another way, because there is not a natural inclination not to
do it. For example, we might say that it is a matter of natural right for
man to be naked, because nature does not give him clothes; but he devises
them by art. In this sense, 'the possession of all things in common and one
liberty for all men' are said to be consistent with natural right: because,
that is, the distinction of possessions and slavery were not brought in by

[204] Art. 4.
[205] *Ibid*.
[206] See pp. 209ff, below.
[207] Ia 105:6 ad 1.

nature, but by human reason for the advantage of human life. And so again the law of nature was not changed in this respect, except by addition.

articulus 6: *Whether the law of nature can be abolished from the heart of man*

It seems that the law of nature can be abolished from the heart of man.

obiectio 1: For a gloss on Romans 2:14, 'When the Gentiles who have not the law', etc. says that 'the law of righteousness, which guilt had blotted out, is inscribed upon the inner man when he is restored by grace'.[208] But the law of righteousness is the law of nature. Therefore the law of nature can be blotted out.

obiectio 2: Moreover, the law of grace is more efficacious than the law of nature. But the law of grace is blotted out by guilt. So much more, therefore, can the law of nature be blotted out.

obiectio 3: Moreover, we regard everything established by [positive] law as being just [in the legal sense].[209] But many things are established by men which are contrary to the law of nature. Therefore [inasmuch as legal justice can be at variance with natural justice,] the law of nature can be abolished from the hearts of men.

sed contra: Augustine says: 'Thy law is written into the hearts of men, which iniquity itself does not blot out.'[210] But the law written into the hearts of men is the natural law. Therefore the natural law cannot be blotted out.

responsio: As stated above,[211] there belong to the natural law, first, certain most general precepts which are known to all; and, second, certain secondary and more particular precepts which are like conclusions derived from first principles. As to those general principles, the natural law can in no way be wholly blotted out from the hearts of men; although it is blotted out with respect to a particular action in so far as the reason is hindered from applying the general principle to a specific act by lust or some other passion, as stated above.[212] But as to the other, secondary, precepts,

---

[208] Peter Lombard, *Collectanea* (*PL* 191:1345).
[209] *Ethics* 5:1 (1129b12).
[210] *Confessiones* 2:4.
[211] Art. 4 and 5.
[212] IaIIae 77:2.

the natural law can be blotted out from the hearts of men: either by evil persuasions, just as in speculative matters errors occur in respect of necessary conclusions; or by vicious customs and corrupt habits, as among certain people robbery, and even vices against nature, as the Apostle says at Romans 1:24, are not considered sinful.

ad 1: Guilt blots out the law of nature in particular cases, but not universally, except perhaps in regard to the secondary precepts of the natural law, in the manner stated in the body of the article.

ad 2: Although grace is more efficacious than nature, nature is nonetheless more a part of the essence of man, and is therefore more inclined to endure.

ad 3: This argument is valid with respect to the secondary precepts of the natural law, against which some legislators have framed certain statutes which are unjust.

(f) *Summa theologiae* IaIIae 95: Human law considered in itself

There are here four things to consider:

1. The usefulness of human law
2. Its origin
3. Its quality
4. Its division

articulus 1: *Whether it was useful for certain laws to be established by men*

It seems that it was not useful for certain laws to be established by men.

obiectio 1: For the intention of every law is that men should be made good by it, as stated above.[213] But men are induced to be good willingly, by admonitions, not through coercion by laws. Therefore it was not necessary to establish laws.

obiectio 2: Moreover, as the Philosopher says, 'men have recourse to a judge as to a kind of animate justice'.[214] But animate justice is better than the

---

[213] IaIIae 92:1 (p. 96, above).   [214] *Ethics* 5:4 (1132a22).

inanimate kind which is contained in the laws. Therefore it would have been better to entrust the execution of justice to the decision of judges rather than to devise laws in addition.

obiectio 3: Moreover, every law is directive of human actions, as is shown by what has been said above.[215] But since human actions consist in particular things, which are infinite in number, matters having to do with the direction of human actions can only be taken into consideration sufficiently by a wise man looking into each of them individually. Therefore it would have been better for human acts to be directed by the judgment of wise men than by the establishing of laws. Therefore it was not necessary to establish human laws.

sed contra: Isidore says: 'Laws were made that human audacity might be held in check by the fear of them, that innocence might be protected in the midst of disorderly men, and that the dread of punishment might restrain the wicked from doing harm.'[216] But these things are very much necessary to the human race. Therefore it was necessary that human laws should be made.

responsio: There is present in mankind a kind of natural aptitude for virtue, as is shown by what has been said above;[217] but some kind of discipline is necessary if that virtue is to reach perfection in a man. In the same way, we see that although man is helped to secure his needs – food and clothing, for example – a degree of effort is necessary also. He has the beginnings of what he needs from nature: that is, reason and hands; but his needs are not fully met by nature, as they are in other animals, to whom nature has given enough in the way of covering and food.[218] Now it is not easy to see how a man might be self-sufficient with respect to this discipline, since the perfection of virtue consists precisely in withdrawing a man from undue pleasures, to which men are especially prone, and especially the young, in whom discipline is more effective. And so men need to receive from another the discipline by which they arrive at virtue.

Now for those young people who are inclined to acts of virtue by a good natural disposition, or by custom, or rather by Divine gift, paternal discipline, which is administered through admonitions, suffices. But because

---

[215] IaIIae 90:1 and 2 (pp. 76ff, above).
[216] *Etymologiae* 5:20 (*PL* 82:202).
[217] IaIIae 63:1; 94:3 (p. 118, above).
[218] Cf. *De regimine principum* 1:1 (p. 6, above).

some are found who are headstrong and prone to vice, and who cannot easily be moved by words, it was necessary for these to be restrained from evil by force or fear, so that they might at any rate desist from evildoing and leave others in peace, and that they themselves, by having habits formed in them in this way, might be brought to do willingly what formerly they did from fear, and so be made into virtuous men. And this kind of discipline, which compels through fear of punishment, is the discipline of the laws.

Hence it was necessary for the sake of peace and virtue for laws to be established: for, as the Philosopher says at *Politics* 1,[219] 'just as man is the best of animals when perfected in virtue, so is he the worst when separated from law and justice'. For man has the weapons of reason, which other animals do not have, for gratifying lusts and brutalities.[220]

ad 1: Men who are well disposed already are better led by admonition than coercion to be willingly virtuous; but men who are ill disposed are not led to virtue except by compulsion.

ad 2: As the Philosopher says at *Rhetoric* 1, 'it is better that all things be regulated by law than left to the decision of judges',[221] and this is so for three reasons. First, because it is easier to find a few wise men who are capable of devising right laws than the many who would be needed to judge each individual case rightly. Second, because those who establish laws devote much time to considering what law to make, whereas judgment on each single case has to be given as soon as the case arises; but it is easier for a man to see what is right by taking many instances into consideration than by considering one case only. Third, because legislators judge in general terms and with the future in mind, whereas men who sit in judgment do so in relation to things present, with respect to which they may be affected by love or hatred or greed of some kind, and so their judgment may be distorted.

Since, then, the 'animate justice' of the judge is not found in many men, and because it can be distorted, it was therefore necessary, whenever

---

[219] *Politics* 1:1 (1253a31).

[220] The Leonine text here has *ad expellendas concupiscentias et saevitias*, which requires the translation 'for expelling lusts and brutalities'; but in view of Aristotle's *Politics*, which St Thomas is clearly paraphrasing (see the previous note), the text surely ought to be read as though the verb were *expleo* rather than *expello*. *Expellendas* is an understandable enough copyist's error for *explendas*. *Expellendas* would make sense, though, i.e.: 'man has the weapons of reason, which other animals do not have, and so is uniquely equipped to expel lusts and brutalities by devising and living by laws'.

[221] *Rhetoric* 1:1 (1354a31).

possible, for the law to determine what the judgment should be, and for very few matters to be entrusted to the decision of men.

ad 3: Certain matters of fact which cannot be determined by the law – for example, whether something has actually been done or not, and other things of this kind – 'must of necessity be committed to judges', as the Philosopher says in the same place.[222]

articulus 2: *Whether every human law is derived from the natural law*

It seems that not every human law is derived from the natural law.

obiectio 1: For the Philosopher says in the *Ethics* that 'the legally just is that which originally was a matter of indifference'.[223] But those things which arise from the natural law are not matters of indifference. Therefore the statutes of human laws are not all derived from the natural law.

obiectio 2: Moreover, positive right is to be contrasted with natural right, as is made clear by Isidore[224] and the Philosopher.[225] But those things which are derived as conclusions from the general principles of the natural law belong to the natural law, as stated above.[226] Therefore those things which belong to human law are not derived from the natural law.

obiectio 3: Moreover, the law of nature is the same for all; for the Philosopher says at *Ethics* v that 'the naturally just is that which has the same force everywhere'.[227] If therefore human laws were derived from the natural law, it would follow that they too are the same for all, which is clearly not so.

obiectio 4: Moreover, it is possible to assign some reason for things derived from the natural law. But, as the Jurist says, 'it is not possible to give a reason for every law established by the mighty'.[228] Therefore not all human laws are derived from the natural law.

---

[222] *Rhetoric* 1:1 (1354b13).

[223] *Ethics* 5:7 (1134b20): 'originally' in the sense of 'before the law made any pronouncement on the subject'. The idea is that 'legal' justice, as distinct from natural justice, has to do with things which are neither right nor wrong in themselves, but merely enacted by the law as matters of convenience and so made 'right' and 'wrong' in a purely conventional sense. See p. 61 n. 17 and p. 119 n. 189, above. The 'wrong' side of the road is wrong only because the law says so. Natural law, by contrast, has to do with what is intrinsically right and wrong.

[224] *Etymologiae* 5:4 (*PL* 82:199).

[225] *Ethics* 5:7 (1134b18).

[226] IaIIae 94:4 (p. 120, above).

[227] *Ethics* 5:7 (1134b19).

[228] *CICiv.: Digesta* 1:3:20.

sed contra: Cicero says in his *Rhetoric* that 'the principles which proceeded from nature and those which had been approved by custom, were
sanctioned by fear and reverence for the laws'.[229]

responsio: As Augustine says,[230] 'that which is not just seems to be no law
at all.' Hence a command has the force of law in so far as it is just. Now
in human affairs a thing is said to be just in so far as it is right according
to the rule of reason. But the first rule of reason is the law of nature, as
is shown by what has been said above.[231] Hence every human law has the
nature of law in so far as it is derived from the law of nature. But if it is
in any respect at odds with the law of nature, it will then no longer be
law, but a corruption of law.

It must be noted, however, that something may be derived from the
natural law in two ways: in one way, as a general conclusion derived from
its principles; in another way, as a specific application of that which is
expressed in general terms. The first way is similar to that by which, in
the sciences, demonstrated conclusions are derived from first principles;
while the second way is like that by which, in the arts, general ideas are
made particular as to details: for example, the craftsman needs to turn the
general idea of a house into the shape of this or that house. Some things
are therefore derived from the principles of the natural law as general
conclusions: for example, that 'one ought not to kill' may be derived as
a conclusion from the principle that 'one ought not to harm anyone';
whereas some are derived from it as specific applications: for example,
the law of nature has it that he who does evil should be punished; but that
he should be punished with this or that penalty is a specific application of
the law of nature. Both modes of derivation, then, are found in the human
law. Those things which are derived in the first way are not contained
in human law simply as belonging to it alone; rather, they have some of
their force from the law of nature. But those things which are derived in
the second way have their force from human law alone.

ad 1: The Philosopher is here speaking of those enactments of positive
law which are by way of determination or specific application of the
general precepts of the natural law.

---

[229] *De inventione* 2:53.
[230] *De libero arbitrio* 1:5.
[231] IaIIae 91:2 ad 2 (p. 86, above).

ad 2: This argument is valid with respect to those things which are derived from the natural law as general conclusions.

ad 3: The general principles of the natural law cannot be applied to all men in the same way because of the great variety of human circumstances; and hence arises the diversity of positive laws among various people.

ad 4: This statement of the Jurist is to be understood as referring to the decisions of 'the mighty' in arriving at specific applications of the natural law; which applications then form the foundations [i.e. the positive laws] upon which the judgment of men of expertise and practical wisdom is based: in so far, that is, as they see at once what is the more suitable decision to reach in a particular case. Hence the Philosopher says in the *Ethics* that in such matters 'we ought to attend to the undemonstrated sayings and opinions of experienced and older people or of people of practical wisdom not less than to demonstrations'.[232]

articulus 3: *Whether Isidore's description of the quality of positive law is appropriate*[233]

It seems that Isidore's description of the quality of positive law is not appropriate when he says at *Etymologies* V: 'Law will be honest, just, possible, according to nature, according to the custom of the country, suitable to place and time, necessary, useful, and clearly expressed, lest it contain some provision harmful by its obscurity; composed for no private advantage, but for the common benefit of the citizens.'[234]

obiectio 1: For previously, in Chapter II, he had expressed the quality of law in three conditions, saying: 'law is anything founded on reason, provided that it is in keeping with religion, conducive to discipline, and productive of welfare'.[235] Therefore it was superfluous subsequently to add further conditions to these.

---

[232] *Ethics* 6:11 (1143b11); i.e. the natural law needs to be applied to particular circumstances by legislators and judges who have wisdom and experience. The point here, in answer to *obiectio* 4, is that it may not be easy to see how particular positive laws are derived from the natural law, but they must nonetheless be so derived.

[233] It should be noted that here and in the next article St Thomas is more concerned with defending the authority of Isidore than with elucidating the character of law.

[234] *Etymologiae* 5:21 (*PL* 82:203).

[235] *Etymologiae* 5:3 (*PL* 82:199). The reference given in the text is incorrect.

obiectio 2: Moreover, justice is a part of honesty, as Cicero says at *De officiis* 1.²³⁶ Therefore, having said 'honest', it was superfluous to add 'just'.

obiectio 3: Moreover, written law is something distinct from custom, according to Isidore himself.²³⁷ Therefore it should not be stated as part of the definition of law that it is 'according to the custom of the country'.

obiectio 4: Moreover, something is said to be 'necessary' in two ways. First, it may be necessary in an absolute sense, that is, because it cannot be otherwise than it is; but that which is necessary in this way is not subject to human judgment, and so necessity of this kind does not arise in relation to human law. But, second, something may be necessary as a means to an end, and this 'necessity' is the same as 'usefulness'. Therefore it is superfluous to say both 'necessary' and 'useful'.

sed contra: There is the authority of Isidore himself, as cited in *obiectio 1*.²³⁸

responsio: In every case where something exists for the sake of an end, its form must be determined according to what is consistent with that end: for example, the form of a saw is of a kind suitable for cutting, as is made clear in the *Physics*.²³⁹ Again, the form of everything that is ruled²⁴⁰ and measured must be consistent with what rules and measures it. Now human law must answer to both these conditions, since it is both something directed to an end, and it is a kind of rule or measure ruled or measured in turn by a higher measure. And this higher measure is twofold, namely, the Divine law and the law of nature, as is shown by what has been said above.²⁴¹

Now the end of human law is to be useful to man, as the Jurist says.²⁴² And so, in describing the nature of law in his first statement, Isidore lays down three conditions, namely: that it be in keeping with religion,

---

²³⁶ *De officiis* 1:7.

²³⁷ *Etymologiae* 2:10; 5:3 (*PL* 82:131 and 199).

²³⁸ I.e. it is *prima facie* unlikely that Isidore will have made a later statement inconsistent with his earlier one.

²³⁹ *Physics* 2:9 (200a10).

²⁴⁰ Reading *regulata* for *recta*.

²⁴¹ Art. 2; IaIIae 93:3 (p. 105, above).

²⁴² *CICiv.*: *Digesta* 1:3:25.

inasmuch as it is consistent with the Divine law; that it be conducive to discipline, inasmuch as it is consistent with the law of nature; and that it be productive of welfare, inasmuch as it is consistent with the advantage of mankind. But all the conditions mentioned by him in the second statement are reducible to these three. For he speaks of law as being 'honest'; but it will be so only insofar as it is 'in keeping with religion'. And when he goes on to say that it should be 'just, possible, according to nature, according to the customs of the country, suitable to place and time', all this is reducible to 'conducive to discipline'. For the character of human discipline is determined, first, by what the order of reason requires; and this is what he means by 'just'. Second, it is determined by what it is feasible for someone to do, because discipline must be adapted to each individual according to what is 'possible' for him, having regard also to what is possible 'according to nature' (for the same burdens should be not laid on children as on grown men); and it must also be according to the human condition, for man cannot live alone in society, without taking others into account. Third, it must be 'suitable to place and time' in that it should be adapted to particular circumstances. The remaining words, 'necessary, useful', etc., mean the same as that the law should be 'productive of welfare': so that 'necessary' refers to the removal of evils; 'useful' to the attainment of good; 'clearly expressed', to the need to prevent any harm arising from [ambiguities in] the law itself. And since, as stated above, law is directed to the common good, he shows this in the final part of his description.

By this the replies to the *obiectiones* are shown.

articulus 4: *Whether Isidore's division of human laws is appropriate* [243]

It seems that Isidore has made a division of human laws, or of human right, which is inappropriate.[244]

---

[243] The reference is a general one, to Isidore's classification of law at *Etymologiae* 5:4–9 (*PL* 82:199f). For the various technical matters touched on in this article see B. Nicholas, *An Introduction to Roman Law* (Oxford, 1992); A. Borkowski, *A Textbook on Roman Law* (London, 1997); D. G. Cracknell, *Roman Law* (London, 1964); W. W. Buckland (rev. ed. P. Stein), *A Text-Book of Roman Law* (Cambridge, 1975). See also *CICiv.: Institutiones* 1:1.

[244] St Thomas's main point in this rather laborious and unconvincing article – that human laws, though formally the same, can be subdivided according to (a) function and (b) the form of government with which they are associated – hardly seems worth the trouble he takes over it. But, once again, it should be remembered that his chief purpose is to defend the authority of Isidore rather than to clarify the nature of human law.

obiectio 1: For under this law he includes the *ius gentium*, so called, as he says, because nearly all nations [*gentes*] use it.[245] But, as he himself says, 'natural law is that which is common to all nations'.[246] Therefore the *ius gentium* is not contained under positive human law, but under natural law. [247]

obiectio 2: Moreover, laws which have the same force seem to differ not formally but only materially.[248] But 'laws, acts of the plebeian assembly, senatorial decrees', and other things of this kind which he mentions[249] all have the same force. It seems, therefore, that they do not differ except materially. But for practical purposes no attention is paid to this kind of distinction, since it can extend into infinity.[250] Therefore this division of human laws is not appropriate.

obiectio 3: Moreover, just as, in the State, there are princes, priests and soldiers, so are there also other offices filled by men. Therefore it seems that, as his description includes a 'military law', and a 'public law' which applies to priests and magistrates,[251] so also it should include other laws pertaining to other offices of the state.

obiectio 4: Moreover, it is not necessary to take notice of those things which arise by accident merely. But it is accidental to [i.e. it is not 'of the essence of'] law that it be devised by this man or that. It is therefore not appropriate to divide laws according to the names of lawgivers: that is, so that one is called the 'Cornelian' law, another the 'Falcidian' law, and so on.[252]

---

[245] *Etymologiae* 5:6 (*PL* 82:200).

[246] *Etymologiae* 5:4 (*PL* 82:199).

[247] The *ius gentium* is not, in fact, identical to the law of nature, but consists of general principles derived from the law of nature and apparently recognised by all peoples, whereas the civil law (*ius civile*) consists of the specific rules derived from such general principles: see *responsio*. According to the *Institutes* of Justinian, the *ius gentium* is, for instance, 'the source of almost all contracts, such as sale, hire, partnership, deposit, loans for consumption, and very many others' (*CICiv.: Institutiones* 1:2:2; and see *responsio*, below): i.e. is the source of those practices which experience shows to be universal to all mankind. *Ius gentium*, although literally the 'right of nations' or 'law of nations', is perhaps best left untranslated, inasmuch as 'law of nations' inevitably suggests to the modern reader some kind of 'international' law. See also IIaIIae 57:3 (p. 163, below) and n. 2 on p. 158, below.

[248] I.e. they are different laws, but not different kinds of law: they have the same 'formal' cause but different 'material' causes. See n. 47 on p. 73, above.

[249] *Etymologiae* 5:9 (*PL* 82:200).

[250] I.e. if we were to treat each single law as if it were a separate kind of law, the classification of law would never come to an end.

[251] *Etymologiae* 5:7; 8 (*PL* 82:200).

[252] *Etymologiae* 5:15 (*PL* 82: 201).

sed contra: The authority of Isidore is sufficient.[253]

responsio: Anything whatsoever can, of itself, be divided [i.e. can be classified] according to something contained in the idea of that thing: for example, 'soul' [*anima*], which is either rational or non-rational, is contained in the idea of 'animal', and therefore 'animal' is properly and of itself divided according to 'rational' or 'non-rational', but not according to 'white' or 'black', which are wholly outside the idea of 'animal'. Now in the idea of human law there are many things according to each of which human law can of itself be properly divided. For, in the first place, part of the idea of human law is that it is derived from the law of nature, as is shown by what has been said above.[254] Accordingly, positive law is divided into the *ius gentium* and 'civil law', according to the two ways in which something may be derived from the law of nature, as stated above.[255] For to the *ius gentium* belong those things which are derived from the law of nature as conclusions from principles – for example, just buyings and sellings and other such things – without which men cannot live together. This kind of law belongs to the law of nature, since, as is proved at *Politics* I, man is by nature a social animal.[256] But those things which are derived from the law of nature as specific applications belong to the civil law, according as each State decides on what suits it best.

Second, part of the idea of human law is that it is directed to the common good of the State. Hence, human law can be divided according to the different kinds of men who work in specific ways to secure the common good: for example, priests, by praying to God for the people; princes, by governing the people; and soldiers, by fighting for the safety of the people. And so certain specific kinds of law are appropriate to these men.

Third, part of the idea of human law is that it is instituted by the governor of the civic community, as shown above.[257] Accordingly, human law can be divided on the basis of the various forms of government. Of these, according to the Philosopher at *Politics* III,[258] one is 'monarchy',

---

[253] St Thomas's usual reason for defending an authority is that he has perceived an apparent discrepancy between it and another or (as in the previous article) an apparent inconsistency within it. But his meaning here seems to be that although the authority of Isidore raises points for discussion, it is not actually at odds with any other authority.

[254] Art. 2.

[255] *Ibid.*; and see n. 247, above.

[256] *Politics* 1:1 (1253a2); and see p. 6 n. 17, above.

[257] IaIIae 90:3 (p. 80, above).

[258] *Politics* 3:5 (1279a26).

that is, when the State is governed by one man; and the kind of law corresponding to this form of government are royal ordinances. Another form of government is 'aristocracy', that is, government by the best men, or men of highest rank; and here the corresponding kind of law is that consisting of authoritative legal opinions and senatorial decrees. Another form of government is 'oligarchy', that is, government by the wealthy and powerful few; and corresponding to this we have the kind of law called 'praetorian' law, which is also called 'honorary'.[259] Yet another form of government is that of the people, which is called 'democracy', and here we have acts of the plebeian assembly. There is also tyranny, which is entirely corrupt, and which therefore has no kind of law corresponding to it. Again, there is a form of government which is a mixture of the other types, and this is the best; and in this case law is made when 'those of high birth sanction something in conjunction with the commons', as Isidore says.[260]

Fourth, it belongs to the idea of human law to be directive of human actions. Accordingly, corresponding to the various matters of which the law treats, there are various laws which are sometimes named after their authors: for example, the 'Lex Julia' concerning adultery,[261] the 'Lex Cornelia'[262] concerning assassins; and there are others differentiated not by their authors, but by the things to which they relate.[263]

ad 1: The *ius gentium* is indeed natural to man in a sense, in so far as he is rational, because it is derived from the natural law in the manner of a conclusion not greatly remote from its first principles, which is why men agree to it so readily. Nevertheless it is distinct from the natural law, and especially so from the natural law which is 'common to all animals'.[264]

---

[259] I.e. the *ius praetorium*, the law consisting of the edicts of the Praetors. Such laws are called 'honorary' 'because those who hold honours in the State have given them their sanction': *CICiv.: Institutiones* 1:2. It is not obvious why the *ius praetorium* should be peculiarly associated with oligarchy, though. See the next note.

[260] *Etymologiae* 5:10 (*PL* 82:200); cf. 2:10 (*PL* 82:130). In his gloss to this paragraph, Fr Gilby remarks that 'The attribution of the various types of law to various types of government is ideological, and need not be pressed historically' (BE 28:115). By 'ideological' he presumably means 'unwarranted but convenient to St Thomas's argument'.

[261] *CICiv.: Digesta* 48:5.

[262] *CICiv.: Digesta* 48:8.

[263] The point, presumably, is that it does not matter what a law is called provided that it is 'directive of human actions'.

[264] Cf. Justinian, *CICiv.: Institutiones* 1:2: 'The law of nature is that which she has taught all animals; a law not peculiar to the human race, but shared by all living creatures, whether denizens of the air, the dry land, or the sea. Hence comes the union of male and female,

The replies to the other *obiectiones* are evident from what has already been said in the body of the article.

(g) *Summa theologiae* IaIIae 96: Of the power of human law

We come next to the power of human law; and here there are six things to consider:

1. Whether human law should be framed for the community
2. Whether human law should restrain all vices
3. Whether it should prescribe all acts of virtue
4. Whether it binds a man in the court of conscience
5. Whether all men are subject to human law
6. Whether those who are subject to the law may go beyond the letter of the law

articulus 1: Whether human law should be framed for the community rather than the individual

It seems that human law should not be framed for the community, but for the individual.

obiectio 1: For the Philosopher says at *Ethics* v that the legally just [i.e. positive law] includes 'all laws passed for particular cases and all those matters which are the subject of decrees'[265] – which are also individual matters, since decrees are issued with reference to particular acts.[266] Therefore law is framed not only for the community, but for the individual also.

obiectio 2: Moreover, law is directive of human acts, as stated above.[267] But human acts have to do with particular things. Therefore human laws should be framed not for the community, but for the individual.

obiectio 3: Moreover, law is a rule and measure of human acts, as stated above.[268] But a measure should be completely exact, as is said at

---

which we call marriage; hence the procreation and rearing of children, for this is a law by the knowledge of which we see even the lower animals are distinguished.' Cf. n. 247, above.

[265] *Ethics* 5:7 (1134b23).

[266] I.e. they are formal pronouncements by an executive authority – in Roman law by the emperor – as to how the general law is to apply in a particular case.

[267] IaIIae 90:1 and 2 (pp. 76ff, above).

[268] *Ibid*.

Metaphysics X.[269] Since therefore in human acts no general proposition can be so exact as not to fail in some particular cases, it seems that laws must necessarily be framed not in general terms but for individual cases.

sed contra: The Jurist says that 'laws should be framed to accommodate what usually happens: the laws are not framed according to what may possibly arise in a particular case'.[270]

responsio: Whatever exists for the sake of an end must necessarily be adapted to that end. Now the end of law is the common good; because, as Isidore says, law should be 'composed for no private advantage, but for the common benefit of the citizens'.[271] Hence human laws should be adapted to the common good. But the common good consists of many things, and so the law must take many things into account, having regard to persons and matters and times. For the community of the State is composed of many persons, and its good is procured by many actions; nor is it established to last only for a short time, but to endure for all time as the citizens succeed one another, as Augustine says at *De civitate Dei* XXII.[272]

ad 1: The Philosopher proposes that the legally just – that is, positive law – has three parts. For some things are laid down simply in a general way; and these are general laws. Of these he says that 'the legally just is that which was originally a matter of indifference, but which, when it has been enacted, is no longer indifferent': for example, the fixing of a prisoner's ransom.[273] But there are some laws which affect the community in one respect and the individual in another. These are called 'privileges' [*privilegia*]: 'private laws' [*leges privatae*][274] as it were, because they have to

---

[269] *Metaphysics* 10:1 (1053a1).
[270] *CICiv.*: *Digesta* 1:3:3; 4.
[271] *Etymologiae* 2:10; 5:21 (*PL* 82:131; 203).
[272] *De civitate Dei* 22:6.
[273] *Ethics* 5:7 (1134b20); and see n. 223, above
[274] Cf. Dist. 3, c. 3: *Privilegiae* (*CIC* 1:5); *Etymologiae* 5:18 (*PL* 82:202). It is possible that St Thomas's use of the expression *leges privatae* will cause confusion here. The distinction between 'public' and 'private' law as *termini technici* of Roman law is as given by Justinian at *CICiv.*: *Institutiones* 1:1: 'The law is divided into public and private. Public law is that concerned with the constitution of the State; private law . . . is collected from natural precepts, from the *ius gentium* and from the civil law of any particular city or State.' Public law (which includes constitutional law, administrative law, criminal law and procedure and the law governing religious observance) regulates public matters; private law (which includes family law, property law, the law of obligations and the law of succession) regulates relations between individuals as such. But what St Thomas means by 'private' laws here are laws which affect individuals only: for example, a law conferring citizenship or a pension or something of the

do with individual persons, and yet their power extends to many matters; and in regard to these he adds, 'and further, all laws passed for particular cases'. Other matters again are called legal not because they are laws, but because they are applications of general laws to particular circumstances, such as decrees which have the force of law; and with regard to these he adds 'all those matters which are the subject of decrees'.

ad 2: That which is directive should be directive of many things. Hence in the *Metaphysics* the Philosopher says that all things belonging to one genus are measured by the one primary member of that genus;[275] for if there were as many rules or measures as there are things measured or ruled, the rules or measures would cease to be of any use, since the usefulness of a rule or measure lies precisely in the fact that it is a single standard which applies to many instances. And so law would be of no use if it did not extend beyond one single act. For whereas the decrees of men of practical wisdom are given for the purpose of directing particular actions, law is a general precept, as stated above.[276]

ad 3: As is said at *Ethics* I, 'We must not look for the same degree of certainty in all things.'[277] Hence in contingent matters, such as natural and human things, a sufficient degree of certainty is achieved when something is true in the majority of cases, even though it sometimes fails to be so in a few.

articulus 2: *Whether it belongs to human law to restrain all vices*

It seems that it does belong to human law to restrain all vices.

obiectio 1: For Isidore says that 'laws were made that man's audacity might be held in check by fear of them'.[278] But it would not be sufficiently held in check unless all evils were restrained by the law. Therefore human laws should restrain all evils.

kind. They are not general laws regulating the community at large, but they define some aspect of the individual's standing in relation to the community. Also, they are binding on everyone with respect to the individual concerned. It is with laws of this kind, which do not on the face of it answer to the proper definition of law because they do not address a common good, that St Thomas is also concerned at IaIIae 90:2:1 (p. 78, above).

[275] *Metaphysics* 9:1 (1052b18); and see IaIIae 90:1 (p. 76, above).
[276] IaIIae 92:2:1 (p. 99, above).
[277] *Ethics* 1:3 (1094b13).
[278] *Etymologiae* 5:20 (*PL* 82:202).

Law

obiectio 2: Moreover, the intention of the legislator is to make the citizens virtuous.[279] But no one can be virtuous unless he is restrained from vice of every kind. Therefore it belongs to human law to restrain all vices.

obiectio 3: Moreover, human law is derived from the natural law, as stated above.[280] But all vices are repugnant to the law of nature. Therefore human law should restrain all vices.

sed contra: Augustine says at *De libero arbitrio* 1: 'It seems to me that the law which is written for the governing of the people rightly permits these things, and that it is Divine providence which punishes them.'[281] But Divine providence punishes nothing but vices. Therefore human law rightly permits some vices, by not restraining them.

responsio: As stated above,[282] law is framed as a rule or measure of human acts. Now a measure should be in keeping with what it measures, as stated at *Metaphysics* x, for different things are measured by different measures.[283] Hence the laws imposed on men should also be in keeping with their condition; for, as Isidore says, law should be 'possible, according to nature, and according to the customs of the country'.[284] Now the power or faculty of action proceeds from an inward habit or disposition; for the same thing is not possible to one who does not have the habit of virtue as is possible to a virtuous man, just as the same thing is not possible to a child as to a grown man: this is why the law is not imposed upon children in the way that it is imposed upon adults, for many things are permitted to children which in adults are punished by the law, or at any rate blamed. And similarly many things are permissible to men who are not perfect in virtue which would not be tolerable in a virtuous man. But human law is framed for a community of men the majority of whom are not men of perfect virtue. And so human laws do not prohibit all the vices from which virtuous men abstain, but only the more grievous ones, from which it is possible for the greater part of the community to abstain; and especially those which do harm to others, without the prohibition of which human society could not be maintained. Thus human law forbids homicide, theft and things of that kind.

---

[279] *Ethics* 2:1 (1103b1).
[280] IaIIae 95:2 (p. 129, above).
[281] *De libero arbitrio* 1:5.
[282] IaIIae 90:1 and 2 (pp. 76ff, above).
[283] *Metaphysics* 10:1 (1053a24).
[284] *Etymologiae* 2:10; 5:21 (*PL* 82:131; 203).

ad 1: 'Audacity' seems to have reference in particular to the attacking of others.[285] Hence it is especially characteristic of those sins by which injury is inflicted upon a neighbour; and these are forbidden by human law, as stated.

ad 2: The intention of human law is to lead men to virtue not suddenly, but step by step. And so it does not immediately impose upon a community of imperfect men the kind of obligation suited to those who are already virtuous: that is, to abstain from all evils. If it did, imperfect men, being unable to bear such precepts, would break out into still greater evils, as is said at Proverbs 30:33: 'He that violently bloweth his nose, bringeth out blood'; and at Matthew 9:17 it is said that if 'new wine', that is, the precepts of a perfect life, 'is put into old bottles', that is, into imperfect men, 'the bottles burst, and the wine runneth out': that is, the precepts are despised, and those men, in their contempt, break out into still worse evils.

ad 3: The natural law is a certain kind of participation in us of the eternal law; but human law falls short of the eternal law. For Augustine says at *De libero arbitrio* I: 'The law which is framed for the government of States allows and leaves unpunished many things that are punished by Divine providence. Nor is the fact that this law does not attempt to do everything a reason why it should be blamed for what it does do.'[286] Hence also human law does not prohibit everything that is prohibited by the natural law.

articulus 3: *Whether human law prescribes all acts of virtue*

It seems that human law does not prescribe all acts of virtue.

obiectio 1: For virtuous acts are the opposite of vicious acts. But human law does not prohibit all vices, as stated above.[287] Therefore nor does it prescribe all acts of virtue.

obiectio 2: Moreover, a virtuous act proceeds from a virtue. But virtue is the end of law; and so that which proceeds from a virtue cannot fall under a precept of law. Therefore human law does not prescribe all acts of virtue.

[285] I.e. because audacity is characteristically 'courage', 'daring', 'boldness', 'rashness'.
[286] *De libero arbitrio* 1:5.
[287] Art. 2.

obiectio 3: Moreover, human law is directed to the common good, as stated above.[288] But some acts of virtue are not directed to the common good, but to a private good. Therefore the law does not prescribe all acts of virtue.

sed contra: The Philosopher says that the law 'prescribes the performance of the acts of a brave man and those of a temperate man and those of an equable man: and similarly with regard to the other virtues and vices, prescribing some acts and forbidding others'.[289]

responsio: The species of the virtues are distinguished according to their objects, as is shown by what has been said above.[290] Now all the objects of the virtues can be directed either to the private good of some person, or to the general good of the community. For instance, acts of courage can be performed by someone either for the preservation of the State or in defence of the rights of a friend; and similarly with the other virtues. But law, as stated above, is directed to the common good. And so there is no virtue whose acts may not [in principle] be prescribed by the law. However, human law does not prescribe all the acts of every virtue, but only those capable of being ordered to the common good either immediately, as when certain things are done directly for the common good, or mediately, as when a legislator ordains certain things pertaining to good order, by which the citizens are instructed so that they may uphold the common good of justice and peace.

ad 1: Human law does not prohibit all vicious acts by the obligation of a precept, just as it does not prescribe all acts of virtue. But it prohibits certain acts of specific vices, just as it prescribes certain acts of specific virtues.

ad 2: An act is said to be an act of virtue in two ways. In one way, from the mere fact that a man does something virtuous: thus an act of justice is to do what is right, and an act of bravery is to do brave things; and in this way the law prescribes certain acts of virtue. In another way, an act is called virtuous when a man does something virtuous in a way that a virtuous man does it.[291] An act of the latter kind always proceeds from

---

[288] IaIIae 90:2 (p. 78, above).
[289] *Ethics* 5:1 (1129b19).
[290] IaIIae 54:2; 60:1; 62:2.
[291] Cf. *Ethics* 2:5 (1105b5).

virtue, and it does not fall under a precept of law, but is the end at which every legislator aims.[292]

ad 3: As stated above, there is no virtue whose act is not capable of being ordered to the common good, either mediately or immediately.

articulus 4: *Whether human law binds a man in the court of conscience*

It seems that human law does not bind a man in the court of conscience.

obiectio 1: For a lower power has no right to impose its law in the court of higher power. But the power of man, which makes human law, is lower than the Divine power. Therefore human law cannot impose itself in a Divine court such as the court of conscience.

obiectio 2: Moreover, the judgment of conscience depends especially upon Divine commandments. But Divine commandments are sometimes made void by human laws, according to Matthew. 15:6: 'You have made the commandment of God of none effect for your tradition.' Therefore human law does not bind a man in conscience.

obiectio 3: Moreover, human laws often inflict calumny and injury upon men, according to Isaiah 10:1f: 'Woe to them that make wicked laws, and when they write, write injustice to oppress the poor in judgment, and do violence to the cause of the humble of my people.' But it is lawful for anyone to avoid oppression and violence. Therefore human laws do not bind a man in conscience.

sed contra: It is said at 1 Peter 2:19: 'This is thankworthy, if for the sake of conscience a man endure sorrows, suffering wrongfully.'

responsio: Laws framed by human beings are either just or unjust. If just, they receive the power to bind in the court of conscience from the eternal law from which they are derived, according to Proverbs 8:15: 'By me kings reign, and lawgivers decree just things.' Now laws are said to be just from their end: that is, when they are directed to the common good; and from their author: that is, when the law that is made does not exceed the power of the legislator; and from their form: that is, when burdens are imposed

---

[292] I.e. we can keep the law (and so be 'just', etc., in an extended or outward sense) without being virtuous; but the end at which every legislator aims is to make men truly virtuous by inculcating good habits as distinct from mere conformity.

upon subjects according to an equality of proportion and with a view to the common good.[293] For since one man is a part of the community, each man belongs to the community in everything that he has and is, just as each part belongs to the whole in everything that it is. Hence nature inflicts a kind of loss on the part in order to preserve the whole. On this account, then, such laws as these, which impose proportionate burdens, are just and binding in the court of conscience, and are legitimate laws.

But laws may be unjust in two ways. In one way, by being contrary to the human good because in opposition to the things mentioned above: either from their end, as when some ruler imposes on his subjects burdensome laws which pertain not to the common good, but rather to his own greed or glory; or from their author, as when someone makes a law which goes beyond the power committed to him; or from their form, as when burdens are imposed unequally on the community even if they are directed to the common good. Laws of this kind are more acts of violence than laws; because, as Augustine says in the book *De libero arbitrio*, 'a law that is not just seems to be no law at all'.[294] Hence such laws do not bind in the court of conscience, except perhaps in order to avoid scandal or disturbance, for which cause a man should give up even what is rightfully his, according to Matthew 5:40f: 'If a man take away thy coat, let him have thy cloak also; and whosoever shall compel thee to go a mile, go with him twain.'

In another way, laws may be unjust by being contrary to the Divine good: for example, the laws of tyrants enjoining idolatry or anything else contrary to the Divine law; and laws of this kind must not be observed in any circumstances, because, as is said at Acts 5:29, 'we ought to obey God rather than man'.

ad 1: As the Apostle says at Romans 13:1f, all human power is from God; 'therefore he that resisteth the power' in matters falling within the scope of that power, 'resisteth the ordinance of God' and accordingly is made guilty in conscience.

ad 2: This argument is valid with respect to those human laws which are established contrary to the commandments of God. The power 'ordained' (Romans 13:1) does not extend to this, and so human laws of this kind should not be obeyed.

[293] Cf. *Ethics* 5:5 (1134a5).   [294] *De libero arbitrio* 1:5.

ad 3: This argument is valid with respect to a law which inflicts unjust harm upon its subjects. The divinely granted order of power does not extend to this, and so a man is not obliged to obey the law in such cases, if he can resist [*resistere*] doing so without scandal or worse harm.[295]

articulus 5: *Whether all men are subject to the law*

It seems that not all men are subject to the law.

obiectio 1: For only those for whom the law is made are subject to the law. But the Apostle says at 1 Timothy 1:9: 'The law is not made for the just man.' Therefore just men are not subject to human law.

obiectio 2: Moreover, Pope Urban says: 'Someone who is guided by a private law[296] need not for any reason be bound by public law.'[297] But all spiritual men,[298] who are the sons of God, are led by the 'private law' of the Holy Spirit, according to Romans 8:14: 'Whosoever are led by the Spirit of God, they are the sons of God.' Therefore not all men are subject to human law.

obiectio 3: Moreover, the Jurist says that 'the prince is not bound by the laws'.[299] But one who is not bound by the law is not subject to the law. Therefore not all men are subject to the law.

sed contra: The Apostle says at Romans 13:1: 'Let every soul be subject to the higher powers.' But it seems that one cannot be subject to a power without also being subject to the laws made by that power. Therefore all men must be subject to human law.

responsio: As is shown by what has been said above,[300] the character of law consists in two things: first, that it is a rule of human acts; second, that it

---

[295] *Resistere* is a stronger word than *defugere, vitare* or *declinare* would have been: i.e. the sense is definitely of resistance rather than mere avoidance or passive disobedience. See Introduction, p. xxix.

[296] The sense of 'private law' in the canon which St Thomas is citing is of guidance given by God to the individual, which overrides the requirements of any merely written – which is what is here meant by 'public' – law. (Cf. n. 274, above.) For instance, Sampson (Judges 16:28ff) and Abraham (Genesis 22:2ff) were both 'privately' commanded by God to do things which would normally be unlawful. See Augustine, *De civitate Dei* 1:21; 26.

[297] C. 19:2:2: *Duae sunt* (*CIC* 1:839).

[298] Cf. 1 Corinthians 2:15.

[299] *CICiv.: Digesta* 1:3:31.

[300] IaIIae 90:1 and 2; 3 ad 2 (pp. 76ff, above).

has coercive force. A man may therefore be subject to law in two ways. In one way, as ruled is subject to ruler; and, in this way, all who are subject to a power are subject to the law made by that power. But there are two ways in which it may happen that someone is not subject to a power. First, by being absolutely exempt from subjection to it: hence the subjects of one city or kingdom are not bound by the laws of the prince of another city or kingdom because they are not under his lordship. Second, in so far as they are ruled by a still higher law. For example, if someone is subject to the proconsul, he should be ruled by his command; but not in those matters where he comes under the direct dispensation of the emperor; for in these matters he is not bound by the command of the lower authority, since he is directed by that of a higher.[301] Accordingly, one who is ordinarily subject to the law may nonetheless not be subject to it in certain matters in respect of which he is ruled by a higher law.

In another way, someone is said to be subject to a law as coerced is subject to coercer. In this way virtuous and righteous men are not subject to the law, but only the wicked, because coercion and violence are contrary to the will, but the will of good men is in harmony with the law, whereas the will of the wicked is discordant with it. And so in this sense only the wicked are 'subject' to the law, and the good are not.

ad 1: This argument is valid with respect to subjection by way of coercion: for law considered under this aspect is not made for just men because 'they are a law unto themselves', since they 'show the work of the law written in their hearts', as the Apostle says at Romans 2:14f. Hence the law does not have the coercive force in relation to them that it does in relation to the unjust.

ad 2: The law of the Holy Spirit is superior to all law devised by man; and so spiritual men, in so far as they are led by the law of the Holy Spirit, are not subject to any law repugnant to the guidance of the Holy Spirit. Nonetheless, the fact that spiritual men are subject to law at all is due to the guidance of the Holy Spirit, according to 1 Peter 2:13: 'Be ye subject to every human creature for God's sake.'

ad 3: The prince is said to be 'not bound by the law' with respect to its coercive force; since, properly speaking, no one is coerced by himself, and law has no coercive force except from the power of the prince. It is in this way, therefore, that the prince is said to be not bound by the law, because

---

[301] Cf. Augustine, *Sermo* 62:5:8ff.

no one can pass a sentence of condemnation on him if he acts against the law. Hence on Psalm 51:4: 'Against Thee only have I sinned', etc., a gloss says that 'there is no man who can judge the deeds of a king'.[302] As to the directive [as distinct from the coercive] force of law, however, the prince is subject to the law by his own will, according to what is said in the *Decretales*: that 'whatever law a man makes for another, he should keep himself'.[303] And the authority of a sage says: 'Obey the law that thou makest thyself.'[304] Moreover, at Matthew 23:3f the Lord reproaches those who 'say and do not', and who 'bind heavy burdens and lay them on men's shoulders, but with a finger of their own they will not move them'. Hence, in the judgment of God, the prince is not unbound by the law with respect to its directive force; but he should fulfil it of his own free will and not under coercion. Yet the prince is indeed above the law inasmuch as he can change the law, and dispense from it in whatever way is expedient to time and place.[305]

articulus 6: *Whether one who is subject to a law may go beyond the letter of the law*

It seems that one who is subject to a law may not go beyond the letter of the law.

obiectio 1: For Augustine says in the book *De vera religione*: 'Although men pass judgment on temporal laws when they make them, when once they are made and confirmed they must pass judgment not on them, but according to them.'[306] But if anyone sets aside the letter of the law, saying that in doing so he is preserving the intention of the legislator, it seems that he passes judgment on the law. Therefore it is not lawful for one who is subject to a law to set aside the letter of the law, even for the sake of preserving the intention of the legislator.

obiectio 2: Moreover, the interpretation of the law belongs only to him whose duty it is to make the law. But those who are subject to the law cannot make the law. Therefore they may not interpret the lawgiver's intention, but should always act according to the letter of the law.

---

[302] Peter Lombard, *Commentarium in psalmos* 51:4 (*PL* 191:486).

[303] X. 1:2:6: *Quum omnes* (*CIC* 2:8).

[304] Ps.-Ausonius, *Septem sapientum sententiae* 11: Pittacus.

[305] A similar argument to this, which St Thomas may have in mind, occurs at John of Salisbury's *Policraticus* 4:2.

[306] *De vera religione* 31.

obiectio 3: Moreover, every wise man knows how to explain his intention in words. But those who have established laws should be considered wise, for [the Divine] wisdom says, at Proverbs 8:15: 'By me kings reign, and law-givers decree just things.' Therefore the intention of the lawgiver should not be judged other than through the letter of the law.

sed contra: Hilary says at *De Trinitate* IV: 'The meaning of what is said must be inferred from the reason why it was said; for things are not subject to speech, but speech to things.'[307] We should therefore take account of the reason which motivated the legislator, rather than of the mere letter of the law.

responsio: As stated above,[308] every law is directed to the common welfare of men. It obtains the force and character of law in so far as this is so, and in so far as it is deficient in this respect it does not have binding force. Hence the Jurist says: 'By no reason of law, or grant of equity, is it permitted for us to render burdensome those beneficial measures which have been introduced for the welfare of mankind by interpreting them harshly, contrary to their beneficent intention.'[309] But it often happens that the observance of a certain law is beneficial to the common welfare in the majority of instances, and yet, in some cases, is very harmful. Since, then, the legislator cannot make provision for every single case, he frames the law according to what happens most frequently, directing his attention to the common good. Hence if a case emerges in which the observance of that law would be damaging to the common welfare, it should not be observed. For example, if in a besieged city there is an established law that the gates of the city are to remain closed, this is beneficial to the common welfare for most of the time: but if it were to happen that the enemy were giving chase to certain citizens by whom the city was being defended, it would be greatly harmful to the city if the gates were not opened to them; and so in that case the gates ought to be opened, contrary to the letter of the law, in order to preserve the common benefit which the lawgiver intended to secure.

It must be borne in mind, however, that if the observance of the law according to the letter does not involve any sudden peril calling for an immediate response, it does not belong simply to anyone at all to expound what is beneficial to the State and what is not beneficial. It belongs only

[307] *De Trinitate* 4 (PL 10:107).
[308] IaIIae 90:2 (p. 78, above); 96:4 (p. 143, above).
[309] *CICiv.*: *Digesta* 1:3:25.

to princes to do this, who have authority to dispense from the laws when such cases arise. If, on the other hand, the peril is so sudden as not to brook the delay involved in having recourse to a superior, the mere necessity has a dispensation annexed to it, because necessity is not subject to law.

ad 1: He who in a case of necessity goes beyond the letter of the law does not judge the law itself, but only the particular case in which he sees that the letter of the law should not be observed.

ad 2: He who follows the intention of the legislator [rather than the letter of the law] is not interpreting the law [as one entitled to do so] as a matter of course, but only because a case has arisen where it is clear on the ground of manifest harm that the legislator intended otherwise. If there is any doubt he must either act according to the letter of the law, or consult a superior.

ad 3: No man is so completely wise as to be able to take account of every single case; and so he cannot sufficiently express in words all those things that are conducive to the end which he intends. Moreover, even if a legislator were able to take all cases into consideration, it would not be suitable for him to mention them all, in order to avoid confusion; rather, he should frame the law according to what happens in the majority of cases.

(h) *Summa theologiae* IaIIae 97: Of change in the laws

We come next to the question of change in the laws; and here there are four things to consider:

1. Whether human law may be changed
2. Whether it should always be changed when something better arises
3. Whether it may be abolished by custom, and whether custom may obtain the force of law
4. Whether the usual meaning of human law can be altered by dispensation of the ruler

articulus 1: *Whether human law should be changed in any way*

It seems that human law should not be changed in any way.

obiectio 1: For human law is derived from the natural law, as stated above.[310] But the natural law remains immovable. Therefore human law should also remain immovable.

obiectio 2: Moreover, as the Philosopher says at *Ethics* v, a measure must above all be fixed.[311] But human law is the measure of human acts, as stated above.[312] Therefore it should remain immovable.

obiectio 3: Moreover, it is of the essence of law that it be just and right, as stated above.[313] But if something is right once it is right always. Therefore that which is law once should be law always.

sed contra: Augustine says at *De libero arbitrio* i: 'A temporal law, no matter how just it may be, can be justly changed in the course of time.'[314]

responsio: As stated above,[315] human law is a dictate of reason by which human acts are directed. Accordingly, there can be two reasons why human law may be justly changed: one having to do with reason, the other having to do with man, whose acts are regulated by law. As regards reason, it seems natural for human reason to advance gradually from the imperfect to the perfect. Hence in the speculative sciences we see that what the first philosophers taught was in some degree imperfect, and was afterwards made more perfect by their successors. So too in practical matters; for those who first set out to discover something useful for the community of mankind, because they were not by themselves able to take everything into account, made certain imperfect arrangements which were deficient in many ways; and these were changed by their successors, who made other arrangements which would fail to secure the common welfare in fewer cases.

As regards man, whose acts are regulated by law, the law can be rightly changed because of the changed circumstances of man, to whom different things are expedient according to different conditions. An example is proposed by Augustine at *De libero arbitrio* i:

> If the people are well moderated and sober, and are most careful guardians of the common interest, it is right to enact a law allowing

[310] IaIIae 95:2 (p. 129, above).
[311] *Ethics* 5:5 (1133a25).
[312] IaIIae 90:1–2 (pp. 76ff, above).
[313] IaIIae 95:2 (p. 129, above).
[314] *De libero arbitrio* 1:6.
[315] IaIIae 91:3 (p. 87, above).

such a people to create their own magistrates for the administration of the commonwealth. But if, little by little, the same people become so corrupt that they sell their votes and entrust the government to disreputable and wicked men, then the right of bestowing honours [i.e. of appointing to public office] is rightly forfeit to such a people, and the choice devolves to a few good men.[316]

ad 1: The natural law is a kind of participation in the eternal law, as stated above,[317] and therefore remains immovable: a characteristic which it has from the immovableness and perfection of the Divine reason by which the natural order itself is established. But human reason is mutable and imperfect, and so its law is mutable. Furthermore, the law of nature contains certain universal precepts which always remain the same, whereas the law posited by man contains certain particular precepts, according to the various circumstances which emerge.

ad 2: A measure should be as fixed as possible. But nothing can remain entirely immutable among mutable things. And so human law cannot be entirely immutable.

ad 3: In relation to corporeal things the term 'right' is used in an absolute sense, and therefore right, considered as such, always remains right. But the rightness of laws is relative to the common benefit, to which the same thing is not always adapted in the same way, as stated above; and so rightness of this kind is subject to change.[318]

articulus 2: *Whether human law should always be changed when something better arises*

It seems that human law should be changed whenever something better arises.

obiectio 1: For human laws are devised by human reason, just as other productions of art are. But in the other arts, a rule which has been followed down to the present time is changed if something better arises. Therefore the same should be done in the case of human laws.

---

[316] *De libero arbitrio* 1:6.
[317] IaIIae 91:2 (p. 85, above); 96:2 ad 3 (p. 141, above).
[318] I.e. statements of fact are always either right or wrong, but the 'rightness' of laws is dependent upon variables and so is subject to change.

obiectio 2: Moreover, it is by learning from the past that we can make provision for the future. For if human laws had not been changed in response to the discovery of better ways of doing things, many disadvantages would have ensued; for the laws of old were found to contain much that was rudimentary. Therefore it seems that laws should be changed whenever anything better arises to be established.

obiectio 3: Moreover, human laws are enacted with a view to governing the particular acts of man. But we cannot acquire perfect knowledge in particular matters except by experience, which requires time, as is said at *Ethics* 11.[319] Therefore it seems that, with the passage of time, something better may arise to be established.

sed contra: It is said in the *Decretum* that 'It is a ridiculous and quite abominable disgrace that we should suffer to be changed those traditions which we have received from the fathers of old.'[320]

responsio: As stated above,[321] human law is rightly changed in so far as such change is necessary to provide for the common benefit. But a change in the law considered simply as such is detrimental to the common well-being, because custom has great force in securing the observance of laws, inasmuch as what is done contrary to common custom, even in trivial matters, is regarded as grave. Hence, when the law is changed, the binding force of law is diminished to the extent that a custom is abolished. And so human law should never be changed unless there is a corresponding increase in the common welfare to compensate for what has been taken away. Such a compensation may arise either from some great and very evident advantage proceeding from the new statute, or from the greatness of the need for it, either because the content of the present law is clearly wrong, or its observance is manifestly harmful. Hence the Jurist Ulpian says that 'in the matter of establishing new laws, the advantage of doing so should be evident before departing from a law which has long been seen as equitable.'[322]

ad 1: The techniques of an art derive their efficacy simply from reason; and so whenever something better arises, the rule previously followed should be changed. But 'laws derive very great force from custom', as the

---

[319] *Ethics* 2:1 (1103a16).
[320] Dist. 12, c. 5: *Ridiculum est* (*CIC* 1:28).
[321] Art. 1.
[322] *CICiv.*: *Digesta* 1:4:2.

Philosopher says at *Politics* II;[323] and it is for this reason that they should not readily be changed.

ad 2: This argument proves that laws ought to be changed not simply to secure any improvement whatsoever, but for the sake of a great advantage or where there is great necessity, as stated above. This reply applies to the third *obiectio* also.

articulus 3: *Whether custom can obtain the force of law*

It seems that custom cannot obtain the force of law; nor can it abolish a law.

obiectio 1: For human law is derived from the natural law and from the Divine law, as is shown by what has been said above.[324] But the custom of men cannot change either the law of nature or the Divine law. Nor therefore can it change human law.

obiectio 2: Moreover, one good cannot come from many evils. But he who first began to act against the law did something evil. Therefore nothing good is brought about by multiplying similar acts. But a law is something good, since it is a rule of human acts. Therefore law cannot be removed by custom in order to allow custom itself to obtain the force of law.

obiectio 3: Moreover, the task of making laws belongs to those public persons whose business it is to rule the community. Hence private persons cannot make law. But custom grows out of the acts of private persons. Therefore custom cannot obtain the force of law by which a previous law is removed.

sed contra: Augustine says: 'The customs of the people of God and the institutions of our forefathers should be held to as law. And those who despise the customs of the Church should be as much restrained as those who disobey the Divine law.'[325]

responsio: Every law proceeds from the reason and will of a legislator: the Divine and natural laws from the rational will of God; the human law from the will of man, regulated by reason. Now just as the reason and will

---

[323] *Politics* 2:5 (1269a20).
[324] IaIIae 93:3 (p. 105, above); 95:2 (p. 129, above).
[325] *Epistolae* 36:1; Dist 11, c. 7: *In his rebus* (*CIC* 1:25).

of man may be made manifest through speech in practical matters, so may they be made known by action: for it seems that when any man acts he is carrying into effect something which he has chosen as a good. But it is clear that law, in so far as it manifests the inward movement and thought of human reason, can be both changed and expounded by human speech; and so law can be changed and expounded by actions also, especially if they are multiplied so as to bring into being a custom: that is, something can be brought into being which obtains the force of law when the inward movement of the will and the thoughts of reason are effectively expressed by repeated outward actions; for when something is done again and again, it seems to proceed from the deliberate judgment of reason. Accordingly, custom has the force of law, abolishes law, and is the interpreter of law.[326]

ad 1: The natural and Divine laws proceed from the Divine will, as stated above. Hence they may not be changed by a custom proceeding from the will of man, but by Divine authority alone. And so it is that no custom can obtain any force contrary to the Divine or natural laws: for Isidore says: 'Let custom yield to authority: evil customs should be eradicated by law and reason.'[327]

ad 2: As stated above,[328] human laws fail in some cases. Hence it is possible sometimes to go beyond the law – that is, in cases where the law fails – yet the act will not be evil. And when cases of this kind are multiplied because of some change in man's circumstances, custom then shows that the law is no longer useful, just as this might be shown by the verbal promulgation of a law repealing the previous one. If, however, the reason which made the law useful [in the first place] remains the same, then the custom does not override the law, but the law the custom; unless perhaps the law seems useless simply because it is not possible 'according to the custom of the country', which was identified as one of the conditions of law.[329] For it is difficult to set aside the custom of a whole community.

[326] I.e. speech expresses reason and will; but repeated action – which is what custom is – also expresses reason and will; therefore, if law arises from reason and will, it follows that it can arise from custom as well as from speech: as well, that is, as from formal legal utterances. The implication (and see ad 3, below) seems clearly to be that the origin of law is associated with the popular will; but, typically of medieval authors, this is a question which St Thomas leaves vague.
[327] *Synonyma* 2:80 (*PL* 83:863).
[328] IaIIae 96:6 (p. 147, above).
[329] *Etymologiae* 5:21 (*PL* 82:203); IaIIae 95:3.

ad 3: There can be two kinds of community into which the custom is introduced. For if it is a free community which may make its own laws, the consent of the whole community expressed through custom counts in favour of a particular observance far more than does the authority of a prince, who has not the power to make laws except as representing the community. Hence although each single person cannot make laws, yet the whole people can. If, however, the community does not have the free power to make its own laws or to set aside a law made by a superior, nevertheless in such a community a prevailing custom obtains the force of law in so far as it is tolerated by those whose business it is to make laws for that community, since by the very fact of tolerating it they seem to approve of that which the custom has introduced.

articulus 4: *Whether the rulers of a community can dispense from human laws*

It seems that the rulers of a community cannot dispense from human laws.

obiectio 1: For the law is established for the 'common benefit', as Isidore says.[330] But the common good should not be set aside for the private advantage of any person, because, as the Philosopher says at *Ethics* I, 'the good of a nation is more Divine than the good of one man'.[331] Therefore it seems that no one should be given a dispensation to act against the general law.

obiectio 2: Moreover, those who are set over others are commanded at Deuteronomy 1:17: 'Ye shall hear the small as well as the great; ye shall not respect persons; for the judgment is God's.' But to allow someone to do what is generally denied to all seems to be to 'respect persons'. Therefore the rulers of a community cannot make such dispensations, since to do so would be against a precept of the Divine law.

obiectio 3: Moreover, human law, if it is to be righteous, must be in harmony with the natural and Divine laws; otherwise it would not be 'in keeping with religion' nor would it be 'conducive to discipline', which is a requirement of law, as Isidore says.[332] But no man can dispense from

---

[330] *Etymologiae* 2:10; 5:21 (*PL* 82:131; 203).
[331] *Ethics* 1:2 (1094b10).
[332] *Etymologiae* 2:10; 5:3 (*PL* 82:131; 199).

the Divine and natural laws. Nor, therefore, can he dispense from human law.

sed contra: The Apostle says at 1 Corinthians 9:17: 'A dispensation is committed to me.'

responsio: Dispensation, properly speaking, denotes a measuring out to individuals of some common goods. Hence the governor of a family is called a dispenser inasmuch as he distributes the tasks and necessaries of life to each member of the family in proper weight and measure. So, then: in every community there is someone who is said to 'dispense' because he ordains how some general precept is to be fulfilled by each individual.

Now it sometimes happens that a precept which is advantageous to the community in most cases is not suitable for a particular person, or in a particular case, either because it would impede some greater good, or because it would lead to some evil, as has been shown above.[333] But it would be perilous to entrust this question to the judgment of each individual, except perhaps in the event of a clear and present danger, as stated above.[334] And so he who has the task of ruling a community has power to dispense from a human law that rests upon his authority, so that, when the law fails in relation to particular persons or circumstances, he may permit the precept of the law not to be observed.

If however he grants this permission without good reason and by his mere will, he will be unfaithful in his dispensation, or he will be unwise: unfaithful, if he does not intend the common good; unwise, if he ignores the reasons for granting dispensations. Hence the Lord says at Luke 12:42: 'Who, thinkest thou, is the faithful and wise steward [*dispensator*], whom his lord setteth over his family?'

ad 1: When someone is dispensed from observing the general law, this should not be done to the detriment of the common good, but with the intention of advancing the common good.

ad 2: It is not respect of persons if equal measures are not assigned to persons who are themselves unequal.[335] Hence when the condition of any person requires that he should reasonably receive special treatment, it is not respect of persons if a special concession is made in his particular case.

---

[333] IaIIae 96:6 (p. 147, above).
[334] *Ibid*.
[335] Cf. *Ethics* 5:3 (1131a25).

ad 3: From the general precepts of the natural law, which never fail, there can be no dispensation; but from the other precepts which are as it were conclusions drawn from the general precepts, a dispensation is sometimes granted by man: for example, that a loan should not be repaid to a traitor to his country, or something of the kind. But each man comes under the Divine law in the same way as a private person comes under the public law to which he is subject. Hence, just as no one can dispense from public human law except one from whom the law derives its authority, or his delegate, so no one can dispense from the precepts of the Divine law, which come from God, except God or one to whom He gives a special responsibility in such cases.

4

Right, justice and judgment[1]

(a) *Summa theologiae* IIaIIae 57: On right

Here there are four things to consider:

1. Whether right is the object of justice
2. Whether right is suitably divided into natural and positive right
3. Whether the *ius gentium* is the same as natural right
4. Whether paternal right and dominative right should be regarded as distinct species of right

articulus 1: *Whether right* [ius] *is the object of justice* [iustitia][2]

It seems that right is not the object of justice.[3]

---

[1] Readers are advised to make themselves familiar with Book v of Aristotle's *Nicomachean Ethics* before tackling this difficult and technical chapter.

[2] Considered generally, the word 'right', which commonly translates the Latin *ius*, can be misleading. 'Right' is not, as Professor Sigmund suggests, a 'prize mistranslation' of *ius* (*St Thomas Aquinas on Politics and Ethics* (New York and London, 1988), p. xxviii); but it should especially be borne in mind that *iura* are not necessarily, although they are sometimes, 'rights' or entitlements in the familiar sense. Some authors use the word *ius* indistinguishably from *lex*, 'law'. For St Thomas, the two are usually not the same (although he does tend to use the expressions *ius naturale* and *lex naturalis* interchangeably). On the one hand, he says that 'law' is 'a kind of rule and measure of acts, by which someone is induced to act or restrained from acting' (IaIIae 90:1 *responsio* (p. 77, above)). On the other, he here uses the words *ius* or *iustum*, 'right' or 'the just' (which he regards as synonyms), to convey the idea of an objective relationship of equality or reciprocity which *lex* can institutionalise in written form (see art. 1, *responsio*, ad 2, and art. 2:2, below; see also the next footnote). In this sense, *ius* is what *lex* prescribes: 'law is not the same as right, properly speaking, but an expression of the idea of right' (ad 2, below). To put the same point another way, *ius* as a noun here means much the same as we might mean by 'right' as an adjective: i.e. law/justice requires us to do what is right. But it has to be admitted that the subtleties of meaning which St Thomas intends to convey by his various uses of *ius*, *lex* and *iustum* sometimes defy translation.

[3] The point of this article is to show that *iustitia*, 'justice', differs from the other virtues in being concerned with outward relationships of equality or reciprocity considered as distinct from individual or private virtue.

158

obiectio 1: For the jurist Celsus says that 'right is the art of the good and equal'.[4] But an art is not the object of justice, because art is an intellectual virtue in itself.[5] Therefore right is not the object of justice.

obiectio 2: Moreover, Isidore says in the book *Etymologies* that 'Law is a species of right.'[6] But the Philosopher identifies 'legislative wisdom' as one of the parts of practical wisdom [*prudentia*].[7] Hence law is the object not of justice, but of practical wisdom. Therefore right is not the object of justice.

obiectio 3: Moreover, the chief purpose of justice is to make a man subject to God; for in the book *De moribus ecclesiae* Augustine says that 'justice is love serving God alone, and hence governing rightly all things subject to man'.[8] But right [*ius*] does not pertain to things Divine, but only to things human; for Isidore, in the book *Etymologies*, says that '*fas* is the Divine law, and *ius* the human law'.[9] Therefore right is not the object of justice.

sed contra: Isidore in the same place says that '*ius* [right] is so called because it is just [*iustum*]'.[10] But the 'just' is the object of justice, for the Philosopher says that 'all men mean by "justice" the habit which makes men capable of doing just acts'.[11] Therefore right is the object of justice.

responsio: The proper function of justice, as compared with the other virtues, is to direct man in his relations with others. For justice denotes a kind of equality – as the name itself shows, for it is commonly said that things are 'adjusted' to one another when they are made equal – and equality has to do with the relation of one man to another, whereas the other virtues perfect man in those things which pertain only to himself. Accordingly, that which is right in the works of the other virtues, and to which the intention of the virtue tends as to its proper object, depends only upon its relation to the agent. But that which is right in a work of justice is constituted, over and above its relation to the agent, by its relation to others; for what we do is said to be 'just' when it is related to someone else by way of some kind of equality: for example, the payment of the fee due for

---

[4] *CICiv.*: *Digesta* 1:1:1.
[5] On 'art' as an intellectual virtue, see Aristotle, *Ethics* 6:4 (1140a1); and see n. 14, below.
[6] *Etymologiae* 5:2 (*PL* 82:199).
[7] *Ethics* 6:8 (1141b25).
[8] *De moribus ecclesiae* 1:15.
[9] *Etymologiae* 5:2 (*PL* 82:198).
[10] *Etymologiae* 5:3 (*PL* 82:199).
[11] *Ethics* 5:1 (1129a7).

a service rendered. And so a thing is said to be just, as having the rectitude of justice, when it is the outcome of an act of justice, without regard to the way in which that act is done by the agent; whereas in the other virtues nothing is deemed to be right unless it is done by the agent in a certain way.[12] For this reason, justice has its own special object proper to itself over and above the other virtues, and this object is called the just [*iustum*], which is the same as 'right' [*ius*]. Hence it is clear that right is the object of justice.

ad 1: Usage often divests words of their original meaning and makes them signify something else. For example, the original meaning of the word 'medicine' was a remedy for restoring a sick person to health; then it became extended to signify the art by which this is done. So too the word *ius* was first used to signify the just thing itself, but subsequently came to designate the art of knowing what is just; and, further, to signify the place where justice is administered (so that someone is said to appear *in jure*);[13] and, further again, 'justice' [in this extended sense] is done by someone who has the duty of 'administering justice' even if his sentence happens to be unjust.[14]

ad 2: Just as there pre-exists in the mind of the craftsman an idea of the things which are to be made externally by his craft, which idea is called the rule of his craft, so also there pre-exists in the mind an idea of the particular just work which the reason then chooses to perform, and which is a kind of rule of practical wisdom.[15] If this rule is reduced to writing it is called a law, which according to Isidore is 'a written decree'.[16] And so law is not the same as right, properly speaking, but an expression of the idea of right.

ad 3: Justice denotes a kind of equality, but we cannot possibly make an equal repayment to God; and so we cannot make a just return to God

[12] E.g. to pay what we owe is 'just' even if done unwillingly or in a morally neutral frame of mind; but the other virtues are made virtuous by the intention of the agent. You cannot be chaste or temperate merely by complying with a rule. See ad 1, below; see also IIaIIae 60:6 (p. 202, below).

[13] We might say in English that someone 'goes to law'.

[14] I.e. when Celsus says that 'right is the art of the good and equal' (*obiectio* 1), he is using the word 'art' in an extended sense, to mean not, as Aristotle does, 'the intellectual virtue deployed in making things', but 'the activity of applying rules to achieve just outcomes'. This extended sense is, after all, familiar enough to English speakers. We talk about the 'art' of sculpture; but we also find it intelligible to talk about the art of 'making' friends, the martial arts, the Artful Dodger, etc., etc.

[15] See IaIIae 93:1 *responsio* (p. 102, above); 95:2 *responsio* (p. 130, above).

[16] *Etymologiae* 5:3 (*PL* 82:199).

according to the complete sense of the term. It is for this reason that the Divine law is not properly called *ius* but *fas*: because, that is, it is enough for God if we do as much as we can. Nonetheless, justice tends to make a man repay God as much as he can, inasmuch as it subjects his mind to Him totally.

articulus 2: *Whether right is suitably divided into natural right and positive right*

It seems that right is not suitably divided into natural right and positive right.

obiectio 1: For that which is natural is immutable, and is the same for all men. But nothing of this kind is found in human affairs, for all rules of human right fail in some cases, nor do they have force everywhere. Therefore there is no such thing as natural right.

obiectio 2: Moreover, something is called 'positive' when it is posited by the human will. But something is not just merely because it is posited by the human will; otherwise man's will could not be unjust. Since, therefore, 'just' and 'right' are the same, it seems that there is no positive right.

obiectio 3: Moreover, Divine right is not natural right, since it goes beyond human nature. Similarly, nor is it positive right, since it is founded not on human authority, but on Divine authority. Therefore right is not suitably divided into natural and positive.

sed contra: The Philosopher says at *Ethics* v that 'of political justice, part is natural, part legal',[17] that is, established by [positive] law.

responsio: As stated above,[18] a right or just act is one which is 'adjusted' to someone else according to some kind of equality. But something can be adjusted to a man in two ways. In one way, by its very nature, as when someone gives something in order to receive an equivalent amount back in return; and this is called natural right. In another way, when something is adjusted or commensurated to someone else by means of an agreement, or by mutual consent, as when someone declares himself content to receive a stipulated amount [in return for something]. This can be done in two

---

[17] *Ethics* 5:7 (1134b18).   [18] Art. 1.

ways. In one way, by some private arrangement: that is, by an agreement confirmed between private persons; in another way, by public agreement, as when a whole populace agrees that the value of something should be fixed in the same way as if it had been adjusted and commensurated between one person and another, or when this is ordained by the prince who has charge of the people and who bears the public person; and this is called positive right.

ad 1: That which is natural to something which has an immutable nature must indeed be the same always and everywhere. But the nature of man is mutable, and so that which is natural to man can sometimes fail. Thus the practice of restoring a deposit to a depositor has its basis in natural equality, and if human nature were always righteous, this would always have to be done. But since it sometimes happens that a man's will is depraved, there are certain cases in which a deposit should not be restored, lest a man of perverse will make ill use of what was deposited: for example, if a madman or an enemy of the commonwealth were to demand the return of his weapons.[19]

ad 2: The human will can make anything just by common agreement provided that the thing in question has nothing about it which is repugnant in itself to natural justice; and it is in matters of this kind that positive right has its place. Hence the Philosopher says at *Ethics* v that 'in the case of the legally just, it does not matter in the first instance whether it takes one form or another; it only matters when once it is laid down'.[20] But if something is repugnant in itself to natural right, the human will cannot by any means make it just: for example, by decreeing that it is lawful to steal or commit adultery. Hence it is said at Isaiah 10:1: 'Woe to them that make wicked laws.'

ad 3: Divine right is that which is divinely promulgated. Such things are partly those which are naturally just but whose justice is hidden from men, and partly those which are made just by Divine institution. Hence also Divine right can be divided with respect to these two things in the same way that human right can be. For the Divine law commands certain things because they are good, and prohibits others because they are evil,

---

[19] Cf. Plato, *Republic* 331C.

[20] *Ethics* 5:7 (1134b20). Fr Gilby's translation of this quotation (BE 37:9), though a paraphrase, is useful: 'Aristotle says that the legally just is that which is morally neutral in principle and can be decided in one way or the other, though once decided it remains no longer neutral.' See also p. 129 n. 223.

while other things are good only because they are commanded and bad because they are prohibited.[21]

articulus 3: *Whether the 'right of nations'* [ius gentium][22] *is the same as natural right* [ius naturale][23]

It seems that the right of nations is the same as natural right.

obiectio 1: For all men agree only in that which is natural to them. But all men agree as to the right of nations; for the Jurist says that 'the right of nations is that of which all nations make use'.[24] Therefore the right of nations is natural right.

obiectio 2: Moreover, slavery among men is natural, for some men are naturally slaves, as the Philosopher proves at *Politics* I.[25] But 'slavery belongs to the right of nations',[26] as Isidore says. Therefore the right of nations is natural right.

obiectio 3: Moreover, right is divided into natural and positive right, as stated above.[27] But the right of nations is not positive right, for never have all nations agreed to enact any statute by common consent. Therefore the right of nations is natural right.

sed contra: Isidore says that 'right is either natural or civil or the right of nations';[28] and so the right of nations is to be distinguished from natural right.

responsio: As stated above,[29] the naturally right or just is that which by its nature is adjusted to, or commensurate with, someone else. Now this commensuration can arise in two ways. In one way, from the nature of the thing considered simply as such, in the way that the male is by nature commensurate with the female, to beget offspring by her, and a parent is commensurate with a child, to nurture it. In another way, something is naturally commensurate with someone else not because of the nature of

---

[21] Cf. p. 61 n. 17.
[22] See p. 134 n. 247, above.
[23] I.e. is the same as natural law. See n. 2, above.
[24] *CICiv.: Digesta* 1:1:1.
[25] *Politics* 1:4 (1254a15).
[26] *Etymologiae* 5:6 (*PL* 82:199).
[27] Art. 2.
[28] *Etymologiae* 5:6 (*PL* 82:199).
[29] Art. 2.

the thing as such, but by reason of some consequence of its being so: for example, the possession of property. For there is no reason why a piece of land considered simply as such should belong to one man rather than another; but considered with respect to how best to cultivate the land and make peaceable use of it, it has a certain commensuration to be the property of one man rather than another, as the Philosopher shows at *Politics* II.[30]

Now to apprehend something simply [i.e. without engaging in any process of reasoning in relation to it] belongs not only to man but to other animals also;[31] and so the right which is called natural in the first way is common to us and to other animals. On the one hand, then, the right of nations, which is 'common to men only', as the jurist says, is less extensive than the natural right which is 'common to all animals'.[32] On the other hand, to consider something specifically in relation to some consequence of it is a process of reasoning, and this, therefore, is natural to man by virtue of the natural reason which performs it. Hence the jurist Gaius says: 'Whatever natural reason establishes among all men is observed by all equally, and is called the right of nations.'[33] And by this is shown the reply to the first *obiectio*.

ad 2: The fact that this man is a slave rather than that is due not to the nature of the man considered simply as such, but to some advantage consequent upon his being so, in that it is beneficial for a slave to be governed by someone wiser than he, and for a master to be assisted by the slave, as the Philosopher says at *Politics* I.[34] And so slavery belonging to the right of nations is natural in the second way, but not in the first.[35]

ad 3: Natural reason tells us what things belong to the right of nations: in terms, for example, of their closeness to equity.[36] Such matters therefore

[30] *Politics* 2:5 (1263a21).
[31] I.e. both man and other animals can respond unreflectively to the simple natural drives to mate or nurture young.
[32] *CICiv.*: *Digesta* 1:1:1.
[33] *CICiv.*: *Digesta* 1:1:9.
[34] *Politics* 1:6 (1255b5).
[35] I.e. slavery is 'natural', but it arises through natural reason rather than mere instinct, and so is part of the *ius gentium*. It does not arise spontaneously in the way that begetting and rearing offspring does; it comes about when reason reflects on natural differences of capacity and calculates the consequences of one arrangement rather than another. The point is elegantly summarised by R. W. and A. J. Carlyle at *A History of Medieval Political Theory in the West*, vol. v, pp. 21f.
[36] I take it that this is what is meant by *ea quae sunt iuris gentium naturalis ratio dictat, puta ex propinquo habentia aequitatem*. Fr Gilby (BE 37:13) translates the passage as 'Matters of

do not need to be enacted in any specific way, because they are indicated by natural reason itself, as stated by the authority cited above.[37]

articulus 4: *Whether paternal right and dominative right*[38] *should be regarded as different species of right*[39]

It seems that paternal right and dominative right should not be regarded as different species of right.

obiectio 1: For the task of justice is 'to render to each what is due to him', as Ambrose says at *De officiis* I.[40] But right is the object of justice, as stated above.[41] Therefore right belongs equally 'to each'; and so the right of a father and master ought not to be distinguished as different species of right.

obiectio 2: Moreover, law is the rational expression of what is just, as stated above.[42] But law looks to the common good of a city and kingdom,

the *jus gentium* are dictated by natural reason as being closely bound up with equity.' DE here gives 'Since natural reason dictates matters which are according to the right of nations, as implying a proximate equality, it follows that they need no special institution.' I have to confess that I do not see what 'as implying a proximate equality' is supposed to mean, or how it is a translation of *ex propinquo habentia aequitatem*. St Thomas's point seems to be that we identify things as being fair and equitable by natural reason, 'equity' here being the kind of self-evident principle of fairness which recognises, for instance, that exchanges must involve equivalent values: see, e.g., art. 2, *responsio*, above.

[37] I.e. *Digesta* I:I:9.

[38] I.e. the right of someone who is the master of slaves.

[39] St Thomas is here commenting on Aristotle's remark at *Ethics* 5:6 (1134b10): 'The justice of a master and a father resemble, but they are not the same as, the justice of citizens. For there can be no injustice in the unqualified sense towards things that are one's own; but a man's belongings, and his child until it reaches a certain age and becomes independent, are as it were parts of himself, and no one chooses to hurt himself: this is why there can be no injustice towards oneself.' St Thomas's point in this article is as follows. Justice strictly so called – 'in the unqualified sense' – is a political relationship, holding as between the members of a community; and, as we saw in art. 1, 'right is the object of justice'. On the one hand, therefore, 'right' in the strict sense belongs to citizens, related politically by justice, not to individuals *qua* fathers or masters (*obiectiones* 1 and 2). But, on the other hand, we would hardly wish to say that non-political, domestic relations are destitute of any kind of 'right' and therefore of any kind of justice. Therefore we have to postulate lesser or qualified senses of right, to cover relationships between fathers and children, masters and slaves, and husbands and wives. It is not clear why Fr Gilby (BE 37:12) should describe St Thomas's discussion here as a 'period piece'. It may fairly be said, though, that St Thomas makes rather heavy weather of it.

[40] *De officiis* 1:24 (*PL* 16:62). But the *locus classicus* of this definition of justice is, of course, *CICiv.: Institutiones* I:I:I.

[41] Art. I.

[42] Art. I ad 2.

as noted above.[43] It does not look to the private good of a single person, or even of a single household. Therefore there should not be some special kind of dominative or paternal right or justice, since 'master' and 'father' belong to the household [rather than to the city or kingdom], as stated at *Politics* I.[44]

obiectio 3: Moreover, there are many other differences of station among men. For example, some are soldiers, some are priests, some are princes. Therefore [if there is a special dominative and paternal right,] some specific kind of right ought to be assigned to them also.

sed contra: At *Ethics* v the Philosopher specifically distinguishes the right of a master and a father and other such things from the politically just.[45]

responsio: The 'right' or 'just' is defined by the commensuration of one person with another. But 'another' can have a twofold meaning. In one way, it can mean something which is simply 'other': that is, which is entirely different. This is the meaning which appears in the case of two men neither of whom is under the other but both of whom are under a city's one prince; and between these, according to the Philosopher at *Ethics* v, there is 'the just' in an unqualified sense.[46] In another way, something is said to be 'other than' something else not in an unqualified sense, but while still belonging in some way to that something else: and in this way, as regards human affairs, a son belongs to his father, since he is in a certain sense part of him, as stated at *Ethics* VIII,[47] and a slave belongs to his master because he is his instrument, as stated at *Politics* I.[48] Hence a father is not related to his son simply as one man to another; and so between them there is not 'the just' in an unqualified sense, but a kind of just called 'paternal'. By the same token, nor is there 'the just' simply between master and slave, but that which is called 'dominative'.

A wife, however, though she belongs to her husband because he is related to her as to his own body, as the Apostle shows at Ephesians 5:28,

---

[43] IaIIae 90:2 (p. 78, above).
[44] *Politics* 1:3 (1253b5). This objection simply makes the point already made in *obiectio* 1 in a different way.
[45] *Ethics* 5:6 (1134b8).
[46] *Ethics* 5:6 (1134a26).
[47] *Ethics* 8:12 (1161b18).
[48] *Politics* 1:4 (1253b32; 1254a14).

is nonetheless more distinct from her husband than a son is from his father or a slave from his master; for she is received into a kind of social life, that of matrimony.[49] Hence, as the Philosopher says, the relationship between husband and wife has more of the nature of justice than does that between father and son or master and slave, because husband and wife are both related directly to the community of the household, as is shown at *Politics* 1;[50] and so between them there is not political justice in the unqualified sense, but 'domestic' justice.

ad 1: It is the function of justice to render to each his due; but this is on the assumption of a transaction involving different parties; for if someone gives himself what is due to him, this is not properly called 'just'. Since, therefore, what belongs to the son is his father's and what belongs to the slave is his master's, it follows that justice in the proper meaning of the term does not exist as between father and son and master and slave.

ad 2: A son belongs to his father inasmuch as he is a son; and, similarly, a slave belongs to his master inasmuch as he is a slave. But each, considered as a man, is also something having an existence of his own, distinct from that of other men. Insofar as each of them is a man, then, a certain kind of justice belongs to them, and for this reason there are certain laws which govern the relations of father to son and master to slave. But insofar as each is something belonging to another, the complete idea of 'just' or 'right' is lacking as between them.

ad 3: As to other differences between one person and another in a State, these all relate immediately to the community of the State and its prince, and so the kind of 'just' which pertains to them is according to the complete idea of [i.e. the unqualified or 'political' sense of] justice. This 'just' however is expressed differently according to the various offices. Hence when we speak of 'military', or 'magisterial', or 'priestly' right, this is not because these kinds of right fall short of 'right' in the unqualified sense, as is the case when we speak of paternal right or dominative right, but because something proper is due to each class of person according to his particular office.

---

[49] I.e. the husband's relation to his wife is social rather than proprietorial. She is not her husband's equal, but nor is she a mere adjunct or belonging.

[50] *Politics* 1:2 and 5 (1253b6; 1259a39). The wife is related to the community of the household 'in her own right' rather than as an appendage of her husband.

(b) *Summa theologiae* IIaIIae 58: On justice

We come next to justice; and here there are twelve things to consider:

1. What justice is[51]
2. Whether justice is always towards another
3. Whether it is a virtue
4. Whether it is in the will as its subject
5. Whether it is a general virtue
6. Whether, insofar as it is a general virtue, it is in essence the same as every virtue
7. Whether there is a particular justice
8. Whether particular justice has a specific field of concern
9. Whether it is concerned with the passions, or with actions only
10. Whether the mean of justice is an objective mean
11. Whether the act of justice is to render to each his own
12. Whether justice is the foremost of the moral virtues

articulus 1: Whether justice is suitably defined as 'a constant and perpetual will to render to each his right'[52]

It seems that justice has been unsuitably defined by the Jurists as 'a constant and perpetual will to render to each his right'.

obiectio 1: For, according to the Philosopher at *Ethics* v, justice is 'a habit by which someone is disposed to do what is just, and to be just in act and intention'.[53] But 'will' denotes a power, or an act also [but not a habit]. Therefore justice is improperly called a will.

obiectio 2: Moreover, righteousness of will is not the same as will itself; otherwise, if the will were its own righteousness, it would follow that no will would be perverse. But according to Anselm, in the book *De veritate*, 'Justice is righteousness.'[54] Therefore justice is not a will.

obiectio 3: Moreover, only the will of God is perpetual. If, therefore, justice is a 'perpetual will', justice will exist only in God.

---

[51] St Thomas also offers a technical analysis of the other side of this question – i.e. of what injustice is – at IIaIIae 59.
[52] *CICiv.: Digesta* 1:1:10; *Institutiones* 1:1:1.
[53] *Ethics* 5:1 (1129a7).
[54] *Dialogus de veritate* 12 (*PL* 158:480).

obiectio 4: Moreover, everything 'perpetual' is 'constant' because it is immutable. In defining justice it is therefore superfluous to postulate that it is both perpetual and constant.

obiectio 5: Moreover, to render to each his right pertains to the prince. Therefore, if justice renders to each his right, it follows that it does not exist except in the prince; which is an unsuitable conclusion.

obiectio 6: Moreover, Augustine, in the book *De moribus ecclesiae*, says that 'justice is love serving God alone'.[55] Therefore it does not render to each his own.

responsio: The definition of justice given above is suitable if it is rightly understood. For since every virtue is a habit which is the guiding principle of good acts, it is necessary that a virtue be defined in terms of the good acts specific to that virtue. Now justice is properly concerned with those things which have to do with our relations with others, as will be made clear below.[56] Hence by the words 'to render to each his right' justice is defined in terms of both the act specific to it and its object.[57] For, as Isidore says in the book *Etymologies*, 'someone is called just [*iustus*] because he upholds the right [*ius*]'.[58]

But if an act of any kind whatsoever is to be virtuous, it must be voluntary, and it must moreover be stable and unwavering. For the Philosopher says at *Ethics* II that if an act is to be virtuous it must be done, first, knowingly; second, voluntarily and for a proper end; and, third, resolutely.[59] Now the first of these things is included in the second, since, as is said at *Ethics* III, what is done unknowingly is done involuntarily.[60] Hence the definition of justice mentions first the 'will' [*voluntas*], in order to show that an act of justice must be voluntary; and the words 'constant' and 'perpetual' are then added, to indicate that the act must also be unwavering.

The definition given above is, therefore, a complete definition of justice apart from the fact that the act of justice is mentioned instead of the habit which takes its species from acts of that kind: that is, the habit which

---

[55] *De moribus ecclesiae* 1:15.
[56] Art. 2.
[57] I.e. the words identify justice both with right (which is the 'object' of justice: see IIaIIae 57:1 (p. 158, above)) and specifically with the *doing* of right in relation to others.
[58] *Etymologiae* 10 (PL 82:380).
[59] *Ethics* 2:4 (1105a31).
[60] *Ethics* 3:1 (1109b35).

is defined in terms of such acts. And if anyone should wish to reduce it to the proper form of a definition, he might say that 'justice is the habit according to which someone has a constant and perpetual will to render to each his right'. This is, in effect, the same definition as that proposed by the Philosopher at *Ethics* v, where he says that justice is 'a habit according to which someone is disposed to do what is just, and to be just in act and intention'.

ad 1: 'Will' in this case denotes the act rather than the power; and it is a custom among authors to define habits in terms of the kinds of act associated with them. Thus Augustine says that [the habit of] faith is [the act of] 'believing what you do not see'.[61]

ad 2: Justice is not the same thing as righteousness in its essence, but the two are related causally, since justice is the habit according to which someone acts and wills righteously.

ad 3: A will may be called 'perpetual' in two ways. In one way, with respect to an act of will which is eternal in its duration; and in this sense only the will of God is perpetual. In another way, with respect to its object, as when someone wills to do something at all times; and this latter sense is the one required by the nature of justice. For, granted that one seldom finds anyone who wishes to act justly[62] in every case, it is not consistent with the nature of justice that someone should wish to do justice only in some particular case or for some limited time. Rather, what is required is that a man should have the will to observe justice at all times and in all circumstances.

ad 4: Since 'perpetual' does not denote an act of will which is eternal in its duration, it is not superfluous to add 'constant'. For while a 'perpetual' will denotes a purpose of observing justice at all times, 'constant' signifies an unwavering intention to persevere in that purpose.

ad 5: A judge's way of 'rendering to each what is his' is by giving commands and direction, because a judge is 'animate justice' and the prince is the guardian of justice, as is said at *Ethics* v.[63] On the other hand, subjects 'render to each what is his' by carrying out those commands.

---

[61] *In Ioannis evangelium* 8:32.
[62] Reading *iuste* for *iniuste*, which seems to make poor sense.
[63] *Ethics* 5:4; 6 (1132a21; 1134a1).

ad 6: Inasmuch as love of God includes love of neighbour, as stated above,[64] so a man's service of God includes rendering to each of his neighbours what is due to him.

articulus 2: *Whether justice is always towards another*

It seems that justice is not always towards another.

obiectio 1: For the Apostle says (Romans 3:22) that 'the justice of God is by faith of Jesus Christ'. But faith is not defined in terms of how one man is related to another. Nor therefore is justice.

obiectio 2: Moreover, according to Augustine in the book *De moribus ecclesiae*, 'it pertains to justice that a man should direct to the service of God his authority over things subject to him'.[65] But the sensitive appetite is subject to man, as Genesis 4:7 shows, where it is said: 'The lust thereof' – that is, of sin – 'shall be under thee, and thou shalt have dominion over it'. Therefore dominion over one's own appetites pertains to justice; in which case justice will be towards oneself.

obiectio 3: Moreover, the justice of God is eternal. But nothing else is co-eternal with God. Therefore justice is by its nature not towards another.

obiectio 4: Moreover, acts which affect only oneself need to be regulated just as much as do acts which affect someone else. But acts which affect only oneself are regulated by justice, according to Proverbs 11:5: 'The justice of the upright shall make his way prosperous.' Therefore justice is concerned with our dealings not only with others, but with ourselves also.

sed contra: At *De officiis* I Cicero says that 'the purpose of justice is the association of men with one another, and the maintenance of the life of the community'.[66] But this implies a relationship of men with one another. Therefore justice is concerned only with those things that are towards another.

[64] IIaIIae 25:1.
[65] *De moribus ecclesiae* 1:15.
[66] *De officiis* 1:7.

responsio: Because the term 'justice' denotes equality, as stated above,[67] justice is by its very nature concerned with the relation of one thing to another. For nothing is equal to itself, but only to something else. Also, inasmuch as it belongs to justice to regulate human actions, as stated above,[68] the 'otherness' which the nature of justice requires must necessarily be as between different potential sources of action. But actions belong to concrete individuals and wholes [*Actiones autem sunt suppositorum et totorum*][69] and not, properly speaking, to parts and forms or powers. For it is not properly said that the hand strikes, but the man with his hand; nor is it properly said that heat makes something hot, but fire by heat. Such things may be said figuratively, however. Hence justice, properly speaking, requires that there be distinct concrete individuals; and, consequently, it exists only in one man in relation to another. Nonetheless, in one and the same man we may speak figuratively of his various principles of action, such as reason and the irascible and concupiscible appetites,[70] as though these were so many different agents: so that, metaphorically, one and the same man can be said to be just [in himself, as distinct from in relation to another] insofar as his reason commands the irascible and concupiscible appetites and these obey the reason, and, in general, insofar as what is appropriate to each part of the man is distributed to it. Hence the Philosopher, at *Ethics* V, calls this 'metaphorical justice'.[71]

ad 1: The justice which works in us by faith is that by means of which the ungodly man is justified, and it consists in the proper ordering of the parts of the soul, as stated above in treating of the justification of the ungodly.[72] But this pertains to 'metaphorical' justice, which can be found

[67] IIaIIae 57:1 (p. 158, above).

[68] IIaIIae 57:1 (p. 158, above); IaIIae 113:1.

[69] 'Concrete individual' is the only English expression I can think of to translate the Thomist *terminus technicus* 'suppositus'.

[70] See n. 23 on p. 7, above.

[71] *Ethics* 5:11 (1138b6): 'Metaphorically, and by reason of a certain resemblance, there is a kind of justice not, indeed, between a man and himself, but between certain parts of him: not every kind of justice, though, but that of master and servant or husband and wife. For these are the ratios in which the part of the soul that has a rational principle stands to the irrational part; and it is with a view to these parts that people also think that a man can be unjust to himself: that is, because these parts are liable to suffer something contrary to their respective desires. There is therefore thought to be a mutual justice between them as between ruler and ruled.'

[72] IaIIae 113:1.

even in someone who lives a life of solitude. By this the reply to the second *obiectio* is also shown.

ad 3: God's justice is from eternity according to His eternal will and purpose; and it is chiefly in this that justice consists. It is not, however, eternal according to its effect, since there is nothing which is co-eternal with God.

ad 4: Acts which affect only oneself are sufficiently regulated insofar as the passions are governed by the other moral virtues. But acts which affect others need to be regulated not only in relation to the agent whose acts they are, but specifically in relation to the persons towards whom they are directed; and so there is a specific virtue concerned with such acts, and this is justice.

articulus 3: *Whether justice is a virtue*

It seems that justice is not a virtue.

obiectio 1: For it is said at Luke 17:10: 'When you shall have done all these things that are commanded you, say: We are unprofitable servants; we have done that which we ought to do.' But it is not unprofitable to do a work of virtue; for Ambrose says at *De officiis* II: 'We speak of a profit that is estimated not by pecuniary gain but by the acquisition of godliness.'[73] Therefore to do what one ought to do is not a work of virtue. Yet it is a work of justice. Therefore justice is not a virtue.

obiectio 2: Moreover, something done under necessity is not meritorious. But to render to someone what is his, which pertains to justice, is a matter of necessity. Therefore it is not meritorious. Yet it is by virtuous acts that we acquire merit. Therefore justice is not a virtue.

obiectio 3: Moreover, every moral virtue is concerned with acts. But when things are produced externally these things are not acts but products, as the Philosopher shows in the *Metaphysics*.[74] Therefore since it pertains

---

[73] *De officiis* 2:6 (*PL* 16:116).

[74] The reference is possibly to *Metaphysics* 8:8 (1050a30), although the connection is not entirely clear. The objection itself is somewhat obscure, but the point seems to be that whereas moral virtues perfect the acts of the agent (see IIaIIae 57:1, *responsio* (p. 159, above)), justice, because it consists in a kind of relation with someone else, can be actualised only in some state of affairs external to the agent; which suggests that justice is not a moral virtue but the 'art' of producing external outcomes (cf. IIaIIae 57:1:1 and ad 1 (pp. 159 and 160, above)).

to justice to produce externally a work that is just in itself, it seems that justice is not a moral virtue.

sed contra: Gregory says that 'the whole edifice of good works is constructed upon four virtues', namely temperance, prudence, fortitude and justice.[75]

responsio: A human virtue is one which renders a human act good and makes the man himself good;[76] and this definition applies to justice. For a man's act is rendered good through attaining a rule of reason according to which human acts are regulated. Hence, since justice [is a rule of reason which] regulates human acts, it is clear that it renders a man's work good; and, as Cicero says at *De officiis* I: 'Good men are so called chiefly from their justice.' Hence, as he says in the same place: 'The splendour of virtue appears in it [i.e. in justice] above all.'[77]

ad 1: When someone does what he ought, he does not thereby bring benefit to the person to whom he does what he ought, but only abstains from injuring him. He does, however, bring benefit to himself insofar as he does what he ought to do spontaneously and readily, which is what it is to act virtuously. Hence it is said at Wisdom 8:7 that the wisdom of God 'teacheth temperance, and prudence, and justice, and fortitude, which are such things as men' – that is, virtuous men – 'can have nothing more profitable in life'.

ad 2: Necessity is of two kinds. One is the necessity of constraint, and this takes away the quality of merit because it acts in opposition to the will. The second kind of necessity is an obligation arising from a command, or a necessity in relation to an end: that is, when someone cannot achieve the end of virtue other than by doing some particular act. The second kind of necessity does not exclude the quality of merit insofar as someone does willingly whatever is necessary in this sense, although it does exclude the glory of supererogation,[78] according to 1 Corinthians 9:16: 'If I preach the Gospel, it is no glory to me, for a necessity lieth upon me.'

ad 3: Justice does not consist in the production of external things in the way that an art does, but in making use of such things in our relations with others.

[75] *Moralia* 2:49 (*PL* 75:592).
[76] Cf. *Ethics* 2:6 (1106a15); IaIIae 55:2ff.
[77] *De officiis* 1:7.
[78] I.e. the glory which attaches to doing more than one's duty.

articulus 4: *Whether justice is in the will as its subject*[79]

It seems that justice is not in the will as its subject.

obiectio 1: For justice is sometimes called truth. But truth is not in the will, but in the intellect. Therefore justice is not in the will as its subject.

obiectio 2: Moreover, justice is concerned with our dealings with others. But to order one thing in relation to another belongs to reason. Therefore justice is not in the will as its subject, but in the reason.

obiectio 3: Moreover, justice is not an intellectual virtue, because it does not have knowledge as its object [but right];[80] and so the conclusion is left that it is a moral virtue. But moral virtue is located in those faculties which are 'rational by participation': that is, the irascible and concupiscible appetites, as the Philosopher shows at *Ethics* 1.[81] Therefore justice is not in the will as its subject, but in the irascible and concupiscible appetites.

sed contra: Anselm says that 'justice is rectitude of will observed for its own sake'.[82]

responsio: The subject [i.e. the 'seat'] of a virtue is that power whose act the virtue in question has the function of regulating. Now the purpose of justice is not to direct any act of the cognitive power, because it is not through knowing something rightly that we are called just; and so the subject of justice is not intellect or reason, which is the cognitive power. Rather, since we are said to be just through doing something rightly, and because the principle which leads immediately to our doing something is an appetitive power, justice must necessarily be in some appetitive power as its subject. Now the appetite is twofold: namely, the will, which is in the reason, and the sensitive appetite, which follows sense-perception and is divided into the irascible and the concupiscible, as stated in the First Part.[83] But the act of rendering to each what is his cannot proceed from the sensitive appetite, because sense-perception does not extend to a consideration of the relation of one thing to another; rather, to do this is a property of reason. Hence justice cannot be in the irascible or

---

[79] It should be borne in mind that by 'subject' St Thomas here means something like 'seat' or 'location' rather than 'subject matter'; hence Fr Gilby's paraphrase (BE 37:29): 'Is justice seated in the will?'

[80] See IIaIIae 57:1 (p. 158, above).

[81] *Ethics* 1:13 (1102b30); and see p. 7 n. 23, above.

[82] *Dialogus de veritate* 12 (*PL* 158:482).

[83] Ia 81:2.

concupiscible appetites as its subject, but only in the will. And so the Philosopher defines justice as an act of the will, as is shown by what has been said above.[84]

ad 1: Since the will is the rational appetite, when the rectitude of reason, which is called truth, is imprinted on the will by dint of the will's closeness to reason, this impression retains the name of truth; and hence it is that justice is sometimes called truth.

ad 2: The will is directed towards its object as a consequence of that object having been apprehended by the reason. And so, since reason orders one thing in relation to another, the will can will one thing in relation to another; and to do this pertains to justice.

ad 3: It is not only the irascible and concupiscible appetites which are 'rational by participation', but the entire appetitive faculty, as stated at *Ethics* I,[85] because all appetite is subject to reason. But the will is contained in the appetitive faculty, and so it can be the subject [i.e. the 'seat'] of moral virtue.

articulus 5: *Whether justice is a general virtue*[86]

It seems that justice is not a general virtue.

obiectio 1: For according to Wisdom 8:7, justice is classified with other virtues: 'She teacheth temperance and prudence, and justice, and fortitude.' But a genus is not classified or enumerated with the species which are members of that genus. Therefore justice is not a general virtue.

obiectio 2: Moreover, as justice is deemed a cardinal virtue,[87] so are temperance and fortitude. But neither temperance nor fortitude is deemed a general virtue. Nor, therefore, should justice be in any way deemed a general virtue.

obiectio 3: Moreover, justice is always towards others, as stated above.[88] But a sin committed against one's neighbour cannot be a general sin,

---

[84] *Ethics* 5:1 (1129a9); cf. art. 1.
[85] *Ethics* 1:13 (1102b30).
[86] I.e. is justice a genus of which other virtues are species, or is it one of a number of specific virtues? Again, the distinction between 'general' or 'legal' justice and 'particular' justice which St Thomas is proposing to draw comes from Book v of the *Nicomachean Ethics* (1129a1ff).
[87] See p. 59 n. 5, above; see also IaIIae 61.
[88] Art. 2.

because it is classified with sin committed against oneself. Nor, therefore, is justice a general virtue.[89]

sed contra: The Philosopher says at *Ethics* v that 'justice is every virtue'.[90]

responsio: As stated above, justice directs a man in his relations with others. But such direction can be of two kinds. On the one hand, it can direct his relations with others considered as individuals; on the other, it can direct his relations with others considered as members of a community, inasmuch, that is, as he who serves a community serves all the men who are included in that community. Accordingly, justice in its proper meaning can be directed to another in both of these ways. Now it is clear that all who are included in a community are related to that community as parts to a whole. But a part is that which belongs to a whole. Hence whatever is a good of a part can be directed to the good of the whole. It follows therefore that the good of any virtue whatsoever, whether the virtue in question directs a man in relation to himself or in relation to some other individual persons, is ultimately referable to the common good to which justice directs: so that all acts of virtue can pertain to justice insofar as justice directs man to the common good. It is in this sense that justice is called a general virtue. And since it is the function of law to direct to the common good, as noted above,[91] it follows that the justice which is general in this way is called 'legal justice', because by it a man is brought into harmony with the law which directs the acts of all the virtues to the common good.[92]

ad 1: Justice is collected or enumerated together with the other virtues not insofar as it is general, but insofar as it is a specific virtue, as will be stated below.[93]

ad 2: Temperance and fortitude are in the sensitive appetite, that is, in the concupiscible and irascible parts of it. Now powers of this kind are able to desire certain particular goods, as the senses are able to know particular

[89] I.e. injustice is a sin against one's neighbour; but such a sin is not 'general' – i.e. is not a genus – since sins against neighbour and sins against self are both species of a more 'general' kind of sin. This is only a different version of the point made in *obiectio* 1.

[90] *Ethics* 5:1 (1130a9).

[91] IaIIae 90:2 (p. 78, above).

[92] I.e. justice is a 'general' virtue insofar as it directs the other moral virtues to the common good: i.e. insofar as it directs our conduct 'in general'. Such 'general' justice is called 'legal' because it is distinctively embodied in the law.

[93] Art. 7.

things. On the other hand, justice is in the intellective appetite as its subject, and so is able to desire the universal good which the intellect is able to know. Hence justice can be a general virtue, whereas temperance and fortitude cannot.

ad 3: Everything that relates to oneself can relate also to another, especially with reference to the common good. Hence just as legal justice can be called a general virtue insofar as it directs to the common good, so by the same token can injustice be called a general sin.[94] Hence it is said at 1 John 3:4 that all 'sin is iniquity'.

articulus 6: *Whether justice, insofar as it is a general virtue, is the same in essence as all virtue*[95]

It seems that justice, insofar as it is a general virtue, is the same in essence as all virtue.

obiectio 1: For the Philosopher says at *Ethics* v that virtue and legal justice 'are the same as all virtue, but differ as to their mode of being'.[96] But things which differ merely as to their mode of being, or logically, do not differ in essence. Therefore justice is the same in essence as all virtue.

obiectio 2: Moreover, every virtue which is not the same in essence as all virtue is a part of virtue. Now the justice discussed above [i.e. general or 'legal'] is, as the Philosopher says, 'not a part of virtue but the whole of it'.[97] Therefore such justice is the same in essence as all virtue.

obiectio 3: Moreover, the essence of a virtue is not altered when that virtue directs its act to some higher end. For instance, the habit of temperance

[94] I.e. an injustice against one's neighbour is a sin against the whole community of which one's neighbour is a part, and hence 'general' in the sense of 'general' established in the *responsio*.
[95] The point of this article is as follows. On the one hand, courage, temperance, etc. are not simply more specific kinds of justice – i.e. are not 'in essence' the same as justice – because they have different objects or 'fields of concern'. On the other hand, then, if justice is 'general' in the way that the previous article has sought to establish, it must somehow include the other virtues without being the same as them. The answer (*responsio*) is the one already suggested by the previous article: that general or 'legal' justice includes and governs the other virtues insofar as the other virtues are directed to the common good, but is nonetheless distinct from them in essence. We can, however (*responsio*; ad 3), use the expression 'justice' loosely or by extension, to refer to any of the virtues insofar as its acts are directed to the common good; and 'justice' in this extended sense is not in essence distinct from the other virtues.
[96] *Ethics* 5:1 (1130a12).
[97] *Ethics* 5:1 (1130a9).

remains the same in essence even when its act is directed to a Divine [rather than a merely human] good. But the acts of all the virtues pertain to legal justice insofar as they are directed to a higher end, namely, the common good of the community, which is greater than the good of a single individual. Therefore it seems that legal justice is the same in essence as all virtue.

obiectio 4: Moreover, every good of a part can be directed to the good of the whole; hence, if it is not so directed, it seems vain and futile. But that which is in accordance with virtue cannot be such [*non potest esse huiusmodi*: i.e. cannot be vain and futile].⁹⁸ Therefore it seems that there can be no act of any virtue which does not pertain to general justice, which directs to the common good; and so it seems that general justice is the same in essence as all virtue.

sed contra: The Philosopher says at *Ethics* v that 'many are able to make use of virtue in their own affairs who are not able to do so in things relating to others';⁹⁹ and at *Politics* iii he says that 'the virtue of the good man is not the same simply as the virtue of the good citizen'.¹⁰⁰ But the virtue of the good citizen is general justice, by which someone is directed to the common good. Therefore general justice is not the same as virtue in general; rather, it is possible to have one without the other.¹⁰¹

responsio: Something is called general in two ways. In one way, by predication: for example, 'animal' is general [i.e. is generic] in relation to [the species] man and horse and so on; and, in this way, that which is general must be the same in essence as the things in relation to which it is general, because its genus is part of the essence of the species and falls within its definition. In another way, something is called general with respect to the extent of its power. Thus a universal cause is general in relation to all its effects: the sun, for example, is general in relation to all bodies that are

---

⁹⁸ DE renders this passage as follows. 'Further, every good of a part can be directed to the good of the whole, so that, if it be not thus directed, it would seem without use or purpose. But that which is in accordance with virtue cannot be so directed.' But surely the adjectival *huiusmodi*, 'such', refers to 'without use or purpose' rather than 'directed to the good of the whole'; nor have I been able to see why DE's translation makes sense in terms of the point which the *obiectio* is making.

⁹⁹ *Ethics* 5:1 (1129b33).

¹⁰⁰ *Politics* 3:2 (1277a22).

¹⁰¹ I.e. one could be a good citizen, in the sense of having all one's acts directed to the common good by 'general' or 'legal' justice – i.e. by the law – and a bad man in terms of one's own motives; similarly, one could be a good man living under bad laws.

illuminated or changed by its power; and in this sense there is no need for that which is general to be the same in essence as those things in relation to which it is general, since cause and effect are not the same in essence.

Now it is in the latter sense that, according to what has been said,[102] legal justice is called a general virtue: inasmuch, that is, as it directs the acts of the other virtues to its own end [i.e. the common good] by moving all the other virtues by its command. For just as charity can be called a general virtue insofar as it directs the acts of all the virtues to the Divine good, legal justice can also be so called insofar as it directs the acts of all the virtues to the common good. Accordingly, just as charity, which looks to the Divine good as its proper object, is a specific virtue in respect of its essence, so too legal justice is a specific virtue in respect of its essence, insofar as it looks to the common good as its proper object.[103] And so it resides in the sovereign principally and as it were architectonically [i.e. as a 'master-virtue' which gives direction]; whereas it resides in his subjects secondarily and as it were administratively [i.e. as a virtue which receives direction].[104]

However, the name of legal justice can be given [by extension] to every virtue insofar as every virtue is directed to the common good by such legal justice, which, though special in essence, is nonetheless general according to the extent of its power. Speaking in this way, legal justice is the same in essence as all virtue, but differs from it logically; and it is in this sense that the Philosopher speaks.

By this the replies to the first and second *obiectiones* are shown.

ad 3: This argument again takes 'legal justice' [in its extended sense] to mean a virtue commanded by legal justice.

ad 4: Every virtue properly so called directs its activity to the end proper to that virtue. If that activity is always or sometimes directed to a further end also, this is not due to that virtue strictly speaking; rather, there must be some higher virtue which directs it to that end. Consequently there must be one supreme virtue distinct in essence from every other virtue,

---

[102] Art. 5.
[103] I.e. legal justice is a 'general' virtue insofar as it looks to the common good and therefore controls the other virtues by directing them to the common good. It is a 'specific' virtue in the sense that it is concerned with the common good specifically, rather than with temperance, fortitude, and what not.
[104] Cf. IIaIIae 60:1 ad 4 (p. 194 below).

which directs all the virtues to the common good; and this virtue is legal justice.

> articulus 7: *Whether there is a particular justice as well as general [i.e. 'legal'] justice*[105]

It seems that there is not a particular justice as well as general justice.

obiectio 1: For there is nothing superfluous in the virtues, just as there is not in nature.[106] But general justice guides man sufficiently in all his dealings with others. Therefore there is no need for a particular justice.

obiectio 2: Moreover, the species of a virtue does not vary according to whether it is directed towards one person or many. But legal justice directs one man's dealings with another in matters pertaining to the community, as shown above.[107] Therefore there is not another species of justice directing one man's dealings with another in matters pertaining to the individual.

obiectio 3: Moreover, between the individual person and the political community comes the community of the household. If, therefore, in addition to general justice, there were a particular justice corresponding to the individual, there would by the same token have to be a domestic justice directing man to the common good of the household; yet there is not said to be any such justice. Nor, therefore, should there be a particular as well as a legal justice.

sed contra: Chrysostom, commenting on Matthew 5:6, 'Blessed are they that hunger and thirst after justice', says: 'By justice He means

---

[105] I.e. is there a branch of justice which regulates the relations between individuals as such, rather than as members of a community? Since we relate to others not only as fellow citizens but as private individuals, and assuming that we do not wish to say that such private relations are devoid of justice, we have to postulate a 'particular' justice as well as general or legal justice. At IIaIIae 61 St Thomas further divides particular justice into commutative and distributive justice. Distributive justice is that virtue whose object is to distribute rewards and punishments to each according to his merits. It observes a just proportion by comparing one person or fact with another so that neither equal persons have unequal things, nor unequal persons equal things. Commutative justice is that virtue whose object it is to render to every one what is his, as nearly as possible, or which governs contracts. This distinction, like the distinction between 'general' and 'particular' justice itself, depends on Book V of the *Nicomachean Ethics*.

[106] Cf. *Politics* 1:2 (1252b1).

[107] Art. 5 and 6.

---

either the general virtue, or the particular virtue which is opposed to avarice.'[108]

responsio: As stated above,[109] legal justice is not the same in essence as all virtue; rather, in addition to the legal justice which directs man immediately to the common good, there must be other virtues to direct him immediately to particular goods; and these virtues may have reference to himself or to another individual person. Just as, therefore, in addition to legal justice there must be particular virtues to direct man in relation to himself, such as temperance and fortitude, so too, as well as legal justice, there must be particular justice to direct man in his dealings with other individuals.

ad 1: Legal justice does indeed direct man sufficiently in his dealings with others. As regards the common good it does so immediately; but as regards the good of another individual, it does so only mediately [i.e. only insofar as the good of that individual is part of the common good]. And so there must be particular justice to direct a man immediately to the good of another individual as such.

ad 2: The common good of the State and the particular good of the individual differ not only with respect to 'many' and 'few', but also with respect to a formal difference [i.e. they differ not only in quantity, but in species or kind]. For common good differs from individual good as whole differs from part. And so the Philosopher says at *Politics* I, 'they do not speak well who say that the State and the household and so forth differ only with respect to many and few and not in species'.[110]

ad 3: According to the Philosopher at *Politics* I, there are three kinds of relationship within the domestic community: that is, 'of husband and wife, father and son, master and slave'.[111] But in each of these relationships, one person in a sense belongs to the other. And so between such persons there does not exist justice in an unqualified sense, but a special kind of justice, namely 'domestic' justice, as stated at Ethics V.[112]

---

[108] *In Mattheum* 15 (PG 57:227).
[109] Art. 6.
[110] *Politics* 1:1 (1252a7).
[111] *Politics* 1:2 (1253b6).
[112] *Ethics* 5:6 (1134b8). See also IIaIIae 57:4, above, p. 165.

articulus 8: *Whether particular justice has a specific field of concern*[113]

It seems that particular justice does not have a specific field of concern.

obiectio 1: For a gloss on Genesis 2:14, 'The fourth river is Euphrates', says: 'Euphrates signifies "fruitful"; nor is it said through what country it flows, because justice belongs to all parts of the soul.'[114] Now this would not be so, if justice had a specific field of concern, since every specific field of concern pertains to a specific power. Therefore particular justice does not have a specific field of concern.

obiectio 2: Moreover, Augustine, in the book *De diversis quaestionibus octoginta tribus*, says that 'the soul has four virtues by which, in this life, it lives spiritually, namely temperance, prudence, fortitude and justice'. And he says that the fourth, justice, is that 'by which all the other virtues are pervaded'.[115] Therefore particular justice, which is one of the four cardinal virtues, does not have a specific field of concern.

obiectio 3: Moreover, justice directs man sufficiently in matters relating to others. But a man can be directed in relation to others in all things pertaining to this life. Therefore the field of concern of justice is general and not specific.

sed contra: The Philosopher, at *Ethics* V, stipulates that particular justice is concerned specifically with those things which belong to social life.[116]

responsio: As the Philosopher shows at *Ethics* II,[117] moral virtue, which is defined as right reason, has as its field of concern the regulation of everything capable of being regulated by reason. Now reason can regulate not only the inward passions of the soul, but also external actions and those external things of which man makes use. But the relation of one man to another is a matter of external actions and involves those external things by means of which men can communicate with one another; whereas the

---

[113] I.e. is particular justice concerned with a specific kind of activity, or with interpersonal activity as a whole? St Thomas wants to say – see *responsio* – that it has to do with outward actions only, and not with what we should call the 'inner' life. In other words, it concerns itself with what we do and not with what we intend or think. 'Field of concern' is a cumbersome translation of *materia*, but it is better than DE's 'matter', and BE's 'subject-matter' is misleading in view of the sense in which St Thomas uses *subiectus* elsewhere: see, for example, ad 1, below and art. 4, above.

[114] Augustine, *De Genesi contra Manichaeos* 2:10.

[115] *83 quaest.* 1:61.

[116] *Ethics* 5:2 (1130b31).

[117] *Ethics* 2:6 (1107a1).

regulation of a man in himself is a matter of inward passions. And so, since justice is directed towards others, it is not concerned with the whole field of moral virtue, but only with external actions and things, and under a certain specific aspect: that is, in so far as one man is related to another through them.

ad 1: As to its essence, justice belongs to one part of the soul, in which it dwells as in its subject: namely, the will, which moves all the other parts of the soul by its command. And so justice 'belongs to all the parts of the soul' not directly, but by a kind of diffusion.

ad 2: As stated above,[118] the cardinal virtues may be taken in two ways. In one way, as special virtues, each having a determinate field of concern. In another way, as certain general modes of virtue. And it is in this latter sense that Augustine is here speaking [of justice]. For he says that

> prudence is knowledge of those things which are to be sought and avoided; temperance is that which restrains our desire for temporal delights; fortitude is strength of mind in confronting temporal adversities; justice is the love of God and our neighbour by which the other virtues are pervaded: that is, it is the common root of the entire order between one man and another.[119]

ad 3: It is the specific nature of justice to be directed towards another; but the inward passions which are part of the field of concern of morals are not, in themselves, directed towards another; rather, it is their effects – that is, outward actions – which are capable of being directed toward another [and this is done by justice]. Hence it does not follow that the field of concern of justice is general in itself.[120]

articulus 9: *Whether justice is concerned with the passions*[121]

It seems that justice is concerned with the passions.

---

[118] IaIIae 61:3 and 4.

[119] *83 quaest.* 1:61.

[120] I.e. justice is 'general' not in its own 'field of concern', which is specifically to be directed 'towards another' or to the common good, but insofar as it also directs other virtues to the common good.

[121] 'Passions' here in the sense of emotions or feelings arising out of movements of the sensitive appetite. See IaIIae 22:3; see also p. 112 n. 156 and p. 114 n. 166.

obiectio 1: For the Philosopher says at *Ethics* II that 'moral virtue is concerned with pleasures and pains'.[122] Now pleasure – that is, delight – and pain are passions, as was noted above in treating of the passions.[123] Therefore justice, as a moral virtue, is concerned with the passions.

obiectio 2: Moreover, it is by justice that one man's actions in relation to another are regulated. But such actions cannot be regulated unless the passions are regulated first, since disorder in the aforementioned actions arises because of disorder in the passions: for example, adultery proceeds from sexual lust, and theft proceeds from an excessive love of money. Therefore justice must be concerned with the passions.

obiectio 3: Moreover, both particular justice and legal justice are directed towards another person. But legal justice is concerned with the passions; otherwise it would not extend itself to all the virtues, some of which are clearly concerned with the passions. Therefore justice is concerned with the passions.

sed contra: The Philosopher, at *Ethics* V, says that justice has to do with actions [as distinct from passions].[124]

responsio: The truth of this question appears from two sources. First, from the subject [i.e. the 'seat'] of justice, which is the will, the movements or acts of which are not passions, as noted above;[125] for it is only the sensitive appetite whose movements are called passions, and so, unlike temperance and fortitude, justice is not concerned with the passions, which are in the irascible and concupiscible appetites. Second, from its field of concern; for justice is concerned with one man's relations with another, and it is not by the inward passions that we are immediately directed in our relations with another. Therefore justice is not concerned with the passions.

ad 1: Not every moral virtue has pleasure and pain as its particular field of concern: fortitude, for instance, is concerned with fear and boldness. But every moral virtue is directed to pleasure and pain as ends to be acquired; for, as the Philosopher says at *Ethics* VII, 'pleasures and pains are the principal end in respect of which we say that something is bad and

---

[122] *Ethics* 2:3 (1104b8).
[123] IaIIae 23.
[124] *Ethics* 5:1 (1129a3): i.e. justice is about what we do rather than what we feel.
[125] IaIIae 22:3; 59:4.

something is good',[126] and in this way too they belong to justice, since 'a man is not just unless he takes pleasure in just actions'.[127;128]

ad 2: External actions lie, as it were, on a mean between external things, which are their objects, and inward passions, which are their origin. Now it sometimes happens that there is a defect in one of these without there being a defect in the other. For example, someone may steal something belonging to another not through a desire to have that thing, but through the will[129] to do its owner harm; or, on the other hand, he may covet what belongs to someone else without having a will to steal it. Accordingly, the directing of our actions insofar as they tend towards external things belongs to justice, but insofar as they arise from the passions it belongs to the other moral virtues, which are concerned with the passions. Hence justice hinders the theft of another's property insofar as stealing is contrary to the equality that should be maintained in external things, while liberality hinders it insofar as it arises from an excessive desire for riches. But since external acts take their species not from the inward passions but from external things as being their objects, it follows that external acts are essentially the concern of justice rather than of the other moral virtues.[130]

ad 3: The common good is the end of each individual member of a community, just as the good of the whole is the end of each part. On the other hand, the good of one individual is not the end of another individual: hence legal justice, which is directed to the common good, is more

---

[126] *Ethics* 7:11 (1152b2).

[127] *Ethics* 1:8 (1099a18).

[128] I.e. fortitude or courage is the virtue concerned immediately with brave behaviour, which is an action rather than a 'passion'. But bravery pleases us; we call it good because it pleases us; and we take pleasure in being, or in the fact that other people are, brave. This kind of argument can plainly apply to every virtue, and the corresponding argument about pain to every vice. There is, therefore, a sense in which moral virtues are concerned with the passions, but only an indirect sense.

[129] 'Will', it will be recalled, has to do with actions, not passions: see *responsio*; see also art. 4 *responsio*.

[130] I.e. strictly speaking justice is concerned with the regulation of our external actions rather than with the passions which drive them. On the other hand, the other moral virtues are chiefly concerned with inward passions: i.e. with motives rather than directly with outcomes. This disjunction is supported by the consideration that the connection between actions and passions – between what we do and how we feel – is not inevitable or invariable. Sometimes our behaviour in relation to external goods is 'defective' without there being a corresponding 'defect' in our internal passions; sometimes our internal passions are defective, but do not lead to the corresponding defect in our external behaviour.

capable of extending to the internal passions by which a man is in some way disposed in himself, than is particular justice, which is directed to the good of another individual. Nonetheless, legal justice extends to the other virtues chiefly in respect of their external actions: insofar, that is, as 'the law commands us to perform the actions of a courageous person, the actions of a temperate person and the actions of an equable person', as is said at *Ethics* v.[131;132]

articulus 10: *Whether the mean of justice is an objective mean* [medium rei][133]

It seems that the mean of justice is not an objective mean.

obiectio 1: For the character of a genus is preserved in each of its species. But moral virtue is defined at Ethics II as 'a habit of choice lying in a mean relative to ourselves, determined by a rational principle'.[134] Therefore there is in justice a rational rather than an objective mean.[135]

obiectio 2: Moreover, in things which are good absolutely, there is neither excess nor defect, and, consequently, nor is there a mean, as there clearly is in the virtues, as is said at *Ethics* II.[136] But justice has to do with things that are good absolutely, as is said at *Ethics* v.[137] Therefore in justice there is not an objective mean.

obiectio 3: Moreover, the reason why the other virtues are said to observe a rational and not an objective mean is that, in their case, the mean varies according to different persons, since what is too much for one is too little

---

[131] *Ethics* 5:1 (1129b19).

[132] The meaning of this passage seems to be as follows. No individual is (legally) required to will the good of any other individual as such, although each individual is required to will the common good of the whole community. In a sense, therefore, 'legal' justice, as distinct from 'particular' justice, can concern itself with the regulation of individual passions for the common good. Nonetheless, even legal justice is concerned with outward actions rather than underlying motives or feelings. Its concern with 'the internal passions by which a man is in some way disposed in himself' is therefore indirect or contingent only.

[133] 'Objective mean' is the nearest one can come to what St Thomas means by *medium rei*: i.e. a 'mean' which is impersonal or mathematical and therefore not variable according to circumstances or relative to what anyone thinks or wills.

[134] *Ethics* 2:6 (1106b36).

[135] A 'rational mean' is a mean calculated by reason in relation to specific circumstances, and therefore not 'objective' in the way explained in n. 133.

[136] *Ethics* 2:6 (1107a22).

[137] *Ethics* 5:1 (1129b5).

for another, as is said at *Ethics* II.[138] But this seems also to be true of justice; for one who strikes a prince does not receive the same punishment as one who strikes a private person. Therefore in justice also there is not an objective mean, but a rational one.

sed contra: The Philosopher says at *Ethics* V that the mean of justice is to be arrived at 'according to arithmetical proportion', which is an objective mean.[139]

responsio: As stated above,[140] the other moral virtues are concerned chiefly with the passions, the regulation of which cannot be accomplished other than in relation to the circumstances of the particular man whose passions they are: other, that is, than in relation to the specific circumstances in which anger or desire arise. And so the mean in such virtues is arrived at not according to the proportion of one thing to another, but simply in relation to the virtuous man himself. In such cases, therefore, the mean is only that which is fixed by reason in relation to ourselves. But justice takes external action as its field of concern, in so far as an action, or something used in that action, is duly proportionate to another person. And so the mean of justice consists in a certain proportion of equality as between the external thing and the external person. But equality is an objective mean between greater and less, as is said at *Metaphysics* IX.[141] Hence justice observes an objective mean.

ad 1: This objective mean is also a rational mean; and so the [generically rational] nature of moral virtue is also preserved in the [specific] case of justice.

ad 2: There are two ways in which something is said to be good 'absolutely'. In one way, something may be good in every way. It is in this way that the virtues are good, and there is neither mean nor extremes in things that are good absolutely in this sense. In another way, something is said to be good absolutely because it is good in an absolute sense – that is, in its nature – although it may become evil through being abused. Riches and honours are cases in point, and in such things it is possible to find excess, deficiency and mean in relation to men, who can use them well or

---

[138] *Ethics* 2:6 (1106a36).
[139] *Ethics* 5:4 (1132a1).
[140] Art. 9; cf. IaIIae 59:4.
[141] *Metaphysics* 9:5 (1056a22).

ill; and it is in this latter sense that justice has to do with things that are good 'absolutely'.

ad 3: The injury inflicted has a different proportion to a prince from that which it has to a private person; and so it is fitting that the injury in each case be redressed by punishment in a different way: and this pertains to an objective and not merely a rational difference.

articulus 11: *Whether the act of justice is to render to each his own*

It seems that the act of justice is not to render to each his own.

obiectio 1: For Augustine, at *De Trinitate* XIV, attributes to justice the act of giving succour to the needy.[142] But in giving succour to the needy we give them what is not theirs but ours. Therefore the act of justice is not giving to each his own.

obiectio 2: Moreover, Cicero says that 'beneficence, which may be called kindness or liberality', pertains to justice.[143] But liberality, properly speaking, lies in giving to someone else not what is his already, but what is one's own. Therefore the act of justice does not consist in rendering to each his own.

obiectio 3: Moreover, it pertains to justice not only to distribute things in a suitable fashion, but also to restrain harmful acts such as homicide, adultery and so forth. But to render to each what is his seems to belong solely to the distribution of things. Therefore the act of justice is not sufficiently described when it is said to be the act of rendering to each his own.

sed contra: Ambrose says at *De officiis* I: 'Justice is that which renders to each what is his, lays no claim to what is another's, and neglects its own advantage in order to preserve the common equity.'[144]

responsio: As stated above,[145] justice takes external activity as its field of concern insofar as either the activity itself or something that we use in performing it is made proportionate to some other person to whom we are related by justice. Now each person's 'own' is said to be that which is

---

[142] *De Trinitate* 14:9.
[143] *De officiis* 1:7.
[144] *De officiis* 1:24 (*PL* 16:62).
[145] Art. 8 and 10.

due to him according to equality of proportion. Therefore the proper act of justice is nothing else than to render to each his own.

ad 1: Since justice is a cardinal virtue, other, secondary, virtues such as mercy, liberality and so forth are adjoined to it, as will appear below.[146] And so to give succour to the needy, which pertains to mercy or godliness, and to be generously kind, which pertains to liberality, are by a kind of reduction attributed to justice as to their principal virtue. By this is also shown the reply to the second *obiectio*.

ad 3: As the Philosopher says at *Ethics* V, in matters of justice, the word 'gain' is used wherever there is an excess of any kind and 'loss' wherever there is a deficiency.[147] This is because, first and more commonly, justice is exercised in voluntary exchanges of things such as buying and selling, where those terms are used strictly, and the terms are then transferred to all other cases where questions of justice can arise. And the same applies to the rendering to each of what is his own.[148]

articulus 12: *Whether justice is pre-eminent among the moral virtues*

It seems that justice is not pre-eminent among the moral virtues.

obiectio 1: For it belongs to justice to render to each what is his. But it belongs to liberality to give of one's own, and this is more virtuous. Therefore liberality is a greater virtue than justice.

obiectio 2: Moreover, nothing is adorned by something less worthy than itself. But proper pride [*magnanimitas*] is the ornament both of justice and of all the virtues, as is said at *Ethics* IV.[149] Therefore proper pride is nobler than justice.

obiectio 3: Moreover, virtue is concerned with what is 'difficult' and 'good', as is said at *Ethics* II.[150] But fortitude involves more difficult things than justice does, since, as is said at *Ethics* III, it is concerned with those things that imperil life.[151] Therefore fortitude is nobler than justice.

---

[146] IaIIae 80:1.

[147] *Ethics* 5:4 (1132b11).

[148] I.e. 'rendering to each what is his' has come to refer by extension to requital or redress of all kinds, not merely to the distribution of things.

[149] *Ethics* 4:3 (1124a1).

[150] *Ethics* 2:3 (1105a9).

[151] *Ethics* 3:6 (1115a24).

sed contra: Cicero says: 'In justice the splendour of the virtues is at its greatest, and it gives its name to the good man.'[152]

responsio: If we speak of legal justice, it is clear that it is pre-eminent among the moral virtues, inasmuch as the common good is pre-eminent over the individual good of one person. Accordingly the Philosopher, at *Ethics* V, says that 'the most excellent of the virtues seems to be justice, more glorious than either the evening or the morning star'.[153] But even if we speak of particular justice, it is more excellent than the other moral virtues, for two reasons. The first reason can be taken from its subject: from the fact, that is, that justice is in the nobler part of the soul, namely, the rational appetite or will, whereas the other moral virtues are in the sensitive appetite, to which belong the passions which are the concern of the other moral virtues. The second reason is taken from its object, because the other virtues are praised solely in relation to the good of the virtuous man in himself, whereas justice is praised in relation to the virtuous man's being well disposed towards another, so that justice is in a certain sense another's good, as is said at *Ethics* V.[154] Hence the Philosopher says, at *Rhetoric* I: 'The greatest virtues must necessarily be those which are most profitable to others, because virtue is a faculty of doing good to others. For this reason the greatest honours are bestowed upon the brave and the just, since bravery is useful to others in war, and justice is useful to others in both war and peace.'[155]

ad 1: Although the liberal man gives of his own, he nonetheless takes into consideration the good of his own virtue when he does so. When, on the other hand, the just man gives to another what is his, he does so as one considering the common good. Moreover justice is observed towards all, whereas liberality cannot extend to all. Again, liberality, by which one gives of one's own, is founded upon justice, whereby one renders to each what is due to him.

ad 2: When proper pride is added to justice it increases the goodness of the latter. Without justice, however, it would not have the character of virtue at all.[156]

---

[152] *De officiis* 1:7.
[153] *Ethics* 5:1 (1129b27).
[154] *Ethics* 5:1 (1130a3); cf. Plato, *Republic* 343C.
[155] *Rhetoric* 1:9 (1366b3).
[156] I.e. without the kind of proportion which justice embodies, it would not be 'proper' pride.

ad 3: Although fortitude is concerned with the most difficult things, it does not have to do with the best things; for it is useful only in war, whereas justice is useful in both war and peace, as stated above.

(c) *Summa theologiae* IIaIIae 60: On judgment

We come next to Judgment; and here there are six things to consider:

1. Whether judgment is an act of justice
2. Whether it is lawful to judge
3. Whether it is unlawful to judge on the basis of suspicion
4. Whether doubts should be given the more favourable interpretation
5. Whether we ought always to judge according to the written law
6. Whether judgment is rendered perverse by usurpation

articulus 1: *Whether judgment is an act of justice*

It seems that judgment is not an act of justice.

obiectio 1: For the Philosopher says at *Ethics* I that 'everyone judges well of what he knows';[157] and so judgment seems to belong to the cognitive faculty. But the cognitive faculty is perfected by prudence.[158] Therefore judgment pertains more to prudence than to justice, which is in the will, as stated above.[159]

obiectio 2: Moreover, the Apostle says at 1 Corinthians 2:15: 'The spiritual man judgeth all things.' But it is chiefly by the virtue of charity, which 'is poured forth in our hearts by the Holy Spirit Who is given to us', as is said at Romans 5:5, that a man is made spiritual. Therefore judgment pertains more to charity than to justice.

obiectio 3: Moreover, it pertains to every virtue to judge rightly within its specific field of concern; for 'the virtuous man is the rule and measure in everything', according to the Philosopher, in the book *Ethics*.[160] Therefore judgment does not pertain more to justice than it does to the other moral virtues.

---

[157] *Ethics* 1:3 (1094b27).
[158] Cf. IIaIIae 47.
[159] IIaIIae 58:4 (p. 175, above).
[160] *Ethics* 3:4 (1113a32).

obiectio 4: Moreover, judgment seems to pertain only to judges; yet the act of justice is found in all just men. Since, then, not only judges are just men, it seems that judgment is not an act peculiar to justice.

sed contra: It is said at Psalm 94:15: 'Until justice be turned into judgment'.

responsio: Properly speaking, judgment denotes the act of the judge in judging. But a judge [*iudex*] is so called from 'declaring the right' [*ius dicens*]. Moreover, 'right' is the object of justice, as noted above.[161] Judgment, therefore, according to the primary meaning of the term, is a definition or determination of the just or right. But when someone defines something well in matters of virtuous action, such a definition proceeds, properly speaking, from a habit of virtue: for example, a chaste person defines things rightly in matters belonging to chastity. And so judgment, which denotes a right determination of what is just, properly pertains to [the habit of] justice. For this reason the Philosopher says at *Ethics* v that 'men have recourse to a judge as to a kind of animate justice'.[162]

ad 1: The term 'judgment', which according to its primary meaning signifies a right decision as to what is just, has been broadened to signify a right decision in anything at all, whether speculative or practical. Nonetheless, right judgment in all matters requires two things. The first is the virtue itself which pronounces judgment; and in this way judgment is an act of the reason, because it belongs to the reason to pronounce or define. The other is the disposition of the one who judges, upon which depends his capacity for judging rightly. And so judgment in matters pertaining to justice proceeds from justice, just as in matters pertaining to fortitude it proceeds from fortitude. So, therefore, judgment is an act of justice insofar as justice inclines one to judge rightly, and of prudence insofar as prudence pronounces the judgment. Hence also *synesis*,[163] which pertains to prudence, is said to 'judge well', as noted above.[164]

ad 2: The spiritual man, from the fact that he has the habit of charity, has an inclination to judge all things rightly according to Divine rules; and it is in accordance with these that he pronounces judgment through the gift

---

[161] IIaIIae 57:1 (p. 158, above).

[162] *Ethics* 5:4 (1132a20).

[163] *Synesis* = 'sound judgment'.

[164] IIaIIae 51:3. Neither *obiectio* 1 nor its reply are well expressed; but the point seems to be the obvious one that sound judgment requires not only knowledge, but also the will to judge rightly, which is justice (see IIaIIae 58:4, p. 175, above).

of wisdom, just as the just man pronounces judgment through the virtue of prudence in accordance with the rules of the law.

ad 3: The other virtues regulate man in himself, but justice regulates man in his dealings with others, as shown above.[165] Now a man is his own master in things which pertain only to himself, but he is not master in things pertaining to others. Where the other virtues are concerned, therefore, there is no need for any judgment – taking the term 'judgment' in its broader sense, as explained above – other than that of the virtuous man.[166] But in matters pertaining to justice, there is further need for the judgment of some superior, who is 'able to reprove both, and to put his hand between both' (Job 9:33). And for this reason judgment belongs more specifically to justice than to any other virtue.

ad 4: Justice is in the ruler as an architectonic virtue [i.e. as a directive or 'master' virtue]:[167] that is, as commanding and prescribing what is just. But it is in his subjects as an executive and administrative virtue [that is, as carrying out the prince's just commands]. And so judgment, which denotes a definition of what is just, pertains to justice considered as existing chiefly in a ruler.

articulus 2: *Whether it is lawful to judge*

It seems that it is not lawful to judge.

obiectio 1: For punishment is not inflicted for anything except that which is unlawful. But those who judge are threatened with a punishment which those who do not judge will escape, according to Matthew 7:1, 'Judge not, and ye shall not be judged.' Therefore it is unlawful to judge.

obiectio 2: Moreover, it is said at Romans 14:4: 'Who art thou that judgest another man's servant? To his own lord he standeth or falleth.' Now God is the Lord of all. Therefore it is not lawful for any man to judge.

obiectio 3: Moreover, no man is without sin, according to 1 John 1:8: 'If we say that we have no sin, we deceive ourselves.' But it is not lawful for a

---

[165] IIaIIae 58:2 (p. 171, above).
[166] I.e. in matters relating only to such things as chastity, temperance, etc., no judgment is needed beyond one's own judgment (in the broad, non-technical sense mentioned at ad 1) of one's conduct, because no dispute requiring the mediation of an outside judge is involved. Judgment in the strict sense, therefore, belongs to justice: i.e. to the moral virtue which regulates us in our relations with others.
[167] Cf. IIaIIae 58:6 (p. 178, above).

sinner to judge, according to Romans 2:1: 'Thou art inexcusable, O man, whosoever thou art, that judgest; for wherein thou judgest another, thou condemnest thyself, for thou dost the same things which thou judgest.' Therefore it is not lawful for anyone to judge.

sed contra: It is said at Deuteronomy 16:18: 'Thou shalt appoint judges and magistrates in all thy gates, that they may judge the people with just judgment.'

responsio: Judgment is lawful insofar as it is an act of justice. But it is clear from what has been said above[168] that three conditions are required for a judgment to be an act of justice. First, it must proceed from the inclination of justice; second, it must proceed from one who has authority; third, it must be pronounced according to the right reason of prudence. If any one of these conditions is absent, the judgment will be faulty and unlawful. It will be faulty and unlawful in one way when it is contrary to the rectitude of justice, in which case the judgment is said to be perverted or unjust; in another way, when a man judges matters over which he has no authority, and this is called judgment by usurpation; in a third way, when the judgment lacks the certainty of reason, as when someone lightly or conjecturally passes judgment on some matter which is doubtful or hidden, in which case it is called judgment by suspicion or rash judgment.

ad 1: The Lord here forbids us rashly to judge the intention of the heart or other uncertain things, as Augustine says in the book *De sermone Domini in monte*.[169] Alternatively, as Hilary says,[170] He forbids us to judge concerning things Divine, which, because they are above us, we ought not to judge but simply believe. Alternatively, as Chrysostom says, He forbids the judgment which proceeds not from benevolence but from bitterness of spirit.[171]

ad 2: A judge is appointed as a minister of God. Hence it is said at Deuteronomy 1:16: 'Judge that which is just'; and, further on (vs. 17), 'because it is the judgment of God'.

ad 3: Those who are guilty of grievous sins should not judge those guilty of the same or lesser sins, as Chrysostom says, commenting on

---

[168] Art. 1, ad 1 and 3.
[169] *De sermone Domini in monte* 2:18.
[170] *Super Matthaeum* 5 (*PL* 9:950).
[171] *Opus imperfectum in Mattheum* 17 (*PG* 56:725).

Matthew 7:1, 'Judge not.'[172] This is to be understood as applying above all when such sins are public, because scandal would then be produced in the hearts of others. But if they are not public but hidden, and the need arises for someone to give judgment as a matter of duty, he can reprove or judge with humility and fear. Hence Augustine says in the book *De sermone Domini in monte*: 'If we find that we ourselves are guilty of the same sin as someone else, let us deplore the fact together with him, and invite him to join with us in striving against it.'[173] It is not by doing this that a man condemns himself so as to deserve condemnation anew, but when, in condemning another, he shows that he also deserves condemnation for the same or a similar sin.

articulus 3: *Whether it is unlawful to judge on the basis of suspicion*

It seems that it is not unlawful to judge on the basis of suspicion.

obiectio 1: For suspicion seems to be an uncertain opinion as to some evil; hence the Philosopher proposes at *Ethics* VI that suspicion concerns itself with both the true and the false.[174] But it is not possible to have any opinion about contingent and singular matters which is not uncertain. Since, then, human judgment is concerned with human acts, all of which are singular and contingent, it seems that no judgment would be lawful if it were not lawful to judge on the basis of suspicion.

obiectio 2: Moreover, one does one's neighbour an injury by judging him unlawfully. But an evil suspicion consists only in a man's opinion, and so does not seem to pertain to the injury of another. Therefore judgment based on suspicion is not unlawful.

obiectio 3: Moreover, if it is unlawful, it must be reducible to an injustice, since judgment is an act of justice, as stated above.[175] But an injustice is always a mortal sin according to its genus, as noted above.[176] Therefore a judgment based on suspicion would always be a mortal sin if it were unlawful. But this is false, because 'we cannot avoid suspicions', as

---

[172] *In Mattheum* 23 (PG 57:310).
[173] *De sermone Domini in monte* 2:19.
[174] Perhaps *Ethics* 6:3 (1139b17).
[175] Art. 1.
[176] IIaIIae 59:4.

Augustine's gloss on I Corinthians 4:5, 'Judge not before the time', says.[177]
Therefore it seems that a judgment based on suspicion is not unlawful.

sed contra: Chrysostom, commenting on Matthew 7:1, 'Judge not', etc.,
says: 'By this commandment the Lord forbids not that Christians should
correct others out of benevolence, but that Christian should despise
Christian by boasting of his own righteousness, hating and condemning
others for the most part on suspicion alone.'

responsio: As Cicero says, 'suspicion' denotes an evil opinion proceeding
from slight indications. Now this arises in three ways.[178] In one way, from
someone being evil himself; for because of this, as if conscious of his own
malice, he readily forms evil opinions of others, according to Ecclesiastes
10:3, 'The fool when he walketh in the way, wherein he himself is a fool,
esteemeth all men fools.' In another way, it arises when someone is ill
disposed towards another. For when someone despises or hates another,
or is angry with him or envies him, he is led by trivial signs to form an
evil opinion of him; for everyone finds it easy to believe what he wishes
to believe. Third, it arises from long experience. Hence the Philosopher
says at *Rhetoric* II, 'old people are very suspicious, for they have often experienced the faults of others'.[179] The first two causes of suspicion clearly
pertain to perversity of the affections, whereas the third cause diminishes
the nature of suspicion insofar as experience produces certainty, which is
contrary to the nature of suspicion. And so suspicion denotes a certain
degree of vice; and the further suspicion goes, the more vicious it is.

Now there are three degrees of suspicion. The first degree is when
a man begins to doubt the goodness of another from slight indications.
And this is a venial and light sin, for 'it pertains to human temptation,
without which life cannot be conducted at all', according to a gloss on
I Corinthians 4:5, 'Judge not before the time.'[180] The second degree is
when someone, from slight indications, esteems another's wickedness as
certain. This, if it involves some grave matter, is a mortal sin, inasmuch
as it cannot be done without despising one's neighbour. Hence the same
gloss adds: 'If, therefore, we cannot avoid suspicions, because we are men,
we must at any rate restrain our judgment: that is, we must refrain from
forming definite and firm opinions.' The third degree is when a judge

---

[177] *In Ioannis evangelium* 9, on 15:23.
[178] *De inventione* 2; *Tusculanae disputationes* 4:7; cf. Alexander of Hales, *Summa theologiae* 2:117:1.
[179] *Rhetoric* 2:13 (1389b20).
[180] *In Ioannis evangelium* 9, on 15:23.

proceeds to condemn someone on suspicion merely. And this pertains directly to injustice. Hence it is a mortal sin.

ad 1: Some degree of certainty is to be found in human acts; not, indeed, the certainty of demonstration, but enough to be suitable to the matter in hand: for example, when the truth of something is proved by competent witnesses.

ad 2: From the very fact that someone has an evil opinion of another without sufficient cause, he despises him without cause and so does him an injury.

ad 3: Since justice and injustice are concerned with external acts, as stated above,[181] a judgment based on suspicion pertains directly to injustice when it is carried into action externally, and then it is a mortal sin, as stated in the body of the article. An inward judgment belongs to justice insofar as it is related to the external judgment in the way that an inward act is related to an external one: for instance, as lust is related to fornication or anger to homicide.

articulus 4: Whether doubts should receive the more favourable interpretation

It seems that doubts should not receive the more favourable interpretation.

obiectio 1: For judgments should be made according to what happens most often. But what happens most often is that something evil is done, because 'the number of fools is infinite', as is said at Ecclesiastes 1:15; 'for the imagination of man's heart is evil from his youth', as is said at Genesis 8:21. Therefore doubts should receive the worse rather than the better interpretation.

obiectio 2: Moreover, Augustine says: 'he lives piously and justly who is sound in his estimate of things, turning neither to one side nor the other'.[182] But he who interprets a doubtful point in the more favourable way, turns to one side. Therefore this should not be done.

obiectio 3: Moreover, a man should love his neighbour as himself. But with regard to himself, a man should interpret doubtful matters in the worse

---

[181] IIaIIae 58:8, 10, 11 (pp. 183ff, above); 59:1 ad 3.
[182] *De doctrina Christiana* 1:27.

sense, according to Job 9:28, 'I feared all my works.' Therefore it seems that doubtful matters affecting one's neighbour should be interpreted in the worse sense also.

sed contra: A gloss on Romans 14:3, 'He that eateth not, let him not judge him that eateth', says: 'Doubts should be interpreted in the more favourable sense.'[183]

responsio: As stated above,[184] from the very fact that someone has an evil opinion of another without sufficient cause, he injures and despises him. Now no man ought to despise another or harm him in any way without good cause; and so, where clear signs of someone else's malice do not appear, we ought to think well of him, by interpreting doubtful things in the more favourable way.

ad 1: It can happen that someone who adopts the more favourable interpretation will frequently err. But it is better to err frequently through having a good opinion of a wicked man, than to err more seldom through having an evil opinion of a good man; for in the latter case an injury is done to someone, but not in the former.

ad 2: It is one thing to judge of things and another to judge of men. For when we judge of things, the good or evil of the thing of which we are judging is not at issue, since it will suffer no harm no matter what kind of judgment we reach about it. All that is at issue is the good of the man who judges, if he judges truly, and his evil if he judges falsely, since 'the true is the good of the intellect, and the false is its evil', as said at *Ethics* VI.[185] This is why everyone should strive to ensure that his judgment is consistent with the true nature of things. On the other hand, when we judge of men, our good and evil judgment bears especially upon the good of the person who is being judged; for he is deemed worthy of honour from the very fact that he is judged to be good, and of contempt if he is judged to be evil. In this kind of judgment, therefore, we should try to judge a man good unless there appears to be a clear reason to the contrary. And though, in doing this, we may judge a man falsely, our judgment in mistakenly thinking well of another pertains to our kindly feeling and not to the evil of our intellect, because it does not pertain to the perfection

---

[183] Augustine, *De sermone Domini in monte* 1:9.
[184] Art. 3 ad 2.
[185] *Ethics* 6:2 (1139a27).

of the intellect as such to know the truth of contingent individual things.

ad 3: It is possible to interpret something in a worse or a better sense in two ways. In one way, by acting on a particular kind of assumption. For instance, when we have to apply a remedy to some evil, whether our own or another's, it is expedient, in order for the remedy to be applied with greater likelihood of a cure, to assume the worse; since if a remedy is efficacious against a worse evil, it will be all the more efficacious against a lesser evil. In another way, we may interpret something for the best or for the worst by deciding or determining, and in this case when judging of things we should try to interpret each thing as it is, and when judging of persons, to interpret things for the better, as stated above.

articulus 5: *Whether we ought always to judge according
to the written law*

It seems that we ought not always to judge according to the written law.

obiectio 1: For we ought always to avoid judging unjustly. But written laws sometimes contain injustice, according to Isaiah 10:1, 'Woe to them that make wicked laws, and when they write, write injustice.' Therefore we ought not always to judge according to the written law.

obiectio 2: Moreover, judgment must take account of individual circumstances. But no written law can take account of every individual circumstance, as the Philosopher shows at *Ethics* v.[186] Therefore it seems that we are not always bound to judge according to the written law.

obiectio 3: Moreover, a law is written in order to make the intention of the legislator clear. But it sometimes happens that if the legislator himself were present he would judge differently. Therefore we ought not always to judge according to the written law.

sed contra: Augustine says: 'In the case of these earthly laws, though men judge them when they are making them, when once they are established and passed, judges may no longer judge them, but only according to them.'

responsio: As stated above,[187] judgment is nothing other than a kind of definition or determination of what is just. Now something is made just

---

[186] *Ethics* 5:10 (1137b13).   [187] Art. 1.

200

in two ways. In one way, by the very nature of the case, and this is called natural right. In another way, by some agreement among men, and this is called positive right, as stated above.[188] Now laws are written in order to declare both kinds of right, but in different ways. On the one hand, the written law does indeed contain natural right; but it does not establish it, for natural right derives its force not from the [written] law but from nature. On the other hand, the written law both contains positive right and establishes it by giving it the force of authority. And so it is necessary to judge according to the written law; otherwise judgment would fall short either of natural or positive right.

ad 1: Just as the written law does not give force to natural right, so nor can it diminish or remove its force, for the will of man cannot alter nature. And so if the written law contains anything contrary to natural right, it is unjust and has no binding force. For positive right has no place except where it makes no difference to natural right whether things are arranged in one way rather than another, as stated above.[189] Hence such writings are to be called not laws, but rather corruptions of law, as stated above;[190] and so judgment should not be delivered according to them.

ad 2: Whereas, in the nature of the case, wicked laws are either always or mostly contrary to natural right, even laws which are rightly established fail in some cases; and if they were observed in such cases this would be contrary to natural right. Hence judgment should not be delivered in such cases according to the letter of the law; rather, recourse should be had to the equity which the legislator intended.[191] Hence the jurist says: 'By no reason of law, or favour of equity, is it allowable for us to interpret harshly, and render burdensome, those useful measures which have been enacted for the welfare of man.'[192] In such cases even the legislator himself would judge differently, and, if he had thought of it in advance, might have made the law cover it. By this is also shown the reply to the third *obiectio*.

---

[188] IIaIIae 57:2 (p. 161, above).

[189] IIaIIae 57:2 ad 2 (p. 162, above). The 'place' of positive right – i.e. positive law – is either to enact the general principles of the natural law into particular statutes (see IaIIae 91:3 (p. 87, above)) or (what is being referred to here) to regulate things which, in themselves, are morally neutral. Positive law which departs from these functions and contravenes natural right becomes *ipso facto* unjust.

[190] IaIIae 95:2 (p. 129, above).

[191] Cf. IaIIae 96:3 (p. 141, above); IIaIIae 120:1 and 2.

[192] *CICiv.: Digesta* 1:1:3.

articulus 6: *Whether judgment is rendered wrongful by usurpation*

It seems that judgment is not rendered wrongful by usurpation.

obiectio 1: For justice is a certain rightness in matters of action.[193] But truth suffers nothing by being declared, but only by not being accepted; and this is so regardless of who declares it. Therefore also justice suffers nothing by being declared, regardless of by whom; and it is this [i.e. being declared, regardless of by whom] which pertains to the nature of judgment.

obiectio 2: Moreover, it pertains to judgment to punish sins. But, as we read, certain persons are praised because they punished the sins even of those over whom they had no authority: Moses, for example, who slew the Egyptian, as is recorded at Exodus 2:12, and Phineas the son of Eleazar who slew Zambri the son of Salu, as we read at Numbers 25:7–14; and, as is said at Psalm 106:31, 'it was counted unto him for righteousness'. Therefore usurpation of judgment does not pertain to injustice.

obiectio 3: Moreover, the spiritual power is distinct from the temporal. But prelates, who have spiritual power, sometimes intervene in things which pertain to the secular power. Therefore usurped judgment is not unlawful.

obiectio 4: Moreover, just as right judgment requires authority, so also does the judge need justice and knowledge, as shown above.[194] But if someone judges who lacks the habit of justice, or does not have knowledge of the law, these are not in themselves reasons for declaring a judgment unjust. Nor therefore will it always be unjust to judge by usurpation: that is, without authority.

sed contra: It is said at Romans 14:4: 'Who art thou that judgest another man's servant?'

responsio: Since judgment should be pronounced according to written laws, as stated above,[195] he who pronounces judgment interprets the dictate of the law in some way, by applying it to a particular case. Now

---

[193] The point of 'in matters of action' here is that no *moral* judgment is at issue. Legal justice takes account of external acts only, rather than inward motives or righteousness (see above, p. 194); so that, according to the argument being put forward, it does not matter who pronounces it as long as it is pronounced.

[194] Art. 1 ad 1–3; art. 2.

[195] Art. 5.

to interpret the law and to make a law belong to the same authority; and so, just as a law cannot be made except by public authority, so nor can judgment be pronounced save by public authority which extends over all those who are subject to the community. Hence, just as it would be unjust for someone to coerce another into observing a law not sanctioned by public authority, so too is it unjust if someone compels another to submit to a judgment pronounced other than by public authority.

ad 1: The mere fact that the truth is declared does not mean that anyone is compelled to accept it. Rather, everyone is free to accept it or not accept it, as he wishes. Judgment, on the other hand, implies a degree of compulsion; and so it is unjust for anyone to be judged by one who does not have public authority.

ad 2: Moses seems to have slain the Egyptian by an authority received as it were by Divine inspiration. This is seen by what is said at Acts 7:25: that, when Moses smote the Egyptian, 'he supposed his brethren would have understood how that God by his hand would deliver Israel'. Alternatively, it can be said that Moses slew the Egyptian without going beyond the bounds of justified defence,[196] in order to protect someone who was suffering unjustly. Hence Ambrose, in the book *De officiis*, says that 'he who does not fend off a blow against a fellow man when he can is just as much worthy to be blamed as the striker';[197] and he cites the example of Moses. Alternatively, we can say, as Augustine does, that 'just as the earth is praised for its fertility when it produces useless weeds before the useful seeds have sprung up, so this deed of Moses was sinful yet gave a sign of great fertility': insofar, that is, as it was a sign of the power by which he was about to deliver his people. As to Phineas, it must be said that he did this by Divine inspiration, out of zeal for God; or because, though not yet high priest himself, he was nonetheless the high priest's son, and this judgment pertained as much to him as to the other judges to whom it was committed.[198]

ad 3: The secular power is subject to the spiritual as the body is to the soul. And so judgment is not usurped if the spiritual authority intervenes in temporal matters where the secular power is subject

---

[196] Cf. IIaIIae 64:7 (p. 262).
[197] *De officiis* 1:36 (*PL* 16:81).
[198] Cf. Exodus 22:20; Leviticus 20; Deuteronomy 13:17.

to it, or in things which have been relinquished to it by the secular power.[199]

ad 4: The habits of knowledge and justice are perfections belonging to [someone as] an individual person [rather than in his public capacity], and so their absence does not mean that judgment is usurped as it would be in the absence of the public authority which gives judgment its coercive force.

[199] See ch. 7, below.

5

Property relations

(a) *Summa theologiae* IIaIIae 66: On theft and robbery

Here there are nine things to consider:

1. Whether it is natural for man to possess external things
2. Whether it is lawful for anyone to possess something as his own
3. Whether the nature of theft lies in taking someone else's property secretly
4. Whether theft and robbery are sins of different species
5. Whether all theft is sinful
6. Whether theft is a mortal sin
7. Whether it is lawful to steal by reason of necessity
8. Whether all robbery is a mortal sin
9. Whether theft is a more grievous sin than robbery

articulus 1: *Whether it is natural for man to possess external things*

It seems that it is not natural for man to possess external things.

obiectio 1: For no man should claim for himself that which belongs to God. But dominion over all creatures belongs to God, according to Psalm 24:1: 'The earth is the Lord's', etc. Therefore it is not natural for man to possess external things.

obiectio 2: Moreover, Basil, expounding the words of the rich man at Luke 12:18, 'I will gather all my fruits and my goods', says: 'Tell me: Which things are yours? Whence did you call them forth when you brought them to life?'[1] But whatever a man possesses naturally he can properly call his. Therefore man does not naturally possess external goods.

---

[1] *Homilia* 6, on Luke 12:18 (*PG* 31:276).

obiectio 3: Moreover, according to Ambrose in the book *De Trinitate*, 'ownership is a title of power'.[2] But man has no power over external things, for he cannot bring about any change in their nature. Therefore the possession of external things is not natural to man.

sed contra: It is said at Psalm 8:6: 'Thou hast put all things under his feet.'[3]

responsio: External things can be considered in two ways. In one way, with regard to their nature; and this is not subject to human, but only to divine, power, the command of which all things obey. In another way, with regard to the use of them; and, in this way, man has a natural dominion over external things because, by means of his reason and will, he is able to make use of external things to his own advantage, as if they were made for this purpose; for the imperfect always exists for the sake of the perfect, as stated above.[4] And it is by this argument that the Philosopher proves, at *Politics* I, that the possession of external things is natural to man.[5] Moreover, the natural dominion over other creatures which belongs to man by virtue of his reason, in respect of which he is made in God's image, is revealed in the account of man's creation given at Genesis 1:26, where it is said: 'Let us make man in our image and likeness: and let him have dominion over the fish of the sea', etc.

ad 1: God has supreme dominion over all things; and, according to His providence, He has ordained certain things for the support of man's body. For this reason man has a natural dominion over things with regard to the power to make use of them.

ad 2: The rich man is reproached for supposing that external things belong to him principally: that is, as though he had not received them from another: that is, from God.

ad 3: This argument considers dominion over external things with regard to their nature. Such dominion belongs only to God, as stated in the body of the article.

---

[2] *De Trinitate* 1:1 (*PL* 15:553).
[3] I.e. under the feet of man.
[4] IIaIIae 64:1 (p. 251, below).
[5] *Politics* 1:3 (1256b7).

articulus 2: *Whether it is lawful for anyone to possess something
as his own*

It seems that it is not lawful for anyone to possess something as his own.

obiectio 1: For everything contrary to the natural law is unlawful. But according to the natural law all things are held in common, and the possession of [private] property is contrary to this community of goods.[6] Therefore it is unlawful for any man to appropriate any external thing to himself.

obiectio 2: Moreover, Basil, expounding the words of the rich man quoted above, says: 'The rich who help themselves to common property and then deem it to be their own are like those who, going early to a play, prevent others from coming and appropriate to themselves that which is ordained to common use.'[7] But it would be unlawful to put obstacles in the way of others wishing to possess common goods. Therefore it is unlawful to appropriate common property to oneself.

obiectio 3: Moreover, Ambrose says, and his words are noted in the *Decretum*, 'Let no man call his own that which is common property';[8] and the fact that by 'common property' he means external things [as distinct from, for example, spiritual blessings] is clear from the words preceding the ones here quoted.[9] Therefore it seems unlawful for anyone to appropriate any external thing to himself.

sed contra: Augustine says in the book *De haeresibus*: 'The "Apostolici" are those who, in their great arrogance, call themselves by that name because they do not receive into their communion people who make use of marriage or who possess anything of their own, as do many monks and clerics in the Catholic Church.'[10] But these people are heretics because, in separating themselves from the Church, they suppose that those who make use of these things, which they themselves avoid, have no hope of salvation. Therefore it is an error to say that it is not lawful for a man to possess property.

---

[6] Cf. Ambrose, *De officiis* 1:28 (*PL* 16:62); *Enarrationes in psalmos* 118:8:22 (*PL* 15:1303); Augustine, *In Ioannis evangelium* 6:25f; and see n. 8, below.
[7] See n. 1.
[8] *Sermo* 81, on Luke 12:18; Dist. 47, c. 8: *Sicut hi* (*CIC* 1:171).
[9] 'But what injustice is there if, as long as I do not invade another's property, I am all the more careful in looking after my own?'
[10] *De haeresibus* 40.

responsio: Two things pertain to man with regard to external things. One is the power to procure and dispose of them; and, in this regard, it is lawful for man to possess property. Indeed, this is necessary to human life, for three reasons. First, because everyone is more diligent in procuring something for himself than something which is to belong to all or many; for each one, avoiding labour, would leave to someone else [the procuring of] that which was to belong to all in common, which is what happens where there is a multitude of servants. Second, because human affairs are conducted in a more orderly manner if each man is responsible for the care of something which is his own, whereas there would be confusion if everyone were responsible for everything in general. Third, because a more peaceful state of things is preserved for mankind if each is contented with his own. Hence we see that quarrels arise more frequently between those who hold property in common and where there is no division of the things possessed.

The other thing which pertains to man with regard to external things is their use. In this respect man ought to hold external things not as his own, but as common: that is, in such a way that he is ready to share them with others in the event of need. Hence the Apostle says at 1 Timothy 6:17f: 'Charge them that are rich in this world that they be ready to distribute, willing to communicate', etc.[11]

ad 1: Community of goods is attributed to the natural law not because natural right[12] dictates that all things should be possessed in common and that nothing should be possessed as one's own, but because the division of possessions is not according to natural right, but, rather, according to human agreement, which belongs to positive right, as stated above.[13] Hence the ownership of possessions is not contrary to natural right; rather, it is an addition to natural right devised by human reason.

ad 2: One would not act unlawfully if, going early to the play, he prepared the way for others; but he acts unlawfully if by so doing he hinders others from going. Similarly, a rich man does not act unlawfully if he anticipates someone in taking possession of something which was originally common property but then shares it with others; but he sins if he excludes others

---

[11] The important distinction which St Thomas here draws between private ownership and common use – the distinction which will presently enable him to say that, in an emergency, one may meet one's needs by taking the property of another (art. 7, *responsio*) – is derived from Aristotle, *Politics* 2:5 (1263a1).

[12] See p. 158 n. 2. Again, the reader accustomed to the political language of, say, John Locke should remember that by 'natural right' here – *ius naturale* – St Thomas means 'natural law'.

[13] IIaIIae 57:2 and 3 (pp. 161ff, above).

indiscriminately from making use of it. Hence Basil says in the same place: 'Why do you have plenty while another begs, unless it be that the merit of a good stewardship may come to you, and he be crowned with the reward of patience?'[14]

ad 3: When Ambrose says: 'Let no man call his own that which is common', he is speaking of ownership with regard to use. Hence he adds: 'He who spends too much is a robber.'

articulus 3: *Whether the nature of theft lies in taking someone else's property secretly*

It seems that the nature of theft does not lie in taking someone else's property secretly.

obiectio 1: For that which diminishes a sin does not seem to belong to the nature of a sin. But to sin secretly contributes to the diminution of a sin, just as, on the contrary, it is said at Isaiah 3:9, as indicating something that made the sin of certain persons worse: 'They have proclaimed abroad their sin as Sodom, and they have not hid it.' Therefore the nature of theft does not lie in taking someone else's property secretly.

obiectio 2: Moreover, Ambrose says, and his words are noted in the *Decretum*: 'It is no less a crime to refuse to help the needy when you are able and prosperous than it is to take away someone else's property.'[15] Therefore just as theft consists in taking something from another, so also does it consist in withholding it.

obiectio 3: Moreover, a man may secretly take from another even that which is his own: for example, something that he has deposited with another, or that has been taken from him unjustly. Therefore the nature of theft does not lie in taking someone else's property secretly.

sed contra: In the book *Etymologies* Isidore says: 'The thief [*fur*] is so called from *furvus* or *fuscus* [dark], because he takes advantage of the night.'[16]

responsio: Three things taken together constitute the nature of theft. The first pertains to theft insofar as theft is contrary to justice, which gives to each what is his own. In this way, it pertains to theft to seize what

---

[14] See n. 1.
[15] *Sermo* 81, on Luke 12:18: Dist. 47, c. 8: *Sicut hi* (*CIC* 1:172).
[16] *Etymologiae* 10 (*PL* 82:378); see also *CICiv.*: *Institutiones* 4:1:2.

is another's. The second pertains to the nature of theft insofar as theft is distinguished from those sins which are against the person, such as homicide and adultery. And, according to this, it pertains to theft to be concerned with something specifically as possessed. For if someone takes what belongs to another not as a possession but as a part of him (for instance, if he amputates a limb), or as a person conjoined with him (for instance, if he makes off with his daughter or wife), this does not, properly speaking, have the nature of theft. The third difference is that which completes the nature of theft: namely, that it consists in something being taken secretly; and, according to this, it pertains properly to theft that it consists in taking someone else's property secretly.

ad 1: Secrecy is sometimes a cause of sin: for example, when someone uses secrecy in pursuance of sin, as in the case of fraud and deceit. In this way it does not diminish sin, but constitutes a species of it; and this is so in the case of theft. In another way, secrecy is simply a circumstance of sin, and thus it diminishes the sin, both because it is a sign of shame and because it removes scandal.

ad 2: To withhold what is due to another inflicts the same kind of harm as taking something unjustly; and so unjust taking should be understood to include unjust withholding.

ad 3: Nothing prevents something which, strictly speaking, is someone's property from 'belonging' to someone else in some particular way: for example, a deposit belongs strictly speaking to the depositor, but in regard to its custody it is the depositary's; and something stolen 'belongs' to the thief at any rate in the sense that he is for the time being in possession of it.[17]

articulus 4: *Whether theft and robbery are sins of different species*

It seems that theft and robbery are not sins of different species.

obiectio 1: For theft and robbery differ only insofar as the one is secret and the other overt; for theft implies the taking of something secretly, whereas robbery is the taking of something violently and openly. But in other kinds of sin, secrecy and openness do not constitute a difference of species. Therefore theft and robbery are not different species of sin.

---

[17] The point, here, somewhat elaborated at art. 5 ad 3, is that one can do wrong even in reclaiming one's own property from a depositary or by 'taking the law into one's own hands' by removing it from a thief.

obiectio 2: Moreover, moral actions take their species from their end, as stated above.[18] But theft and robbery are directed to the same end: namely, to the possession of what belongs to someone else. Therefore they do not differ in species.

obiectio 3: Moreover, just as something is taken by force in order to possess it, so is a woman taken by force in order to enjoy her; and hence Isidore, in the book *Etymologies*, says that 'the rapist [*raptor*] is so called from "despoiler" [*corruptor*], and the victim of rape [*rapta*] from "despoiled" [*corrupta*]'.[19] But a case of rape is so called whether the woman is taken openly or in secret. Therefore when a possession is taken by force, it does not matter whether this is done secretly or openly. Therefore theft and robbery do not differ.

sed contra: At *Ethics* v, the Philosopher distinguishes theft from robbery, stipulating that theft is done secretly whereas robbery is done openly.[20]

responsio: Theft and robbery are both vices opposed to justice, inasmuch as someone does an injustice to someone else [in committing them]. Now 'no one suffers an injustice willingly', as is proved at *Ethics* v.[21] And so theft and robbery both derive their nature as sins from the fact that something is taken against the will of him from whom it is taken. But something is said to be done against someone's will in two ways: either because it is done by violence, or because he does not know that it is happening, as noted at *Ethics* iii.[22] Therefore the sinful nature of robbery differs from that of theft; and for this reason they differ in species.

ad 1: In other kinds of sin the nature of the sin does not depend upon the fact that something is done against someone's will, as it does in the case

---

[18] IaIIae 1:3; 18:6.

[19] *Etymologiae* 10 (*PL* 83:392). The example – and see also ad 3, below – derives much of its force from the fact that the same word, *raptor*, is used in this article to mean both 'robber' and 'rapist'. The verb *rapio*, and its grammatical relatives, conveys the general idea of seizing, plundering, preying, and so lends itself to a range of translation. DE gives the following rendering: 'Further, just as a thing is taken by force for the sake of possession, so a woman is taken by force for pleasure: wherefore Isidore says (*Etym.* x) that "he who commits a rape is called a corruptor, and the victim of the rape is said to be corrupted".' This is not a happy translation of the quotation from Isidore (although, as so often, Isidore's etymology is almost certainly incorrect). *Corrumpo*, and hence *corrupta*, derived from it as an adjective, certainly does not here carry any connotation of 'corruption' in the ordinary sense.

[20] *Ethics* 5:2 (1131a6).

[21] *Ethics* 5:9 (1138a12).

[22] *Ethics* 3:1 (1109b35).

of sins opposed to justice; and so [in the case of sins opposed to justice], where there is a different kind of involuntariness there is a different species of sin.

ad 2: The ultimate end of robbery and theft is the same. But this does not suffice to make them identical in species, because there is a difference of proximate ends. For the robber wishes to obtain something by his own power, and the thief by cunning.[23]

ad 3: The rape of a woman cannot be a secret from the woman who is raped. And so even if it is done secretly in relation to other people, a rape still has the nature of robbery from the standpoint of the woman to whom the violence is done.

articulus 5: Whether theft is always a sin

It seems that theft is not always a sin.

obiectio 1: For no sin is commanded by God; for it is said at Ecclesiasticus 15:21: 'He hath commanded no man to do wickedly.' But we find that God has commanded theft, for it is said at Exodus 35:36: 'And the children of Israel did as the Lord had commanded Moses, and they despoiled the Egyptians.' Therefore theft is not always a sin.

obiectio 2: Moreover, one who finds something that is not his and takes it seems to commit theft, for he takes someone else's property. Yet this seems lawful according to natural equity, as the jurists say.[24] Therefore it seems that theft is not always a sin.

obiectio 3: Moreover, one who takes something that is his own seems not to sin; for he does not act against justice, because he does not detract from its [principle of] equality.[25] Yet someone commits a theft if he secretly takes even his own property which is detained by or in the custody of another.[26] Therefore it seems that theft is not always a sin.

---

[23] In scholastic moral philosophy, 'proximate' ends are those which are not desired for themselves, but only in so far as they are steps towards the attaining of ultimate ends. Strictly speaking, proximate ends are not ends, but means. Ultimate ends are desired for their own sake and therefore are not subservient to anything else. For instance, the obtaining of medical care is proximate in relation to the ultimate end of health.

[24] *CICiv.*: *Institutiones* 2:1:39.

[25] I.e. he does not treat himself unequally by taking more than is due to him.

[26] *CICiv.*: *Digesta* 47:15.

sed contra: It is said at Exodus 20:15: 'Thou shalt not steal.'

responsio: If anyone considers the nature of theft, he will find that it has the nature of sin in two ways. In one way, because it is contrary to justice, which renders to each what is his own. Thus theft is contrary to justice because it involves taking what belongs to another. In another way, by reason of the deceit or fraud committed by the thief in taking someone else's property secretly and by stealth. Hence it is clear that every theft is a sin.

ad 1: Whether he does it secretly or overtly, it is not theft for someone to take another's property by order of a judge who has commanded him to do so; for it then becomes due to him by the fact that it was awarded to him by the sentence of the court. Hence still less was it theft for the children of Israel to take away the spoils of the Egyptians at the Lord's command, Who decreed that they should do this by way of compensation for the suffering which the Egyptians had inflicted upon them without cause. As a sign of this it is said at Wisdom 10:19: 'The just took away the spoils of the wicked.'

ad 2: With regard to things found, there is a distinction to be made. For some things were never anyone's property, such as the stones and gems found on the seashore; and one who finds such things may keep them.[27] The same applies to treasure buried in the ground long ago, of which no one is the owner; except that, if he finds it on the land of another, the finder is bound by civil law to give half of it to the owner of the land.[28] This is why, in the Gospel parable at Matthew 13:44, it is said of the finder of the treasure hidden in a field that he 'bought the field', as if to acquire the right of possessing the whole treasure. On the other hand, things may be found in the vicinity of someone else's property, and then, if anyone takes them with the intention not of keeping them but of returning them to the owner who does not regard them as unclaimed, he is not guilty of theft.[29] Similarly, if things found appear to be unclaimed, and if the finder believes this to be so, he does not commit theft even if he keeps them. In any other case the sin of theft is committed. Hence, as Augustine says in a certain homily, and as is noted in the *Decretum*: 'If you have found something and not returned it, you have stolen it.'[30]

[27] Cf. *CICiv.*: *Institutiones* 2:1:18; *CICiv.*: *Digesta* 1:8:3.
[28] *CICiv.*: *Institutiones* 2:1:39; *CICiv.*: *Codex* 10:15:1.
[29] For example, if one were to impound straying animals with a view to returning them to their owner.
[30] *Sermo* 178:8; C. 14:5:6: *Si quid invenisti* (*CIC* 1:739).

ad 3: He who by stealth takes back his own property which was deposited with another places the depositary, who is bound either to restore it or show that he is innocent, in a serious position.[31] Hence it is clear that he sins, and is bound to rescue the depositary from his plight. Again, he who by stealth takes back his own property which has been unjustly detained by another, also sins: not because he injures the detainer (and he is therefore not bound to make restitution or recompense), but he sins against general justice by usurping to himself judgment in the matter of his property, thereby setting aside the order of justice. And so he is bound to make satisfaction to God and to take pains to allay the scandal he may have given to his neighbours.[32]

articulus 6: Whether theft is a mortal sin

It seems that theft is not a mortal sin.

obiectio 1: For it is said at Proverbs 6:30: 'The fault is not great when a man hath stolen.' But every mortal sin is a great fault. Therefore theft is not a mortal sin.

obiectio 2: Moreover, mortal sin deserves to be punished with death. But the penalty inflicted by the law for theft is not death but only indemnity, according to Exodus 22:1, 'If any man steal an ox or a sheep he shall restore five oxen for one ox, and four sheep for one sheep.' Therefore theft is not a mortal sin.

obiectio 3: Moreover, theft can be committed in respect of small things as well as great. But it seems unfitting for someone to be punished with eternal death for stealing something small, like a needle or a pen. Therefore theft is not a mortal sin.

sed contra: No one is condemned by the Divine judgment save for a mortal sin. Yet one is condemned for theft, according to Zachariah 5:3: 'This is the curse that goeth forth over the face of the earth; for every thief shall be judged as is there written.' Therefore theft is a mortal sin.

responsio: As noted above,[33] a mortal sin is one that is contrary to charity, which is the spiritual life of the soul. Now charity consists principally in

---

[31] Cf. *CICiv.*: *Institutiones* 3:14:3.
[32] See n. 17, above.
[33] IaIIae 72:5; IIaIIae 59:4.

love of God, and secondarily in love of neighbour, to which it pertains that we should wish and do our neighbour well. But by theft we harm our neighbour in his property; and if men were to steal from one another indiscriminately, human society would perish. Therefore theft, as being contrary to charity, is a mortal sin.

ad 1: It is said that theft is not a great fault in cases of two kinds. First, when a person is led to steal through necessity, which diminishes sin or removes it entirely, as we shall show below.[34] Hence the text goes on (Proverbs 6:30): 'For he stealeth to fill his hungry soul.' Second, theft is said to be not a great fault as compared to the guilt of adultery, which is punished with death.[35] Hence the text goes on (vv. 31f) to say of the thief that 'if he be taken, he shall restore sevenfold, but he that is an adulterer shall destroy his own soul'.

ad 2: The punishments of this present life are more curative than retributive. For retribution is reserved to the Divine judgment which is passed upon sinners 'according to the truth' (Romans 2:2). And so according to the judgment of this present life the punishment of death is inflicted not for every mortal sin, but only for those which inflict an irreparable injury, or, again, for those involving some horrible depravity. Hence according to the present judgment the punishment of death is not inflicted for theft which does not inflict irreparable harm, but only when it is aggravated by some grievous circumstance: as in the case of sacrilege, which is the theft of a sacred object; of peculation, which is theft of common property, as Augustine shows;[36] and of kidnapping, which is theft of a man, for which the punishment of death is inflicted.[37]

ad 3: Reason counts that which is little as though it were nothing. A man therefore does not consider himself injured in very trivial matters, and anyone who takes such things can assume that this is not against the will of him whose things they are. And if someone takes such very little things, he can to that extent be excused from mortal sin. If, however, his intention is to steal from his neighbour and inflict harm on him, there can be mortal sin even in such very little things, just as there may be in consent by thought alone.

[34] Art. 7.
[35] Leviticus 20:10; Deuteronomy 22:22.
[36] *In Ioannis evangelium* 12:6.
[37] Cf. Exodus 21:16.

articulus 7: *Whether it is lawful to steal by reason of necessity*

It seems that it is not lawful to steal by reason of necessity.

obiectio 1: For penance is not imposed except upon a sinner. But it is said in the *Decretales*: 'If anyone under the necessity of hunger or nakedness has stolen food, clothing or an animal, let him do penance for three weeks.'[38] Therefore it is not lawful to steal by reason of necessity.

obiectio 2: Moreover, the Philosopher says at *Ethics* II that 'there are certain acts whose very name implies wickedness',[39] and he places theft among these. But that which is wicked in itself cannot be done for the sake of some good end. Therefore no one can lawfully steal in order to supply a necessity.

obiectio 3: Moreover, a man should love his neighbour as himself. But, according to Augustine in the book *Contra mendacium*, it is not lawful to steal in order to assist one's neighbour by giving him alms. Nor therefore is it lawful to steal in order to supply one's own necessities.

sed contra: In cases of necessity all things are common property. And so there seems to be no sin in taking another's property when need has made it common.

responsio: Things pertaining to human right cannot take anything away from natural right or Divine right. Now according to the natural order established by Divine providence, lower things are ordained for the purpose of supplying man's necessities. And so the division and appropriation of such things which proceeds from human law does not cancel out the fact that man's necessities must be supplied by means of those things. And so whatever anyone has in superabundance is due under the natural law to the poor for their succour. Hence Ambrose says, and his words are noted in the *Decretum*: 'It is the hungry man's bread that you detain; the naked man's cloak that you store away; the poor man's ransom and freedom that is in the money which you bury in the ground.'[40] Since there are many people in need and not all of them can be succoured from the same source, the dispensing of his own property is entrusted to the judgment of each man, so that out of it he may succour those who suffer need. If, however, there is a necessity so urgent and clear that it is obvious that the necessity

---

[38] X 5:18:3: *Si quis* (*CIC* 2:810).
[39] *Ethics* 2:6 (1107a9).
[40] Dist. 47, c. 8 (*CIC* 1:172).

must be met at once by whatever means are to hand – for example, if a person is in immediate danger and no other help is available – anyone can then lawfully supply his own need from the property of another by taking from it either openly of in secret; nor, properly speaking, does this have the character or theft or robbery.

ad 1: This decretal refers only to cases in which there is no question of urgent necessity.

ad 2: Properly speaking, to take and use another's property secretly in a case of extreme necessity does not have the character of theft, because that which someone takes in order to support his own life becomes his own by reason of that necessity.

ad 3: In a case of similar necessity someone can also take another's property secretly in order to succour his neighbour in need.

articulus 8: *Whether robbery may be committed without sin*

It seems that robbery may be committed without sin.

obiectio 1: For the spoils of war are taken by violence, which seems to belong to the nature of robbery, according to what has been said.[41] But it is lawful to take spoils from the enemy; for Ambrose says in the book *De Patriarchis*: 'When the spoils have come into the victor's power, military discipline requires that they should all be reserved to the king':[42] that is, so that he may distribute them. Therefore in certain cases robbery is lawful.

obiectio 2: Moreover, it is lawful to take from someone that which does not belong to him. But the things which unbelievers have do not belong to them; for Augustine says in the book *Ad Vincentium Donatistam*: 'You call such things yours falsely, for you do not possess them justly, and according to the laws of earthly kings you are required to forfeit them.'[43] Therefore it seems that anyone may lawfully rob unbelievers.

obiectio 3: Moreover, the princes of the earth extort many things from their subjects by force, which seems to belong to the nature of robbery. But it seems a grave thing to say that they sin in this regard, because, if so, nearly all princes would be condemned. Therefore in some cases robbery is lawful.

[41] Art. 4.
[42] *De Abraham* 1:3 (*PL* 14:449).
[43] *Epistolae* 93:12; see also Dyson, *The Pilgrim City*, ch. 3.

sed contra: Anything acquired lawfully can be offered to God in sacrifice or oblation. But this cannot be done with things taken by robbery, according to Isaiah 61:8: 'For I the Lord love judgment, and hate robbery for burnt offering.' Therefore it is not lawful to take anything by robbery.

responsio: Robbery implies a certain violence and coercion used to remove from someone unjustly that which belongs to him. Now in the society of men no one can employ coercion except by public authority. And so if someone who is a private person takes another's property by violence, not using public authority, he acts unlawfully and commits robbery, as bandits do. In the case of princes, the public power is entrusted to them so that they may be the custodians of justice. And so it is not lawful for them to use violence or coercion except in the course of justice, either when fighting against the enemy or punishing citizens who are malefactors. Whenever something is taken by violence of this kind, this does not have the character of robbery, since it is not contrary to justice. But to use public authority to take other people's property violently and against justice, is to act unlawfully and to commit robbery; and anyone who does this is bound to make restitution.

ad 1: In the matter of spoils a distinction must be made. For if those who despoil an enemy are waging a just war, the things which they acquire in the war by violence become theirs. This does not have the character of robbery, and so they are not bound to make restitution. Nonetheless, even those who are waging a just war may sin in taking spoils through greed arising from an evil intention: if, that is, they fight principally not for justice but for spoils. For in the book *De verbo Domini* Augustine says that 'it is a sin to fight only for the sake of spoils'.[44] If, moreover, those who take spoils are waging an unjust war, they commit robbery and are bound to make restitution.[45]

ad 2: Unbelievers possess their goods unjustly insofar as they are commanded by the laws of earthly princes to forfeit them. And so they may be removed from them by violence: not by private initiative, however, but by public authority.

ad 3: If princes exact from their subjects that which is due to them according to justice for the preservation of the common good, this is not

---

[44] *Sermones supposititii* 82. The sermon is on Luke 3:13ff. The reference to *De verbo Domini* is possibly due to a defective memory or a scribal error.
[45] See IIaIIae 40 (pp. 239ff, below).

robbery even if they employ violence in doing so. But if princes extort by violence something which is not due to them, they commit robbery just as much as the bandit does. Hence Augustine says at *De civitate Dei* IV: 'Justice removed, then, what are kingdoms but great bands of robbers? What are bands of robbers themselves but little kingdoms?'[46] And it is said at Ezekiel 22:27: 'Her princes in the midst of her are like wolves ravening the prey.' Hence they are bound to make restitution, just as robbers are; and by so much do they sin more grievously than robbers, as their actions bring into a greater and more general peril the public justice whose custodians they are appointed to be.

articulus 9: *Whether theft is a more grievous sin than robbery*

It seems that theft is a more grievous sin than robbery.

obiectio 1: For theft joins fraud and deceit to the taking of another's property, and these things are not found in robbery. But fraud and deceit have the character of sin in themselves, as noted above.[47] Therefore theft seems to be a more grievous sin than robbery.

obiectio 2: Moreover, shame is fear in relation to an evil deed, as is said at *Ethics* IV.[48] But men are more ashamed of theft than they are of robbery. Therefore theft is more wicked than robbery.

obiectio 3: Moreover, the more people a sin harms the more grievous it seems to be. But theft may harm great and small alike, whereas only the weak can be injured by robbery, since it is only against them that violence can be employed. Therefore theft seems to be a more grievous sin than robbery.

sed contra: According to the laws robbery is to be more severely punished than theft.[49]

responsio: As stated above,[50] robbery and theft are sinful because, in each case, something is taken from someone against his will. In a case of theft, however, it is 'against his will' in the sense that he does not know that it is

---

[46] *De civitate Dei* 4:4.
[47] IIaIIae 55:4 and 5.
[48] *Ethics* 4:9 (1128b11; 22).
[49] *CICiv.: Institutiones* 4:2.
[50] Art. 4 and 6.

being done; whereas in a case of robbery it is 'against his will' because done by violence. Now something done to someone by violence is more 'against his will' than something done without his knowledge, because violence is more directly in opposition to the will than is mere ignorance. Therefore robbery is a more grievous sin than theft. There is also another reason: that robbery not only inflicts a loss on someone in his property, but also causes humiliation and injury to his person, and this is a more grievous matter than the fraud or deceit which belong to theft. By this the reply to the first *obiectio* is shown.

ad 2: Men who cling to external things think more highly of the external strength which is exhibited in robbery than of the inward virtue which is lost through sin; and this is why they are less ashamed of robbery than of theft.

ad 3: Although more people may be injured by theft than by robbery, more grievous injuries may be inflicted by robbery than by theft; and for this reason also robbery is the more odious crime.

(b) *Summa theologiae* IIaIIae 78: On the sin of usury[51]

We come next to the sin of usury, which is committed in relation to loans. And here there are four things to consider:

1. Whether it is a sin to take usury for a loan of money
2. Whether one may ask for some other kind of consideration for a loan of money
3. Whether someone is bound to restore whatever profits he has made out of money lent upon usury
4. Whether it is lawful to borrow money upon usury

articulus 1: *Whether it is a sin to take usury for a loan of money*

It seems that it is not a sin to take usury for a loan of money.

obiectio 1: For no man who follows the example of Christ sins. But the Lord said of Himself at Luke 19:23: 'At my coming I might have required

---

[51] By 'usury' St Thomas means the taking of interest on loans – i.e. the charging of a fee for the use of money – or anything which is tantamount to doing so. He is not referring merely to the taking of excessive interest.

mine own' – that is, the money lent – 'with usury'.[52] Therefore it is not a sin to take usury for a loan of money.

obiectio 2: Moreover, according to Psalm 19:8, 'The statutes of the Lord are right': that is, because they forbid sin. But usury of a kind is permitted under the Divine law, according to Deuteronomy 23:19f: 'Thou shalt not lend upon usury to thy brother; usury of money, usury of victuals, usury of anything that is lent upon usury. Unto a stranger thou mayest lend upon usury.' Indeed, it is even promised as a reward for observing the law, according to Deuteronomy 28:12: 'Thou shalt lend to many nations, and thou shalt not borrow.' Therefore it is not a sin to take usury.

obiectio 3: Moreover, what is just in human affairs is decided by the civil laws. But according to these laws the taking of usury is permitted.[53] Therefore it seems that it is not unlawful.

obiectio 4: Moreover, we are not obliged to keep the counsels on pain of sin.[54] But at Luke 6:35 we are told, as one of several counsels, to 'Lend, hoping for nothing thereby.' Therefore it is not a sin to take usury.

obiectio 5: Moreover, it does not seem sinful in itself to receive payment for doing what one is not bound to do. But someone who has money is not bound in every case to lend it to his neighbour. Therefore it is lawful for him sometimes to receive payment for lending it.

[52] This is an odd misunderstanding of the parable told at Luke 19:12ff, where the 'Lord' to whom the words quoted are attributed is not Jesus, but 'a certain nobleman [who] went into a far country to receive for himself a kingdom'.

[53] Despite *CICiv.: Institutiones* 2:4:2 (see ad 3, below), Roman law in practice permitted the taking of interest on loans from earliest days. The Twelve Tables – the oldest Roman law code of all – fixed (Table 8) a legal maximum of 12% per annum. It was subsequently reduced to 6% and abolished altogether in 341 BC by the *Lex Genucia*; but interest was again recognised during the Republic, and the maximum rose once more to 12%. Justinian established rates at between 4% and 12% depending on circumstances (*CICiv.: Codex* 4:32:26). See *The Institutes of Justinian* (ed. T. C. Sandars, London, 1948), p. 325.

[54] The 'counsels' or 'evangelical counsels' are those parts of Christ's teaching regarded as supererogatory rather than as binding upon all. They do not state necessary conditions of salvation, but give advice to those who wish to do more than the minimum and to aim at the highest attainable standard of Christian perfection on earth. Therefore we do well if we follow them, but we do not sin if we do not. The distinction between counsels and commandments is a traditional one, introduced into the Church at an early stage as a way of escaping the conclusion towards which a literal interpretation of scripture seems to point: that we can only be saved if we give away all our property, are persecuted and despised, etc. See IIaIIae 184:3; see also *NCE* 4, *s.v.* 'Counsels, Evangelical'.

obiectio 6: Moreover, silver made into coins does not differ in species from silver made into a vessel. But it is lawful to receive payment for the loan of a silver vessel. Therefore it is also lawful to receive payment for the loan of a silver coin. Therefore usury is not in itself a sin.

obiectio 7: Moreover, anyone can lawfully receive a thing which its owner gives him voluntarily. But he who accepts a loan gives the usury voluntarily. Therefore he who lends may lawfully receive the usury.

sed contra: It is said at Exodus 22:25: 'If thou lend money to any of my people that is poor, that dwelleth with thee, thou shalt not be to him as an usurer, neither shalt thou lay upon him usury.'

responsio: To take usury for a loan of money is unjust in itself, because to do so is to sell something which does not exist, and this is to create a manifest inequality, which is contrary to justice.[55] To make this clear, it must be noted that there are certain things the use of which consists in their consumption. For example, we consume wine when we use it for drink, and we consume wheat when we use it for food. In things of this kind, then, the use of the thing must not be counted as something separate from the thing itself. Rather, whoever is granted the use of the thing is granted the thing itself; and, for this reason, to lend things of this kind is to transfer their ownership. If, therefore, someone wanted to sell wine separately from the use of the wine, he would be selling the same thing twice, or he would be selling something which does not exist. Hence, clearly, he would commit a sin of injustice. Similarly, he commits an injustice who lends wine or wheat and asks to be paid twice: that is, once by the return of an equal amount of the thing, and again by charging a price for its use, which is called usury.

There are, however, things the use of which does not consist in their consumption. For example, to use a house is to dwell in it, not to destroy it. And so in cases of this kind the two things may be granted separately: for instance, someone may hand over the ownership of his house to someone else while reserving to himself the use of it for the time being; or, conversely, he may grant the use of the house to someone else while retaining ownership of it to himself. For this reason a man may lawfully receive payment for the use of his house, and, in addition, may also claim back the house which he has lent, as happens in the renting and letting of a house.

---

[55] For the Roman law basis of this argument, see n. 59, below; for Aristotle's version of it, see *Politics* 1:10 (1258a38).

222

But money, according to the Philosopher at *Ethics* v and *Politics* I,[56] was invented principally for the purpose of exchange; and so the proper and principal use of money is to be consumed or used up by being expended in the process of exchange. For this reason it is in the nature of the case unlawful to receive payment for the use of money, which is called usury; and just as a man is bound to restore other things which he has acquired unlawfully, so is he bound to restore money which he has taken in usury.

ad 1: 'Usury' is here to be taken figuratively, to mean the increase of spiritual goods which God exacts from us; for He wishes us always to profit from the goods which we receive from Him; but this is for our own advantage, not His.

ad 2: The Jews were forbidden to take usury from their brethren: that is, from other Jews. But by this we are to understand that to take usury from anyone at all is evil simply; for we must regard everyone as our neighbour and brother, especially in the condition of the Gospel to which all are called. Hence it is said unconditionally at Psalm 15:5: 'He that putteth not out his money to usury'; and at Ezekiel 18:8: 'Who hath not taken usury.' They were allowed to take usury from strangers, but this was not granted to them as something lawful; rather, it was permitted in order to avert a greater evil: lest, that is, they should take usury from the Jews, who were worshippers of God, because of the avarice to which, as is noted at Isaiah 56:11, they were prone.[57] Where we find it promised to them as a reward that 'Thou shalt lend [*faenerabis*] to many nations', etc., 'lend' is here to be understood broadly, as lending without interest [*faenus ibi large accipitur pro mutuo*], as at Ecclesiasticus 29:10, where we read: 'Many have refused to lend [*faenerati*]', that is, to lend without interest [*mutuaverunt*], 'fearing to be defrauded'. The Jews, therefore, are promised abundant wealth as their reward, so that they might be able to 'lend' [*mutuare*] to others.[58]

ad 3: Human laws allow certain sins to remain unpunished because of the condition of men who are imperfect, and who would be hindered in the

---

[56] *Ethics* 5:5 (1133a29); *Politics* 1:10 (1258a38).

[57] 'Yea, they are greedy dogs which can never have enough, and they are shepherds that cannot understand. They all look to their own way, every one for his gain, from his quarter.'

[58] St Thomas is here trying to exploit the fact that Roman lawyers use the terms *faenus* and *mutuum* to denote a loan with and without interest respectively. It has to be admitted that the scriptural texts upon which he is commenting do not readily support the interpretation that he wishes them to bear.

pursuit of many benefits if all sins were strictly forbidden them and punishments appointed. And so human law has permitted usury not because it deems it as being in accord with justice, but lest the benefit of many should otherwise be impeded. Hence in civil law it is stated that 'those things which are consumed by being used, do not admit of usufruct either according to natural reason or civil law', and that 'the Senate did not and could not appoint a usufruct to such things, but established a quasi-usufruct': that is, by permitting usury.[59] Moreover the Philosopher, led by natural reason, says at *Politics* I that 'it is greatly against nature to make money by usury'.[60]

ad 4: A man is not always bound to lend, and for this reason lending is placed among the counsels. But it has the character of a commandment [rather than a counsel] that a man should not seek to derive profit from lending (although considered in relation to the maxims of the Pharisees, who considered some kinds of usury to be lawful, this can be called a counsel in the same way that love of one's enemies is a counsel).[61] Alternatively, He speaks here not of the hope of usurious gain, but of the hope which is put in man. For we ought not to lend or do any good deed through hope in man, but only through hope in God.

ad 5: One who is not bound to lend may accept repayment for what he has done, but he must not exact more. Rather, he is repaid according

---

[59] The law from which St Thomas is quoting is *CICiv.: Institutiones* 2:4:2f. Broadly speaking, 'usufruct' is the right to enjoy the 'fruits' of property belonging to someone else. In the ordinary way, this is a right for which one might expect to have to pay. Most obviously, one might pay rent for an orchard or a vineyard. But Roman law provides that, save by a kind of legal fiction called quasi-usufruct, it is not possible to have a usufruct in *res fungibilia*: that is, in things like corn, wine and money, the use of which consists in their being consumed. It is not possible to enjoy, and therefore not possible to buy or sell the right to enjoy, the fruit of such things, precisely because they have no fruit. Anyone who purported to charge a fee for such enjoyment – for example, anyone who sold a loaf of bread and the right to eat it separately – would therefore be selling something which does not exist. This point – made also by Aristotle – is the main non-scriptural basis of the medieval Church's objection to usury. See *NCE* 14 *s.v.* 'Usury'; see also the works mentioned in n. 243 on p. 133, above.

[60] *Politics* 1:10 (1258a38).

[61] I.e. not taking usury was a 'counsel' to the Pharisees, to whom it was permitted by the law, and was to that extent optional in the sense explained in n. 54. The words in parentheses do not, however, fit comfortably into the grammar of the sentence. I suspect that 'although considered in . . . is a counsel' was originally a gloss written, perhaps interlinearly, by some unknown reader and then interpolated into the text by scribal accident. Such interpolations are quite common in medieval texts.

to the equality of justice if he is repaid as much as he lent. Hence if he exacts more for the usufruct of a thing which has no other use than the consumption of its substance, he exacts a price for something which does not exist, and so the exaction is unjust.

ad 6: The principal use of a silver vessel is not the consumption of it, and so one can lawfully sell the use of it and retain the ownership. But the principal use of silver money is to be expended in exchange for something. Hence it is not lawful for anyone to sell its use and then to want the amount of the loan to be repaid also. It must be noted, however, that the secondary use of silver vessels may be an exchange, and such use may not be lawfully sold. Similarly, there can be some secondary use of silver money. For instance, a man might lend coins for show, or to be used as security; and this kind of use of money a man can lawfully sell.[62]

ad 7: One who gives usury does not simply give it voluntarily, but under a certain necessity, insofar as he needs to borrow money which he who has it will not lend without usury.

articulus 2: *Whether one may ask for some other kind of consideration for a loan of money*

It seems that one may ask for some other kind of consideration for a loan of money.

obiectio 1: For it is lawful for anyone to take steps to indemnify himself against loss. But sometimes someone suffers loss through lending money. Therefore it is lawful for him to ask, or even to exact, something else besides the money lent, to cover the risk of loss.

obiectio 2: Moreover, as is said at *Ethics* v, one is bound by a debt of honour to recompense someone who has done him a favour.[63] But to lend money to someone who is in need is to do him a favour for which he ought to be grateful. Therefore he who receives a loan is bound by a natural debt to make some recompense [for the favour in addition to repaying the loan, to show his gratitude]. But it does not seem unlawful to bind someone to do that which he is already bound to do as a matter of natural right.

---

[62] *CICiv.: Digesta* 17:1:28. [63] *Ethics* 5:5 (1133a4).

Therefore it does not seem unlawful for someone who lends money to another to oblige him to make some sort of recompense.[64]

obiectio 3: Moreover, just as there is material remuneration, so there is 'remuneration of the tongue' and 'remuneration by service', as the [interlinear] gloss on Isaiah 33:15, 'Blessed is he that shaketh his hands from all bribes', says.[65] But it is lawful to accept service or praise from one to whom one has lent money. Therefore, by the same reasoning, it is lawful to accept any other kind of remuneration.

obiectio 4: Moreover, the relation of gift to gift seems to be the same as that of loan to loan. But it is lawful to accept money for money given. Therefore it is lawful to accept repayment by loan in return for a loan granted.

obiectio 5: Moreover, a lender, by transferring his ownership of a sum of money, alienates it from himself more completely than does one who entrusts it to a merchant or craftsman [i.e. than one who invests it in somebody's business]. But it is lawful to take a profit on money entrusted to a merchant or craftsman. Therefore it is also lawful to receive usury for money lent.

obiectio 6: Moreover, a man can accept a pledge for money lent, the use of which pledge he might sell for a price: as when someone mortgages his land or the house in which he lives. Therefore it is lawful to receive usury for money lent.

obiectio 7: Moreover, it sometimes happens that a loan is repaid by the lender selling goods to the borrower at a higher price, or buying goods from him at a lower price; or, again, the price of something may be raised if payment is delayed or lowered in order to secure payment more quickly. In all such cases there seems to be payment for a loan of money; nor does this appear to be obviously unlawful. Therefore it seems to be lawful to expect or exact some consideration for money lent.

---

[64] The argument here is that, if you lend me money, you are doing two things: lending me money, and doing me a favour. It is therefore not wrong to expect me to repay the favour in addition to repaying the loan.

[65] The *glossa interlinearis* is the scriptural commentary (begun by Anselm of Laon (d. 1117)) customarily written between the lines of the text in copies of the Vulgate produced from the twelfth century onwards. It is to be distinguished from the *glossa ordinaria* (written in the top and side margins) and (from the fourteenth century) the *postilla* of Nicholas of Lyra and *additiones* of Paulus Brugensis, written at the foot of the page. These various glosses appear also in some early printed versions of the Vulgate.

sed contra: Among the other things requisite in the just man it is said at Ezekiel 18:17 that he 'hath not taken usury and increase'.

responsio: According to the Philosopher at *Ethics* IV, something is reckoned as money 'if its value can be measured by money'.[66] Thus, just as it is a sin against justice if, by tacit or express agreement, someone takes money in return for lending money or anything else that is consumed by being used, as stated above,[67] so too is it similarly a sin to take anything, by tacit or express agreement, whose value can be measured by money. It would not, however, be a sin to receive something of this kind not as exacting or receiving it as though it were due under some tacit or express agreement, but as a gift: for one might, after all, lawfully accept a gift even before lending money, and so not then be left worse off by the loan. Moreover, it is lawful to exact recompense for a loan in the shape of things not measured by money: for example, benevolence, love for the lender, and so forth.

ad 1: A lender can without sin make an agreement with a borrower that [in addition to repayment of the loan] the borrower will compensate him for any loss by which the lender is deprived of something that he should rightly have. It can also happen in such circumstances that the borrower avoids a greater loss than the lender incurs, and in this event the borrower may compensate the lender out of what he has gained [without this being a case of usury].[68] But a lender cannot enter into an agreement compensating him merely for the fact that he will not make a profit from his money if he lends it; for he may not sell something which he does not yet have, and which he might, indeed, be prevented by many things from ever having.

ad 2: Recompense for a favour may be made in two ways. In one way, as a debt of justice, which someone can be bound by a formal contract to repay. In such a case, the amount to be repaid is according to the amount of benefit received. And so the borrower of money or of anything the

---

[66] *Ethics* 4:1 (1119b26).

[67] Art. 1.

[68] Suppose, for instance, the borrower uses the lender's money to pay off creditors, thereby avoiding ruin but rendering himself unable to repay the loan by the due date. In this case, the lender has suffered a loss – the money owed is not available to him after the agreed date; but the borrower has avoided a greater loss: i.e. going out of business. When the borrower's business has recovered sufficiently, he may not only repay the loan, but also make an additional payment to the lender in compensation for the loss occasioned by the delay. This would be compensation for a genuine loss rather than usury on the loan, and therefore not unlawful.

use of which lies in its consumption is not bound to repay more than he received on loan. Hence if he is required to repay more than he borrowed, this is contrary to justice. In another way, someone can be bound to make recompense for a favour as a debt of friendship, and what is due in this case is related more to the affection with which the favour was conferred than to the greatness of the favour itself. The latter kind of debt does not involve a civil obligation to repay it: that is, an obligation to repay it as a matter of necessity rather than from spontaneous choice.

ad 3: If someone were to expect or exact, as though under a tacit or express agreement, repayment for a loan of money in the form of some remuneration of service or words, this would be the same as expecting or exacting some material remuneration, for a monetary value can be assigned to both, as is seen in the case of those who sell their labour by hand or by tongue. If, however, remuneration by service or words is given not as an obligation but as a favour, which is not to be evaluated in monetary terms, it is lawful to take it, exact it,[69] and expect it.

ad 4: Money cannot be sold for a sum greater than the amount lent, which must be repaid; nor should a loan be made with a demand for anything, or in expectation of anything, apart from a sentiment of goodwill on the part of the borrower, to which a monetary value cannot be assigned: a sentiment which might indeed prompt the borrower to lend something in return of his own free will. But an obligation to lend in return at some future time is repugnant to this sentiment. Moreover, an obligation of this kind has a monetary value [and so is usurious, because it amounts to paying for the use of money with money]. And so it is lawful for the lender to borrow something else at the same time, but it is not lawful for him to bind the borrower to grant him a loan at some future time.

ad 5: One who lends money transfers the ownership of the money to the borrower. Hence the borrower holds the money at his own risk, and is bound to repay it in its entirety. The lender therefore must not exact more. But he who entrusts his money to a merchant or craftsman so as to form a kind of company does not transfer the ownership of his money to him. Rather, it remains his, so that it is at his risk that the merchant speculates with it, or the craftsman uses it for his work; and so the lender

---

[69] The verb is *exigere*. It is difficult to see how one might translate this word by anything less forceful than 'exact'; but it is also difficult to see how one could 'exact' a favour, or why such an 'exaction' would not be usurious within the terms of the argument. Perhaps St Thomas has in mind something like moral suasion.

may lawfully demand, as something belonging to him, a share of the profits derived from the money.

ad 6: If, in return for money lent to him, someone pledges something to which a monetary value can be assigned, the lender must regard the use of that thing as counting towards the repayment of the loan. Otherwise, if he wishes to have the free use of the thing in addition to repayment, this is the same as if he took money for lending, which is usury; unless perhaps it were the kind of thing that friends usually lend one another freely, as in the case of the loan of a book.

ad 7: If someone holds off the repayment of a loan by the purchaser so that he may be able to sell goods to him at a price higher than the just one, this is plainly a case of usury; for the postponement of payment has the character of a loan, and whatever he demands beyond the just price in consideration of this delay is therefore like a price for a loan, which pertains to the nature of usury. Similarly, if a buyer pays for goods before they can be delivered because he wishes to buy them at a price lower than the just one, this is the sin of usury; because, again, this payment of money in advance has the character of a loan, the price of which is the reduction of the just price of the goods sold. If, however, someone is willing to reduce the just price so that he may have his money sooner, he does not commit the sin of usury.

articulus 3: *Whether someone is bound to restore whatever profits he has made out of money lent upon usury*

It seems that one is bound to restore whatever profits he has made out of money lent upon usury.

obiectio 1: For the Apostle says at Romans 11:16: 'If the root be holy, so are the branches.' By the same token, therefore, if the root be rotten, so are the branches. But the root was the sin of usury. Therefore whatever profit is made from it is also usurious. Therefore he is bound to restore it.

obiectio 2: Moreover, it is said in the *Decretales*: 'Property acquired through usury must be sold and its value repaid to those from whom the usury was extorted.'[70] By the same token, therefore, whatever else is acquired from lending money upon usury must be restored.

---

[70] X. 5:19:5: *Quum tu sicut asseris (CIC 2:812).*

obiectio 3: Moreover, that which someone buys with money acquired through usury is due to him because he paid the money for it. Therefore he has no more right to the thing bought than he had to the money with which he paid for it. But he was bound to restore the money gained through usury. Therefore he is also bound to restore what he acquired with it.

sed contra: Someone can lawfully keep what he has legitimately acquired. But that which is acquired by the proceeds of usury is sometimes legitimately acquired.[71] Therefore it can be lawfully kept.

responsio: As stated above,[72] there are certain things whose use is their consumption and which do not admit of usufruct according to law.[73] And so if such things – for example, money, wheat, wine and things of that kind – are extorted by means of usury, a lender is not bound to restore more than he received, since what is acquired by such things is the fruit not of the thing itself but of human industry; unless perhaps the other party, by losing some of his own goods, is injured through the lender retaining them: for then the lender is bound to compensate him for the loss. On the other hand, there are certain things whose use is not their consumption; and such things do admit of usufruct: for example, a house and land and other such things. And so if someone has by usury extorted from another his house or land, he is bound to restore not only the house or land but also the fruits accruing to him from it, since they are the fruits of something which is the property of another, and so are owed to the other.

ad 1: A root has not only the character of matter, as money acquired by usury does; it also has something of the character of an active cause, insofar as it provides nourishment. And so the comparison is not apt.

ad 2: Property acquired by the proceeds of usury does not belong to the parties who paid usury, but to him who bought it. But the parties who paid usury have a claim on that property, just as they do on the other goods of the usurer. And so whereas it is not required that the property itself should be handed over to the parties who paid usury – for the property may, after all, be worth more than they have paid in usury – it is nonetheless required that the property should be sold and the value restored to them: according, that is, to the amount taken from them in usury.

---

[71] I.e. is acquired without breaking any law.
[72] Art. 1.
[73] *Ibid.*, ad 3; and see n. 59, above.

ad 3: That which someone buys with money acquired through usury is due to him who bought it not by reason of the usurious money as instrumental cause, but by reason of his own industry as principal cause. And so he has more right to the goods acquired with usurious money than to the usurious money itself.[74]

articulus 4: *Whether it is lawful to borrow money upon usury*

It seems that it is not lawful to borrow money upon usury.

obiectio 1: For the Apostle says at Romans 1:32: 'they are worthy of death: not only they that do the same, but they also that consent to them that do them'. But he who borrows money upon usury consents to the sin of the usurer and gives him an occasion of sin. Therefore he sins also.

obiectio 2: Moreover, no one should for any temporal advantage give an occasion of sin to another; for this pertains to the nature of active scandal, which is always a sin, as stated above.[75] But he who asks a loan of a usurer gives him an occasion of sin. Therefore he is not excused by any temporal advantage.

obiectio 3: Moreover, it seems no less necessary sometimes to deposit money with a usurer than to borrow from him. But it seems completely unlawful to deposit money with a usurer, just as it would be unlawful to leave a sword with a madman or a maiden with a libertine or food with a glutton. Nor therefore is it lawful to borrow from a usurer.

sed contra: One who suffers an injury does not sin, according to the Philosopher at *Ethics* v,[76] for justice is not a mean between two vices, as is said in the same book.[77] But the usurer sins by doing an injury to the person who borrows from him upon usury. Therefore one who receives a loan upon usury does not sin.

---

[74] The purport seems to be that there is no reason why he should not keep the goods provided that he repays the money taken as usury.

[75] IIaIIae 43:2 cf. IIaIIae 53:1. 'Active scandal' is a word or action, evil in itself, which incites another to sin; 'passive scandal' is found in the person who is the victim of the incitement. But because no one sins except willingly, the immediate effect of scandal can be only a temptation to sin, not sin itself.

[76] *Ethics* 5:11 (1138a34).

[77] *Ethics* 5:5 (1133b32). Aristotle's, and therefore St Thomas's, point here is that justice is a 'mean', but not in a way that other virtues are. Courage, for example, is a mean between rashness and cowardice. But justice is a mean not between being too just and not just enough, but between doing injustice and suffering it. Injustice is therefore not a vice on the part of the one who suffers it.

responsio: It is in no way lawful to induce a man to sin, but it is lawful to make use of another's sin to bring about a good end; for God Himself uses all sins to some good purpose, since He brings forth some good from every evil, as is stated in [Augustine's] *Enchiridion*.[78] And so when Publicola asked whether it is lawful to make use of the oath of someone who has sworn by false gods – which is clearly a sin, since it gives Divine honour to them – Augustine replied: 'Whoever uses the oath of someone who has sworn by false gods, but for a good purpose rather than a bad, associates himself not with his sin in swearing by demons, but with his good compact, by which he kept his word.'[79] If, however, he were to induce him to swear by false gods, he would sin.

So too it must be noted in the same vein that it is in no way lawful to induce someone to lend upon usury, but that it is lawful, for some good purpose such as the relief of one's own or someone else's need, to borrow upon usury from someone who is already prepared to lend and who will exact usury: just as it is lawful for a man who has fallen among thieves to save his life by revealing to them the whereabouts of his property, which they then sin in taking, after the example of the ten men who said to Ishmael: 'Kill us not: for we have stores in the field', as is said at Jeremiah 41:8.

ad 1: One who borrows upon usury does not consent to the usurer's sin; rather, he makes use of it. Nor is it the lender's taking of usury which pleases the borrower, but his lending, which is a good.

ad 2: One who borrows upon usury gives the usurer an occasion not for taking usury, but for lending. It is the usurer himself who finds occasion for sin, in the malice of his own heart. Hence there is passive scandal on the usurer's part, but there is no active scandal on the part of the individual in asking for the loan. Nor, if he is in need, should the borrower refrain from borrowing because of this passive scandal; for such passive scandal arises not from weakness or ignorance, but from malice.

ad 3: If someone were to deposit money with a usurer who had no other means of practising usury, or with the intention of investing it so as to make a greater profit from his money through usury, he would be giving a sinner the means of sinning. Hence, he would be a sharer in his guilt. But if the usurer in question has other means of practising usury, there is

---

[78] *Enchiridion* 11.   [79] *Epistolae* 47.

no sin in depositing money with him so that it may be in safer keeping, since this is to use a sinful man to good purpose.

(c) The letter to the Duchess of Brabant 'On the government of Jews'[80]

I have received your Grace's letter [litteras], from which [ex quibus][81] I have fully understood your pious solicitude for the government of your subjects and the devout love which you have for the brethren of our order; and I thank God, Who has sown into your heart the seeds of such great virtue. It is difficult for me to write in response to your several points, as you ask in the same letter: partly because of the demands made on my time by the work of teaching, and partly because I should have liked it better had you sought the advice of others more learned in such things than I. But because it would, as I think, be unseemly were I to be found negligent in assisting you in your anxieties, or thought ungrateful for your esteem, I have tried, in the present letter, to answer the points you raise, though without prejudice to a better opinion.

First, therefore, your Grace asked whether at any time, and [if so] at what time, it is lawful to exact tribute of Jews. To this question, put without qualification in this way, it can be replied that, as their sins deserve, the Jews are, or have been, given over into perpetual slavery, as the laws state,[82] so that earthly lords may take their property as though it were their own, provided only that the things necessary to sustain life are not withdrawn from them. However, because we ought to walk honestly even before those who are outcast, lest the name of the Lord be blasphemed, as the Apostle admonishes the faithful, by his own example, to give no offence to Jews or Gentiles or to the Church of God (1 Corinthians 10:32): it seems, having regard to this, that forced service should not be exacted of them where it has not been customary to do so in past time; for that which

---

[80] See Introduction, p. xix.

[81] It is quite usual for plural forms to be used in this way in referring to a single letter. There is therefore no reason to suppose that St Thomas is replying to several letters. The Duchess's letter is, however, not extant.

[82] What St Thomas probably has in mind here is the canon X. 5:6:13: *Etsi Judaeos* (*CIC* 2:775f); but canon law is full of legislation relating to the Jews, not all of it hostile. On this large question generally see especially S. Simonsohn, *The Apostolic See and the Jews* (Toronto, 1989); also S. Grayzel, *The Church and the Jews in the Thirteenth Century* (New York, 1989); W. Pakter, *Medieval Canon Law and the Jews* (Abhandlungen zur rechts-wissenschaftlichen Grundlagenforschung, 68: Ebelsbach, 1988).

is unaccustomed usually disturbs men's minds all the more. According to this reasoning, therefore, you can exact tribute of the Jews according to the custom of your predecessors, provided that there is no other reason why you should not do so.

But, so far as I have been able to gather from your next enquiry, it seems that your doubts in this regard are heightened by the fact that the Jews of your country appear to have nothing apart from what they have acquired through the wicked practice of usury. You therefore go on to ask whether it is lawful to exact from them monies which, because thus extorted, ought to be restored. It seems, then, that the answer to be given here is this: that since the Jews may not lawfully retain what they have taken from others by usury, it follows that you may not lawfully retain it if you take it from them, except, perhaps, in the case of monies which they may have extorted from you or your forebears. If they have goods which they have extorted from others, you ought to restore them to those to whom the Jews themselves are bound to make restitution.[83] Hence if you can find the specific persons of whom usury has been extorted, you must make restitution to them. Otherwise, the goods in question should be put to pious use, according to the advice of diocesan bishops and other men of probity; or used for the general benefit of your country, to relieve need or serve the interest of the community. Nor, subject to the customs of your predecessors, would it be unlawful for you to exact such goods from the Jews as a new thing, provided that you have the intention of expending them in the manner just described.

Second, you ask if Jews should be punished for offences by monetary fines, given that they have nothing apart from the proceeds of usury. According to the principles just set forth, the answer here seems to be this: that it is expedient to punish them by means of a monetary fine in order to ensure that no advantage is obtained from iniquity. Also, it seems to me that a Jew, or any other usurer, should be punished by a heavier fine than anyone else, since they are known to have less right to the money thus removed from them. Also, other penalties can be added as well as fines, lest it should seem to be a sufficient punishment merely to restore what is owed to others already. But money from fines levied on usurers cannot be retained if it has no other source than usury; rather, it must be expended in the ways described above. If it be said that the princes of the earth suffer loss by doing this, they have only themselves to blame for such loss,

---

[83] Cf. X. 5:19:5: *Quum tu sicut asseris* (*CIC* 2:812).

which arises from their own negligence. They would do better to compel the Jews to work for honest profit, as is done in parts of Italy, rather than allowing them to live in idleness and grow rich by usury, thereby defrauding their lords of their proper revenues. In the same way, and by their own fault, princes would be defrauded of their proper revenues if they were to permit their subjects to enrich themselves by robbery or theft; for then they would be just as much bound to make restitution of anything that they exacted from such subjects.

Third, you ask whether it is lawful to accept money, or some gift, freely offered by them. To which the reply seems to be this: that it is lawful to receive such things, but that, if it has no source apart from usury, it is expedient that anything thus received should be restored to its rightful owner or, otherwise, expended in the manner stated above.

Fourth, you ask what should be done with the balance if more is taken from a Jew than is owed by him to Christians. The answer to this is clear from what has been said already. A surplus in excess of what is owed to Christians can arise for two reasons. Either the Jew may have some property apart from the proceeds of usury, and, in this case, subject to what has been said above, it is lawful for us to keep what is levied; and it seems that the same must be said if [the surplus has arisen because] those who have paid usury have subsequently made a free gift to the Jew in addition, provided that the proceeds of usury themselves are first repaid. It may, however, happen that those from whom usury has been taken have meanwhile been removed either by death or because they now dwell in other lands. In this case, restitution must be made [wherever possible], but if it is not apparent who the persons are to whom restitution should be made, the procedure should be as described above.

What has been said of Jews should be understood as applying also to *cavorsini*[84] and to all others who persist in the wicked practice of usury.

Fifth, with regard to your bailiffs and other officials, you ask if it is lawful to sell their offices to them or take from them some agreed sum by way of deposit, which they will then receive back from the proceeds of their office. We must say here, it seems, that this question appears to involve two difficulties. The first concerns the sale of offices. As to this, it

---

[84] DuCange (*Glossarium mediae et infimae Latinitatis*) gives various spellings of this word: *caorcini, catucini, caursini, cawarsini, corsini* and *cahoursini*. They are, he says, 'Italian merchants noted for usurious loans, especially in France', where, he adds, several laws were passed against them. The name apparently derives from their association with the town of Cahors. According to Matthew Paris, cited by DuCange, they were active in England also.

seems that we must consider what the Apostle says (1 Corinthians 6:12): that many things are lawful which are not expedient. Since what you entrust to your bailiffs and officials is nothing more than the power belonging to a temporal office, I do not see that it is unlawful for you to sell such offices, provided that you sell them to people of whom it may be supposed that they will exercise their office beneficially, and not to those who offer so high a price for the office that they will not be able to recoup it without burdening your subjects. It seems, however, that the sale of such offices is not expedient. For one thing, it is frequently the case that those who are best fitted to exercise such offices are poor, and so not able to buy them; and even if they were rich, the best men are not ambitious for such offices, nor do they wish to profit from acquiring them. It would follow, then, that offices in your lands would often be filled by the worst kind of people, ambitious and lovers of money, who would probably oppress your subjects and so not faithfully procure your advantage. Hence it would seem more expedient to choose good and capable men to receive your offices, if necessary even compelling them to do so if they are unwilling. For by their goodness and industry greater good will accrue to you and your subjects than you could manage to acquire from the sale of offices. This was the counsel given to Moses by his kinsman. He said (Exodus 18:21f): 'Provide out of all the people able men, such as fear God, men of truth, hating covetousness: and place such over them, to be rulers of thousands, and rulers of hundreds, rulers of fifties, and rulers of tens: and let them judge the people at all seasons.'

The second doubt arises with regard to the matter of a deposit. It seems that we must say here that if someone agrees to pay a deposit in order to receive an office, this agreement is beyond doubt usurious, since he receives the power of an office in return for a loan. Hence in a case of this kind you would be giving occasion for sin, and the officials in question would be bound to resign any office thus obtained. If, however, you were to give them the office freely and afterwards accept a deposit from them which they could then recover from the proceeds of office, this can be done without any sin.

Sixth, you ask if it would be lawful to levy tribute of your Christian subjects. Here, you should consider that the princes of the earth are instituted by God not so that they may seek profit for themselves, but to procure the common benefit of the people. For in condemnation of certain princes it is said at Ezekiel 22:27: 'Her princes in the midst thereof are like wolves ravening the prey, to shed blood and to destroy souls, to get dishonest gain.' And elsewhere it is said by the same[85] prophet (Ezekiel 34:2f): 'Woe be to the shepherds of Israel that do feed themselves! Should not the shepherds feed the flocks? Ye eat the fat and ye clothe you with the wool, ye kill them that are fed: but ye feed not the flock.' Therefore a revenue is established for earthly princes, so that they may live and abstain from despoiling their subjects. Hence at the Lord's command it is said by the same prophet (Ezekiel 45:8): 'To the king shall be given a certain possession in Israel, and princes shall no more oppress my people.' But sometimes it happens that princes do not have revenues sufficient to protect their lands or to perform other tasks which might reasonably be expected of princes; and in such a case it is just that their subjects should be called upon to furnish whatever is necessary to secure the common welfare. Hence it is that there is an ancient custom in some lands for lords to impose certain taxes upon their subjects, and if these are not immoderate, this can be done without sin; for, according to the Apostle (1 Corinthians 9:7), 'Who goeth a warfare any time at his own charges?' Therefore a prince who fights for the common benefit can live at the community's expense and make a charge upon the business of the community either through the established forms of taxation or, if these are not in place, or if they are not sufficient, by levying a charge on individuals. A similar principle seems to apply when some new circumstance arises such that it is necessary to spend more than usual for the common benefit or to preserve the honourable standing of the prince, and the normal revenues or customary exactions are not sufficient: if, for example, enemies invade the land, or if some similar case arises. Earthly princes may then lawfully demand from their citizens sums beyond the normal exactions for the common benefit. If, however, they wish to make exactions in addition to what is usual out of the mere desire for money or to meet inordinate and immoderate expenses, this is entirely unlawful. Hence John the Baptist said to the soldiers who came to him (Luke 3:14): 'Do violence to no man, neither calumniate any man, and be content with your pay.' The revenues of princes are as it were their 'pay', with which they should be content. They should not demand more, save for the reasons just discussed and for the sake of the common benefit.

Seventh, you ask what you should do if your officials have extorted from your subjects something beyond what the law requires, whether the sums have come into your hands or not. As to this, the answer is plain. If

---

[85] Reading *eundem* for *quemdam*.

the sums have come into your hands, you should return them, if possible, to the specific persons from whom they came, or, if the specific persons cannot be found, you should expend them in pious uses or for the common benefit. If, however, they have not come into your hands, you must compel your officials to make the same kind of restitution, lest they profit from their injustices, even if the specific persons from whom the exactions were made are not known to you. Indeed, such officials should be punished all the more severely by you, so that others may abstain from such offences in the future; for, as Solomon says (Proverbs 19:25), 'The wicked man being scourged, the fool shall be wiser.'

Finally, you ask if it is good that the Jews in your province should be required to bear some distinctive sign to distinguish them from Christians. As to this, the answer is plain and according to the statute of a general council: that Jews of both sexes in all Christian provinces and at all times should be distinguished from other people by some particular form of dress.[86] This is in any case commanded by their law: that is, that they should wear a fringed four-cornered cloak, by which they might be told apart from others.[87]

These, O illustrious and religious lady, are my replies for the time being to your questions; but I do not wish to impose my opinion in such matters upon you: indeed, I would rather persuade you to take the advice of others more learned than I. May your reign long prosper.

[86] The 'General Council' is the fourth Lateran Council of 1215. See X. 5:6:15: *In nonnullis* (*CIC* 2:15f); and see also n. 82, above.
[87] Numbers 16:38f; Deuteronomy 22:12.

6

War, sedition and killing

(a) *Summa theologiae* IIaIIae 40: On war

We come next to war; and here there are four things to consider:

1. Whether it is a sin to wage war
2. Whether it is lawful for clerics to fight
3. Whether it is lawful for those who wage war to make use of ambushes
4. Whether it is lawful to wage war on holy days

articulus 1: *Whether it is always a sin to wage war*

It seems that it is always a sin to wage war.

obiectio 1: For punishment is not inflicted for anything except sin. But those who wage war are threatened by the Lord with punishment, according to Matthew 26:52: 'All that take the sword shall perish by the sword.' Therefore all war is unlawful.

obiectio 2: Moreover, whatever is contrary to a Divine precept is a sin. But to wage war is contrary to a Divine precept, for it is said at Matthew 5:39: 'But I say unto you, That ye resist not evil', and at Romans 12:19: 'Dearly beloved, avenge not yourselves, but rather give place unto wrath.' Therefore to wage war is always a sin.

obiectio 3: Moreover, nothing is contrary to an act of virtue except sin. But war is contrary to peace. Therefore war is always a sin.

obiectio 4: Moreover, every kind of legitimate contest is lawful, as is clear in the case of contests of reason.[1] But the martial contests which take place in tournaments are prohibited by the Church, for those who die in

---

[1] I.e. the disputations which formed so important a part of the medieval university education. See, e.g., L. J. Daly, *The Medieval University, 1200–1400* (New York, 1961).

such events are deprived of ecclesiastical burial.[2] Therefore it seems that war is a sin absolutely.

sed contra: Augustine, in a sermon on the centurion's son, says: 'If Christian teaching condemned war altogether, those who sought wholesome counsel in the Gospel would have been told to cast aside their arms and withdraw altogether from the military profession; whereas it was said to them: "Do violence to no man and be content with your wages" (Luke 3:14). If He commanded them to be content with their wages, He did not forbid them to be soldiers.'[3]

responsio: If a war is to be just, three things are required. First, the authority of the prince by whose command war is to be waged. For it does not pertain to a private person to declare war, because he can prosecute his rights at the tribunal of his superior; similarly, it does not pertain to a private person to summon the people together, which must be done in time of war. Rather, since the care of the commonwealth is entrusted to princes, it pertains to them to protect the commonwealth of the city or kingdom or province subject to them. And just as it is lawful for them to use the material sword in defence of the commonwealth against those who trouble it from within, when they punish evildoers, according to the Apostle (Romans 13:4), 'He beareth not the sword in vain: for he is the minister of God, a revenger to execute wrath upon him that doeth evil': so too, it pertains to them to use the sword of war to protect the commonwealth against enemies from without. Hence it is said to princes at Psalm 82:4: 'Deliver the poor and needy: rid them out of the hand of the wicked.' Hence also Augustine says: 'The natural order accommodated to the peace of mortal men requires that the authority to declare and counsel war should be vested in princes.'[4]

Second, a just cause is required: that is, those against whom war is to be waged must deserve to have war waged against them because of some wrongdoing. Hence Augustine says in the book *Quaestiones in heptateuchum*: 'A just war is customarily defined as one which avenges injuries, as when a nation or state deserves to be punished because it has neglected

---

[2] The reference is evidently to Canon 16 of the second Lateran Council (1139), repeating a prohibition first stated at the Synod of Clermont (1130). See n. 12 below.

[3] Not a sermon *De puero centurionis*, as the text seems to suggest, but *Epistolae* 138:2 (*Ad Marcellinum*).

[4] *Contra Faustum* 22:75.

either to put right the wrongs done by its people or to restore what it has unjustly seized.'[5]

Third, it is required that those who wage war should have a righteous intent: that is, they should intend either to promote a good cause or avert an evil. Hence Augustine says: 'Among true worshippers of God, those wars which are waged not out of greed or cruelty, but with the object of securing peace by coercing the wicked and helping the good, are regarded as peaceful.'[6] For it can happen that even if war is declared by a legitimate authority and for a just cause, that war may be rendered unlawful by a wicked intent. For Augustine says in the book *Contra Faustum*: 'The desire to do harm, the cruelty of vengeance, an unpeaceable and implacable spirit, the fever of rebellion, the lust to dominate, and similar things: these are rightly condemned in war.'[7]

ad 1: As Augustine says: 'He "takes the sword" who arms himself to shed another's blood without the command or permission of a superior or lawful power.'[8] But one who, as a private person, makes use of the sword by the authority of the prince or judge, or, as a public person, through zeal for justice, as if by the authority of God, does not 'take the sword', but uses it as one commissioned by another, and so does not deserve to suffer punishment. Even those who use the sword sinfully are not always slain by the sword; yet they always 'perish' by their own sword nonetheless, for, unless they repent, they are punished eternally for their sinful use of the sword.

ad 2: As Augustine says, one should always be prepared in spirit to observe precepts of this kind: that is, a man should always be prepared not to resist or not to defend himself if need be.[9] But it is sometimes necessary to act otherwise than this for the common good: even, indeed, for the good of those against whom one is fighting. Hence Augustine says:

> Many things must be done which are against the wishes of those whom we have to punish with, as it were, a kindly severity. When we take away from someone the freedom to do wrong, it is beneficial for him that he should be vanquished, for nothing is more unfortunate

[5] *Quaestiones in heptateuchum* 4:10; and see Dyson, *The Pilgrim City*, ch. 4.
[6] Cf. *De civitate Dei* 19:12; C. 23:1:6: *Apud veros* (*CIC* 1:893).
[7] *Contra Faustum* 22:74.
[8] *Contra Faustum* 22:70.
[9] *De sermone Domini in monte* 1:19.

than the happiness of sinners, when impunity nourishes guilt and an evil will arises like an enemy within.[10]

ad 3: Those who wage just wars intend to secure peace, and so they are not opposed to any peace except that evil peace which the Lord 'came not to send' upon the earth (Matthew 10:34). Hence Augustine says: 'We do not seek peace in order to wage war; rather, we wage war in order to achieve peace. Be peaceful, therefore, in making war, so that, in vanquishing those against whom you fight, you may lead them to the benefit of peace.'[11]

ad 4: Men are certainly not forbidden to engage in every kind of exercise involving feats of arms, but only in those exercises which are disorderly and perilous and which lead to slaying and looting.[12] Among the people of antiquity warlike contests were held without such perils, and so were called 'armed practice' or 'wars without blood', as Jerome states in one of his letters.[13]

articulus 2: *Whether it is lawful for clerics and bishops to fight*

It seems that it is lawful for clerics and bishops to fight.

obiectio 1: For, as stated above,[14] wars are lawful and just insofar as they defend the poor and the commonwealth as a whole from injury by enemies. But to do this seems to pertain to prelates above all, for Gregory says in a certain homily: 'The wolf comes upon the sheep when any unjust and predatory man oppresses those who are faithful and humble. But he who

---

[10] *Epistolae* 138:2.

[11] *Epistolae* 189.

[12] Canon 16 of the second Lateran Council says: 'We absolutely condemn those detestable jousts or tournaments at which knights are accustomed to assemble by agreement and, to display their strength and boldness, foolishly engage in contests which are often the cause of death to men and of danger to souls. If anyone taking part in these should meet his death, he is to be deprived of Christian burial, although penance and the Viaticum are not to be withheld if he should ask for them.' This is a rather more unequivocal prohibition than St Thomas's comment seems to suggest. In general, though, the Church was opposed to tournaments not as such, but inasmuch as they tended to become occasions for settling grievances and exacting revenge. The fourth Lateran Council (1215) and the second Council of Lyons (1274) both forbade tournaments absolutely for a period of three years on pain of excommunication, for fear that they might distract participants from the duty of fighting in the crusades. See J. D. Mansi, *Sacrorum conciliorum nova et amplissima collectio* (Florence and Venice, 1757–98), 22:953–1068.

[13] The reference does not seem to be to any letter of St Jerome now extant; but cf. Vegetius, *Rei militaris instituta* 1:9ff; 2:23.

[14] Art. 1.

seemed to be the shepherd and was not, leaves the sheep and flees, for while he fears danger to himself, he does not dare to resist the injustice of another.'[15] Therefore it is lawful for prelates and clerics to fight.

obiectio 2: Moreover, Pope Leo writes: 'Because adverse tidings had often come from the Saracen side, some said that the Saracens were coming secretly and furtively to the port of Rome; and for this reason we commanded our people to assemble, and ordered them to go down to the seashore.'[16] Therefore it is lawful for bishops to fight.

obiectio 3: Moreover, the same principle seems to be involved whether a man does something himself, or consents to its being done by someone else, according to Romans 1:32: 'They which commit such things are worthy of death, and not only they that do the same, but they also that consent to them that do them.' Now those who induce others to do something certainly consent to it. But it is lawful for bishops and clerics to induce others to go to war; for it is said that: 'Charles began to wage war against the Lombards at the exhortation and prayers of Hadrian, bishop of Rome.'[17] Therefore it is also lawful for them to fight.

obiectio 4: Moreover, that which is honest and meritorious in itself is not unlawful for prelates and clerics. But it is sometimes honest and meritorious to wage war; for it is said that 'if someone die for the true faith and the salvation of his country, or in defence of Christians, he will receive from God a heavenly reward'.[18] Therefore it is lawful for bishops and clerics to fight.

sed contra: It was said to Peter as representing bishops and clerics (Matthew 26:52): 'Put up again thy sword into his place.' Therefore it is not lawful for them to fight.

responsio: A number of things are necessary for the good of human society, and some are better and more swiftly done by many people than by one, as the Philosopher shows in his *Politics*.[19] But certain tasks are so much at odds with one another that they cannot suitably be performed at the same time, and so those deputed to great tasks are forbidden to engage in small ones. Thus, according to human laws, soldiers, who are deputed

---

[15] *Homilia in evangelia* 1:14 (*PL* 76:1128).
[16] C. 23:8:7: *Igitur* (*CIC* 1:954f).
[17] C. 23:8:10: *Hortatu* (*CIC* 1:955).
[18] C. 23:8:9: *Omni timore* (*CIC* 1:955).
[19] *Politics* 1:1 (1252b3).

to warlike tasks, are forbidden to engage in commerce.[20] Now warlike tasks are entirely repugnant to the offices to which bishops and clerics are deputed, for two reasons. The first is a general reason: that warlike tasks have a greatly unquiet character, and hence much distract the mind from the contemplation of Divine things and from praising God and offering prayers for the people, which belong to the duties of clerics. Thus, just as commercial ventures are forbidden to clerics because such things too much entangle the mind, so also are warlike activities, according to 2 Timothy 2:4: 'No man being a soldier to God, entangleth himself with the affairs of this life.'

The second reason is a particular one: that all clerical orders are ordained to the ministry of the altar, upon which the Passion of Christ is represented under the sacrament, according to 1 Corinthians 11:26: 'As often as ye eat this bread and drink this cup, ye do show the Lord's death till He come.' And so it is not fitting for them to slay or shed blood. On the contrary, it is proper for them to be prepared to pour out their own blood for Christ, and so imitate in deed what they represent in their ministry. And it is for this reason decreed that those clerics who shed blood even without sin become irregular.[21] But it is not lawful for any man who has been deputed to some duty to do something by which he is rendered unfit to perform his duty. And so it is entirely unlawful for clerics to wage war, because war is directed to the shedding of blood.

ad 1: Prelates ought to resist not only the wolf who slays the flock spiritually, but also predators and tyrants who vex it in body: not, however, by making use of material arms in their own person, but by spiritual means, according to what the Apostle says at 2 Corinthians 10:4: 'The weapons of our warfare are not carnal, but mighty through God.' These weapons include wholesome admonitions, devout prayers, and, for the pertinacious, the sentence of excommunication.

ad 2: Prelates and clerics may take part in wars by the authority of their superiors: not, however, by fighting with their own hands, but by giving spiritual assistance to those who fight justly, by exhortation and absolution and other such spiritual aids. Thus in the Old Testament the priests were commanded to sound the sacred trumpets in the midst of the battle.[22] It was for this purpose that bishops or clerics were first permitted to go to

---

[20] *CICiv: Codex* 12:35.
[21] Dist. 50, c. 4: *Miror* (*CIC* 1:178).
[22] Joshua 6:4; Numbers 10:9.

war; but it is an abuse of this permission if any one of them fight with his own hand.

ad 3: As noted above,[23] every power or art or virtue which exists for the sake of an end must also dispose the things which are directed to the attaining of that end. Now among the faithful people, carnal wars should be considered as having as their end the Divine spiritual good which clerics are deputed to secure. And so it pertains to clerics to dispose and lead other men to prosecute just wars. For they are forbidden to wage war themselves not because it is a sin to do so, but because such activity is not in keeping with their duty.

ad 4: Although it is meritorious to wage just war, the fact of their being deputed to works more meritorious still renders it unlawful for clerics to do so. Thus the act of marriage can be meritorious, yet it is rendered blameworthy in those who have taken a vow of virginity, by reason of their obligation to a still greater good.

articulus 3: *Whether it is lawful to make use of ambushes in war*

It seems that it is unlawful to make use of ambushes in war.

obiectio 1: For it is said at Deuteronomy 16:20: 'That which is altogether just shalt thou follow.' But ambushes, since they are a kind of deception, seem to pertain to injustice. Therefore it is unlawful to use ambushes even in a just war.

obiectio 2: Moreover, ambushes and deceptions seem to be opposed to fidelity in the same way that lies are. But since we must keep faith with all men, no man is to be lied to, as Augustine shows in the book *Contra mendacium*.[24] Therefore, since 'faith should be kept with an enemy', as Augustine says in his letter *Ad Bonifacium*,[25] it seems that one must not use ambushes against enemies.

obiectio 3: Moreover, it is said at Matthew 7:12: 'Whatsoever ye would that men should do to you, do ye even so to them'; and this is to be observed in relation to all our neighbours. But our enemy is our neighbour. Therefore, since no one wishes to have ambushes or deceptions prepared for him, it seems that no one ought to carry on war by means of ambushes.

[23] IIaIIae 23:4 ad 2.
[24] *Contra mendacium* 15.
[25] *Epistolae* 189.

sed contra: Augustine says: 'when the war is just, it does not matter from the point of view of justice whether it be carried on openly or by ambushes';[26] and he proves this by the authority of the Lord, Who commanded Joshua to lay ambushes for those who dwelt in the city of Ai, as noted at Joshua 8:2.

responsio: The purpose of ambushes is to deceive enemies. But there are two ways in which someone may be deceived by what someone else does or says. In one way, by being told something false or by not having a promise kept; and this is always unlawful. No one ought to deceive an enemy in this way, for there are certain rights of war and covenants which should be observed even among enemies, as Ambrose says in the book *De officiis*.[27] In another way, someone may be deceived by what we say or do because we do not reveal our thoughts or intentions to him. But we are not always bound to do this, for even in sacred doctrine many things are to be kept hidden, especially from unbelievers, lest they mock them, according to Matthew 7:6: 'Give not that which is holy unto the dogs.' So much more, then, ought our preparations against the enemy to be kept hidden. One of the most important parts of a military education, therefore, as is clear from Frontinus's book *Strategemata*, is the art of concealing one's plans lest they come to the enemy's knowledge.[28] And the planning of ambushes, which may lawfully be used in a just war, belongs to this art of concealment; nor can such ambushes properly be called deceptions; nor are they repugnant to justice or to a rightly-ordered will, for a man would have a disordered will if he were unwilling that anything should be hidden from him by others.

By this the replies to the *obiectiones* are shown.

articulus 4: *Whether it is lawful to fight on holy days*

It seems that it is unlawful to fight on holy days.

obiectio 1: For holy days are ordained to provide rest for things divine. They are therefore understood to be included in the Sabbath observance prescribed at Exodus 20:8; for the word 'sabbath' means 'rest'. But wars are occasions of the greatest unrest. Therefore it is in no way lawful to wage war on holy days.

---

[26] *Quaestiones in heptateuchum* 6:10.
[27] *De officiis* 1:29 (*PL* 16:68).
[28] *Strategemata* 1:1.

obiectio 2: Moreover, certain persons are reproached at Isaiah 58:3f because on fast-days they insisted on having their debts paid, and engaged in strife and smote with the fist. It is all the more unlawful, therefore, to wage war on holy days.

obiectio 3: Moreover, no wrongful act should be done to avoid temporal harm. But waging war on a holy day seems to be wrongful in itself. Therefore no one should wage war on a holy day even if there is a need to avoid temporal harm.

sed contra: It is said at 1 Maccabees 2:41: 'The Jews rightly determined saying: Whosoever shall come up against us to fight on the Sabbath-day, we will fight against him.'

responsio: The observance of holy days does not impede those things which are ordained for man's safety, even that of his body. Thus the Lord argued with the Jews, saying at John 7:23: 'Are ye angry at me because I have made a man every whit whole on the Sabbath-day?' Hence it is that physicians may lawfully treat men on a holy day. But it is a more pressing task to preserve the health of the commonwealth – to prevent the slaughter of many and innumerable other ills both temporal and spiritual – than the bodily health of one man. In order to defend the commonwealth of the faithful, therefore, it is lawful to wage just war on holy days, provided only that it is necessary to do so: for it would be to tempt God if one were to abstain from war even in the face of such necessity. But as soon as the need ceases it is no longer lawful to fight on a holy day, for the reasons given.

By this the replies to the *obiectiones* are shown.

(b) *Summa theologiae* IIaIIae 42: On sedition

We come next to sedition, and here there are two things to consider:

1. Whether it is a specific sin
2. Whether it is a mortal sin

articulus 1: *Whether sedition is a specific sin distinct from others*

It seems that sedition is not a specific sin distinct from others.

obiectio 1: For, as Isidore says in the book *Etymologies*, 'a seditious man is one who causes dissent among minds, and begets discord'.[29] But one who

---

[29] *Etymologiae* 10 (*PL* 82:394).

causes a sin to be committed does not himself sin by any other kind of sin than that which he caused to be committed. Therefore it seems that sedition is not a specific sin distinct from discord.[30]

obiectio 2: Moreover, sedition implies a kind of division. But 'schism' takes its name from *scissura* ['separation'], as stated above.[31] Therefore it seems that the sin of sedition is not distinct from the sin of schism.

obiectio 3: Moreover, every specific sin which is distinct from others is either a capital vice or arises from some capital vice.[32] But sedition is reckoned neither among the capital vices nor among those vices which arise from them, as appears from *Moralia* 31, where the vices of both kinds are enumerated.[33] Therefore sedition is not a specific sin distinct from others.

sed contra: At 2 Corinthians 12:20 seditions are distinguished from other sins.[34]

responsio: Sedition is a specific kind of sin, resembling war and strife[35] in certain ways but differing from them in others. It resembles them in so far as it implies a kind of opposition. But it differs from them in two respects. First, because war and strife signify actual fighting with one another, whereas sedition can be said to involve either actual fighting or preparation for such fighting. Hence the [interlinear] gloss on 2 Corinthians 12:20 says that seditions are 'tumults leading to conflict': because, that is, certain persons are preparing and intending to fight.[36] Second, they differ in that, properly speaking, war is carried on against external enemies, being as it were between one community and another, whereas strife occurs between one individual and another, or between a few people on one side and few on the other, while sedition, properly so called, arises as between parts of a single community who dissent from one another, as when one part of the city rises in tumult against another. And so, since sedition is opposed to a special kind of good, namely the unity and peace of a community, it is therefore a special kind of sin.

---

[30] See IIaIIae 37 for St Thomas's discussion of discord.

[31] IIaIIae 39:1.

[32] A 'capital' vice or sin is one which induces someone to commit other sins arising from it.

[33] Gregory, *Moralia* 31:45 (*PL* 76:621).

[34] 'For I fear lest perhaps when I come I shall not find you such as I would, and that I shall be found by you such as you would not. Lest perhaps contentions, envyings, animosities, dissensions, detractions, whisperings, swellings, seditions, be among you.'

[35] Cf. IIaIIae 41.

[36] See n. 65 on p. 226, above.

ad 1: A seditious man is said to be one who incites sedition in others; and since sedition denotes a kind of discord, a seditious man is therefore one who creates discord, not of any kind, but as between the parts of a community. But the sin of sedition is not only in him who sows discord, but also in those who dissent from one another inordinately.

ad 2: Sedition differs from schism in two respects. First, schism is opposed to the spiritual unity of a community, that is, ecclesiastical unity; whereas sedition is opposed to the temporal or secular unity of a community: for example, of a city or kingdom. Second, schism does not imply any preparation for bodily fighting, but is a matter of spiritual dissension only, whereas sedition does imply preparation for bodily fighting.

ad 3: Sedition, like schism, is contained under discord, since each is a kind of discord not between one individual and another, but between the parts of a community.

articulus 2: *Whether sedition is always a mortal sin*

It seems that sedition is not always a mortal sin.

obiectio 1: For sedition implies 'a tumult leading to conflict' as the gloss quoted above shows.[37] But conflict is not always a mortal sin: indeed it is sometimes just and lawful, as noted above.[38] So much more, therefore, can there be sedition without mortal sin.

obiectio 2: Moreover, sedition is a kind of discord, as stated above.[39] But there can be discord without mortal sin, and sometimes indeed without any sin at all. Therefore the same is true of sedition.

obiectio 3: Moreover, they are praised who deliver a community from the power of a tyrant. But this cannot easily be done without some dissension in the community while one part of the community is striving to retain the tyrant and another to get rid of him. Therefore there can be sedition without sin.

sed contra: The Apostle forbids 'seditions' along with other things which are mortal sins.[40] Therefore sedition is a mortal sin.

[37] Art. 1.
[38] IIaIIae 40:1 (p. 239, above); 41:1.
[39] Art. 1 ad 3.
[40] 2 Corinthians 12:20.

responsio: As stated above, sedition is contrary to the unity of a community, that is, of the people of a city or kingdom. But Augustine says at *De civitate Dei* II that the wise understand the term 'people' to mean 'not any indiscriminate multitude, but an assembly of those united by agreement as to what is right and by a common interest'.[41] Hence it is clear that the unity to which sedition is opposed is a unity of right and common interest; and so, clearly, sedition is opposed to justice and the common good. Therefore by reason of its genus it is a mortal sin, and it will be so much the more grievous in proportion as the common good which is attacked by sedition is greater than the private good which is attacked by strife.

The sin of sedition therefore pertains first and foremost to those who stir up sedition, who sin most grievously; and, second, to those who are led by them to disturb the common good. But those who resist them in order to defend the common good are not to be called seditious themselves, just as no one is to be called quarrelsome because he defends himself, as stated above.[42]

ad 1: It is lawful to fight for the sake of the common benefit, as stated above.[43] But sedition is contrary to the common good of the community. Hence it is always a mortal sin.

ad 2: Discord from that which is not a manifest good can be without sin, whereas discord from that which is a manifest good cannot be without sin. But sedition is a discord of this latter kind, for it is contrary to the benefit of the community, which is a manifest good.

ad 3: Tyrannical rule is not just, because it is not directed to the common good but to the private good of the ruler, as the Philosopher shows at *Politics* III and *Ethics* VIII.[44] Disruption of such a government therefore does not have the character of sedition, unless perhaps the tyrant's rule is disrupted so inordinately that the community subject to it suffers greater detriment from the ensuing disorder than it did from the tyrannical government itself. Indeed it is the tyrant who is guilty of

[41] *De civitate Dei* 2:21, quoting Cicero, *De republica* 1:25.
[42] IIaIIae 41:1.
[43] IIaIIae 40:1 (p. 239, above).
[44] *Politics* 3:5 (1279b6); *Ethics* 8:10 (1160b8).

sedition, since he nourishes discord and sedition among his subjects in order to be able to dominate them more securely. For this is tyranny: a form of government directed to the private good of the ruler and the injury of the community.

(c) *Summa theologiae* IIaIIae 64: On homicide

Here there are eight things to consider:

1. Whether it is lawful to kill any living thing
2. Whether it is lawful to kill sinners
3. Whether this is lawful for a private, or only for a public, person
4. Whether this is lawful for clerics
5. Whether it is lawful for someone to slay himself
6. Whether it is lawful to slay a just man
7. Whether it is lawful for someone to kill a man in self-defence
8. Whether it is a mortal sin to kill someone

articulus 1: *Whether it is unlawful to kill any living thing*

It seems that it is unlawful to kill any living thing.

obiectio 1: For the Apostle says (Romans 13:2) that those who resist the ordinance of God receive to themselves damnation. But, according to Psalm 147:8f, by the ordinance of Divine providence, 'Who maketh grass to grow upon the mountains; Who giveth to beasts their food', all living things should be preserved. Therefore it seems unlawful to kill any living thing.

obiectio 2: Moreover, homicide is a sin because it deprives a man of life. But life is common to all animals and plants. Therefore for the same reason it seems to be a sin to slay brute beasts and plants.

obiectio 3: Moreover, a specific punishment is not appointed in the Divine law for anything except sin. But a punishment is appointed in the Divine law for one who kills another's ox or sheep, as is shown at Exodus 22:1. Therefore the killing of brute beasts is a sin.

sed contra: Augustine says at *De civitate Dei* 1: 'When we hear it said, "Thou shalt not kill", we do not take this as applying to trees, for they have no sensation, nor to non-rational animals, because they have no fellowship with us. The conclusion remains, therefore, that we are to take "Thou shalt not kill" as applying to man.'[45]

responsio: There is no sin in using something for its proper purpose. Now in the natural order of things, imperfect things exist for the sake of perfect, just as, in the process of generation, nature proceeds from the imperfect to the perfect. Hence, just as in the generation of man there was first a living thing, then an animal, and finally a man,[46] so too such things as plants, which merely have life, all exist for the sake of animals, and all animals exist for the sake of man. And so it is not unlawful if man makes use of plants for the benefit of animals, and animals for the benefit of men, as the Philosopher shows at *Politics* I.[47] But among the possible uses, the most necessary seems to be that animals use plants, and men animals, as food; and this cannot be done without killing them. And so it is lawful both to kill plants for the use of animals, and animals for the use of men; and this, indeed, is by Divine ordinance, for it is said at Genesis 1:29f: 'Behold I have given you every herb and all trees to be your meat, and to all beasts of the earth.' Again, it is said at Genesis 9:3: 'Everything that moveth and liveth shall be meat for you.'

ad 1: The life of animals and plants is preserved by Divine ordinance not for their own sake, but for man's. Hence, as Augustine says at *De civitate Dei* I, 'by the most just ordinance of their Creator, both their life and death are subject to our needs'.[48]

ad 2: Brute beasts and plants do not have a life governed by reason so that they can set themselves to work. Rather, they are always set to work at the behest, as it were, of another, by a certain impulse of nature. And this is a sign that they are naturally enslaved and accommodated to the uses of others.

ad 3: He who kills another's ox sins not with regard to the killing of the ox, but because he has injured a man with respect to his property. Hence

---

[45] *De civitate Dei* 1:20.
[46] The reference is to the story of creation at Genesis 1, where God created first plants, then animals, and finally man.
[47] *Politics* 1:3 (1256b15).
[48] *De civitate Dei* 1:20.

this is not contained under the sin of homicide[49] but under the sin of theft or robbery.

articulus 2: *Whether it is lawful to kill sinners*

It seems that it is not lawful to kill men who have sinned.

obiectio 1: For in a parable (Matthew 13:29f) the Lord forbade the uprooting of the tares which in the same place (vs. 38) are said to be 'the children of the wicked one'. But everything forbidden by God is a sin. Therefore it is a sin to kill a sinner.

obiectio 2: Moreover, human justice takes its form from Divine justice. But according to Divine justice sinners are reserved for repentance, according to Ezekiel 18:23 and 33:11, 'I desire not the death of the sinner, but that the wicked turn from his way and live.' Therefore it seems altogether unjust for sinners to be killed.

obiectio 3: Moreover, as Augustine shows in the book *Contra mendacium* and the Philosopher at *Ethics* II, that which is evil in itself should not be done even for the sake of a good end. But to kill a man is evil in itself, for we must have charity towards all men, and 'we wish our friends to live and to exist', as is said at *Ethics* IX. Therefore it is in no way lawful to kill a man who has sinned.[50]

sed contra: It is said at Exodus 22:18, 'Thou shalt not suffer a witch to live', and at Psalm 101:8: 'I will early destroy all the wicked of the land.'

responsio: As stated above,[51] it is lawful to kill brute beasts insofar as they are naturally ordained to man's use as imperfect is ordained to perfect. Now every part is directed to the whole as imperfect to perfect; and so every part naturally exists for the sake of the whole. For this reason we see that if the health of the whole body requires the removal of some member, perhaps because it is diseased or causing the corruption of other members, it will be both praiseworthy and wholesome for it to be cut away. Now

---

[49] The translation looks odd: no one has supposed, even mistakenly, that killing an ox might be a form of homicide; but *unde non continetur sub peccato homicidii* is what the text says. What it means is that killing an ox is not to be compared with killing a man, but is a kind of theft or robbery.
[50] *Contra mendacium* 7; *Ethics* 2:6 (1107a14); *Ethics* 9:4 (1166a4).
[51] Art. 1.

every individual person stands in relation to the whole community as part to whole. And so if some man is dangerous to the community, causing its corruption because of some sin, it is praiseworthy and wholesome that he be slain in order to preserve the common good; for 'a little leaven corrupteth the whole lump' (1 Corinthians 5:6).

ad 1: The Lord commanded them to abstain from uprooting the tares in order to spare the wheat, that is, the good. This commandment applies when the wicked cannot be slain without at the same time also slaying the good, either because the wicked lie hidden among the good, or because the wicked have so many followers that they cannot be killed without endangering the good, as Augustine says.[52] Hence the Lord teaches that it is better that the wicked be suffered to live and vengeance reserved to the Final Judgment than that the good be slain together with the wicked. When, however, the good incur no peril, but rather are protected and saved by the slaying of the wicked, then the latter may lawfully be slain.

ad 2: According to the order of His wisdom, God sometimes slays sinners at once, in order to deliver the good, and sometimes grants them time for repentance, according as He knows what is expedient for His elect. And this also human justice imitates as far as it can; for it slays those who are dangerous to others, while it reserves for repentance those who sin without grievously harming others.

ad 3: By sinning, man withdraws himself from the order of reason, and in so doing falls away from the dignity of his humanity, by which he is naturally free and exists for himself, and descends instead towards the slavish condition of the beasts: becoming liable, that is, to be disposed of in whatever way is useful to others, according to Psalm 49:20: 'Man, when he was in honour, did not understand; he hath been compared to senseless beasts, and made like to them'; and it is said at Proverbs 11:29: 'The fool shall serve the wise.' And so although it is evil in itself to slay a man while he remains in his dignity, it can nonetheless be good to slay a man who is a sinner, just as it can be to slay a beast. For a wicked man is worse than a beast, and does more harm, as the Philosopher says at *Politics* I and *Ethics* VII.[53]

---

[52] *Contra Parmenianum donatistam* 3:2.   [53] *Politics* 1:1 (1253a32); *Ethics* 7:6 (1150a7).

articulus 3: Whether it is lawful for a private person to kill a man who has sinned

It seems that it is lawful for a private person to kill a man who has sinned.

obiectio 1: For nothing unlawful is commanded in the Divine law. But at Exodus 32:27 Moses commanded: 'Let every man kill his brother, and friend, and neighbour' because of the sin of the molten calf. Therefore it is lawful for even private persons to kill a sinner.

obiectio 2: Moreover, as stated above,[54] man, on account of sin, 'hath been compared' to the beasts. But it is lawful for any private person to kill a wild beast, especially a harmful one. Therefore he may for the same reason kill a man who has sinned.

obiectio 3: Moreover, a man, even if he is a private person, is worthy of praise if he does something beneficial to the common good. But the slaying of malefactors is beneficial to the common good, as stated above.[55] Therefore it is praiseworthy for even private persons kill malefactors.

sed contra: Augustine says: 'A man who, without exercising any public office, kills a malefactor, shall be judged guilty of homicide, and all the more so since he has not feared to usurp a power which God has not granted him.'

responsio: As stated above, it is lawful to kill a malefactor insofar as doing so is directed to the health of the whole community; but so to do pertains only to him to whom the task of preserving the community's health has been entrusted, just as it pertains to the physician to cut off a decayed member when he has been entrusted with the care of the health of the whole body. Now the care of the common good is entrusted to princes having public authority; and so they alone, and not private individuals, can lawfully kill malefactors.

ad 1: As Dionysius shows at *De caelesti hierarchia* XIII, responsibility for an act belongs to the person by whose authority the act is done.[56] And so, as Augustine says at *De civitate Dei* I, 'He does not slay who is the servant of one who commands him, just as the sword is only the instrument of him who wields it.'[57] Hence those who slew their neighbours and friends

[54] Art. 2 ad 3.
[55] Art. 2
[56] *De caelesti hierarchia* 13 (*PG* 3:305).
[57] *De civitate Dei* 1:21.

at the Lord's command seem not to have done this themselves, but by His authority, just as the soldier slays the enemy by the authority of the prince and the executioner the robber by that of the judge.

ad 2: A beast is distinct by nature from man. Hence no one needs to be authorised to kill a wild beast, whereas such authorisation is necessary in the case of domestic animals: although not for their sake, but only by reason of the owner's loss. But a man who is a sinner is not distinct by nature from righteous men; and so public authorisation is needed if he is to be condemned to death for the common good.

ad 3: It is lawful for any private person to do something for the common benefit provided that no harm is thereby done to anyone; but if anyone is harmed, this cannot be done except by the judgment of him to whom it pertains to decide what is to be taken away from the parts in order to secure the welfare of the whole.

articulus 4: *Whether it is lawful for clerics to kill malefactors*

It seems that it is lawful for clerics to kill malefactors.

obiectio 1: For clerics especially must fulfil what the Apostle says at 1 Corinthians 4:16: 'Be ye imitators of me, as I also am of Christ', by which we are called upon to imitate God and His saints. But God Himself, Whom we worship, slays malefactors, according to Psalm 136:10: 'Who smote Egypt with their firstborn'. Again, Moses caused the Levites to slay twenty-three thousand men because of the worship of the calf, as recorded at Exodus 32:28; the priest Phineas slew the Israelite who went in to a woman of Midian, as recorded at Numbers 25:6ff; Samuel slew Agag, king of Amalek;[58] Elijah slew the priests of Baal;[59] Mattathias slew the man who went up to sacrifice;[60] and, in the New Testament, Peter slew Ananias and Sapphira.[61] Therefore it seems that even clerics may kill malefactors.

obiectio 2: Moreover, the spiritual power is greater than the temporal and is more fully united with God. But the temporal power lawfully slays malefactors as God's minister, as is said at Romans 13:4. So much more,

---

[58] 1 Samuel 15:33.
[59] 1 Kings 18:40.
[60] 1 Maccabees 2:24.
[61] Acts 5:3.

therefore, may clerics, who are God's ministers and have spiritual power, slay malefactors.

obiectio 3: Moreover, whoever lawfully receives an office can lawfully perform the duties pertaining to that office. But it pertains to the office of earthly princes to slay malefactors, as stated above. Therefore those clerics who are earthly princes[62] may lawfully slay malefactors.

sed contra: It is said at 1 Timothy 3:2f: 'A bishop then must be blameless, not given to wine, no striker.'

responsio: It is not lawful for clerics to kill, for two reasons. First, because they are elected to the ministry of the altar, upon which is represented the Passion of the slain Christ 'Who when He was struck did not strike' (1 Peter 2:23). And so it is not fitting for clerics to strike or kill, for ministers should imitate their lord, according to Ecclesiasticus 10:2: 'As the judge of the people is himself, so also are his ministers.'

The other reason is that clerics are entrusted with the ministry of the New Law, in which no punishment of death or bodily mutilation is appointed; and so they should abstain from such things so that they may be 'fitting ministers of the New Testament' (2 Corinthians 3:6).

ad 1: God does what is right universally and in all things, but He does so in each one according to the manner fitting to it. And so everyone should imitate God in that which is especially fitting to him. Hence, though God indeed slays malefactors in body, it is not fitting that everyone should imitate Him in this. Again, Peter did not slay Ananias and Sapphira by his own authority or with his own hand. Rather, he pronounced the Divine sentence of death which had been passed upon them. Again, the priests or Levites of the Old Testament were the ministers of the Old Law, according to which bodily penalties were inflicted; and so it was fitting for them to slay with their own hands.

ad 2: The ministry of clerics is ordained to better things than bodily slayings: that is, to those things which pertain to spiritual health; and so it is not fitting for them to involve themselves with small matters.

ad 3: Ecclesiastical prelates accept the office of earthly princes not so that they may inflict the judgment of blood themselves, but so that this may be done by others acting on their authority.

---

[62] I.e. who are bishops and archbishops and therefore have temporal responsibilities in addition to their spiritual ones.

articulus 5: *Whether it is lawful for someone to slay himself*

It seems that it is lawful for someone to slay himself.

obiectio 1: For homicide is a sin inasmuch as it is contrary to justice. But no one can do injustice to himself, as is proved at *Ethics* v.[63] Therefore no man sins by slaying himself.

obiectio 2: Moreover, it is lawful for one who has public authority to slay malefactors. But he who has public authority is sometimes a malefactor himself. Therefore it is lawful for him to slay himself.

obiectio 3: Moreover, it is lawful for a man to choose to undergo a lesser peril in order to avoid a greater peril. For example, it is lawful for someone to amputate a diseased limb even from himself in order to save his whole body. But sometimes, by slaying himself, someone avoids a greater evil, such as a life of misery or the disgrace of some sin. Therefore it is lawful for someone to slay himself.

obiectio 4: Moreover, Samson slew himself, as is recorded at Judges 16:30, yet he is numbered among the saints, as Hebrews 11:32 shows. Therefore it is lawful for someone to slay himself.

obiectio 5: Moreover, it is said at 2 Maccabees 14:42 that a certain Raziah slew himself, 'choosing rather to die manfully than to come into the hands of the wicked, to be abused otherwise than beseemed his noble birth'. But nothing done manfully and bravely is unlawful. Therefore to slay oneself is not unlawful.

sed contra: Augustine says at *De civitate Dei* I: 'What remains, then, is this: that, when it is said, "Thou shalt not kill", we must understand this as applying to man, and hence to mean "neither another nor thyself"; for he who kills himself kills what is no other than a man.'[64]

responsio: It is altogether unlawful to slay oneself, for three reasons. First, because everything naturally loves itself, and to this belongs the fact that everything naturally preserves itself in being and resists corruption as far as it can. And so for anyone to slay himself is contrary to the inclination of nature, and contrary also to charity, whereby every man should love himself. To slay oneself is therefore always a mortal sin, as being contrary to the natural law and to charity. Second, because every part, as such,

---

[63] *Ethics* 5:11 (1138a4).   [64] *De civitate Dei* 1:20.

belongs to the whole. Now every man is part of a community, and so, as such, belongs to that community. Hence one who slays himself does injury to the community, as the Philosopher shows at *Ethics* v. Third, because life is as it were a divine gift bestowed upon man, and is subject to the power of Him Who kills and makes alive. Hence he who deprives himself of life sins against God, just as he who slays another's slave sins against the master of that slave, and just as he sins who usurps judgment to himself in a matter not entrusted to him. For it pertains to God alone to pronounce sentence of death and life, according to Deuteronomy 32:39: 'I kill and I make alive.'

ad 1: Homicide is a sin not only because it is contrary to justice, but also because it is contrary to the charity which a man ought to have towards himself. It is in this respect that to slay oneself is a sin in relation to oneself. In relation to the community and to God, it is a sin by reason of its being also opposed to justice.

ad 2: One who has public authority may lawfully slay a malefactor because he can pass judgment on him. But no one is judge of himself. Hence it is not lawful for one who exercises public authority to slay himself for any sin whatsoever. He may, however, hand himself over to the judgment of others.

ad 3: Man is made master of himself through free will; and so a man can lawfully dispose of himself with regard to those things which pertain to this life, which is ruled by man's free will. But the transition from this life to another happier one is subject not to man's free will but to the Divine power. And so it is not lawful for a man to slay himself so that he may pass to a happier life.

Similarly, it is not lawful to do so in order to avoid any misery of this present life. For the ultimate and most terrible evil of this life, as the Philosopher says at *Ethics* III, is death.[65] And so to bring death upon oneself in order to avoid the other afflictions of this life is to embrace a greater evil in order to avoid a lesser.

Similarly again, it is not lawful to slay oneself because one has committed a sin. For one thing, in doing this one does oneself the greatest harm, because one deprives oneself of the time necessary for repentance; for another, it is not lawful to slay a malefactor except by the judgment of a public authority.

[65] *Ethics* 3:6 (1115a26).

Similarly again, it is not lawful for a woman to kill herself in order to avoid being dishonoured by another; for she ought not to commit against herself the very great sin of killing herself in order to avoid another's sin. For a woman who is violated by force commits no crime if her own consent is not present, since, as the blessed Lucy says, there is no iniquity of body without consent of mind.[66] Now it is clear that fornication and adultery are less grievous sins than homicide, especially against oneself; for it is the most grievous sin of all to harm oneself, to whom one owes the greatest love. Moreover it is the most perilous, because no time remains in which it may be expiated by penance.

Similarly again, it is not lawful for anyone to slay himself for fear of consenting to sin; for we must not do evil 'that good may come' (Romans 3:8) or that evil may be avoided: especially a small and uncertain evil; for it is not certain that anyone will consent to sin in the future, since God is able to deliver a man from sin no matter how great the temptation.[67]

ad 4: As Augustine says at *De civitate Dei* I: 'That Samson crushed himself and his enemies under the ruins of the house is not to be excused other than by the fact that the Holy Spirit, Who had worked many miracles through him, secretly commanded him to do this.'[68] He assigns the same reason to the case of certain holy women whose memory is celebrated in the Church, who slew themselves in time of persecution.[69]

ad 5: If someone does not shrink from being slain by another for the sake of the good of virtue and in order to avoid sin, this pertains to fortitude. But for someone to inflict death upon himself in order to avoid painful evils, though it has the appearance of fortitude (which is why some, including Raziah, have slain themselves in the belief that they were acting out of fortitude), is not true fortitude. Rather, it is a kind of weakness of a spirit unable to bear painful evils, as the Philosopher shows at *Ethics* III[70] and Augustine at *De civitate Dei* I.[71]

---

[66] St Lucy's retort to Paschasius, Roman Governor of Sicily, when he threatened to have her imprisoned in a brothel. The association of the sentiment with St Lucy is a hagiographical commonplace. See the Biographical Glossary *s.v.* 'Lucy'; see also St Augustine, *De civitate Dei* 1:18.
[67] In the whole of this reply, St Thomas clearly has in mind Augustine, *De civitate Dei* 1:16ff.
[68] *De civitate Dei* 1:21.
[69] *De civitate Dei* 1:26.
[70] *Ethics* 3:7 (1116a12).
[71] *De civitate Dei* 1:22f.

articulus 6: *Whether it is lawful to kill the innocent*

It seems that it is in some cases lawful to kill the innocent.

obiectio 1: For the fear of God is never shown through a sinful act; rather, 'The fear of the Lord driveth out sin', as is said at Ecclesiasticus 1:27. But Abraham was commended for his fear of the Lord because he was willing to slay his innocent son. Therefore one can without sin slay the innocent.

obiectio 2: Moreover, among those sins which are committed against one's neighbour, the greater sins seem to be those which do the greater harm to the one sinned against. Now to be slain does greater harm to a sinner than to one who is innocent, since by death the latter passes immediately from the misery of this life to the glory of heaven. Since, therefore, it is in certain cases lawful to slay a sinner, so much more is it lawful to slay one who is innocent or righteous.

obiectio 3: Moreover, that which is done according to the order of justice is not a sin. But sometimes one is compelled to slay an innocent man according to the order of justice: for example, when a judge, who has to judge according to the evidence, condemns to death someone whom he knows to be innocent but who has been traduced by false witnesses; and, similarly, the executioner who in obedience to the judge slays the man who has been unjustly sentenced.

sed contra: It is said at Exodus 23:7: 'The innocent and righteous thou shalt not slay.'

responsio: A man can be considered in two ways. In one way, in himself; in another way, in relation to something else. If a man be considered in himself, it is unlawful to kill anyone, since in everyone, even the sinner, we ought to love the nature which God has made, and which is destroyed by slaying him. On the other hand, as stated above,[72] the slaying of a sinner becomes lawful in relation to the common good, which is corrupted by sin, whereas the common good is conserved and promoted by the life of righteous men, for they are the foremost part of the community. Therefore it is in no way lawful to slay the innocent.

ad 1: God has lordship over death and life, for it is by His ordinance that both the sinful and the righteous die. And so he who slays the innocent at God's command does not sin, any more than God does, at Whose behest

[72] Art. 2.

he acts: indeed, his fear of God is shown by his willing obedience to His commands.

ad 2: In weighing the gravity of a sin, consideration must be given to what is essential rather than accidental. Hence one who slays a righteous man sins more grievously than one who slays a sinner: first, because he injures one whom he ought to love more, and so acts more against charity; second, because he inflicts an injury on someone who is less deserving of one, and so acts more against justice; third, because he deprives the community of a greater good; fourth, because he despises God more, according to Luke 10:16, 'He that despiseth you despiseth Me.' But it is accidental to the slaying that the righteous man who is slain is received by God into glory.

ad 3: If the judge knows that someone has been convicted by false witnesses and is innocent, he must examine the witnesses more carefully, so that he may find occasion for letting the blameless man go free, as Daniel did (Daniel 13:51). If he cannot do this, he should remit him for judgment to a higher court. If he cannot do this either, he does not sin if he pronounces sentence according to the evidence; for it is not he who kills the innocent man, but they who asserted his guilt. Again, if the sentence contains an intolerable error, the executioner who is to carry out the sentence of the judge who has condemned an innocent man should not obey him; otherwise the torturers who slew the martyrs would be excused. If, however, the sentence does not contain a manifest injustice, he does not sin if he carries out the judge's command, for has no right to scrutinise the judgment of his superior; nor is it he who slays the innocent man, but the judge at whose behest he acts.

articulus 7: *Whether it is lawful to kill someone in self-defence*

It seems that it is not lawful to kill someone in self-defence.

obiectio 1: For Augustine says to Publicola: 'I do not like the advice that one may kill someone in order to avoid being killed by him: unless, however, one is a soldier carrying out a public function, in which case one acts not for oneself but for others, with power to do whatever is consistent with one's duty.'[73] But he who kills someone in self-defence kills him to avoid being killed by him. Therefore this would seem to be unlawful.

[73] *Epistolae* 47; C. 23:5:8: *De occidendis* (*CIC* 1:932).

obiectio 2: Moreover, at *De libero arbitrio* I he says: 'How are they free from sin in the sight of Divine providence, who are polluted by human slaughter for the sake of things which ought to be despised?'[74] And, as is shown by what occurs earlier in the same passage, among the 'things which ought to be despised' are 'those things which men may lose against their will', one of which is the life of the body. Therefore it is not lawful for anyone to take another's life in order to preserve the life of his own body.

obiectio 3: Further, Pope Nicholas says, and this is noted in the *Decretum*:

> Concerning the clerics about whom you have consulted us, namely, those who have killed a pagan in self-defence, as to whether they may after penance return to their former state or rise to a higher one: know that it is in no case lawful for them to kill any man in any circumstances whatsoever, nor can anyone give them licence to do so.[75]

But clerics and laymen alike are bound to observe moral precepts. Therefore nor is it lawful for laymen to kill anyone in self-defence.

obiectio 4: Moreover, homicide is a more grievous sin than simple fornication or adultery. But no one may lawfully commit simple fornication or adultery or any other mortal sin whatsoever to save his own life; for the life of the spirit is to be preferred to that of the body. Therefore no one may lawfully take another's life in self-defence in order to preserve his own life.

obiectio 5: Moreover, if the tree is evil, so will the fruit be also, as is said at Matthew 7:17. But self-defence itself seems to be unlawful, according to Romans 12:19: 'Dearly beloved, avenge not yourselves.' Therefore the slaying of a man which proceeds from it is unlawful also.

sed contra: It is said at Exodus 22:2: 'If a thief be found breaking into an house and be smitten that he die, he that struck him shall not be guilty of blood.' But it is much more lawful to defend one's life than one's house. No one, therefore, is guilty if he slays a man in defence of his own life.

responsio: Nothing prevents a single act from having two effects, only one of which is intended while the other is beside the intention. Now moral acts take their species from what is intended, not from what is beside the

---

[74] *De libero arbitrio* 1:5.
[75] *Epistolae* 138 (*PL* 119:1131); Dist. 50, C. 6: *De his clericis* (*CIC* 1:179).

intention, since this is accidental, as explained above.[76] Accordingly, an act of self-defence may have two effects, one of which is the saving of one's own life while the other is the slaying of an attacker. If one's intention is to save one's own life, the act is not unlawful, because it is natural for everything to keep itself in being as far as possible. Yet an act may be rendered unlawful even though proceeding from a good intention if it is out of proportion to the end. Hence if a man uses more violence in self-defence than is necessary, this will be unlawful, whereas if he repels force with force in moderation, his defence will be lawful because, according to the laws, 'it is lawful to repel force by force, provided that one does not exceed the limits of blameless defence'.[77] Nor is it necessary to salvation that a man refrain from an act of moderate self-defence in order to avoid killing another man, since one is bound to take more care of one's own life than of another's. But since it is unlawful for anyone to take a man's life except a public authority acting for the common good, as stated above,[78] it is not lawful for one man to intend to kill another in self-defence, except in the case of those who have public authority, who, though intending to kill a man in self-defence, refer this to the public good: for instance, a soldier fighting against the enemy and a minister of the judge fighting with robbers; although even these sin if they are motivated by private animosity.

ad 1: The authority of Augustine is to be understood here as referring to a case where one man intends to kill another in order to save himself from death. The passage from *De libero arbitrio* [quoted in the second *obiectio*] is to be understood in the same sense. It is precisely to indicate this kind of intention that he says, 'for the sake of things [which ought to be despised]'. By this the reply to the second *obiectio* is also shown.

ad 3: Irregularity[79] is a consequence of the act, even though sinless, of taking a man's life, as appears in the case of a judge who justly condemns a man to death. For this reason a cleric, if he brings about the death of someone in self-defence, is irregular, even if he intended not to kill him, but only to defend himself.

---

[76] IIaIIae 43:3; IaIIae 72:1.

[77] X. 5:12:18: *Significasti* (*CIC* 2:800).

[78] Art. 3.

[79] 'Irregularity' in the sense used here is a technical term denoting a canonical impediment directly impeding the reception of tonsure and Holy Orders or preventing the exercise of orders already received. It is called a 'canonical' impediment because introduced in ecclesiastical law. See *NCE* 7, *s.v.* 'Holy Orders, Irregularities Affecting'.

ad 4: The act of fornication or adultery is not necessarily directed to the preservation of one's own life, as is the act which sometimes results in the taking of someone's life.

ad 5: The defence forbidden in this passage is that which is accompanied by vengeful spite. Hence a gloss says: 'Avenge not yourselves – that is, do not strike your enemies back.'[80]

articulus 8: *Whether one incurs the guilt of homicide through slaying a man by chance*

It seems that one does incur the guilt of homicide through slaying a man by chance.

obiectio 1: For we read that Lamech slew a man believing himself to be slaying a wild beast, and that he was reputed guilty of homicide.[81] One who slays a man by chance therefore incurs the guilt of homicide.

obiectio 2: Moreover, it is said at Exodus 21:22f that: 'If one strike a woman with child, and she miscarry indeed, if her death ensue thereupon, he shall render life for life.' But this can be done without any intention of killing her. Therefore one is guilty of homicide through killing someone by chance.

obiectio 3: Moreover, in the *Decretum* there are several canons which prescribe punishments for unintentional homicide.[82] But punishment is not due to anything except guilt. Therefore he who slays a man by chance incurs the guilt of homicide.

sed contra: Augustine says to Publicola: 'God forbid that guilt should be imputed to us if, when we do something for a good and lawful purpose, we cause harm to anyone without intending to.'[83] But it sometimes happens that someone is killed by chance as a consequence of something done for a good purpose. Therefore guilt is not to be imputed to the person who did it.

responsio: According to the Philosopher at *Physics* II, 'chance is a cause which acts beyond anyone's intention'.[84] Strictly speaking, therefore,

---

[80] Peter Lombard, *Collectanea*, on Romans 12:19 (*PL* 191:1502).
[81] This is a traditional Jewish interpretation of Genesis 4:23. See *Encyclopaedia Iudaica* (Jerusalem, 1971), vol. X, *s.v.* 'Lamech'.
[82] Dist. 50, *passim* (*CIC* 1:178ff).
[83] *Epistolae* 47.
[84] *Physics* 6:5 (197b18).

things which happen by chance are neither intended nor voluntary. And since every sin is voluntary, according to Augustine,[85] it follows that chance occurrences, as such, are not sins. It does happen, however, that something which is not voluntary and intended actually and of itself is voluntary and intended accidentally, inasmuch as he who removes an obstacle to something happening is an accidental cause of it. Hence he who does not remove something from which homicide results will, if he ought to have removed it, be in that sense guilty of voluntary homicide. This happens in two ways. In one way, when someone brings about another's death by occupying himself with unlawful things which he ought to avoid; in another way, when he does not take proper care. And so, according to the laws, if anyone does what he may lawfully do and takes due care, yet someone loses his life as a result, he does not incur the guilt of homicide; whereas if he is occupied with some unlawful pursuit, or even if he is occupied with something lawful but without due care, he does not escape the guilt of homicide if a man's death follows as a result of what he does.

ad 1: Lamech did not take sufficient care to avoid taking a man's life, and so he did not escape the guilt of homicide.

ad 2: One who strikes a woman with child does an unlawful act. And so if the death either of the woman or of her unborn child results, he will not avoid the crime of homicide, especially since death may so easily result from such a blow.

ad 3: According to the canons, a penalty is imposed upon those who cause death unintentionally through doing something unlawful or not taking due care.

[85] *De vera religione* 14.

7

Religion and politics

(a) *Summa theologiae* IIaIIae 10: On relations with unbelievers

articulus 8: *Whether unbelievers ought to be coerced into the faith* [1]

It seems that unbelievers ought by no means to be coerced into the faith.

obiectio 1: For it is said at Matthew 13:28f that the servants of the householder in whose field tares had been sown asked him: 'Wilt thou then that we go and gather them up?' And he replied: 'Nay, lest while ye gather up the tares, ye root up also the wheat with them.' Commenting on this, Chrysostom says: 'The Lord speaks thus in order to prevent the slaying of men. For it is not right to slay heretics, because if you kill them you will necessarily destroy many holy persons also.'[2] For the same reason, therefore, it seems that unbelievers ought not to be coerced into the faith.

obiectio 2: Moreover, it is said in the *Decretum*: 'Concerning the Jews, the holy synod prescribes that henceforth none are to be brought to believe by force.'[3] Nor, therefore, for the same reason, ought other unbelievers to be coerced into the faith.

---

[1] This *quaestio* has twelve articles, of which only 8, 10 and 11 are here translated. The others are as follows:

1. Whether unbelief is a sin
2. Where it is located
3. Whether it is the greatest of sins
4. Whether every act of the unbeliever is a sin
5. Concerning the species of unbelief
6. Their comparison with one another
7. Whether the faith is to be discussed with unbelievers
9. Whether communication is to be had with them
12. Whether the children of unbelievers are to be baptised against their parents' wishes

[2] *In Mattheum* 46 (*PG* 58:477).
[3] Dist. 45, c. 5: *De Judaeis* (*CIC* 1:161).

obiectio 3: Moreover, Augustine says that although a man can do many things unwillingly, 'he cannot believe unless he is willing'.[4] But the will cannot be compelled. Therefore it seems that unbelievers ought not to be coerced into the faith.

obiectio 4: Moreover, it is said at Ezekiel 18:32, as though God were speaking: 'I desire not the death of the sinner.' But we ought to conform our will to the Divine will, as stated above.[5] Therefore again we should not desire unbelievers to be slain.

sed contra: It is said at Luke 14:23: 'Go out into the highways and hedgerows and compel them to come in.' But men 'come in' to the house of God – that is, into the Church – by faith. Certain persons therefore ought to be compelled into the faith.

responsio: There are some unbelievers who have never received the faith, such as the heathens and the Jews. These are in no way to be compelled into the faith, so that they may believe; for belief is an act of will. If the means to do so are present, however, they should be coerced by the faithful lest they hinder the faith by blasphemies or evil persuasions, or, indeed, by open persecutions.[6] And it is for this reason that Christ's faithful frequently wage war against unbelievers: not, certainly, to coerce them to believe, for even if they were to conquer them and take them captive they should still leave them the liberty to believe if they wish; but to prevent them from hindering the faith of Christ. But there are other unbelievers who have at some time accepted the faith and professed it, such as heretics and apostates of all kinds. These should be compelled even by bodily means to keep their promises and hold fast to what they once received.

ad 1: Some have understood the words of the gospel to forbid the slaying of heretics but not their excommunication. This is shown by the quoted authority of Chrysostom. Also, Augustine says of himself:

> My opinion at first was that no one ought to be coerced into the unity of Christ: that we should act only by words, fight only by arguments, and conquer by reason alone. But this opinion of mine was overcome not by the words of those who opposed it, but by the examples to

---

[4] *In Ioannis evangelium* 26, on 6:44.
[5] IaIIae 19:9 and 10.
[6] Cf. Dist. 45, c. 5: *De Judaeis* (*CIC* 1:162).

which they could point by way of demonstration. For fear of the law has been so profitable that many now say, Thanks be to the Lord, Who has burst our bonds asunder.[7]

Therefore when the Lord says, 'Suffer both to grow until the harvest', this is to be understood according to the words which are then added: 'lest while ye gather up the tares, ye root up also the wheat with them'. For as Augustine says:

> Here it is shown clearly enough that where there is no fear of this [i.e. of rooting up the wheat with the tares] – that is to say, where a crime is so notorious and so execrable to all men that it has no defenders, or at any rate none who might give rise to schism – the severity of discipline should not sleep.[8]

ad 2: Those Jews who have not in any way received the faith, ought not to be coerced into the faith. If, however, they have already received the faith, 'they ought to be compelled to keep it', as is stated in the same canon.

ad 3: Just as 'taking a vow is a matter of will and keeping it a matter of obligation',[9] so acceptance of the faith is a matter of will, but keeping it once received is a matter of obligation. And so heretics should be compelled to keep the faith. For Augustine says: 'What do these men mean by their accustomed cry, "We are free to believe or not believe: Whom did Christ compel?"? Let them know that Christ first compelled Paul, and then taught him.'[10]

ad 4: As Augustine says in the same letter:

> None of us wishes any heretic to perish. But the house of David did not deserve to have peace unless his son Absalom were killed in the war which he had raised against his father. Thus if the Catholic Church gathers together some at the cost of the perdition of others, she heals the sorrow of her maternal heart by the delivery of so many peoples.[11]

---

[7] *Epistolae* 93:5.
[8] *Contra Parmenianum donatistam* 3:2.
[9] Peter Lombard, *Commentarium in psalmos* 75:11 (*PL* 191:709).
[10] *Epistolae* 185:6.
[11] *Epistolae* 185:8.

articulus 10: *Whether unbelievers may have authority or dominion over the faithful*

It seems that unbelievers may have authority or dominion over the faithful.

obiectio 1: For the Apostle says at 1 Timothy 6:1: 'Whosoever are servants under the yoke, let them count their masters worthy of all honour'; and it is clear that he is here speaking of unbelieving masters, for he then adds (vs. 2): 'But they that have believing masters, let them not despise them.' Again, it is said at 1 Peter 2:18: 'Servants, be subject to your masters with all fear, not only to the good and gentle, but also to the ill disposed.' But this would not be commanded by Apostolic teaching unless unbelievers might have authority over the faithful. Therefore it seems that unbelievers may have authority over the faithful.

obiectio 2: Moreover, whoever is a member of a prince's household is subject to him. But certain of the faithful have been members of unbelieving princes' households; for it is said at Philippians 4:22: 'All the saints salute you, especially they that are of the household of Caesar', that is, of Nero, who was an unbeliever. Therefore unbelievers can have authority over the faithful.

obiectio 3: Moreover, as the Philosopher says at *Politics* 1, a slave is his master's instrument in those things which pertain to human life, just as a craftsman's labourer is his instrument in those things which pertain to the performance of his craft. But in such things a believer can be subject to an unbeliever: he may, for instance, work on an unbeliever's farm. Therefore unbelievers can have authority over the faithful extending even to mastery.

sed contra: It pertains to those who are in authority to pronounce judgment on those over whom they are placed. But unbelievers cannot pronounce judgment on the faithful, for the Apostle says at 1 Corinthians 6:1: 'Dare any of you, having a matter against another, go to law before the unjust', that is, before unbelievers, 'and not before the saints?' Therefore it seems that unbelievers may not have authority over the faithful.

responsio: We can speak of this matter in two ways. In one way, we can speak of the dominion or authority of unbelievers over the faithful as though it were about to be established for the first time. This should not by any means be permitted, because it would give scandal and imperil the faith. For, unless they are persons of great virtue, those who are placed under the jurisdiction of others are easily influenced by those to whom they are subject, to comply with their commands. Similarly, unbelievers despise the faith if they know that the faithful are falling short of it, which is why the Apostle forbade the faithful to go to law before an unbelieving judge. And so the Church in no way permits unbelievers to acquire dominion over the faithful, or to have any kind of preferment over them in any office.

In another way, we can speak of dominion or authority as being already in existence. Here we must note that dominion and authority are institutions of human right, whereas the distinction between the faithful and unbelievers arises from Divine right. Now Divine right, which comes from grace, does not abolish human right, which comes from natural reason. And so the distinction between the faithful and unbelievers, considered in itself, does not abolish the dominion and authority of unbelievers over the faithful. Nonetheless this right of dominion or authority can be justly abolished by the sentence or ordinance of the Church, as having the authority of God: because unbelievers, by reason of their unbelief, deserve to lose their power over the faithful, who are made children of God.[12] But the Church sometimes does this, and sometimes she does not. For among those unbelievers who are subject to the Church and her members even in temporal matters, the Church has established it as a law that if the slave of a Jew becomes a Christian, he should immediately be released from servitude without payment of a price if he is a *vernaculus* – that is, if he was born in servitude – and similarly if, while yet an unbeliever, he was bought for his service: if, however, he was bought to be sold, his master is bound to offer him for sale within three months.[13] Nor does the Church do injustice in this; for since the Jews themselves are slaves of the Church, she can dispose of their property, just as secular princes also have enacted many laws in relation to their own subjects in favour of liberty.[14] But the Church has not applied the above law to those unbelievers who are not subject to her or to her members in temporal matters, even though, as of right, she could do so, because she wishes to avoid scandal: as the Lord did at Matthew 17:25f, where He showed that He could be excused from paying tribute because 'the children are free', yet commanded that the tribute be paid nonetheless, to avoid giving scandal. So too Paul, having said that servants should honour their masters, goes on (1 Timothy 6:1): 'lest the name of God and His doctrine be blasphemed'.

---

[12] Cf. Romans 8:16.

[13] *Gregorii I Registrum* (ed. Ewald Hartmann) 6:29, reprinted at Simonsohn, *The Apostolic See and the Jews*, vol. 1, pp. 12f.

[14] See p. 233 n. 82, above.

By this the reply to the first *obiectio* is shown.

ad 2: The authority of Caesar existed before the distinction between believers and unbelievers did. Hence it was not dissolved by the conversion
of some to the faith. Moreover, it was advantageous that there should be
some believers in the emperor's household, so that they might protect the
rest of the faithful. Thus the Blessed Sebastian, remaining concealed by
his soldier's cloak, comforted the souls of those Christians whom he saw
weakening under torture in the house of Diocletian.[15]

ad 3: Slaves are subject to their masters for the whole of their lives, and are
subject to their overseers in every respect; but the craftsman's labourer
is subject to him only in respect of certain specific tasks. Hence it would
be more perilous for unbelievers to have dominion or authority over the
faithful than for them to employ them in some craft. And so the Church
permits Christians to cultivate the land of Jews, because this does not
involve the necessity of close association with them. Thus Solomon re-
quested the King of Tyre to send master craftsmen to hew the trees, as
recorded at 1 Kings 5:6. If, however, there is any reason to fear that the
faithful will be undermined by such association or communication, it
should be forbidden absolutely.

articulus 11: *Whether the rites of unbelievers ought to be tolerated*

It seems that the rites of unbelievers ought not to be tolerated.

obiectio 1: For it is clear that unbelievers sin in observing their rites. But
one who does not prevent a sin when prevention of it is possible seems
to consent to it, as noted in a gloss on Romans 1:32, 'Not only they that
do them, but they also that consent to them that do them.'[16] Therefore
those who tolerate their rites sin.

obiectio 2: Moreover, the rites of the Jews are compared to idolatry; for
a gloss on Galatians 5:1, 'Be not held again under the yoke of bondage',
says: 'The bondage of that law was not lighter than that of idolatry.'[17] But
it would not be tolerated if anyone were to perform the rites of idolatry:
indeed, Christian princes first closed the temples of the idols, and then

[15] *Acta sanctorum*, Jan., II: 621ff; and see Bibliographical Glossary, *s.v.* 'Sebastian'.
[16] Ambrose, *Commentaria in epistolam ad Romanos* 1:32 (*PL* 17:63).
[17] Peter Lombard, *In epistolam ad Galatas* 5:1 (*PL* 192:152); cf. Augustine, *Contra Faustum* 9:18.

destroyed them, as Augustine relates at *De civitate Dei* XVIII.[18] Therefore, again, the rites of the Jews must not be tolerated.

obiectio 3: Moreover, unbelief is the most grievous of sins, as stated above.[19] But other sins such as adultery, theft and so forth, are not tolerated, but are punished by the law. Therefore also the rites of unbelievers ought not to be tolerated.

sed contra: Gregory, speaking of the Jews, says: 'They should have licence to observe and celebrate all their festivals, just as they and their forefathers have observed them for long ages gone by.'[20]

responsio: Human government is derived from the Divine government, and ought to imitate it. But although God is omnipotent and the Supreme Good, He nonetheless permits certain evils, which He might prevent, to occur in the universe, lest, if they were removed, greater goods might be taken away or greater evils ensue. So, then, in human government also, those who rule rightly tolerate certain evils, lest certain goods be impeded or certain worse evils incurred. For example, Augustine says at *De ordine* II: 'If you banish whores from human affairs, everything will be disrupted by lust.'[21] Hence, though unbelievers sin in performing their rites, they can be tolerated either because of some good which results from their doing so, or in order to avoid some evil.

Thus from the fact that the Jews observe their rites in which, of old, the truth of the faith which we hold was prefigured, there follows this good: that even our enemies bear witness to our faith, and that what we believe is represented to us as in a figure.[22] And so they are tolerated in the performance of their rites. But the rites of other unbelievers, which contain neither truth nor advantage, are not to be tolerated in any way, except perhaps to avoid some evil: that is, to avoid the scandal or dissension that might otherwise arise, or some hindrance to the salvation of those who, if they were tolerated, might gradually be converted to the faith. For this reason the Church has sometimes tolerated the rites even of heretics and pagans, when there was a great multitude of unbelievers.

By this the replies to the *obiectiones* are shown.

---

[18] *De civitate Dei* 18:54.
[19] Art. 3.
[20] Dist. 45, c. 3: *Qui sincera* (*CIC* 1:160).
[21] *De ordine* 2:4.
[22] Cf. Augustine, *De civitate Dei* 4:34.

(b) *Summa theologiae* IIaIIae 11: On heresy

articulus 3: *Whether heretics ought to be tolerated*[23]

It seems that heretics ought to be tolerated.

obiectio 1: For the Apostle says at 2 Timothy 2:24ff: 'The servant of the Lord must not strive, but be gentle unto all men, in meekness instructing them that oppose themselves, if God peradventure will give them repentance to the acknowledging of the truth, and that they may recover themselves out of the snare of the devil.' But if heretics are not tolerated, but put to death, the opportunity of repentance is taken away from them. Therefore this seems to be contrary to the Apostle's command.

obiectio 2: Moreover, whatever is necessary in the Church should be tolerated. But heresies are necessary in the Church; for the Apostle says at 1 Corinthians 11:19: 'There must be heresies, that they who are reproved may be manifest among you.' Therefore it seems that heretics should be tolerated.

obiectio 3: Moreover, the Lord commanded his servants at Matthew 13:30 to suffer the tares 'to grow until the harvest', that is, until the end of the world, as is explained in the same place (vs. 39). But according to the exposition of this given by the saints, the tares signify heretics.[24] Therefore heretics should be tolerated.

sed contra: The Apostle says at Titus 3:10f: 'A man that is an heretic after the first and second admonition, reject, knowing that he that is such is subverted.'

responsio: With regard to heretics two things are to be considered: one on their own side, the other on the side of the Church. On their own side there is the sin by which they deserve not only to be separated from the Church by excommunication, but also cut off from the world by death. For it is a much more grievous thing to corrupt the faith which gives life to the soul than to forge money, which supports temporal life. Hence if forgers of money or other malefactors are at once justly condemned

---

[23] This *quaestio* has four articles, of which only the third is translated here. The others are:

1. Whether heresy is a species of unbelief
2. In what it consists
4. Whether those who recant are to be received

[24] Cf. Chrysostom, *In Mattheum* 46 (*PG* 58:477).

to death by secular princes, so much more should heretics be not only excommunicated but even justly put to death as soon as they are convicted of heresy. On the side of the Church, however, there is mercy, which seeks the conversion of those who err; and so she condemns not at once, but 'after the first and second admonition', as the Apostle directs. After that, if the heretic is found to be pertinacious still, the Church, no longer hoping for his conversion, looks to the salvation of others by separating him from the Church through the sentence of excommunication; and, further, she hands him over to the secular tribunal to be removed from the world by death. For Jerome, on Galatians 5:9, 'A little leaven', says: 'Cut away the rotten flesh, expel the diseased sheep from the fold, lest the whole house, the whole dough, the whole body, the whole flock, burn, perish, rot, die. Arius was but a little spark in Alexandria; but because that spark was not quenched forthwith, the whole world was laid waste by its flame.'[25]

ad 1: It is precisely this meekness which requires that the heretic be admonished a first time and a second; but if he is not willing to recant, he must be regarded as already 'subverted', as the quoted authority of the Apostle shows.

ad 2: The advantage which comes about as a result of heresy is something apart from the intention of the heretics: that is, the constancy of the faithful is tested, as the Apostle says, and, as Augustine says, we are made to shake off our sloth and search the scriptures more diligently.[26] But what the heretics themselves intend is to corrupt the faith, which is harmful in the highest degree. And so we should look to what is their true intention, and exclude them, rather than to what is apart from their intention and tolerate them.

ad 3: According to the *Decretales*, 'to be excommunicated is not to be uprooted: someone is excommunicated so that his "spirit may be saved in the day of the Lord", as the Apostle says at 1 Corinthians 5:5'.[27] Yet even if heretics are entirely uprooted, by death, this is not contrary to the Lord's command, which is to be taken as applying in circumstances where the tares cannot be gathered up without rooting up the wheat also, as stated above, in treating of unbelievers in general.[28]

---

[25] *In epistolam ad Galatas* 3 (*PL* 26:403).
[26] *De Genesi contra Manichaeos* 1:1.
[27] X. 5:7:9: *Ad abolendam* (*CIC* 2:780).
[28] IIaIIae 10:8 ad 1.

(c) *Summa theologiae* IIaIIae 12: On apostasy

articulus 2*: Whether a prince forfeits his dominion over his subjects by reason of his apostasy from the faith, so that they are no longer bound to obey him*[29]

It seems that a prince does not forfeit his dominion over his subjects by reason of his apostasy from the faith, so that they are no longer bound to obey him.

obiectio 1: For Ambrose says that the Emperor Julian, though an apostate, nonetheless had under him Christian soldiers who obeyed him when he said, 'Form a line and defend the commonwealth.'[30] Therefore subjects are not absolved from the dominion of their prince by reason of his apostasy.

obiectio 2: Moreover, an apostate from the faith is an unbeliever. But we find that some of the saints served unbelieving masters. For instance, Joseph served Pharaoh,[31] Daniel served Nabuchodonosor,[32] and Mordecai served Ahasuerus.[33] Therefore apostasy from the faith does not detract from the obedience owed to the prince by his subjects.

obiectio 3: Moreover, by apostasy from the faith a man turns away from God; but he does this by every other sin as well. If, therefore, by reason of apostasy from the faith, princes were to lose their right to command those of their subjects who are believers, they would by the same token lose it by reason of other sins also. But this is clearly false. Therefore we ought not to withhold obedience from a prince by reason of his apostasy from the faith.

sed contra: Gregory VII says: 'Holding fast to the institutions of our holy predecessors, we, by apostolic authority, absolve from their oath those who are bound in fealty or by oath to excommunicated persons, and we forbid them to show fealty to such persons in any way whatsoever until they shall have made amends.'[34] But apostates from the faith, like heretics, are excommunicate, according to the decretal.[35] Therefore princes who have apostatised from the faith should not be obeyed.

---

[29] This *quaestio* has two articles, the first of which is 'Whether apostasy belongs to unbelief'.

[30] Despite the text, the reference is clearly to Augustine, *Enarrationes in psalmos* 124:3. The incorrect attribution is due to C. 11:3:94: *Iulianus* (*CIC* 1:669).

[31] Genesis 41ff.

[32] Daniel 2ff.

[33] Esther 2ff.

[34] C. 15:6:4: *Nos sanctorum* (*CIC* 1:756).

[35] X. 5:7:9: *Ad abolendam* (*CIC* 2:780).

responsio: As stated above,[36] unbelief is not in itself inconsistent with dominion, since dominion was introduced by the *ius gentium*, which is a human law, whereas the distinction between believers and unbelievers is made according to Divine right, which does not cancel out human right. Nevertheless one who sins by unbelief may be sentenced to the loss of his right of dominion, as is also sometimes possible because of other sins. Now according to the Apostle at 1 Corinthians 5:12 – 'What have I to do to judge them that are without?' – it does not pertain to the Church to punish those who have never received the faith. She can, however, pass sentence of punishment upon the unbelief of those who have received the faith. It is moreover fitting that by this punishment they should be no longer able to command the faithful as their subjects; for, otherwise, great corruption of the faith might occur, since, as stated above,[37] 'the man who is an apostate deviseth evil with a wicked heart, and soweth discord' (Proverbs 6:12ff), intending to separate men from the faith. And so, as soon as the sentence of excommunication is passed upon someone by reason of apostasy from the faith, his subjects are *ipso facto* absolved from his lordship and from the oath of fealty by which they were bound to him.

ad 1: At that time the Church was in her infancy and did not yet have the power to restrain earthly princes; and so she allowed the faithful to obey Julian the Apostate in those things which were not against the faith, in order to avoid greater peril to the faith.

ad 2: As stated in the body of the article, we are not here concerned with those unbelievers who have never received the faith.

ad 3: Apostasy from the faith separates a man from God totally, as stated above,[38] but this is not true of any other kind of sin.

(d) *Scripta super libros sententiarum* II, Dist. 44, quaest. 3

articulus 4: *On spiritual and temporal power*

There are two ways in which a higher power and a lower can be related. In one way, the lower power may be completely derived from the higher, and the whole power of the lower will then be founded upon the power

---

[36] IIaIIae 10:10 (p. 270, above).
[37] IIaIIae 1:2.
[38] Art. 1.

of the higher; in which case we should obey the higher power before the lower simply and in all things . . . And it is in this way that God's power is related to every created power. In this way also is the power of the emperor related to that of the proconsul. In this way again is the power of the pope related to every spiritual power in the Church, because the different degrees of dignity within the Church are both disposed and ordered by the pope himself; and so his power is as it were the foundation of the Church, as is shown at Matthew 16:18: 'Thou art Peter, and upon this rock I will build my Church' . . . In another way, a higher and lower power can be such that each arises from some supreme power which arranges them in relation to each other as it wishes. In this case, the one will not be subject to the other save in respect of those things in which it has been subjected to the other by the supreme power; and only in such things are we to obey the higher power before the lower. It is in this way that the bishops and archbishops of the Church, whose power descends from the pope, are related to each other . . .

Spiritual and secular power are both derived from the Divine power, and so secular power is subject to spiritual power insofar as this is ordered by God: that is, in those things which pertain to the salvation of the soul. In such matters, then, the spiritual power is to be obeyed before the secular. But in those things which pertain to the civil good, the secular power should be obeyed before the spiritual, according to Matthew 22:21: 'Render to Caesar the things that are Caesar's.' Unless perhaps the spiritual and secular powers are conjoined, as in the pope, who holds the summit of both powers: that is, the spiritual and the secular, through the disposition of Him Who is both priest and king, a priest for ever according to the order of Melchizedek,[39] the King of kings and Lord of lords, Whose power shall not fail, and Whose kingdom shall not pass away for ever and ever. Amen.[40]

---

[39] Psalm 110:4; Hebrews 5:6.

[40] Some commentators have found remarkable what St Thomas says at *Quaestiones quodlibetales* 12:19, that: 'The times are different now, for kings are wise and clearly serve the Lord Jesus Christ with fear; and so in this present time kings are vassals of the Church. The condition of the Church now is therefore different from what it was then; yet she is not a different Church.' The key words here are *in isto tempore reges vassali sunt ecclesiae*. If this means, 'nowadays there are kings who are vassals of the Church' – i.e. that there are kings who hold their kingdoms as papal fiefs – it is a completely uncontroversial statement. If it means 'all kings are now vassals of the Church', it is a statement of the most extreme papalist or 'hierocratic' position. It seems unlikely, in view of St Thomas's generally mild and conservative outlook, that on this one occasion only, and for no apparent reason, he should have taken the latter kind of stance. In my view, therefore, the former interpretation is correct.

Biographical glossary

Alexander of Macedon: Alexander 'the Great' (356–323 BC); son of King Philip II of Macedon. Between the ages of thirteen and sixteen he was tutored by Aristotle. He succeeded his father after the latter's assassination in 336 BC. Enormously ambitious, he was a military commander of genius who inherited an efficient military machine from his father. In the decade between 334 BC and 324 BC he created the Macedonian empire encompassing Greece, Egypt, Asia Minor, and Asia up to western India. He founded over seventy cities and diffused Hellenic culture throughout the known world. After his death, the empire was divided up into the 'Hellenistic' kingdoms by his generals.

Ambrose: St Ambrose was born in 339 into an aristocratic family of Roman Christians and educated at Rome in law and the liberal arts. His forensic abilities earned him advancement to the consular governorship of Liguria and Æmilia with a residence at Milan. Called upon in 374 to mediate between Catholics and Arians in a violent dispute over the vacant see of Milan, Ambrose dealt with the affair so tactfully that, at the age of thirty-five, and much against his wishes, he found himself acclaimed Bishop of Milan by both Catholics and Arians. His first act as bishop was to give his property to the poor; but the most notable event of his episcopate was his infliction of public penance on the Emperor Theodosius. He was a friend and mentor of St Augustine, and the eloquence of his sermons was a factor in Augustine's conversion. He died on 4 April 397.

Anselm: St Anselm of Canterbury; the most distinguished theologian and philosopher of the eleventh century. He was born in 1033 and entered the Benedictine Abbey at Bec in 1060, becoming prior in 1063 and abbot in 1078. His works while at Bec include the *Proslogion*, in Chapter 2 of which occurs the 'ontological argument' or *argumentum Anselmi* for which he is best remembered. He became Archbishop of Canterbury in 1093. Despite recurrent conflict with William Rufus and Henry I, he maintained a formidable literary output. He died on 21 April 1109. He was canonised in 1494 and named a Doctor of the Church by Pope Clement XI in 1720.

Archelaus: More properly Herod Archelaus; born 23 BC; ruler of Samaria, Judea and Idumea between 4 BC and AD 6. He was the son of Herod 'the Great' (q.v.) and his wife Malthace. He and his brothers Herod Antipas and Philip were educated in Rome. His father's will appointed him king, but the Emperor Augustus allowed him to assume only the title of Ethnarch of Samaria, Judea and Idumea. Antipas and Philip became Tetrarchs of Galilee and the north-eastern parts of the kingdom respectively. Archelaus's arbitrariness and incompetence made him universally unpopular, and both Jews and Samaritans appealed to Rome to have him removed. According to St Matthew's Gospel (2:22), Jesus's parents settled in Galilee because they were afraid to go into the territories ruled by Archelaus. In AD 6, Augustus exiled him to Vienne in Gaul (not Lyons, as St Thomas says at *De regimine principum* 1:7) and Judea became a Roman province.

Aristotle: Greek philosopher, active in, though not a native of, Athens; almost always called 'the Philosopher' by St Thomas, evidently as a mark of esteem. Aristotle was born in 384 BC in Stagira, a Greek colony of Thrace. He was a member of Plato's Academy from 367 BC to Plato's death in 347, first as a student, then as a teacher. Aristotle left the Academy after Plato's death and in 343 BC accepted a position in the court of Philip II of Macedon as tutor to the future Alexander the Great (q.v.). He returned to Athens in 335 BC and opened his own school, the Lyceum. His connection with Alexander made him unpopular with Athenian patriots after Alexander's death in 323 BC, and he again left the city. He died at Chalcis in Euboea in 322 BC. He was a prolific author whose interests range over an enormous field: physics, metaphysics, biology, logic, ethics, politics. Almost all his original works have perished. Ancient library catalogues indicate that what we now call the 'works' of Aristotle consist mostly of rough drafts and lecture notes written up and edited after his death.

Arius: The Presbyter of the Church in Alexandria with whose name is associated the Arian heresy, which denies the divinity of Christ.

Arianism so emphasises the distinct hypostasis of the Father and the Son that the Son is reduced to a mere created being, subordinate to and different in essence from the Father, and only called God in a lower sense. Arius began to teach this heresy in *ca.* 318, in response to what he considered to be the Sabellianism of Bishop Alexander of Alexandria. The first ecumenical council of the Church, at Nicaea in 325, was convoked by the Emperor Constantine to try to settle the questions raised by Arianism. The council upheld the Godhood of the Son and asserted the 'consubstantiality' of the Son with the Father. Arius and his followers were banished to Galatia and Illyricum, but Arianism continued to be professed in some form for another fifty years and more.

Augustine: St Augustine was born at Thagaste – modern Suk Ahras, in Algeria – in 354. His mother, Monica, was a Christian. She tried to bring up her son accordingly, but Augustine disliked the moral de- mands of Christianity and thought the scriptures unsophisticated. As a young man he admired Cicero and Plotinus; he retained a strongly Platonist outlook throughout his life. Longing for certainty, he experi- mented with Manichaeism and Scepticism, but found neither of them satisfactory. Having in 384 accepted a position at Milan as a teacher of rhetoric, he came under the influence of prominent Christians in that city, especially the bishop, St Ambrose (q.v.). After a prolonged mental struggle, he was baptised by St Ambrose on Holy Saturday, 387. He was ordained priest in 391, and five years later became Bishop of Hippo. (Hippo is the modern Algerian town of Annaba.) He remained in that office for more than thirty years, engaged in continuous debate with heretics and schismatics. His literary output extends to 113 books and treatises, over 200 letters and more than 500 sermons. He died in 430.

Augustus: Gaius Julius Caesar Octavianus, first Emperor of Rome (27 BC–AD 14), the 'Caesar Augustus' of Luke 2:1. He was the great- nephew and adopted son and heir of Julius Caesar (q.v.). With Mark Antony and Lepidus he was victorious in the civil war against Caesar's assassins Brutus and Cassius. He subsequently quarrelled with Antony and defeated him at the battle of Actium in 31 BC. Thereafter, he was effectively in sole command at Rome and began to use the name 'Augustus' in place of his given name Octavian. He increased his personal power slowly and cautiously. He organised the army with himself at the head, and used it both to strengthen Rome's frontiers and to extend her possessions into Spain, Gaul, Egypt and Armenia. His military and administrative abilities enabled him to construct a strong empire out of the tatters of the Roman republic; although he claimed only to have 'restored' the republic and was careful to have his position periodically confirmed by the Senate.

Bias: Bias of Priene, one of the 'seven sages' listed by Diogenes Laertius (1:13) and by Plato at *Protagoras* 343A. He lived during the first half of the sixth century BC. Such biographical details as we have are at Diogenes Laertius 1:82ff. He is also mentioned by Plato at *Hippias Major* 281C–E and *Republic* 335E.

Cato: The Cato to whom St Thomas refers at *De regimine principum* 1:8 is Marcus Porcius Cato the younger, called 'Uticensis' (94–46 BC), a Stoic philosopher, noted for 'the inflexible rectitude of his life' (Sallust, *Iugurth.* 53:4). An ally of Pompey, he committed suicide after Julius Caesar's defeat of Pompey's supporters at the battle of Thapsus in 46 BC. He is not to be confused with his great-grandfather of the same name, M. Porcius Cato 'the Censor' (234–149 BC), also a byword for puritanism and austerity.

Celsus: Publius Iuventius Celsus; Roman jurist. The dates of his birth and death are unknown, but he was a distinguished public servant of the second century AD: Praetor in AD 106 or 107; Governor of Thrace between 107 and 117; Consul in 128; and finally Proconsul of Asia. He also served on the council of the Emperor Hadrian. His major work was a *Digesta* in thirty-nine books. As a jurist he is noted for a remarkably independent and non-conforming spirit which often put him at odds with colleagues.

Charles: The 'Charles' mentioned at IIaIIae 40:2:3 is Charlemagne, King of the Franks from 768 and Emperor of the restored Western Roman empire from 800 until his death in 814. The elder son of Pepin III 'the Short' and Bertrada, he was born *ca.* 742. When Pepin died in 768, Charlemagne became King of the Franks jointly with his brother Carloman. Carloman's death in 771 left him as sole king. For the next twenty-eight years, he united most of the lands of Western Europe by wars of conquest, ruling the Frankish empire thus created by means of a loosely centralised government relying on the loyalty of local nobles. Unusually learned, he took an interest in matters of theology and ecclesiastical government. On Christmas Day 800, Charlemagne was crowned Roman Emperor by Pope Leo III. This coronation, by which the Pope supposedly 'translated' the empire from East to West, must rank as one of the most politically significant events of the Middle Ages.

Chrysostom: St John 'Chrysostom' (i.e. 'Goldenmouth', because of his eloquence); a saint and martyr of the Greek Church and commentator on the scriptures. He was born at Antioch in 354 into a wealthy family and educated there in philosophy and rhetoric. He became a monk in 375, but his health did not allow him to pursue the eremitical life which was his first choice. He was ordained priest in 386 and, reluctantly, consecrated Archbishop of Constantinople *ca.* 398. As archbishop, he was noted for his concern with social issues, charitable works and zeal for moral reform in the Church. This last, and his outspokenness in pursuit of it, made him unpopular with influential people. He fell foul of Theophilus, Patriarch of Alexandria, and the Empress Eudoxia, who removed him from office and in 404 sent him into exile. He was much persecuted, and died on 14 September 407.

Cicero: Marcus Tullius Cicero (106–43 BC); Roman orator, statesman, philosopher and man of letters; Consul in 63 BC. He is often referred to by late classical and medieval authors as Tullius; hence the 'Tully' of older English translations. He admires Greek thought, but his own philosophy is eclectic, superficial and inconclusive. He attached more importance to the active than the contemplative life, and wrote philosophy only when prevented from taking part in politics. The back-handed compliment which St Augustine pays him at *De civitate Dei* 2:27, that he 'was a distinguished man and by way of being a philosopher', is not unjust. He was embroiled in the political turmoils which marked the end of the Roman republic, and assassinated (7 December 43 BC) by order of Mark Antony, who caused his head and hands to be nailed to the Speaker's Rostrum in the Senate.

Damascene: St John Damascene – i.e. 'of Damascus' – was born in AD 690. His father was John al-Mansur, a Christian official in the court of the Caliph Abdul Malek. John succeeded to his father's office, but in 730 political intrigues occasioned by the Iconoclast controversy cost him the Caliph's favour and he and his old tutor Cosmas became monks at the monastery of St Sabas near Jerusalem. Cosmas eventually became Bishop of Majuma, but John remained in the monastery for the rest of his life, devoting himself to study and writing. He died in about 755. The work to which St Thomas refers, *De fide orthodoxa*, was translated into Latin by Burgundius of Pisa in 1150 at the request of Pope

Eugenius III. Our only biographical source is the very unsatisfactory tenth-century *Life* by John, Patriarch of Jerusalem (*PG* 94:429–90).

Damon and Pythias: The version of the famous story of Damon and Pythias given at *De regimine principum* 1:11 is paraphrased from Valerius Maximus (q.v.). The tradition is that Damon and Pythias were Pythagorean philosophers and that Pythias, alternatively called Phintias, was condemned to death for plotting against Dionysius the Younger of Syracuse (q.v.). See also Cicero, *De officiis* 3:10:45.

Dinocrates: The Dinocrates whose name is misspelt as Xenocrates at *De regimine principum* 2:3 is Dinocrates (or Deinocrates) of Rhodes. Despite the slightly discreditable story which St Thomas repeats from Vitruvius (q.v.), Dinocrates was one of the most distinguished architects of the ancient world. He was commissioned by Alexander the Great (q.v.) in 332 BC to design the city of Alexandria. In collaboration with the sculptor Scopas, he was also responsible for building the famous Temple of Artemis at Ephesus.

Diocletian: Gaius Aurelius Valerius Diocletianus. Initially an ordinary soldier called Diokles, he was proclaimed Emperor by the army in 284. He held the principate jointly with his friend Maximian from 284 to 305, when they both abdicated. These two further divided the Empire with Constantius I (from 286) and Galerius (from 293). Diocletian moved his capital from Rome to Nicomedia, from where he governed the eastern portion of the Empire. He was responsible for important administrative and fiscal reforms, considerably strengthening the power of the Emperor in relation to the Senate. During a principate of two decades, he succeeded in restoring a degree of order to an empire seriously disrupted by political and military upheaval. He was initially tolerant of Christianity, but in 303 ordered the burning of scriptures and the destruction of churches. A general persecution ensued, and continued after his abdication. He died in 316.

Dionysius (1): Dionysius is the name of two tyrants of the city-state of Syracuse. (i) Dionysius the Elder ruled from 407 to 367 BC. He was a military despot who by his conquests of Sicily and southern Italy made Syracuse the most powerful Greek city west of Greece itself. He saved Sicily from conquest by Carthage through four arduous wars. The story told by St Thomas at *De regimine principum* 1:7 relates to this Dionysius. (ii) His son Dionysius the Younger (*fl.* 368–344 BC) ended the war with Carthage but was far less gifted as an administrator and soldier than his father. He wrote poetry and philosophy and was a

patron of the arts. It was this Dionysius whom Plato, at the suggestion
of Dionysius's uncle Dion, tried to mould into a philosopher-ruler,
but without success. The story of Damon and Pythias (q.v.) belongs
to the reign of the younger Dionysius. He was expelled by the people
of Syracuse in 344 BC and spent most of the rest of his life in Corinth,
where he is said to have been a teacher of rhetoric.

Dionysius (2): Dionysius 'the Areopagite', now usually called Pseudo-
Dionysius, is a pious fraud of the fifth century who wishes us to think
that he is the Dionysius converted to Christianity by St Paul at Athens
(Acts 17:34). He was also erroneously believed to have been the same
person as the martyr Dionysius/Denys who was the first Bishop of
Paris. His true identity is unknown. He is the author of a number of
works which, because of their emphasis on the ideas of hierarchy and order, are much quoted by medieval political authors: *De divinis nominibus*,
De caelesti hierarchia, *De ecclesiastica hierarchia* and *Theologia mystica*.
Several other works, either specious or now lost, are referred to in the
Pseudo-Dionysian writings. It is obvious on internal grounds that these
writings are not productions of the first century. Their authenticity was
first seriously challenged by the Renaissance scholar Lorenzo Valla.

Domitian: Titus Flavius Domitianus, the second son of the Emperor
Vespasian (q.v.). He had himself proclaimed Emperor in AD 81 as his
older brother Titus lay dying of a fever. There are many stories of his
ruthlessness, sexual rapacity and horrifying cruelty; he is commonly
supposed to have been deranged. He was a persecutor of Christians,
but contemporary pagan sources (Juvenal, Tacitus, Suetonius and the
younger Pliny) speak ill of him too. He lived in constant and justified
fear of conspiracies. He was assassinated in AD 96.

Fabius: Quintus Fabius Maximus Verrucosus 'Cunctator' (d. 203 BC);
Roman military commander and noted opponent of the Carthaginian
general Hannibal. He was Consul five times (233, 228, 215, 214,
209) and appointed dictator after the Carthaginian victory at Lake
Trasimene in 217 BC. The name Cunctator – 'Delayer' – comes from
his tactic of constantly harassing and demoralising the enemy without
ever allowing himself to be drawn into battle against superior forces.
When the Romans grew tired of this and relieved him of his command
in 216, the result was the disaster of Cannae: the worst military defeat
ever sustained by Rome.

Frontinus: Sextus Iulius Frontinus; Roman soldier, politician, and author. Born in Sicily in AD 35, he lived an active and distinguished life of

public service. He was Praetor Urbanus in 70; Consul in 73; Governor of Britain 74–8; served with Domitian in Germany in 83; Proconsul of Asia in 84; Consul twice more, in 98 and 100; and Curator Aquarum under Nerva or Trajan. While in this last post he wrote the work for which he is chiefly remembered, *De aquis urbis Romae*. The work to which St Thomas refers, *Strategemata*, is a compendium of short accounts of how distinguished military commanders of the past dealt successfully with fifty different classes of matters which arise in war. He died in 104.

Gaius: Roman jurist (*ca.* AD 110–80). Little is known of his personal details. He was active during the principates of Hadrian, Antoninus Pius, Marcus Aurelius and Commodus: i.e. at the time when the Roman Empire was at the height of its power and prosperity. He is best known as the author of the *Institutes*, a complete exposition in four books of the elements of Roman law. Many quotations from the works of Gaius occur in the *Digesta* of Justinian, and a comparison of the *Institutes* of Justinian with those of Gaius shows that the whole method and arrangement of the later work, and, indeed, a number of passages verbatim, were copied from the earlier. He is one of the five jurists – the others being Papinian (q.v.), Ulpian (q.v.), Modestinus and Paulus – formally recognised by the Emperor Justinian as being the authoritative sources of Roman law.

Gratian: Iohannes Gratianus; celebrated as the founder of the science of canon law. He compiled the earliest systematic collection of Canons, the *Concordantia discordantium canonum*, more usually called the *Decretum* or *Decretum Gratiani*, which forms the first part of what is now known as the *Corpus iuris canonici*. He was born in Italy, perhaps at Chiusi, in Tuscany, in about 1100. He became a monk and taught at Bologna in the monastery of Saints Felix and Nabor at Bologna. The *Decretum* was compiled probably between 1140 and 1150. He died between 1160 and 1180. It will be seen from these imprecise dates that little is known of his life. There is a monument to him in the church of St Petronius at Bologna, although we do not even know how much of his life he spent in that city.

Gregory: Pope St Gregory I, 'The Great' (540–604; Pope from 590). Born into a wealthy Sicilian family, Gregory was educated as a lawyer and possessed considerable skill as an administrator. In 574 he gave up a promising career in public life to become a monk, and thereafter lived a life of great austerity. He brought to the papal office a higher degree of spiritual and temporal authority than it had ever previously enjoyed. He is rightly regarded as the founder of the medieval papacy. Large numbers of works are spuriously attributed to him; but the *Regula pastoralis* and *Moralia*, to which St Thomas refers, are genuine. It is a curious fact that his mother Sylvia and two of his aunts, Tarsilla and Æmilia, are also saints.

Hadrian: The Hadrian mentioned at IIaIIae 40:2:3 is Pope Hadrian I (*pont.* 772–95). His pontificate of twenty-three years, ten months and twenty-four days has at the time of writing been surpassed in length only by that of Pius VI (1775–99). He is chiefly remembered for his determined resistance to Lombard political ambitions in Italy. He was a close friend of Charles, known as 'Charlemagne' (q.v.), upon whose assistance he called to deliver Rome from the threat of Lombard invasion in 773. It was probably during his pontificate that the so-called Donation of Constantine was confected. In co-operation with the Empress Irene, he laboured to repair the damage done by the Iconoclast Controversy to relations between the Eastern and Western Churches. He presided over the second Council of Nicaea in 787, in which the Catholic view regarding the use and veneration of images was definitively stated. He was responsible for a great deal of building work in Rome, upon which he is said to have expended enormous sums of money.

Herod: Herod, the King of the Jews mentioned at *De regimine principum* 1:7, is Herod 'the Great' (73–6 BC). A protégé of Mark Antony, he became Governor of Galilee at the age of only sixteen (47 BC). He was made Tetrarch of Galilee in 42 BC, and installed in Jerusalem as King in 37 BC, after Mark Antony's defeat of the Parthians. His non-Jewish origins – his father, Antipater, was Idumaean and his mother the daughter of an Arabian prince – were much resented by his subjects. His political adroitness enabled him to survive the fall of Mark Antony, but he was always a client king, dependent on the support of Rome. His major achievement was the rebuilding of the city of Jerusalem after the earthquake of 31 BC and the construction of the port of Caesarea. His later years were marked by the atrocities chronicled by Josephus; although Josephus does not mention the 'massacre of the innocents', for which St Matthew's Gospel is our only authority. After his death, the kingdom was divided between his three sons (Herod) Archelaus (q.v.), Herod Antipas and Philip.

Hilary: St Hilary of Poitiers. He was born in Poitiers at the beginning of the fourth century, apparently into a pagan family. As a young man, he conceived a strong desire to understand why and by Whom we are given the gift of life. He came across the Christian scriptures by chance, and began to study them. He was converted to Christianity, and became Bishop of Poitiers in about 350. Apart from the years 359–61, which he spent in Constantinople, he remained in Poitiers for the rest of his life. He was an active participant in the Arian controversy, and suffered a good deal of persecution as a result. He died in 368; he was proclaimed a Doctor of the Universal Church by Pius IX in 1851.

Isidore: Isidore of Seville; born in Cartagena, Spain, in about 560 AD. A man of remarkably broad learning, he succeeded his older brother Leander as Archbishop of Seville in 600 or 601. His younger brother, St Fulgentius, was Bishop of Astigi and his sister Florentina was a nun who was at one point in charge of over forty convents. Isidore played an important part in the second Council of Seville (619) and the fourth Council of Toledo (633), through both of which he exercised great influence over the intellectual and educational development of the Spanish Church. He also devoted himself, during the lifetime of Leander, to the conversion of the Visigoths from the Arian heresy. A prolific author, he is best remembered for his *Etymologiae*, or *Origines*, as it is sometimes called: a compendium of learning which was used as a textbook throughout the Middle Ages and which was still being reprinted in the sixteenth century. He died on 4 April 636.

Jerome: Saint and Father of the Church; editor and translator of the Vulgate. He was born in Dalmatia in 347 and educated there and in Rome, where he was baptised by Pope Liberius in *ca.* 366. After much travel, he lived for two years as a hermit in the desert of Chalcis. From 377 to 379 he was in Antioch, where he studied biblical texts and translated the works of Origen and Eusebius. Between 382 and 385 he lived in Rome as secretary to Pope Damasus, who encouraged him to begin his translation of the New Testament. His devotion to asceticism and an outspoken manner made him unpopular, and in 385 he moved to Bethlehem, where he remained until his death. Famously industrious and a gifted linguist, he wrote numerous biblical commentaries and tracts against Pelagianism and other heresies. His edition and translation of the scriptures was completed in 406. He died in 419, with his head resting on the manger where the infant Christ had lain.

Julius Caesar: Roman patrician, general, statesman, historian. He was born (100 BC) into a poor but noble Roman family; he claimed to be descended on his mother's side from Aeneas of Troy. He made his reputation first as a soldier. He became Praetor in 62 BC and Consul in 59 BC. Between 58 and 54 BC he waged a series of brilliant military campaigns in Gaul. His war memoirs, *De bello Gallico*, are still extant. As a member of the 'First Triumvirate' with Pompey and Crassus, he was one of the most powerful men in Rome. Ultimately, he fought a civil war with Pompey for mastery of Rome. After his defeat of Pompey at Pharsalus in 48 BC he ruled for four years in Rome as sole dictator. Always regarded as dangerously ambitious, he was assassinated by a conspiracy of senators on the Ides of March – i.e. 15th March – 44 BC.

Leo: The Pope Leo mentioned at IIaIIae 40:2:1 is Pope St Leo IV (*pont.* 847–55). He became Pope at a time when Rome was under immediate threat of Saracen invasion. He had seen the Saracen attack on Rome in 846, and to prevent its recurrence fortified the city and its suburbs. He built a wall around the Vatican and established and fortified the part of Rome still called the Leonine City. These fortifications were finished in 852. Shortly after they were begun, another attempted Saracen invasion occurred (848), and the Pope personally led an army to Ostia as part of the successful Italian military and naval effort to repulse it. This is the incident to which St Thomas refers.

Lucy: St Lucy of Syracuse, a virgin and martyr of the fourth century, recognised by both the Eastern and Western Churches. The only information that we have is unsubstantiated hagiography. Born *ca.* 283, she consecrated her virginity to God, but was betrothed against her will to an unsuitable young man. In the year 303, during the persecution of Diocletian, her mother Eutychia, a wealthy widow, was miraculously cured of a haemorrhage. Lucy persuaded her to distribute her wealth to the poor. This gesture enraged the young man whom Lucy was to marry, and he denounced her as a Christian to Paschasius, Governor of Sicily. Condemned to imprisonment in a brothel, she was saved by divine intervention. An attempt to burn her alive was similarly thwarted; but a second attempt to kill her, this time with a sword, succeeded. Before she died she made an edifying speech foretelling the death of Diocletian and the end of the persecution.

Nero Caesar: Nero Claudius Caesar Augustus Germanicus (AD 37–68), Roman Emperor from 54 to 68. After a promising beginning, his principate became a byword for extravagance, vanity and cruelty as power, the love of pleasure and an increasing fear of conspiracy unhinged his mind. This, at any rate, is the standard view; although much of what we know of him comes from hostile sources, and his bad press is partly due to his persecution of the Christians in 65. He is said also to have been an artist and a musician, and he was responsible for a great deal of building work in Rome. St Augustine, whom St Thomas is paraphrasing at *De regimine principum* 1:8, took him as an illustration of the principle that God sends tyrants into the world to punish sinners. He had his stepbrother Britannicus poisoned in order to remove a political threat, and in 59 arranged the death of his own mother, Agrippina. He is also said to have been responsible for the fire which devastated Rome in 64.

Nicholas: Pope St Nicholas I (*pont.* 858–67). He considerably extended and consolidated the power of the papacy. His uncompromising stand in relation to the marital affairs of Lothar II of Lorraine included one of the earliest assertions of a papal right to judge temporal rulers when they sin. His intervention in the affairs of the Archdiocese of Rheims, when Archbishop Hincmar deposed Bishop Rothad of Soissons in 862, helped to strengthen the authority of the Apostolic See over the sees of the West. A similar attempt to intervene in the Photian schism in the East was less successful, and led only to an acrimonious and prolonged quarrel during which a Synod convoked by Photius in 867 purported to depose the Pope.

Ninus: The legendary eponymous founder of the Assyrian city of Nineveh; traditionally supposed to have invented the art of warfare and to have been the first to assemble armies for the sake of conquering his neighbours. In referring to Ninus at *De regimine principum* 1:14, St Thomas probably has in mind Augustine, *De civitate Dei* 4:6 and 16:17.

Octavian Augustus: *See* Augustus.

Papinian: Aemilius Papinianus (d. 212); Roman jurist. He held high office under the Emperor Septimius Severus (193–211), of whom he was a close friend; but he perished as a political casualty when Severus's son Caracalla succeeded to the principate in 212. Papinian was a jurist of great learning and reputation, noted also for his stern moral character. His opinions, along with those of Paulus, Gaius (q.v.), Ulpian (q.v.) and Modestinus, formed the basis of the codified Roman law of the fifth century. His main works, now known through quotations in the *Codex Theodosianus* and in the *Digesta* of the *Corpus iuris civilis*, were *Quaestiones* (thirty-seven books), *Responsa* (nineteen books), *Definitiones* (two books), and *De adulteriis* (two books).

Plato: Plato (427–347 BC) was born into an aristocratic and well-connected Athenian family. His real name was Aristocles ('Plato' is a nickname meaning 'broad': presumably a reference to his physique).

His early adulthood coincided with the period of political dislocation following the defeat of Athens by Sparta in the Peloponnesian War of 431–404 BC. He almost took part in the oligarchical government – the 'thirty tyrants' – installed in Athens after the war; but, becoming disillusioned with politics, he devoted himself to philosophy instead. In 387 he founded the school in Athens known as the Academy. Its curriculum embraced astronomy, biology, mathematics, political theory and philosophy. Aristotle (q.v.) was the Academy's most distinguished student. Almost all of Plato's surviving works are 'dialogues': reports of real or fictitious philosophical conversations. In the majority of them the most important protagonist is his teacher Socrates, condemned to death by the Athenian people in 399 BC. Each dialogue has a theme which is explored by a long process of question and answer. The result is sometimes artificial and lacking in precision, and it is often difficult to escape the conclusion that the argument is prearranged so that Socrates will win. The breadth and originality of Plato's thought nonetheless establish him as the founding figure of Western philosophical enquiry.

Pythias: *See* Damon and Pythias.

Romulus: Romulus and his twin brother Remus are the legendary founders of Rome. They were the sons of Mars and the Vestal Rhea Silvia. Thrown into the river Tiber by their uncle Amulius, they were washed ashore, suckled by a she-wolf, and eventually found and brought up by the shepherd Faustulus. Having slain their uncle, they founded the city of Rome; but, in a quarrel over precedence, Romulus killed Remus and became sole king. Romulus peopled Rome by establishing a place of refuge for all fugitives on the Capitol.

Sallust: Gaius Sallustius Crispus (86–34 BC); Roman politician and historian. He was a friend of Julius Caesar, who made him Governor of Numidia. Having made his fortune there, Sallust returned to Rome and devoted himself to writing history. He concentrated in his writings on an analysis of the critical stages in the decline of the Roman republic. Only two of his works, *Bellum Catilinae* and *Bellum Iugurthinum*, are extant in more than fragmentary form.

Sebastian: According to the traditional hagiographies, for which there is no appreciable historical corroboration, St Sebastian was the son of a wealthy Roman or Milanese family and a member of the imperial bodyguard of Diocletian. During Diocletian's persecution of the Christians, Sebastian visited them in prison, bringing food and encouragement. He is said to have healed the wife of a fellow soldier by making the Sign of the Cross over her. Discovered and charged with being a Christian, Sebastian was tied to a tree, shot full of arrows, and left for dead. He survived, recovered – thanks, it is said, to the miraculous intervention of St Irene – and returned to preach to Diocletian, who had him beaten to death.

Seneca: Lucius Annaeus Seneca (4 BC–AD 65); Stoic philosopher and uncle of the poet Lucan. He was born in Spain but educated in Rome, where he spent most of his life. He had a discreditable affair with the niece of the Emperor Claudius, who in AD 41 banished him to Corsica. Allowed to return in 49, he became Praetor the following year. Having spent some years as tutor and advisor to the Emperor Nero, in 65 he became involved in the unsuccessful conspiracy of C. Cornelius Piso against him, and was required by the Emperor to commit suicide. The fortitude of his end is famously described by Tacitus at *Annales* 15. His philosophical work is seen at its best in his 124 *Epistulae morales*. The medieval Christian belief, supported by a spurious collection of letters, that Seneca knew St Paul is false.

Suetonius: Gaius Suetonius Tranquillus; Roman biographer and antiquarian. He was a civil servant in the entourage of the Emperor Hadrian (AD 117–138). He wrote biographies, most of which are lost, of men of letters, and the extant *De vita Caesarum*, 'Lives of the [first twelve] Caesars', for which he is best known. He is an indiscriminate and uncritical collector of material, and an inveterate gossip; but his *Lives* are written in an attractive style and contain much valuable information. After his death, his work was carried on by an anonymous author under the title *Historia Augusta*; but these biographies of later emperors down to Diocletian are of little historical worth.

Tarquin the Proud: Lucius Tarquinius Superbus; the last of Rome's seven kings. He came to the throne by murdering his father-in-law Servius Tullius. The Roman dislike of kings is traditionally attributed to the cruel and tyrannical behaviour by which his reign was distinguished. He was king from *ca.* 534 to 510 BC. His son, Tarquinius Sextus, raped Lucretia, wife of Lucius Tarquinius Collatinus, who then took her own life. This event sparked the revolt of Junius Brutus, the expulsion of the kings from Rome and the establishment of the consulate.

Tiberius Caesar: Roman Emperor from AD 14 to 37. He was the son of Tiberius Claudius Nero and Livia, but by the marriage of his mother to the Emperor Augustus (q.v.) he became Augustus's stepson, and was formally adopted by him in AD 4. In AD 10 he was appointed co-regent with Augustus and became Emperor in AD 14. Hostile sources – especially Tacitus – depict him as increasingly tyrannical and merciless, but his principate was not without a strong positive side. Like Augustus he reformed and improved every department of government, and promoted the prosperity of the Empire of which Augustus had laid the foundation. He consolidated the imperial power by declining to have his authority renewed from time to time by the Senate, as Augustus had done. The ministry and death of John the Baptist and Jesus occurred during the principate of Tiberius (see e.g. Luke 3:1).

Titus: *See* Vespasian.

Torquatus: Titus Manlius Imperiosus Torquatus (*fl.* 4th cent. BC); Roman general, dictator and consul; he served against the Gauls (361 BC), slaying one of them in single combat. As a trophy he took the Gaul's *torquis* or collar, hence the name Torquatus. In 340, with his colleague, Publius Decius Mus, he defeated the Latins near Vesuvius and at Trifanum. It is Livy (7:7) who tells us that Torquatus had his own son executed for disobeying orders not to engage in single combat with the enemy. This remarkable story tends to be cited by Christian authors with admiration (see, e.g., St Augustine, *De civitate Dei* 1:23; 5:18).

Ulpian: Domitius Ulpianus; Roman jurist. He was born at Tyre in Phoenicia, but the year of his birth is not known. He was a close associate of the jurist Papinian (q.v.), with whom he taught at the famous law school at Berytus and whose works he annotated. He wrote extensively, and about two-fifths of the *Digesta* of Justinian consists of extracts from his writings. He became Praetorian prefect (i.e. chief adviser to the emperor and commander of his bodyguard) in AD 222 and is said to have exercised considerable influence over Alexander Severus, who was only thirteen when he became Emperor in that year. His political influence was resented and he was assassinated by soldiers of the Praetorian Guard, probably in 288.

Urban: The Pope Urban to whom St Thomas refers at IaIIae 96:5 is Pope Urban II (1042–99; elected March 1088). His given name was Otho, Otto or Odo of Lagery. By preference a monk (he was professed at Cluny *ca.* 1070), circumstances decreed for him a life of ecclesiastical diplomacy. In 1078 he became Cardinal Bishop of Ostia and therefore *ex officio* Dean of the College of Cardinals and chief counsellor to Pope

Gregory VII. Between 1082 and 1085 he was papal legate in France and Germany. He was a vigorous supporter of Gregory in his disputes with the Emperor Henry IV, by whom he was imprisoned for a short while during 1083. Towards the end of his life, in response to the suggestion of the Christian Emperor Alexius I, he sponsored the first Crusade to recover Jerusalem from the Muslims. He was beatified by Leo XIII on July 14 1881.

Valerius Maximus: Roman author of miscellanies (*ca.* 20 BC–*ca.* AD 50). His *Factorum ac dictorum memorabilium libri* IX ('Nine Books of Memorable Deeds and Sayings') was written in about AD 30. As the name suggests, it is a miscellany of anecdotes on a variety of subjects. The material is arranged in short chapters, each devoted to a particular virtue, vice, religious practice or custom. His purpose, Valerius Maximus tells us, is to provide people looking for illustrative examples with a handy compendium of material drawn from famous writers. The book was much admired during the Middle Ages and Renaissance. It remains interesting as a source of information on first-century Roman attitudes toward religion and moral values.

Vegetius: Flavius Vegetius Renatus (*fl. ca.* AD 385–400); Roman military writer; author of the military handbook called *Epitoma rei militaris*, also known as *Rei militaris instituta*. The work was of little importance in its own day, but had considerable influence on the military and strategic thought of the Middle Ages and Renaissance. It is also an important source of information about the military system of the later Roman empire.

Vespasian: The senior of the two Roman emperors, father and son, called Titus Flavius Vespasianus. Both enjoyed distinguished military careers. Vespasian emerged from the political and military imbroglio which followed the death of Nero (whom he annoyed by falling asleep during his concerts) and was Emperor from AD 69 to 79. His son, usually called Titus, succeeded him in 79 and was Emperor until 81. Titus had a scandalous affair with Queen Berenice of Judea. It was during the principate of Titus that there occurred the disastrous eruption of Vesuvius which buried Pompeii and Herculaneum. Both emperors were noted for moderation, clemency and generosity, although Titus was responsible for the destruction of Jerusalem in AD 70.

Vitruvius: Marcus Vitruvius Pollio was a contemporary and protégé of the Emperor Augustus (q.v.), who appointed him, first, as his chief military engineer and then as architect of the new public buildings constructed in Rome during his principate. During his tenure of the latter office, Vitruvius wrote *De architectura*, a technical manual which, intended to be used by workmen, was written in straightforward Latin rather than the Greek of intellectuals. This fact helped to ensure that the work remained in use throughout the European Middle Ages. The influence of Vitruvius is therefore seen in much Gothic architecture, distinguishing it from the later Graeco-Roman architecture characteristic of the East.

Xenocrates: *See* Dinocrates.

Index

CAMBRIDGE TEXTS IN THE HISTORY
OF POLITICAL THOUGHT

Titles published in the series thus far

Bayle *Political Writings* (edited by Sally L. Jenkinson) 0 521 47677 1 paperback

Beccaria *On Crimes and Punishments and other writings* (edited by Richard Bellamy) 0 521 47982 7 paperback

Bentham *Fragment on Government* (introduction by Ross Harrison) 0 521 35929 5 paperback

Bernstein *The Preconditions of Socialism* (edited by Henry Tudor) 0 521 39808 8 paperback

Bodin *On Sovereignty* (edited by Julian H. Franklin) 0 521 34992 3 paperback

Bolingbroke *Political Writings* (edited by David Armitage) 0 521 58697 6 paperback

Bossuet *Politics Drawn from the Very Words of Holy Scripture* (edited by Patrick Riley) 0 521 36807 3 paperback

The British Idealists (edited by David Boucher) 0 521 45951 6 paperback

Burke *Pre-Revolutionary Writings* (edited by Ian Harris) 0 521 36800 6 paperback

Christine De Pizan *The Book of the Body Politic* (edited by Kate Langdon Forhan) 0 521 42259 0 paperback

Cicero *On Duties* (edited by M. T. Griffin and E. M. Atkins) 0 521 34835 8 paperback

Cicero *On the Commonwealth* and *On the Laws* (edited by James E. G. Zetzel) 0 521 45959 1 paperback

Comte *Early Political Writings* (edited by H. S. Jones) 0 521 46923 6 paperback

Conciliarism and Papalism (edited by J. H. Burns and Thomas M. Izbicki) 0 521 47674 7 paperback

Constant *Political Writings* (edited by Biancamaria Fontana) 0 521 31632 4 paperback

Dante *Monarchy* (edited by Prue Shaw) 0 521 56781 5 paperback

Diderot *Political Writings* (edited by John Hope Mason and Robert Wokler) 0 521 36911 8 paperback

The Dutch Revolt (edited by Martin van Gelderen) 0 521 39809 6 paperback

Early Greek Political Thought from Homer to the Sophists (edited by Michael Gagarin and Paul Woodruff) 0 521 43768 7 paperback

The Early Political Writings of the German Romantics (edited by Frederick C. Beiser) 0 521 44951 0 paperback

The English Levellers (edited by Andrew Sharp) 0 521 62511 4 paperback

Erasmus *The Education of a Christian Prince* (edited by Lisa Jardine) 0 521 58811 1 paperback

Fenelon *Telemachus* (edited by Patrick Riley) 0 521 45662 2 paperback

Ferguson *An Essay on the History of Civil Society* (edited by Fania Oz-Salzberger) paperback 0 521 44736 4

Filmer *Patriarcha and Other Writings* (edited by Johann P. Sommerville) 0 521 39903 3 paperback

Fletcher *Political Works* (edited by John Robertson) 0 521 43994 9 paperback

Sir John Fortescue *On the Laws and Governance of England* (edited by Shelley Lockwood) 0 521 58996 7 paperback

Fourier *The Theory of the Four Movements* (edited by Gareth Stedman Jones and Ian Patterson) 0 521 35693 8 paperback

Gramsci *Pre-Prison Writings* (edited by Richard Bellamy) 0 521 42307 4 paperback

Guicciardini *Dialogue on the Government of Florence* (edited by Alison Brown) 0 521 45623 1 paperback

Harrington *A Commonwealth of Oceana* and *A System of Politics* (edited by J. G. A. Pocock) 0 521 42329 5 paperback

Hegel *Elements of the Philosophy of Right* (edited by Allen W. Wood and H. B. Nisbet) 0 521 34888 9 paperback

Hegel *Political Writings* (edited by Laurence Dickey and H. B. Nisbet) 0 521 45979 3 paperback

Hobbes *On the Citizen* (edited by Michael Silverthorne and Richard Tuck) 0 521 43780 6 paperback

Hobbes *Leviathan* (edited by Richard Tuck) 0 521 56797 1 paperback

Hobhouse *Liberalism and other writings* (edited by James Meadowcroft) 0 521 43726 1 paperback

Hooker *Of the Laws of Ecclesiastical Polity* (edited by A. S. McGrade) 0 521 37908 3 paperback

Hume *Political Essays* (edited by Knud Haakonssen) 0 521 46639 3 paperback

King James VI and I *Political Writings* (edited by Johann P. Sommerville) 0 521 44729 1 paperback

Jefferson *Political Writings* (edited by Joyce Appleby and Terence Ball) 0 521 64841 6 paperback

John of Salisbury *Policraticus* (edited by Cary Nederman) 0 521 36701 8 paperback

Kant *Political Writings* (edited by H. S. Reiss and H. B. Nisbet) 0 521 39837 1 paperback

Knox *On Rebellion* (edited by Roger A. Mason) 0 521 39988 2 paperback

Kropotkin *The Conquest of Bread and other writings* (edited by Marshall Shatz) 0 521 45990 7 paperback

Lawson *Politica sacra et civilis* (edited by Conal Condren) 0 521 39248 9 paperback

Leibniz *Political Writings* (edited by Patrick Riley) 0 521 35899 x paperback

The Levellers (edited by Andrew Sharp) 0 521 62511 4 paperback

Locke *Political Essays* (edited by Mark Goldie) 0 521 47861 8 paperback

Locke *Two Treatises of Government* (edited by Peter Laslett) 0 521 35730 6 paperback

Loyseau *A Treatise of Orders and Plain Dignities* (edited by Howell A. Lloyd) 0 521 45624 x paperback

Luther and Calvin on Secular Authority (edited by Harro Höpfl) 0 521 34986 9 paperback

Machiavelli *The Prince* (edited by Quentin Skinner and Russell Price) 0 521 34993 1 paperback

de Maistre *Considerations on France* (edited by Isaiah Berlin and Richard Lebrun) 0 521 46628 8 paperback

Malthus *An Essay on the Principle of Population* (edited by Donald Winch) 0 521 42972 2 paperback

Marsiglio of Padua *Defensor minor* and *De translatione Imperii* (edited by Cary Nederman) 0 521 40846 6 paperback

Marx *Early Political Writings* (edited by Joseph O'Malley) 0 521 34994 x paperback

Marx *Later Political Writings* (edited by Terrell Carver) 0 521 36739 5 paperback

James Mill *Political Writings* (edited by Terence Ball) 0 521 38748 5 paperback

J. S. Mill *On Liberty*, with *The Subjection of Women* and *Chapters on Socialism* (edited by Stefan Collini) 0 521 37917 2 paperback

Milton *Political Writings* (edited by Martin Dzelzainis) 0 521 34866 8 paperback

Montesquieu *The Spirit of the Laws* (edited by Anne M. Cohler, Basia Carolyn Miller and Harold Samuel Stone) 0 521 36974 6 paperback

More *Utopia* (edited by George M. Logan and Robert M. Adams) 0 521 52540 3 paperback

Morris *News from Nowhere* (edited by Krishan Kumar) 0 521 42233 7 paperback

Nicholas of Cusa *The Catholic Concordance* (edited by Paul E. Sigmund) 0 521 56773 4 paperback

Nietzsche *On the Genealogy of Morality* (edited by Keith Ansell-Pearson) 0 521 40610 2 paperback

Paine *Political Writings* (edited by Bruce Kuklick) 0 521 66799 2 paperback

Plato *The Republic* (edited by G. R. F. Ferrari and Tom Griffith) 0 521 48443 x

Plato *Statesman* (edited by Julia Annas and Robin Waterfield) 0 521 44778 x paperback

Price *Political Writings* (edited by D. O. Thomas) 0 521 40969 1 paperback

Priestley *Political Writings* (edited by Peter Miller) 0 521 42561 1 paperback

Proudhon *What is Property?* (edited by Donald R. Kelley and Bonnie G. Smith) 0 521 40556 4 paperback

Pufendorf *On the Duty of Man and Citizen according to Natural Law* (edited by James Tully) 0 521 35980 5 paperback

The Radical Reformation (edited by Michael G. Baylor) 0 521 37948 2 paperback

Rousseau *The Discourses and other early political writings* (edited by Victor Gourevitch) 0 521 42445 3 paperback

Rousseau *The Social Contract and other later political writings* (edited by Victor Gourevitch) 0 521 42446 1 paperback

Seneca *Moral and Political Essays* (edited by John Cooper and John Procope) 0 521 34818 8 paperback

Sidney *Court Maxims* (edited by Hans W. Blom, Eco Haitsma Mulier and Ronald Janse) 0 521 46736 5 paperback

Sorel *Reflections on Violence* (edited by Jeremy Jennings) 0 521 55910 3 paperback

Spencer *The Man versus the State* and *The Proper Sphere of Government* (edited by John Offer) 0 521 43740 7 paperback

Stirner *The Ego and Its Own* (edited by David Leopold) 0 521 45647 9 paperback

Thoreau *Political Writings* (edited by Nancy Rosenblum) 0 521 47675 5 paperback

Tönnies *Community and Civil Society* (edited by José Harris and Margaret Hollis) 0 521 56119 1 paperback